For The Ca[...]
family from
their loving
friend Nanny

DASHIELL HAMMETT

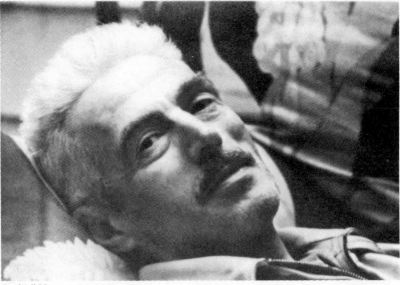

Dashiell Hammett, c. 1946.

The Life of

DASHIELL HAMMETT

DIANE JOHNSON

CHATTO & WINDUS
THE HOGARTH PRESS
LONDON

Published in 1984 by
Chatto & Windus · The Hogarth Press
40 William IV Street, London WC2N 4DF

British Library Cataloguing in Publication Data
Johnson, Diane
The life of Dashiell Hammett.
1. Hammett, Dashiell-Biography   2. Authors,
American-20th Century-Biography
I. Title
813'.52   PS3515.A4347
ISBN 0–7011–2766–X

Printed in Great Britain by
Redwood Burn Limited
Trowbridge, Wiltshire

Special acknowledgment is made to the following for permission to
reprint previously unpublished material: Jean Potter Chelnov, Frederick V. Field, Franklin Folsom, William C. Glackin, David Goldway, Jeremy Gury, Frances Goodrich and Albert Hackett, Lillian
Hellman, Morris Hershman, Nancy Bragdon Hughes, Humanities
Research Center at the University of Texas at Austin, Edward Langley, Mildred Le Vaux, Josephine H. Marshall, Mary Jane Miller,
Dorothy (Mrs. L. Frederick) Nebel, and Emanuel J. Rosenberg.

Grateful acknowledgment is made to the following for permission
to reprint previously published material:
    Alfred A. Knopf, Inc.: Excerpts from *The Letters of Nunnally
Johnson*, edited by Dorris Johnson. Copyright © 1981 by Dorris
Johnson. Reprinted by permission of Alfred A. Knopf, Inc.
    Alfred A. Knopf, Inc. and Random House, Inc.: Excerpts from
three works by Dashiell Hammett. *The Big Knockover*. Copyright
© 1962 by Dashiell Hammett. *The Glass Key* and *The Thin Man*.
Both Copyright © 1972 by Dashiell Hammett. Used by permission
of the publishers.

*For my family
and for all my forbearing friends*

Everybody has twenty-fours hours a day, no more and seldom less, and one way of putting in the time seems as filling to me as another, depending of course on your own nature . . .

—DASHIELL HAMMETT

ACKNOWLEDGMENTS

This book could not have been written without the cooperation of Hammett's friend and executrix, Lillian Hellman. I am grateful to Miss Hellman for giving her time and for her permission to use their voluminous correspondence. She herself has written about her long, complicated relationship with Hammett, and I have ventured very seldom into this preserve, depending for my account, instead, on what he has written, and on his letters, which make plainer than any commentator could his affection and admiration, and also the tensions of two strong natures. I should explain that passages which refer to Hammett's thoughts or feelings are based throughout on these letters; I have not ventured to imagine or invent anything. In many cases the diction is Hammett's too even where I have hoped by paraphrase to avoid too much direct quotation.

I am immensely grateful, also, to Hammett's daughter Josephine Hammett Marshall, who has provided recollections and correspondence; and for my opportunity to talk to his other daughter, Mary Hammett Miller, and to the late Mrs. Hammett. I greatly hope, but cannot expect, that my version of Hammett's life will do justice to their experience and impressions.

Many other people who knew Hammett have been kind enough to talk with me or write to me about what they remember and felt about this elusive man. Merely to mention them in a list, as here, is very inadequate thanks, I am afraid, for their thoughtful help: Dr. Abraham Abeloff, Howard S. Benedict, Mary Benet, James Benet, Alvah Bessie, William Blackbeard, Robert Boltwood, Jean Potter Chelnov, Lester Cole, Frederick Dashiell, Hugh Eames, Harold Edinberg, Rose Evans, Frederick V. Field, Franklin Folsom, William C. Glackin, Herbert Gold, David Goldway, Joe Gores, Larry Gottlieb, Jeremy Gury, Frances Goodrich and Albert Hackett, Charles Haydon, Morris Hershman, Serrell Hillman, Nancy Bragdon Hughes, Robert Kempner, Mary Kaufman, Hal Kierce, Charles Kossman, Howard Lachtman, Leslie Lamont, Ring Lardner, Jr., Mildred Le Vaux, Saul Levin, Patricia Neal, Dorothy Nebel, S. J. Perelman, Mary Marguerite Riordan, Helen and Samuel Rosen, Emanuel J. Rosenberg, Richard Roth, Herbert

Ruhm, Alvin Sargent, William Sibilia, Edward Teicher, Robert Treuhaft, Larry Washburn, John Waters, Peggy and Jerome Weidman, Hannah Weinstein, Edward Wellen, David Werman, Phyllis White (Mrs. Anthony Boucher), John P. Wirtz and Selma Wolfman.

A number of people helped me with the research and preparation of the manuscript: Frances Anderson; Gary Fisketjon and Beverly Haviland at Random House; David Madden and Tom Venturino; Stephen Talbot and Martha Ruddy, at KQED; William Koshland at Knopf; and Professor Steven Marcus, who kindly turned over to me his earlier researches. Many friends have been supportive and encouraging, and have given me invaluable suggestions: Alice Adams, Catherine Carver, Barbara Epstein, Robert Gottlieb, Alison Lurie, Leonard Michaels, William Abrahams and John Murray. And, finally, great thanks to Jason Epstein, the principal editor, for his encouragement and help from the beginning.

CONTENTS

INTRODUCTION

In the month of Dashiell Hammett's death, January 1961, John Crosby observed in the New York *Herald Tribune* that the television air was full of imitation Sam Spades: "As a matter of fact, they are imitations of imitation Sam Spades: the 77 *Sunset Strip* and the rest of them are now distilled by a whole batch of Hollywood hacks who have never been inside a police station. The stuff is turned out like salt-water taffy now, rather sexy and violent stuff, but nevertheless as commercial as anything sold at Atlantic City. Only the corruption remains; the talent has long since fled."[1]

Now, twenty years after Hammett's death, this is all the more true. We take the hard-boiled hero for granted—he's as much a part of daily life as Superman—but we have nearly lost sight of the extent to which he was Hammett's creation, descended from Sam Spade, and from Sam's predecessor, a short, fat little man called the Continental Op.

These tough and taciturn heroes also derive, no doubt, from our national character, from our history and from earlier fiction, from Natty Bumppo to Race Williams, Spade's contemporary in the work of Carroll John Daly. The hard-boiled hero does not express his emotions (though he possesses them), and assumes himself to be outside a society that is itelf corrupt and has disappointed him. He devises a course of action and sticks to it even though it is invariably at odds with the approved course and may even be illegal. As Oscar Wilde said, Americans are great hero-worshipers and draw their heroes from the criminal classes. We admire a hard-boiled hero who is determined, in a world devoid of values, to do what his code of honor tells him must be done, and his code

derives from an earlier and simpler world—the world B.C. as Hammett called it—before credit and the crisis of 1918. Many Americans have internalized the point of view of the Hammett hero and
see public officials and the official structures of society as inevitably
corrupt.

Students of the detective story have explained the flourishing of
this genre as an expression of the conflicts of late-nineteenth- and
early-twentieth-century society. The detective story is essentially
an allegory, usually a Freudian allegory, with the detective as the
superego and the criminal as the id—both aspects of the same personality. The crime is a symbolic enactment of some innate human
impulse of lust or greed, and its solution, at least in the traditional
story, represents the reintegration of the personality with society,
its lawless impulses quelled so that society can again function
smoothly. This is also the form of comedy, and the detective story
is essentially a comic form. In Hammett's peculiar version, society
is returned to its former state, but that itself is shown to be corrupt
and false.

That the hunter and the hunted in tales of this kind are two
aspects of the same personality is both metaphorically true and
related to the fact that policemen and their prey understand each
other and are in a strange way comfortable with each other. The
private eye has a foot in each camp. But from the point of view of
the criminal he is a bit too straight, and from that of the law a bit
too seedy. He is at once a crook and a competitor. Even the title,
"private eye," is a perfect metaphor for an inhabitant of the psychological territory that Sam Spade and the Op inhabit—territory
vastly different from that inhabited by the public "I." To see crime
as an aspect of the unconscious has led to changes in our attitudes
toward it; the mission of the private eye is sometimes tempered by
his sense of complicity, and sometimes his punitive zeal is intensified
by his anxiety about this ambiguity.

The question of paternity is central to Hammett's work. This
theme, or issue, involves the conflict between generations, identity,
the handing down of skill and wisdom, the usurpation of authority,
the transfer of power. In some of his early stories, set in the tuberculosis hospital where Hammett was sent after his military service,
a young, powerless soldier ("I" or "Slim") joins others in defying
or combating figures of authority—doctors or orderlies—and in
situations where they cannot win they drift off like yearlings from
a herd. Hammett's first detective, the Op, is as plump and nameless

as a newborn; he exists only in relation to a powerful father, the Old Man of the Continental Agency, whose rules are "rather strict" and who, like an implacable god, has "no feelings at all on any subject." And like the Old Man, other fathers in Hammett's early work prevail over sons; it may be the father who is sexually involved with a young woman, like Leopold Gantvoort in "The Tenth Clew"; or a father who is a sexual rival of his son. Most strangely—for it is a theme unusual in literature—the central crime in two of his novels, *The Glass Key* and *Red Harvest*, is the murder of a son by his father.

This vision of authority as evil and menacing also forms the basis of Hammett's politics and may even provide a clue to why he stopped writing—as an unconscious means of defying the fatherly editors who so enthusiastically fostered and championed him. His stories are dramatizations of conflict with authority born of the discovery that authority is flawed. Fathers are not gods; they kill; the law is corrupt; and the rich and powerful are the worst people.

Hammett was a Marxist, and this fact has encouraged various critics to identify his and other hard-boiled detective stories with Marxism (and sometimes fascism). It is true that *Red Harvest* can be seen as an indictment of capitalist society, but it presents no socialist program and no real idea of social change. The point is to describe the corruption and observe the protagonist in his attempt to make little temporary corrections for the sake of the endeavor, without much hope that they will endure, and to do this by the rules he makes up, which are not the rules of society.

Tough-guy politics might better be described as disillusioned populism. The methods adopted by the Op and others continue to appeal to us because they begin from a widespread perception of society and authority: "Available though it is to the appeal of patriotism during times of national crisis, much of the political sentiment of Americans remains crystallized in the image of little people, lost now without a party or a program. . . . The neopopulists' politics is that of frustration and a desire to set things right, at least temporarily, by any means, the simpler the better."[2] And so the Op retains his charm today. The more complex mutations of Hammett's hero into Spade, Ned Beaumont and Nick Charles arise from Hammett's personal history and dramatize his attitude to authority.

During his life, Dashiell Hammett was a popular figure, often identified with his creations. He was like the hero of a book—tall, handsome, talented and flamboyant, a former private eye turned writer and playboy. Eventually he was to be regarded as a political villain dedicated to the overthrow of the government, and he would finally lead the life of a forgotten and penniless recluse. During all these phases he was the same person, always his own man. But he was also the embodiment of certain contradictions and tensions typical of his generation and nationality, an individual, yet curiously typical too. His fascination for so many is perhaps like that of Humphrey Bogart, especially the Bogart as Spade, world-weary and unsurprised, a survivor.[3]

Like other men born in the nineteenth century within the traditions of the Catholic Church, Southern manhood and American patriotism, Hammett was heir to beliefs and values that, though they did not seem appropriate to the world he found, he believed in and could not abandon. To make sense of a contradictory world, he embodied the contradictions in his own life; his behavior was both virtuous and libertine. He was to be rich and poor; unfaithful while faithful; a patriotic Communist, an ascetic hedonist. All of these contradictions gave his life a certain fascination, and, even more, a certain familiarity. There was something peculiarly American about it that can be better presented perhaps than summarized. At each decade of his life he did the American thing—went West before World War I when young men went West, joined the army, went West again to San Francisco during the twenties and the heyday of gangsters and prohibition, went to Hollywood in the glamorous thirties, when Hollywood was at its peak, to war again in the forties, and in the fifties, during the witch-hunts, to jail. He presented himself gamely to history and bore its depredations cheerfully, for he had a strange and sweet nature and knew what the Continental Op knew when he woke up beside the dead body of Dinah Brand with an ice pick in his hand: no one is to be trusted, least of all yourself.

Hammett was not the only American novelist to be troubled by the confusions of two worlds and misled by the general tone of the American twenties and thirties, which Dorothy Parker later called the smartypants stage of our history. Among the people he knew, Fitzgerald was a virtual suicide, and Hemingway an actual suicide; only William Faulkner, also alcoholic, was able to survive. And these were college-educated, middle-class men. Hammett, a poor boy with a grade-school education, had far to travel, but he seemed for a brief time to have got where he was going. He made himself an innovator and the master of a genre and developed techniques of fiction writing to go on with. He had glamour and money—more than he had ever imagined and as much as he wanted. The heroism of his life lay not in his Horatio Alger success but in the long years after success, when money and gifts were gone. It is the long blank years that prove the spirit.

DASHIELL HAMMETT

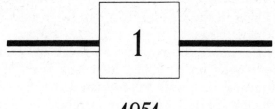

1

1951

IN PRISON

This begins in a federal prison in Ashland, Kentucky, the fall of 1951, on the second of November, a day much like the other days since Dashiell Hammett came here, for the days are not various in prison: he writes to his daughter Josephine that there is, of course, no news.[1] Hammet is fifty-seven years old, and will live another nine years. He is already ill, thin and old-looking, and as skinny as Gandhi. In his granny glasses he has strangely come to resemble Gandhi, though he used to look like an actor or a dancer, tall and handsome, in houndstooth checks with a swagger stick. Now his thinness worries the guards and other prisoners. They give this old guy easy indoor jobs to do, cleaning the toilets or pushing a broom or a mop.[2]

Hammett was brought here on a special guarded bus in late September and first put into a cell by himself. Before that he was in a jail in New York City; he has been locked up since early July. The Ashland Federal Correctional Institution confines a few income-tax evaders and forgers but mostly moonshiners and thieves and young fellows sent up on the Mann Act. Hammett and his companion, Frederick Vanderbilt Field, are political prisoners; Hammett is doing six months for contempt of court, and Field is doing nine, because they wouldn't answer questions in a Communist-hunting case.

The countryside around the prison is a little like St. Marys County, Maryland, near where Hammett was born and spent his childhood. Outside the prison, hunters walk in the woods and along the ditches. He can hear their guns in the early morning, men out after pheasant and rabbit. He envies the hunters their solitary stalking in the woods. He'd like to go hunting. It is the freedom he most misses.

Now, in November, the mornings are foggy and cold, and Hammett wakes himself up coughing; his cough is the first thing he hears, and then, as they walk to breakfast across the courtyard, he hears the shotguns in the woods. After breakfast he does his chores. This particular day is Friday, a mop day. He notices that "the mop handle felt kind of good in my hand . . . and I realized I'd been looking forward to mopping . . . and I guess either I was feeling better or I am going crazy—or both." He pushes the mop around the dormitory and reflects that he'll be out on December 9, "so I'll at least get a couple of weeks of duck shooting"; and when he has finished sweeping and mopping the floor, some of the boys come in and throw cigarette butts down on it. They grind the butts under their heels and laugh, and Hammett curses them and starts again with the broom. His dustpan is a folded newspaper with the edge moistened, a clever trick the guards taught the prisoners. This is a ritual, the littering and the curses. The boys like Hammett and he likes them. They are hillbillies, mostly from West Virginia and Tennessee, or from the countryside right around the prison.

Many of the inmates seem to like the prison: some of them say they never had it so good—it's better than home. The food's better and there's enough of it, and in prison they teach you to read and write if you can't. Many of them can't. There is a committee—Hammett and Fred Field serve on it—to help teach the new fellows how to use the toilets and the showers. It shocks Fred Field, the descendant of Commodore Vanderbilt, to think that there are American white men who don't know how to use indoor toilets: this shocks even Hammett, who has been in the army twice and seen everything.

Hammett and Field had their radical politics, but they didn't do any preaching in the prison. But Hammett spoke plainly about other things. It made Fred nervous sometimes when Hammett would tease the other men, "What does a murderer like you know?" or "What do you expect from a thief?" Fred feared he'd say it to someone unbalanced; after all, this was a prison, and things happen. When Hammett did try a little sermon on tolerance or equality, it never got very far. "It's not that I'm prejudiced," the kid from South Carolina said when they tried to talk about race relations, "because I've got no reason to dislike niggers, but I just hate 'em."[3]

The blacks were kept elsewhere and separate, and Dr. Alpheus Hunton, who had been sentenced for the same reasons as Hammett and Field, had been taken to an entirely segregated and separate prison in Virginia.

Sometimes a man is worried and tortured beyond belief by the mere fact of confinement. He chafes and repines, sometimes sickens. But others aren't bothered as much, and they are said to do "easy time." This was Hammett: "The time goes very rapidly," he assured his daughter Jo. His case had just been heard in the circuit court of appeals and would probably be taken to the Supreme Court. Hammett felt an interest, as one does in one's own case, but it was becoming clear to him that by the time the lawyers and judges got done with all the hearings and pleadings he'd be out anyhow, and he'd hate to have to come back again to serve a week or two if things went against him. So he'd just as soon stay here another month; it wasn't so bad. As the boys said, you can do five months without taking your shoes off.

Coming to prison had been in its way a festival event, like a public hanging, with the accompanying hoots of the attendant press, the eyes of the curious following the bus that transported him, the stares in the elevator at the West Street jail in New York at the nice-looking men in handcuffs. On the way to Kentucky they'd stopped overnight in Ohio at a boys' prison in Chillicothe, a gloomy place, but even in the silence of the dining hall, where it was forbidden to make a noise with your fork against your metal plate, the stares of the sullen boys were comradely, and in their cells they found the day's papers and the *Saturday Evening Post*, and Cokes, magically bespeaking brotherhood. Arriving at Ashland, they'd been given intelligence tests, as if entering a new school, and Hammett had been able to do things, like dividing fractions, which impressed the others.

His spirits had improved at Ashland, because his health had improved. When he first got there, after the hot jail in New York, he was run-down or something, he didn't know what, and fainted in the food line. He was embarrassed by this, and he told Fred Field, who caught him as he toppled over, that he had low blood pressure, though he didn't. Hammett had had these episodes a few other times in the past. Now the doctors had put him for a few weeks in the prison hospital.

Sometimes, pitying his weakness and admiring his literary reputation, the correctional staff put him to work in the prison library. Hammett got a kick out of the person in charge there, a kid, John

Waters, who took the library very seriously and worried about whether Hammett should work in a library where his own books were, for fear there might be something wrong with this, conflict of interest or something. Hammett promised to be very fair in passing out books: "One of mine for every one of the others."[4]

Some mornings Hammett went back to bed for a couple of hours, and sometimes he did this in the afternoon too, and slept the

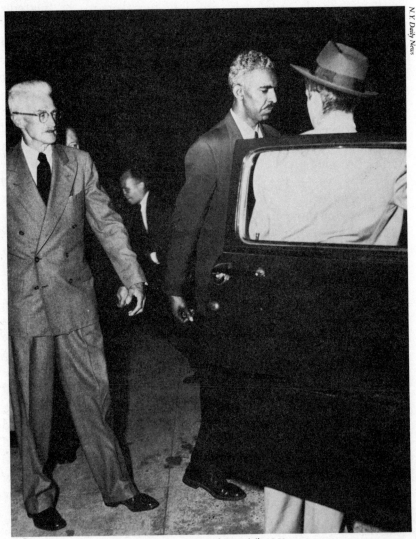

N Y Daily News

Dashiell Hammett and Alpheus Hunton being taken to jail, 1951.

day away. In the late morning the prisoners could go to the little canteen and with their five dollars' monthly allowance could buy cigarettes or pipe or chewing tobacco, or a two-dollar watch. With five dollars a month, Hammett and Fred Field with all his wealth were in the same boat with the hillbilly kids. Fred gave up cigarettes to buy pipe tobacco; Hammett bought chewing tobacco and cigarettes. There was no booze, of course, which didn't matter to Hammett, who had been on the wagon now for three years. It mattered to the others; they talked about whiskey almost as much as they talked about women.

They talked a lot about the food too. The food wasn't so bad here, and Hammett had by now actually put on a pound or two. The main meal was at noon; they might have fresh pork steak or bacon from the prison-farm pigs, and corn fritters, cream pie and coffee. The meat was good, but the fritters and hot-cakes and rolls usually came out doughy and everyone would complain. Sometimes Hammett would write to Jo and his other daughter, Mary, about the food because there wasn't much else to write about—there was no news in prison, just life from day to day, and the mail was censored.

Getting the mail was a big event each day. Both his daughters wrote, and Jo sent a lot of snapshots of her baby, Ann, his first grandchild. Jo and Mary were on an approved list of next of kin who were allowed to write, and the officials sometimes also let through letters from his wife, Josephine, although she was not strictly approved, and once they let through a letter from his friend Lillian Hellman, who was also disapproved. Hammett could write only to Jo and Mary and his lawyer, Charles Haydon. His letters to them were censored in theory, but nothing ever had to be crossed out. Like many professional writers, he was not an enthusiastic writer of letters but stuck to a bland, affectionate style that didn't bother the prison censors at all, a tone of exemplary sweetness and calm.

On the outside his friends imagined him ill and despondent. They were obliged to get news of him from Jo, and send it the same way. His friends questioned Charlie Haydon after his visits on the state of Hammett's color, his weight, his cough. Lillian Hellman and Jo and Hammett's secretary, Muriel Alexander, shared the feminine conviction that baby pictures would be cheering, so a lot of his mail consisted of those.

Muriel wrote Jo detailed instructions about Polaroid film, for which she had a standing monthly order at Abercrombie and Fitch: "What's most important is that a steady stream of pictures of that wonderful child are sent to your father."[5] Muriel used to go down to the West Street jail in New York and hold up pictures 'from her side of the visitors' room, and she could see how much he loved to see them.

Hammett acknowledged these baby pictures very courteously: "I don't want to sound too much like the doddering grandfather I am, but it seems to me that Ann becomes lovelier in almost every snapshot you send."[6] But he kept these baby pictures out of sight in one of the two drawers of his bunk. They were not exactly in keeping with the tone of the rest of the pictures in the dormitory, though one indeed was a nude baby picture, and Jo had had to get special permission to send it.

The daily mail. An afternoon nap. Supper, at five, which might be cheese sandwiches and then after supper, at seven, you were counted and you turned in your socks and handkerchief for clean ones, except on Saturdays and Sundays when you had to make do.

This afternoon, November 2, he heard a rumor that the circuit court of appeals had turned down his and Fred's appeal for bail and that it had upheld the ruling of the federal court. Hammett took some comfort in one small dissenting voice, "occupying itself with some sort of technicalities which may (or may not)" do him and the others some good. This meant, he realized, that he would have to decide whether or not to go to the Supreme Court. He was inclined to take his case as far as possible, and so was Fred. His friend Lillian Hellman thought this a wise though probably an expensive decision. He was not after justification—he was not given to vengeful brooding in prison. It was more that he was interested in how it would turn out.

For instance, would the Supreme Court, which he respected, really feel he had had no right to keep silent about something he didn't know about anyway? And had the courts really turned into Inquisitions? What would happen? "This letter won't get to you in time or I might ask you and Ann to be praying your heads off about two-thirty Eastern time,"[7] he writes to Jo. He found himself thinking how nice it would be to have supper in New York, oysters on the half shell, quail and sweetbreads, as a free man. But he didn't think it would happen.

· · ·

This is Friday and the Sam Spade program is on the radio to-night. Some of the men go off after dinner to practice for an amateur show they are giving, but there is a crowd of Spade fans who gather up to the radio. Hammett is known to the other cons not only as a famous writer but as someone who hasn't ratted on others, and although the second thing is more important to them than the first, being a famous writer and successful in the world impresses them too. The voice of Sam Spade comes over the radio, and the men imagine him as looking tall and tough, as once Hammett must have looked, even though he is now thin and shrunken, with a cough and false teeth. And what must impress them even more is that when the voice of Spade comes over the radio, he, Hammett, is making money even while he lies there smoking on his bunk in prison.

That he was making money even though he was a Communist was above all things what seemed to infuriate people on the outside. Walter Winchell, the radio gossip, gloated that "Dashiell Hammett must be very itchy cooped up in the sneezer. Call him Dashiell Hammett and sickle."

"He took crime out of the gutter. And now it looks as though he has followed it there," said the *Knickerbocker* (N.Y.) *News*.

"He's written a lot of paragraphs, but this was his first sentence," said the Philadelphia *Inquirer*.

Harrisburg *Patriot*: "He started his career by putting others in jail, and now he's ending it there, in jail!"

"Call him Samovar Spade," said Walter Winchell:

It is sickening to the lovers of mystery plays via the networks to read where one of the most prolific authors of these whodunits is a fair-haired boy for the communists. Hammett has become a wealthy man in America, but after making his millions he has suffered a dislike for our form of government; with the usual run of shoddy no-good American reds, it's hardly worthwhile to ponder who they are. Track them down, yes, and show them up for what they are, surely, and impose on them any legal penalty that's called for. But most usually there's a bunch of faceless nonentities who would fail as miserably under the communists' system as they have under the democratic. But every now and then some reasonably well-known name pops up—some man or woman usually connected with the film industry who has reaped a fortune from decent American pocketbooks.

The next time "The Thin Man" comes to town—or the next time you hear of any other book or movie play by Dashiell Hammett—you might pause and remember the gratitude you've got from him for your previous donations.

A bigger mystery than any which his fertile brain ever conceived is this: Why will a man who has enjoyed every luxury of life under the American system be caught running with those who would stomp that system out of existence?

The inheritor of great wealth made in America, the man Field, and the writer of mysteries who has also grown wealthy because he could write as he pleases, the man Hammett, flout the American tradition when they refuse to answer lawful questions in court. They are properly, we think, sentenced for contempt of that court. [Oxnard, Calif., *Press*].

There is no law that requires anybody to add one dollar to Hammett's revenue and patriotic Americans will refuse to read or listen to a line that has ever come from that guy. We are through with him and anyone that ever had a tie-up with the Russian gang. He had his day in court and showed exactly what kind he is. . . . Why should we give these guys a break? [Port Chester, N.Y., *Guide*]

There was only one newspaper, beyond the red newspapers where he was predictably praised, that had anything reasonable to say. It was a paper in Alabama, whose columnist Alan Rankin said he didn't care about an author's politics.[8]

After the Sam Spade broadcast was over, the men would talk as usual about women. Hammett's life was bounded by female connections—his daughters, Jo and Mary; his secretary, Muriel; his best friend, Lillian; and even his pet turtle, Willy, who turned out to be Wilhelmina. But none of these were women in the sense that the men in the dormitory meant. Hammett told a story or two now and then, but not often, and when he thought about women in the sense the other men did, it was of Patricia Neal, a pretty young actress. She was no intellectual, but pretty and sweet. On the subject of smart women and sweet ones Hammett's mind had always been divided. He sent Pat Neal a message, via Jo, that it was easy to be a little in love with her from prison,[9] for prison encourages sentiment. She didn't love him, of course. He was a famous writer but too old.

On the way to the prison from the New York jail where they'd

been held, their bus had broken down. It was an ordinary Grey-
hound-style bus but the driver was caged off and a guard was in
another cage. This bus had broken down in front of a high school
in New Jersey. The transmission had gone. The bus had FEDERAL
BUREAU OF PRISONS written on the side, so the high school kids
came and gawked. But it was the girls who hung around longest,
giggling or looking dreamy-eyed, lured by the idea of outlaws.
Perhaps they were attracted by the good-looking Field and wondered what he'd done. They hadn't looked much at skinny old
Hammett with his scruffy mustache and little granny glasses. Yet
there was a time when women right and left fell into bed with
Hammett.

In prison he had shaved off his mustache, according to the rules.
He had worn it for twenty-five years, and at first his bare face
shocked him, it seemed so long and pale between the nose and the
upper lip. But now after a month he liked being without it. It was
more comfortable, and there was something to having a new face
with which to start anew. Although he had no future plans. He
wrote to Jo that only popular pressure would make him regrow
lip hair.[10]

Tonight he was reading, for the first time, *Jane Eyre*, which he
found in the prison library. While in prison he also read, among
other books, Gogol's *Dead Souls*, which he thought a very funny
book, Meyer Levin's *Citizens*, which it seemed to him he had read
before, Cerletti's *Wind over Wisconsin*, and *The Last of the
Mohicans*, and he reread *Tess of the D'Urbervilles, Jude the Ob-
scure, The Return of the Native, Crime and Punishment* and *Les
Misérables*.[11]

Lights out at ten o'clock. When he first got there he would
drop off to sleep immediately when the lights were turned out, but
lately it took him a couple of hours to get to sleep. They were
seldom unpleasant hours, and, as a matter of fact, he looked forward to them sometimes. He lay there and thought pleasantly of
things about which he didn't have to come to any conclusions.

He came to no conclusions about the future. He had no plans.
Maybe he'd go to the Coast to see the baby. He thought more
about the past, and in particular about his reputation as a writer,
which now stuck to him like the shirt of Nessus, a poison gift, for
he no longer wrote. It had been seventeen years since his last novel
was published.

Since then his reputation had not waned but grown, catching

heat from films based on his books, from glimpses others had
caught of the man himself, stylish and taciturn, going into "21,"
the smart New York restaurant, from gossip columns, from the
admiration of French critics.

André Gide, in particular, was on his mind in prison. Hammett
invoked Gide to challenge that kid, John Waters, who ran the
prison library and had been to the New School for Social Research
in New York and who thought detective stories were trash. "Have
you read Gide?" Hammett snapped at him. "Know who Gide
thinks the great American writers are now? Faulkner and Hammett."

After that John Waters read Hammett too. And Hammett wrote
to Jo that Gide had compared him with Balzac, something he had
heard from Lillian, who was in France. "André Gide had said
among other things that I was as good a writer as Balzac, which
of course pleased me immensely."[12] Then, in the same sentence, he
adds that on the fourteenth of last month three judges of the
circuit court heard their appeal against their sentences. The con-
junction of these two unlikely conditions, that of being a great
writer and a prisoner, is on his mind, and probably troubles him.
Above all, does Gide know what he is talking about? What if he
does? What if he doesn't? A present of fame, of literary reputation, was like a hot coal in his pocket, reassuring, hand-warming,
but if he drew it out to look at it, it turned into cinders. The
greater his reputation, the more trivial to him seemed the stories
from which it arose, the more incumbent upon him to write differ-
ently and better and greater and more, and the more impossible to
do any of this. And so, lights out at ten, and he would lie there
in his cot a couple of hours before dropping off to sleep, trying
not to think of writing.

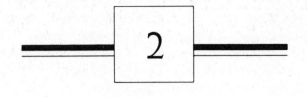

1894–1917

EARLY LIFE

He did not think of the future any more than was necessary, but he thought about the past. When he got out of prison, he tried to write about it, but the past was not his subject. It didn't work for him; he did not understand it well; it was mysterious to him. He did know that he had more in common with the inmates of the prison, and with the guards and wardens, than he did with many other people in his recent life. Here were Southerners and untaught people, as he himself had been, guards and watchers, as he himself had been and as his father had been, and farm people, like the people he came from.

He had never expected to go to prison, though there were relations back in St. Marys County who, remembering him, were not surprised—a tall, red-haired boy who bragged about the city where they'd gone to live, and thought that St. Marys County was the sticks and told everybody so, though he liked to visit his grandpa well enough, and to wander in the woods. In the city he smoked cigarettes and worked for the railroad; these were times when a likely boy could expect to get ahead.

On both sides, Hammett and Dashiell, his people had been in America since the eighteenth century. Roughly speaking, the Hammetts were farmers and the Dashiells sailors, all working people and artisans, with material ups and downs. Hammett was born May 27, 1894, on a farm called Hopewell and Aim, in the house of his grandfather, Samuel Hammett, where his mother and father were living. It was a tobacco farm, with a big three-story farmhouse. Hammett's father, Richard Thomas, helped his own father, Samuel, with the farming, and here also lived the grandfather's new young wife, Lucy, and Hammett's mother, Annie Bond Dashiell Hammett, and Hammett's older sister, Aronia Rebecca— they called her Reba. And eventually Lucy would produce some new babies, and Hammett would get a baby brother, Dick.[1]

Richard Thomas didn't think much of farming. He thought it hard work and countrified, and he cherished a wish to get ahead. He thought it might be possible to get ahead in a big city like Philadelphia or Baltimore, where his wife's people lived. Annie Dashiell was a fragile, hard-working, imaginative woman who held herself above the Hammetts. The climate in St. Marys County aggravated her cough—she had a "chest," as they said, and she welcomed the idea of city life again. So Richard took her and his three children and went first to Philadelphia to seek their fortune and, not finding it there, to Baltimore, where they moved in with Annie's mother, Mrs. Dashiell.

The move was meant to be temporary. Mrs. Dashiell lived in a rented house at 212 North Stricker with Aunt Aronia, her daughters, a boarder named Mrs. Croswell and her son, a clerk. The Dashiells were fixed pretty much like everybody else on North

Photo by O V Wooten. Courtesy of Frederick Dashiell

"Long Hill," built in 1683, with nineteen graves of Dashiells.

Stricker Street. One family, at 224, was better off; only four people lived in this house, which they owned, and they had a black servant to help them, the only servant on the street and the only black. One other family on the street owned its house, but everybody else rented, and most people had boarders. In the alleys and in nearby blocks were many black families.

It was a real American street. The parents of almost everyone had been born in America, and even their parents and grandparents had. No one was rich, but they were hardworking. Women worked as seamstresses and saleswomen, dressmakers and hat makers. Hammett's grandmother worked as a saleslady. The men were tailors or clerks or watchmen, and there was a young man apprenticed at the picture framer's and a man who made cigars. The street was not paved, and the toilets were out back.[2]

This was in 1898. Hammett's father had a job as a clerk and wore vests and braces and bands around his sleeves. In 1899 he worked as a salesman, and the next year things picked up so that he could move his family to a better place, on Poplar Street, and the next year they moved to Sixtieth Street. Then his luck turned bad and back they went to North Stricker to live with Mrs. Dashiell again. Hammett's father didn't keep a job long, he was too full of plans. He worked now as a salesman, now as a bus conductor, now as a foreman in a lock factory. Hammett, his sister and younger brother went to Public School 72 when it was time. They went now and then to the country to visit the Hammett relatives, and Hammett's grandfather would take the boy out to hunt or fish or walk around the fields. Hammett's grandfather with his new wife began to have a new family of little children too.

When Hammett and his father Richard, smartly dressed in city clothes, would go back to the farm to visit, Hammett, who had grown tall and likely-looking, would tell all these farm people about life in the city, and the farm people, looking at his father's striped suits, looking at his father's motor car, concluded that things were going all right, or, if Richard Thomas had not made much of himself, strictly speaking, the boy, Dashiell, looked like he figured to.[3]

After the boy learned to read, he would sit far into the night reading trash, mysteries, whatever he could find, and good books too. Sometimes what he read would confuse him. When he was thirteen, seeking all answers to everything, he read Kant's *Critique of Pure Reason.* He didn't understand it, and it didn't reveal all answers to life, but he read it all the way through. Throughout his life he would like books of that kind, on abstract subjects, which attempted to explain things clearly, even if they couldn't.

In 1908, when he was fourteen, he started high school, at the Baltimore Polytechnic, a school where bright children could get a good start, might even enter college as sophomores when they finished. Hammett took algebra, American literature, English composition, history, mechanical drawing and physics. He was best at history, but he would always be good at drawing and have a liking for mathematics and technical subjects. He was not allowed to study them further now, for he had to leave school almost as soon as he began.

Richard T. was not doing well financially, and as Dashiell was so tall and self-assured, his father felt that he should bring in his share, like the other boys in the 200 block of North Stricker—the printer's apprentice, the jeweler's apprentice, the boy who was learning picture frames. So Hammett left school and got a job as a messenger boy for the B & O Railroad. He hated it.

In 1910, when he was sixteen, he was living at 212 North Stricker with his father, who was working as a clerk, all of them working hard.[4] In 1912, when Richard, his little brother, turned sixteen, he became a clerk too. In 1911 Hammett's grandfather Samuel died. There was some hope at first of profit—Samuel left more than $2,000—but this would have to be split up among Samuel's new children too, and then a creditor of Richard T.'s, a J. Freeman, insisted on having his $84.13, so in the end Richard T. got only $67.70, and this wasn't enough to keep him from going under once again.[5]

It was at this period that Hammett began to row with his father and come home drunk. His father was in a teetotaling phase,[6] but his sober habits didn't help him as far as Hammett could see, and Hammett's wild habits didn't impede *him*. Sometimes he'd be late to his job, for it was hard to get up after a night of drinking. "We'll keep you this time," a man at the railroad said, "but promise not to be late again." "I can't promise," Hammett said. "Oh well," said the railroad man, "stay on anyway; at least you're honest."

Hammett was honest, but restless and curious. Down at the railroad yard, he heard stories about the West. He watched dice games and card games, and learned to play them, and he bet his money on horses, trains and fights. Whores hung around the bars near the railroad yard, and he went with them sometimes and came to like them, though he caught gonorrhea when he was twenty. This was a natural hazard; he was a handsome boy and women liked him. His grandmother, who went to the movies every Saturday afternoon, thought he looked like Wallace Reid, her favorite movie star. Weekdays she worked. His brother, Richard, worked too, and his sister, Reba, was learning to do secretarial work and typing —they all worked hard. Even so, it wasn't easy for people like the Hammetts, clinging to the upper fringe of the lower class, the working class, native-born and respectable, being constantly challenged by rambunctious immigrants trying to better themselves —Irish or Germans pushing themselves into the clerk jobs, the salesman jobs. In 1915 Richard Thomas was dealing in oysters, and at this time Hammett had a pretty good job with the Pinkerton operatives, where he'd started earlier as a clerk and now that he was twenty was on the way to being an operative himself. He was brave and intelligent, and could do things men much older couldn't do. Around the office they thought he'd make a good operative—discreet, patient, and he'd uphold the rules. The pay was twenty-one dollars a week. Hammett liked the work.

"We never sleep" was the Pinkerton National Detective Agency's motto. It had the nation under watch, from coast to coast. It had begun in the mid-nineteenth century at a time when other police agencies, municipal or federal, were unformed and ineffective. Alan Pinkerton, the founder, had established both a detective network and a philosophy against crime: Pinkerton operatives were to solve crimes and prevent them. By Hammett's day they were also to protect private property, often factories and mines in labor disputes. Pinkerton men were soldiers, watchmen, enforcers, team players, loners. The head of the Baltimore office, a little fat man named James Wright, whom the Op was to resemble, taught Hammett the rudiments of shadowing, an essential detective skill that Hammett took to. Hammett explained how it was done:

> You simply saunter along somewhere within sight of your subject, and, barring bad breaks, the only thing that can make you lose him is over-anxiety on your part. Even a clever criminal may be shadowed for weeks without suspecting it. I knew one operative who shadowed a wily old forger for more than three months without arousing his suspicion. I myself trailed one for six weeks, riding trains and making half a dozen small towns with him; and

I wasn't exactly inconspicuous, standing an inch over six feet. You don't worry about a suspect's face. Tricks of carriage, ways of wearing clothes, general outline, individual mannerisms—all as seen from the rear—are much more important to the shadow than faces.[7]

A Pinkerton man was self-reliant, vigilant, stuck to the old way of wits and patience.

Many devices of "scientific" detecting are excellent when kept to their places, but when pushed forward as infallible methods, they become forms of quackery, and nothing else. The trouble is that criminals are so damned unscientific, and always will be so long as the most marked criminal trait is the childish desire for a short cut to wealth. The chemist and the photographer and the rest make excellent assistants to our old friend, the flat-footed, low-browed gumshoe, but he's the boy who keeps the jails full of crooks in the long run. . . . There is no doubt that fingerprints are a valuable part of the anti-criminal arsenal, but they are only a part of it. As evidence goes, I favor what is usually called "circumstantial evidence" as against the testimony of witnesses. . . . Neither have I much faith in experts who claim infallibility in any field except, perhaps, abstract mathematics.[8]

He was sent West. A Pinkerton man would get money for his train ticket, not for the pullmans, but for sitting up throughout the drafty long ride. On the train young Hammett saw the flat stretches of the Great Plains, then the Rockies, bleak landscapes one after another, and the little train towns, and mining camps, and lonesome farmhouses. He had not realized before how big America was. He would have Pinkerton money for the train food and to stay in a small hotel or boardinghouse in the town where he had to do his job. Back in Baltimore, on Stricker Street, he had a home, but his real home now was the Gladstone valise of the homeless, of the traveler. He had to learn all the ways to get a suit cleaned, a shirt done, clothes washed. He was tidy, a careful packer.

The boardinghouses of the small Western towns were a matter of chance. Sometimes the food was good, sometimes not, sometimes there was a pretty daughter or good talk, but usually not. Rooms were fifty cents or a dollar. The towns were full of strangers going through, and lots were young, like Hammett, young men going West, hopping trains and picking up jobs, sleeping in boardinghouses.

Hammett, earliest known photos.

It was in such a boardinghouse in Butte, Montana, in 1917 that the owner, Mrs. Nora Byrne, was awakened one night by voices in the room next to hers, room 30, men's voices saying there must be some mistake here, and then feet in the hall, then men at her door, pushing it open, and Mrs. Byrne, having jumped out of bed, held her door with all her strength as some men with guns pushed it in anyway. They held the gun on her, saying, "Where is Frank Little?" and she told them. Then they went away again, and kicked down the door of room 32 and went in and woke the man sleeping there, who made no outcry or objection and demanded no explanation. Because he had a broken leg, they had to carry him out.

Then, in the morning, he was found hanging from the trestle with a warning to others pinned to his underwear. Some people said his balls had been cut off. The warning came from the Montana vigilantes, though it was hard to see what the citizens of Montana stood to gain from the death of this poor man. Only the mine owners stood to gain from the death of this agitator, a Wobbly. Wobblies were stirring up a lot of trouble among the miners at Butte.

"These Wobblies," said the mine owner's lawyer a few days later, "snarling their blasphemies in filthy and profane language; they advocate disobedience of the law, insults to our flag, disregard of all property rights and destruction of the principles and institutions which are the safeguards of society."[9] He was trying to show that Mr. Little had brought his lynching on himself. "Why, Little, the man who was hanged in Butte, prefaced his seditious and treasonable speeches with the remark that he expected to be arrested for what he was going to say." Perhaps he had not expected, however, to be hanged, but what were decent Americans to do with such rascals?

The mine owner's lawyer, noticing no contradiction, inconsistency or irony, proclaimed that the Wobblies "have invariably shown themselves to be bullies, anarchists and terrorists. These things they do openly and boldly," unlike (he did not add) all the decent American vigilantes who came masked by night. The young Hammett, in Montana at the time, noticed the ironies and inconsistencies with particular interest because men had come to him and to other Pinkerton agents and had proposed that they help do away with Frank Little.[10] There was a bonus in it, they told him, of $5,000, an enormous sum in those days.

Hammett's inclinations had probably always been on the side of law and order. His father had once been a justice of the peace and always went to the law when necessary with confidence, for instance, when his buggy was damaged by the potholes on the public road; and he worked for a lock-and-safe company, and at other times as a watchman or a guard. There was thus in the family a brief for caring about the property of others, putting oneself at risk so that things in general should be safe and secure.

But at some moment—perhaps at the moment he was asked to murder Frank Little or perhaps at the moment that he learned that Little had been killed, possibly by other Pinkerton men—Hammett saw that the actions of the guards and the guarded, of the detective and the man he's stalking, are reflexes of a single sensibility, on the fringe where murderers and thieves live. He saw that he himself was on the fringe or might be, in his present line of work, and was expected to be, according to a kind of oath of fealty that he and other Pinkerton men took.

He also learned something about the lives of poor miners, whose wretched strikes the Pinkerton people were hired to prevent, and about the lies of mine owners. These things were to sit in the back of his mind.

And just as he learned about the lot of poor miners, and about the aims of trade unions, so at some point he learned about the rich. He saw their houses—maybe as a Pinkerton man, or maybe it was back in Baltimore that he noticed the furniture and pictures in rich people's houses, different from the crowded parlor on North Stricker Street, or from the boardinghouses and cheap hotels he stayed in. He learned to prefer the houses of the rich. He must also have noticed the clothes of women, and the difference between silk and flannel, and learned the rituals an expensive woman required to keep beautiful, and how much she cost.

He himself was easy with women by now, and he usually got what he wanted. He also got another dose of clap, this same year, 1917, which he did not write home about, but he took it as one of the risks, more or less cheerfully, and certainly didn't change his ways.

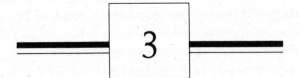

1918–1921

HOSPITAL

In the view of the radical American workingmen who belonged to the Industrial Workers of the World and who called themselves Wobblies, the great war in Europe was just a plot to enrich the makers of munitions and the owners of mines. To the Wobblies, it was the international struggle of labor that mattered, and at first Hammett, who had seen the struggling miners at firsthand, was inclined to take the Wobbly view of it. The war seemed far away from Montana, though the mine owners and the papers talked of it: "Full production is what is needed for the war effort, and no strikes." "Our main anxieties and thoughts since our country was precipitated into the great European struggle have been with the brave boys, among whom each of us has son, brother, close relative or friend who have been called to the front to bear their share of the dangers and horrors of modern warfare . . . and if any of us fail in our duties [to work the mines] he is a more despicable slacker than any able-bodied young man who, without excuse, avoids the call to arms,"[1] said the mine owners. Eventually Hammett took this view of it himself, and made his way back to Baltimore and said good-bye to his family and joined up.

He was now Private Hammett of the 34th Company, 9th Training Battalion, 154th Depot Brigade. After three weeks of training in June 1918, he was sent to the Motor Ambulance Company. By October he had caught the flu that rampaged through the troops and around the world, and of which millions died. He lay in the base hospital for three weeks, feverish, unable to sit up, wracked with coughing. Perhaps he had not known until now that he had contracted his mother's TB, the common affliction of city people brought up in crowded houses.

He was let out of the hospital and then in a few months was back in again, and again in a few months after that, and by the next May, in 1919, the army had decided he would never be cured or fit enough to be a soldier, and discharged him with a pension of $40 a month. It had not been much of a military career, spent being ill, fifteen miles from home. Of his time in the army he said later only that he had overturned an ambulance and people had been hurt. He decided he would never drive again, and he never did, or only rarely.[2]

Two other times in his life he had hurt someone, and each time it filled him with horror. Once, when he was a little boy playing hockey he had hit another boy in a fury. The boy was winning, and this seemed at the moment unendurable. So Hammett hit him with a stick, and made his chin bleed. Seeing the boy's blood terrified him, and he ran away. He was ashamed.

And then when he was a Pinkerton man, he was once guarding a powder magazine and had used a gun. He hadn't wanted or meant to, but it was his responsibility, and his partner was off somewhere else. A thief came creeping up and began to scale the fence and wouldn't stop when Hammett shouted, so there was no recourse but to follow instructions and fire. The man dropped off the fence cursing, clutching himself, and ran away. Hammett felt terror again at the sight of blood, at the fragility of life.

He would try never to carry a gun again except for hunting and would not kill except to eat what he killed, and would try never to drive a car again, for which you had to be sober and aggressive. Guns and cars were weapons he did not use against others.

Hammett came out of the army with the rank of sergeant, weighing only a hundred and forty, twenty pounds less than when he'd gone in, and he had tuberculosis, which he hadn't known about before. He was twenty-five. He went home to Baltimore to his family and back to his job with Pinkerton's.

At home things were the same; only he wasn't the same—he was ill and restless, and felt cramped living with his family. So when he felt a little better, he got on the train again for Pinkerton and went West again, this time to Spokane, Washington, and from that office was once more sent into the mining country. In the summer mountain air he felt almost well and gained weight, but in the autumn he became ill again, thinner than ever, weaker, sicker. He went to the Public Health Service hospital in Tacoma, where he was declared completely disabled, his health ruined beyond repair.

It was about this same time that a young girl named Josephine Annis Dolan, from Anaconda, Montana, who had worked in the war as a Red Cross nurse, wrote to the Red Cross officials for another assignment, hoping to become a Public Health Service nurse. She wanted to leave Montana and go somewhere else as soon and as far as she could.

When their parents died,[3] Josephine Annis Dolan, aged seven, and her little brother, aged six, were put in an old-fashioned Montana orphanage founded like many other nineteenth-century orphanages with the view that to be an orphan was somehow indicative of a moral defect, or of congenital bad luck. An orphan should not get her hopes up, should not expect happiness. The orphanage would train the hopes out of you by making you scrub and wash clothes. Scullery work was good for a child.

But the dead Mrs. Dolan had a sister-in-law, Mrs. Kelly, there in Anaconda, and one night Mrs. Kelly had a dream in which the shade of her dead sister Mrs. Dolan came to her, wailing and lamenting the fate of her children confined in an orphanage, and Mrs. Kelly awoke in a sweat of self-reproach. She knew what people had been saying about her for allowing her sister's children to be put in the home like that and she went around to the orphanage directly.

At first the people at the orphanage could not find Josephine. She'd been locked in the coal cellar for being bad and defiant, locked in there and forgotten. So Aunt Kelly knew the dream was an omen and a sign that had come just in time, and she took Josephine home with her—though not the little brother. Josephine, a small but strong girl, could be a help around the house.

Josephine did work hard and helped Aunt Kelly, who had so many children of her own she could scarcely look after them all. There was a baby, who fell to Josephine's special care, whom Josephine seemed to love. She took it into her bed and comforted it when it cried. Josephine also helped with the washing and scrubbing, and said nothing when Uncle Kelly put his hands on her where it seemed to her he shouldn't. Each year she got a new dress when the Kelley girls got new dresses, for it wouldn't do to dress the orphan more shabbily than the real daughters—people would notice that. New dress or no, Josephine was happy when she became fifteen and could go to the hospital and learn to be a nurse.

Being a nurse was respectable, and a way to get along. For a girl who had to make her own way it wasn't bad, but Josephine didn't like it. She didn't like the smell of the hospital, and she didn't like sleeping there in a narrow bed that was like the one in the orphanage, and she didn't like blood or the sounds of people dying. But she did like being safely away from Uncle Kelly. She wore white dresses and smart caps, and when the war came, she joined the army and became a second lieutenant.

After the war she was accepted as a public health nurse, and went off first to New Mexico and then to Tacoma, Washington, to a hospital, out on Pulyallup Road, and it was there that she met Hammett. He came from Baltimore. She thought him very clever and handsome and admired his neatness and the tidy military

Josephine Annis Dolan.

Courtesy of Josephine Hammett Marshall

way he made his bed. He was not like the others. He kept his covers and bureau neat, and wore his hair in a pompadour. He would help the other sick people, as though he were not one of the sick himself.

Hammett wrote about the hospital time, almost the only period of his life about which he wrote directly, first in some little stories and later in the unfinished novel "Tulip":

I'm in a lung hospital in 1921, out in a converted Indian school on Puyallup Road in the fringes of Tacoma, Washington.[4] Most of us were what came to be known as disabled veterans of World War I, but the Veterans Administration hadn't any hospitals of its own in those days—maybe hadn't even been organized under that name—so the United States Public Health Service took care of us in its hospitals. In this one about half of us were lungers; the other half what was then called shell shock victims, segregated as far as sleeping quarters and eating were concerned because I suppose some sort of control was kept over them—we didn't have much—and because they might catch t.b. from us. It was a nice sloppily run hospital, and I think most of us who took it easy beat the disease—it's the lungers I'm talking about; I don't know how the shell shocks (goofs in our language) made out—while the more conscientious ones, those who chased the cure, died of it. The major in charge of the hospital was reputed to be a lush, but I don't remember any evidence of that. I remember, though, that he was afraid of the newly formed American Legion and we used that to beat him over the head with whenever he tried to get strict, though I think most of us belonged to another organization called the Disabled Veterans. Our standard defense against any and all attempts to impose anything approaching control over us was the statement—made sulkily or triumphantly, mumbled or shouted, depending on who made it and what the circumstances were—*We're not in the Army now!* Our doctors and nurses—most of them freshly out of the Army themselves—got pretty tired of hearing it, but it was a long long time before we got tired of saying it. We got either eighty or sixty dollars a month compensation from the government—I can't remember the exact figure—though I suppose it must have varied with our degree of sickness, since thermometers were called compensation sticks; enough free cigarettes to help out, though not enough to keep a reasonably heavy smoker fully supplied; free room and board, of course; and we didn't need many clothes. It wasn't a bad life. All liquor was bootleg then—except for the occasional snort you could wheedle out of a nurse or doctor—

and the stuff we bought was pretty bad but it was strong; lights were put out at probably ten o'clock, but the room I shared with a kid from Snohomish had been a matron's room in the old Indian-school days and was on the same electric light circuit as the toilet, so we had only to hang a blanket over the window to play poker as late as we wished; as I remember it we came into and went out of the hospital as we liked, needing a pass only for overnight trips to Seattle and such, though there may have been certain times we were supposed to be on hand. Anyhow most of us found it a lot better than working for a living. Sometimes we were broke; I remember Whitey Kaiser—a powerfully built squat blond Alaskan with most of the diseases known to man; he could hit like a pile driver, but his knucklebones would crumble like soda crackers—borrowing a blackjack from me—I had come to the hospital from working for a detective agency in Spokane and you're always picking up things like that when you're young— and giving it back to me the next morning with ten bucks. When I read in an afternoon paper about a man being slugged and robbed of a hundred and eighty dollars on the Puyallup Road— it ran from Tacoma to Seattle—the night before, I showed it to Whitey, who said people who were robbed always exaggerated the amounts. Sometimes we were flush; there was a lean hatchet-faced dark boy named Gladstone who finally got his bonus from the Army—a sizable sum, though I don't remember the amount any more—and spent it all for two used cars and the collected works of James Gibbons Huneker because he wanted culture and I'd told him Huneker had it. Most of the time we were bored. I supposed we bored pretty easily.[5]

The wild Whitey fascinated Hammett. He himself was ill and wild. He and Hammett went into Tacoma to see Pavlova, and for a couple of weekends the citizens of Tacoma came out to visit the hospital as a patriotic duty. There had been a newspaper story or a campaign: Visit the wounded veterans. Ungratefully the veterans terrified the visitors with gruesome stories, or they threw pie pans over the curtains of their wards to frighten shell-shocked men. They were cruel to their comrades because their situation was cruel—both terrified and bored, they were waiting to die.

Perhaps this was the first time that Hammett had thought of death as something coming to him. He had seen dead men before, had even seen them die, but such things had seemed unlikely to happen to a healthy young person full of ideas. Now when he coughed, blood spurted from his lungs, and he had horrible intimations of mortality. He saw too that the army believed he would die, and didn't care. He was only twenty-seven, and he hadn't done what he knew he could do, and it would be a shame to die before he did it. The heat was terrible that summer of 1921, and men died of diseases like measles and mumps.

Hammett believed that you could fight death or at least not lie down before it. You could live your life and keep on your feet, and in particular drink whiskey. The ones that just lay about, as he said, seemed to him to die sooner, maybe from docility.

He kept himself going, went into Tacoma or down to Seattle, drank and gambled. He took the little nurse Jose—to rhyme with "dose"—out to dinner or the movies. She was a credulous little girl from Anaconda, and he pitied her. She'd been on her own almost as long as he had, and he felt women shouldn't be on their own like that. She was Catholic, like his mother, and with no more schooling than Annie Hammett had but with the same plucky attitude, and she said what she thought.

He would write twice in the next few years of a soldier in a hospital making love to a little nurse:

> We would leave the buildings in early darkness, walk a little way across the desert, and go down into a small canyon where four trees grouped around a level spot. The night dampness settling on earth that had cooked since morning would loose the fragrance of ground and plant around us. We would lie there until late in the night, our nostrils full of world-smell, the trees making irregular map-boundary division among the stars. Our love seemed dependent on not being phrased. It seemed if one of us had said, "I love you," the next instant it would have been a lie. So we loved and cursed one another merrily, ribaldly, she usually stopping her ears in the end because I knew more words.[6]

He kept thinking about it, and wrote a revised version:

> She wasn't pretty, but she was a lot of fun, a small-bodied wiry girl with a freckled round face that went easily to smiling. . . . the trees that made maps among the stars . . . Our lovemaking was a thing of rough and tumble athletics and jokes and gay repartee and cursing. She usually stopped her ears in the end because I knew more words.[7]

Jose was really scared when she found out she was in trouble, and about that time Hammett was sent off to another hospital down in Southern California. And she didn't feel well, she was sick, maybe just scared sick. They sent her to Helena, Montana, and gave her a discharge from the Public Health Service. She wrote a letter to Hammett in California.

Hammett was to write later, in "Tulip," about the hospital in Southern California, mostly about the high jinks and the train ride there.

Then the government opened, or reopened, a hospital down near San Diego—the old Army hospital in what had been Camp Kearney—and fourteen of us were transferred down there, mostly the undesirable cut-ups, I reckon. We went down in a private sleeping car, picking up a few more members at Portland. We had a couple among us who thought, or said, they were hopheads, a one-legged chap named Austen—they thought he had a tubercular infection of the bone and kept whittling pieces off his leg— and an ugly redhead named Quade with tubercular intestines. Whitey and I were broke, but among his diseases he had something wrong with his kidneys and the doctor at Tacoma had given him some white powders to take, folded up in bundles just like dope, so we peddled them to Austen and Quade throughout the trip and they sniffed them and got—or thought they got—a good bang out of them all the way to San Diego. In the Camp Kearney hospital we ran into our enemy—regulations. We got there late at night and were wakened at an early hour by a night orderly who wanted urine specimens before he went off duty. That was easy, of course: we told him where to go for his urine specimens and went back to sleep and he went off-duty without the specimens. Then we found out that not only would we have to have passes to leave the hospital—Tijuana, wide open just across the border, had been a major reason for our willingness to come here: Agua Caliente hadn't been opened yet—but they were issued only stingily, and, on top of that, we as newcomers would have to spend two weeks in a quarantine ward before we were eligible for anything, even for permission to wander around the hospital. So we revolted happily and announced that we were leaving the hospital for San Diego. The management had us over for a conference, cut the quarantine period to ten days, as I now remember it, but stuck to the other rules, and we went outside

for our own conference, by this time most of us cheerfully looking forward to San Diego and Tijuana with the local Red Cross
to throw ourselves on when we were broke. And then up the
duck walk past us came one of the hospital's civilian employees,
a pretty little girl in a striped shirtwaist and dark skirt with nice
legs in silk stockings that had a run up the back of one, and our
revolt went blooey: we decided maybe the hospital wouldn't be
so bad after all—and we could always leave when we wanted to
—and sent Whitey, who had become our spokesman by now, in
to tell the commanding officer we were staying. (None of us
ever got anywhere with the pretty little girl; I'm not sure any of
us tried very hard.) One of us—I've forgotten which—had by
this time got himself sincerely convinced there was some principle
involved in our revolt and vanished San Diegoward. The rest of
us settled down to the new routine of a new hospital. Whitey
wasn't with us long; after a few weeks he and another chap came
back from the city pretty tight one night and he slugged a doctor
—I think because the doctor had given Whitey's companion a
shot of apomorphine for his drunkenness—and got thrown out.
There was some talk about our leaving with him, but nothing
came of it and he went on his way.

Whitey continued to fascinate him; he was what Hammett was
not—dumb, brutal, succinct, and quick to act. Hammett was
shortsighted, more like a writer than a hero. If his glasses fell off,
he couldn't see much. He took off his glasses around women or for
a picture. Hammett wrote another story about Whitey.

Whitey shouldn't have hit the doctor, but he did. He poked
him in the fat mouth and the doctor fell down on the board walk
and squalled. An orderly came running from the nearest ward.
He was a red-faced meaty fellow with pop eyes. He ran up behind Whitey with his hands out while Whitey was standing over
the doctor cursing him because he wouldn't get up to be hit
again. . . .
I got between Whitey and the orderly and pushed the orderly
back. He let himself be pushed back. Whitey turned around and
said: "Smack him, Slim." That wasn't necessary. The orderly
didn't want to fight, but it was easier to smack him than to argue
with Whitey, so I hit him where he looked softest.
He staggered back against the rail complaining: "What's the
matter with you guys?"
Whitey went over to him.
"What do you think's the matter with us? There's nothing the

matter with us. There's not a God-damned thing the matter with us. What the hell's the matter with you?"

The orderly mumbled: "Aw, for Christ's sake, brother."

Whitey's coat bunched over his shoulders and he struck the orderly in the face twice, savage left-and-right-hand punches with all the weight of Whitey's thick body and all the thrust of his thick legs behind them. The orderly's head and body rocked far back over the rail. Whitey took him by the neck and threw him over the rail to the gravel six or eight feet below.

The doctor had disappeared.

I said "Well, we've lost a home."

Whitey spit on the back of his left hand, rubbed it, and said: "I popped a knuckle on that bum."[8]

After this period he thought about Whitey, and missed him. Twenty years later, when he was in the army again, happy, back in the army, he would sometimes sign his letters "Whitey," though he was probably thinking of his hair, which had turned white by then.

The new hospital was on the edge of the desert. There wasn't much to do here either. They caught horned toads and Gila monsters and staged rattler–Gila monster fights in any empty boxcar standing nearby on an unused track.

The Gila monsters always won, but most of the sucker money backed the rattlers at first, and when there was no rattler money to be had we stopped staging the fights—there was Tijuana to hit every couple of weeks. I still don't remember much about San Diego except that it was nice to look at riding downhill towards it between pink and pale-blue stucco houses, the U.S. Grant Hotel and the tonic stores where in those Prohibition days you bought and drank from a great variety of high-alcohol-content patent medicines. I suppose I read a good deal in the hospital but I can't remember a single thing I read there. I know I had a good time in Camp Kearney, but when the races closed at Tijuana—in May, I think—I asked for a discharge from the hospital and they gave it to me. They couldn't say I was an arrested case—I didn't finally lick my t.b. until five or six years later—so they wrote *maximum improvement reached* and let me go.[9]

He did a lot of reading at this time, and it must have been here that he got the letter from the scared little nurse from the hospital in Tacoma.

4

1921-1923

STARTING OUT
IN SAN FRANCISCO

When Josephine came home from Tacoma disgraced, the Kellys had plenty to say to her, not that they were surprised, for she had developed chirpy, frank ways after she got out on her own, and had learned fast talk in the army. They were not surprised, only embarrassed, scandalized and sad. But they had taken her in before and would not abandon her now. They were surprised, though, and somewhat skeptical when she said she was going off to San Francisco to get married to the man who was responsible.

Josephine took the train from Helena, Montana, and was met by Hammett, whom she had not seen for some months. They were glad to see each other, even though they didn't know each other very well. Neither of them had anyone else.

Decorously, they took separate lodgings. Hammett stayed in the rooming house, the Woodstock Rooms, where he'd been living, on Ellis Street, and he put Jose up at the Golden West, a hotel around the corner on Powell. Then they applied for their marriage license on July 6, and on the seventh went around to St. Mary's Cathedral on Van Ness in a taxi and got married, though not before the high altar. Hammett brought her flowers. She hadn't known he was a Catholic, and she thought it was a good omen.

Their new apartment on Eddy Street[1] had two furnished rooms and a bath. In the kitchen there was a big table, where Hammett would work sometimes, a laundry tub with a wooden cover over it, a stove and a sink. In the living room was a bed that folded down and a table that folded out, but not both at once. If Josephine did the wash in the kitchen, he had to work or read in the living room, or if the baby (when she came) cried in the living room, he'd work in the kitchen. The furniture was not very nice, old scraps hauled in by the manager, but someday they planned to have better. Hammett liked the little place and was a help. He cooked steaks and ham and omelettes. Downstairs, below them, were bootleggers. Lying in bed at night, they could hear the bottles clinking. But the police raid one night was so quiet they barely heard it at all.[2]

Hammett was working at this time for Pinkerton's, and Jose thought it was bad for him to work in the cold and foggy San Francisco summer; he had to lurk long hours in doorways or go out of town or shadow people for days on end, whole nights through. He too wanted to change his work and had applied to the Federal Board for Vocational Education for some other sort of training. He was told that he was approved for training, but also that the doctors didn't think he was well enough—not "in proper physical condition to successfully carry on in training"—so he had to go on shadowing and waiting and coughing and getting weaker.

San Francisco was a wide-open place in those days, run by crooks and mobsters. There was every kind of vice, and everything was for sale. Hammett loved it, loved the bars and the docks, and the fights and the races, the beauty.

Mary Jane was born October 16, 1921. Hammett was amazed by her and rocked her when she cried. They shifted her from room to room with them in her little basket crib and washed diapers in the laundry tub and hung them on the roof. They were happy.

Downtown at the fanciest hotel in San Francisco, at the St. Francis, film people from Los Angeles had a wild party with bath-tub gin and showgirls and models and starlets. One of them died. Another of them, Mrs. Bambina Maud Delmont, denounced Fatty Arbuckle, the popular fat movie star. She said he had raped the girl, Virginia Rappe—pressed his huge body down on her. Mrs. Bambina Maud Delmont had seen him opening Miss Rappe's bedroom door, standing in his pajamas with Miss Rappe's Panama hat on his head, and heard Miss Rappe screaming, "He did it. I know he did it. I have been hurt! I am dying!"

Others couldn't understand at first why she was screaming with pain. "Portions of the statement," apologized a newspaper, "have been omitted as unfit for publication." Something had burst inside Virginia Rappe, and later she died, and Fatty Arbuckle was arrested, as the world agreed he deserved to be.

"Roscoe Arbuckle owns three Cadillac cars, one special built,

Hammett in San Francisco,
perhaps on the roof of 620
Eddy Street, c. 1921.

valued at $25,000," the *Chronicle* told its fascinated readers, "and
a house on West Adams Street for which he paid $100,000 about a
year ago." His stepmother revealed that "Arbuckle never aided his
family." "She added that Roscoe's brother, Clyde, had aided her,"
reported the censorious press.[3]

ARBUCKLE TELLS PARTY STORY: ACTOR ASSERTS HE ONLY AIDED
VIRGINIA RAPPE was the headline for a follow-up story.

Pinkerton men were in on it, checking things out for Fatty's
lawyers, and Hammett told people later how he had been one of
them. He wrote a little anecdote:

> I sat in the lobby of the Plaza, in San Francisco. It was the day
> before the opening of the second absurd attempt to convict
> Roscoe Arbuckle of something. He came into the lobby. He
> looked at me and I at him. His eyes were the eyes of a man who

expected to be regarded as a monster but was not yet inured to it. I made my gaze as contemptuous as I could. He glared at me, went on to the elevator still glaring. It was amusing. I was working for his attorneys at the time, gathering information for his defence.[4]

Fatty stayed in Hammett's mind for years. Other detectives told him that the girl had the clap. Her insides had burst with clap. Detectives get the real story. It wasn't Fatty's fault.

Hammett thought the D.A. was trying to frame Fatty; he talked to Jose about it, and when his daughters were big enough he talked to them about it, all the horrible details about things done to Virginia Rappe with bottles, though they didn't want to hear. It stayed with him. Fat villains were to appear in his tales.

A few days after the Arbuckle case began, on the twenty-fourth of November, he was involved with another case: the liner *Sonoma* sailed into San Francisco from Sydney, missing $125,000 that had been locked away in strongboxes in the strong room and mysteriously stolen during the voyage. When the theft was discovered, Pinkertons and police were assigned to guard the ship and search it. First Assistant Engineer Carl Knudsen was credited by the newspaper with finding some gold sovereigns—nearly $28,000 worth—in the ventilating pipes. Another $75,000 was found attached to oil cans floating near the stern by "private operatives." "Finding of the gold on my part was the result of figuring out possible hiding places for the gold along with the others. The report that I dreamed where the treasure was stored is not true, and furthermore, I have never talked with a newspaper man from any paper since the gold was found to be missing," said Knudsen. Perhaps Hammett was one of "the others." He had been promised the job of sailing out on the *Sonoma*, to watch the crew, but it didn't happen because the gold was found.[5]

He thought of the *Sonoma* gold case as his last case. Now he was really too ill to work for Pinkerton's. And the job no longer suited his ambitions. He had had a glimpse beyond it.

But the Hammetts needed money. At Pinkerton's he'd been making six dollars a day and paid for a seven-day week whether or not he was on a case or recovering from one, like the time he sat two days in a chair after he was stunned by a brick. He would have been paid six dollars a day all the way to Australia on a long sea voyage looking for the stolen gold if it hadn't been found. He would always cherish a wish to go to Australia.

He bought a new suit and went job hunting. Josephine wondered where he got the money for the suit—he must have been saving it up. The jobs he found were part time, mostly in advertising, and the rest of the time he spent at the library. Here, as at the hospital or on the train, he read. Uneducated, he had no grounds for choosing this book over that. He chose them all, read everything, and when he struck something good, he knew it, and thrilled to it. He recognized trash, and instinctively knew that his judgment was as reliable on writing as it was in the matter of clothes. He read pulps and Aristotle and Henry James. He also read the French—in particular, Anatole France and Flaubert. He read the realistic Icelandic sagas of the thirteenth century with special interest, recognizing in their laconic and grim realism, their mannered but compelling narratives, their sophisticated appreciation of society and greed and honor, something that had to do with himself and with the way he could hope to write. It was to James, he would say later, that he owed his conceptions of literary style and his ideas of method,[6] and to the sagas some ideas of tone.

He began writing and sending out stories and poems, and he began to think of himself, timidly at first, as an aspiring writer. He wrote to his father about his ambition and to ask for money to buy time, to get established. His father wrote back, sending good wishes but no money, and whatever resentment Hammett had felt toward Richard T. now became stronger. He never quite forgave his father for abandoning him at this time.

DASHIELL—on April 15, 1921 ANNIE wife of the late John V. Dashiell. Relatives and friends are invited to attend the funeral services at the residence of her son-in-law Richard T. Hammett 1119 W. Lexington Street, Monday 2 P.M.

—Baltimore *Evening Sun*, APRIL 16, 1921

HAMMETT—on August 3, 1922 ANNIE B. DASHIELL HAMMETT beloved wife of Richard T. Hammett. Funeral from the parlor of George J. Smith, 1000 West Fayette Street on Saturday August 5 at 11 A.M. Interment on Sunday August 6 at St. Marys Co. Md.

—Baltimore *Evening Sun*, AUGUST 4, 1922

His grandmother had died the year before; his crisis of feeling about his parents was intensified by the death now of his mother. Hammet did not go East for his mother's funeral, but he grieved, he felt as orphaned as Jose. He signed some of his first stories "Peter Collinson"; in the underworld, Peter Collins was a name for nobody, a John Doe, so Peter Collinson meant nobody's son.[7]

In February 1922 he entered Munson's Business College, a secretarial school, to learn newspaper reporting. His tuition and a small stipend were paid by the Vocational Rehabilitation Bureau. He also managed to get a small sum for Jose and the baby. His negotiations with the Veterans Bureau became, as well as a necessity, an obsession.

At his sickest, in the hospital in Tacoma, Hammett had received $80 a month, which was reduced to $40 a month when he went to the convalescent hospital in San Diego. When he left the hospital, probably in May of 1921, he was given $20 a month, as though he were better; but "Maximum improvement achieved" wasn't the same as better—in fact, it implied he would never be better. Later the rehabilitation people had told him that though he was accepted in Vocational School, he wasn't well enough for Vocational School. The illogic, the indifference of this, infuriated him. Sitting in a lonely room in Seattle,[8] he wrote the Veterans Bureau, and he continued to do so after he and Jose had moved to Eddy Street. But he could not make the government see the unfairness that he saw: that he was now a sick person, likely to die, who had had wonderful plans and aims. The boy who took to the road at fourteen, veteran of stakeouts and mining camps and wide-open towns, must now lead the quiet and semi-invalid life of a secretarial student, would-be writer and advertising man—all pursuits that kept him indoors at his typewriter. Here he was, in a tiny, dingy apartment over bootleggers, with a new baby, a trustful little nurse wife, and no money. He was twenty-eight and would soon be thirty. He had the artist's indignation at the world's indifference, its inability to distinguish him from the other rowdy soldiers, the other little boys at the blacking factory. He, this precious I, this distinct, perceptive being. Like Dickens' complaints, years after he had worked in the blacking factory, Hammett's injured tone creeps into his letters to indifferent bureaucrats, and sounds in his stories: "Paul left the post-office carrying his monthly compensation check, in its unmistakeable narrow manila envelope with the mocking bold-faced instructions to postmasters should the addressee have died meanwhile."⁹

Loyal service got you nothing, not from the government, not from Pinkerton's. He would always hate the government, and people in authority. If you were faithful to the job you said you'd do for them, it was only because you had pride in your word and your work. This was the way he himself behaved, expecting nothing, and the way his fictional heroes would behave. They would expect nothing, would not be surprised at the indifference of the higher-ups to the private soldier, the miner, the member of the guild, the operative on his cold watch. And yet these lonely servants took pride in their lot to serve if the higher-ups were on the side of higher good. Hammett was in every sense an enlisted man. He knew better than to ask for anything in return. Yet if driven by need he would sometimes ask, and it was his fate that he would always be denied.

> WANTED a high class experienced newspaper advertising salesman for two months intensive work; must be familiar with special work; to right man may lead to permanent position; give previous experience and references, which will be treated confidentially. Address box 146403 Examiner.
>
> —San Francisco *Examiner*, NOVEMBER 5, 1921¹⁰

He now took a part-time advertising job with Samuels Jewelry, run by Al Samuels, upon whom Hammett would fasten if not orphan love, at least wild gratitude. Samuels was the one person who helped Hammett now.

Samuels Jewelry, with two stores, one on Market, one on Kearny, was having a big year under Al's dynamic leadership. Samuels was a great believer in the power of advertising and took out long newspaper ads in the chatty fashion of those days. Perhaps he was running out of chat when he found the young Hammett to ghostwrite for him. He was fond of saying that he never hired anyone who wasn't smarter than himself, and he liked the look of Hammett.

And Hammett, always responsive to *esprit de corps*, liked the family way the business was run. Newspaper readers were told, for instance, "that if you want to see us at our best, come in next Tuesday, the 28th (Nov. 1922). We'll be all dolled up, preparatory to our annual dinner and dance as Mr. Samuels' guest at the Hotel Whitcomb in the evening. There will be twice as many as last year, and the girls all have new dresses."[11]

Hammett perfectly understood the values of the world of the twenties, in which men bought diamonds for women and a good watch for themselves, and an engaged couple was a new stable social unit, and people wanted to trade "up" and "amount to something" and they wanted other people to know how well they were doing:

> She loved him dearly—there was no doubt about it. If she had not respected his feelings so much she might have given him some intimation of her disappointment regarding the diamond he had placed on her finger when their troth was plighted.
>
> But she just could not think of hurting him. So she smiled bravely, and assured him that she was the happiest girl in the world. However, she was *ashamed* to compare her dull, lifeless stone with the flawless brilliant, blue-white diamonds that her girl friends had received from their intended husbands.
>
> How had he come to unwittingly place her in this humiliating position? It was simply an error in judgement. He could not afford to pay over a certain sum and he had bought "size" instead of "quality." If he had only asked her, he would have learned this fact:
>
> All intelligent women of refinement prefer small gems of fine quality, to diamonds that may be larger yet not so pure and scintillating. . . .[12]

> Every young man knows that the diamond ring he chooses for the lady of his heart must run the gauntlet of critical friends and relatives. It behooves him, therefore, to make his selection with great care, choosing a diamond ring that will reflect his good taste—a tribute to the girl he loves.[13]

> It's nothing unusual to find a man of position and excellent standing who is temporarily short of cash. The average man figures a long time ahead on the spending of his income. Besides his fixed expenses of rent, meals, clothing and recreation, he usually carries some kind of an investment, a savings account or life insurance, that pretty well takes care of all he earns. So when he finds himself engaged he may not have the cash necessary for the ring.
>
> We try to take care of men like that. . . .[14]

Sometimes the ads were little detective stories, which were sometimes signed "Albert S. Samuels," and sometimes "The Advertising Manager":

> Here's a true story told by a conductor of the San Francisco Municipal Street Railway: One day a few weeks ago a woman passenger was about to alight from a crowded car when she noticed a gentleman's watch and chain dangling on the button of her coat. How, when or where she had unconsciously become in possession of the timepiece, she was at a loss to explain. She gave her watch to the conductor who turned it in to the Lost and Found Department. Later, it was claimed. How the watch was lifted from the owner's pocket without his knowledge is told for the benefit of all.
>
> A man wore his watch on one end of his chain and a pocket knife on the other end. It was his custom to keep the watch in one lower vest pocket and the knife in the other one. *He did not run the chain through a button-hole of his vest* but let it swing with a careless ease and grace, all unsupported and unprotected. When the woman swept by him in the crowded car, the chain became looped over the button of her coat. Being unanchored in any fashion, both watch and knife were lifted neatly from their resting place. . . .[15]

Hammett, poor, ambitious, isolated in San Francisco, knew that somewhere else there was a Smart Set, epitomized by H. L. Mencken's magazine of that name—peopled by witty, beautifully dressed women and rich young men of the kind that were usually the villains in his stories. Somewhere else was money and good talk. It was to this imaginary Smart Set, and to the magazine of the same name, that Hammett mailed his first attempts at writing—little stories, accounts of his life as a detective, witty little poems.[16]

On May 23, 1923, he finished at Munson's Business College. In need of money he wrote to the Veterans Bureau:

620 Eddy Street
June 11, 1923

Mr. Allan Carter
Chief, Claims Division
U.S. Veterans Board
883 Market Street
San Francisco

Dear Mr. Carter:

I have your letter of June 8th notifying me that from May 31st my compensatory disability is rated at less than 10%.

Mr. Bourne, of your division, told me this afternoon that this rating was based upon my last physical examination: made by a Dr. Seid, I think, some time last month.

I do not feel that my condition at this time—which is certainly no better than it was before I entered training—justifies this rating and I wish to appeal from it.

If possible I should like another examination, preferably by a lung specialist, so that we may know definitely where we stand without putting me to the expense of getting the opinions of outside specialists.

Sincerely yours,

Samuel D. Hammett

In October of 1922, when Mary Jane was already a year old, Hammett had succeeded in winning a retroactive "additional compensation" for Jose—$2.50 a month, making a total of $16.21—and then a few months later the bureau wrote warning him that when he was through with the Vocational School in May of 1923 the compensation would stop altogether. Hammett was outraged. He wasn't through, rehabilitated or well. His publications were not enough to support them. He needed more time. He wrote letters, he went around to the office, he insisted. He kept telling them he was not better and wanted an examination so they would all know whether he could expect to live or die.

His enemy in the United States Veterans Bureau, a Mr. Carter, chief of the Claims Division, now threw up his hands about the difficult Mr. Hammett and sent the entire file to the District Board of Appeals, from whom Hammett heard nothing for three months.

He wrote them more letters. Much of the frustration inherent in his situation—rejection slips, financial hardship, enforced idleness—focused itself in his need to prove that despite the opinion of doctors he was more than 10 percent disabled. He knew he was continuing to have something the matter with him. His subsequent medical history would show that he and not the doctors was right. Mr. Carter dickered endlessly:

> The file does not contain a certified copy of the public record of your marriage but merely a photostat copy thereof. This is not satisfactory under the rules now in force and consequently we must request you to submit a certified copy of the public record of your marriage, duly certified by the Recorder in and for the City and County of San Francisco. This document should have the impression of his official seal on it. Also, in view of the time which has elapsed since compensation has been paid, please submit the affidavit of two witnesses stating that you have not been separated or divorced from your wife, if this is the case.
>
> October 31, 1923

Hammett grimly complied with this latest set of requirements in November of 1923, and in April earned a retroactive award of $51.68. It was not much, but they needed it. Two weeks later the vengeful Mr. Carter informed him that his last check would be in May. More protests elicited another $9 for June, and then even the determined Hammett was defeated. The bureau said he was rehabilitated, but he grew steadily sicker. He would continue his angry correspondence with the Veterans Bureau for the rest of his life, and would never change his view of vindictive authority.

The first acceptance is a great moment for a writer. For Hammett, to receive worldly reward, however tiny, for his thoughts was admission into a smart set. In October 1922 Hammett's short story "The Parthian Shot" was accepted by Mencken's magazine *Smart Set*, and he was beside himself with relief, joy. He and Jose had dinner sent in from a restaurant—but perhaps he was too ill to go out.

After that he began to receive acceptances right and left. He read all kinds of magazines—poetry magazines, literary magazines, pulps—and sent them what they wanted. He discovered a particular knack for doing what the pulps wanted, and he found that his experience with Pinkerton's provided him with lots of ideas. Not only the pulps but the smart set thought that a literate detective was a glamorous thing.

In 1920 H. L. Mencken and his partner, George Jean Nathan, had started another magazine, called *Black Mask*, in which to publish mystery and crime fiction. They wanted to cash in on the public appetite for pulp magazines, and they wanted to subsidize *Smart Set*. The venture was successful. People who bought Westerns, dime novels and pulp magazines bought *Black Mask* too, and soon Mencken and Nathan could sell it at a profit. Other good editors—Phil Cody, Harry North, George Sutton, Fanny Ellsworth and Joseph T. Shaw—took it over in turn, each contributing something to its personality and to the eminence it was gaining in its field.[17]

Hammett was a reader of *Black Mask*. He felt on the one hand that he could write better stuff than this, and on the other that it had something, it was trying for something. He began to try for it too. He had some interest in the work of Carroll John Daly,[18] whose hardboiled detective, Race Williams, had begun to appear in *Black Mask* four months before Hammett's first story appeared. But old-fashioned detective stories had always struck him as ridiculous: the brainy sleuth seldom leaving his rooms divines from esoteric clues the murderer. Hammett had waited in too many cold doorways and been taken too often by surprise, and he knew how often a detective was absolutely floored when trying to find out who had done what. And he knew detectives were not upper-class men of leisure with orchid hothouses and nice lives but low-priced drudges. He knew a few more things too that he thought he could contribute to the literature of the detective story. It wasn't so much that he knew how to do things, for he hadn't after all been a detective very long—it was that he knew what being a detective meant.

Hammett's earliest detective was Waldron Honeywell, famous for a treatise proving that "the mysteries confronting Sherlock Holmes would have been susceptible to the routine methods of an ordinary policeman," for frustrating a bomb plot at Versailles, finding the assassin of the emperor of Abyssinia and sundry other feats.[19] But to tell some of his stories he invented a little short, fat, fortyish detective—the opposite, that is, of himself, and a little like his description of his first boss, Jimmy Wright, back in the Baltimore Pinkerton's. Hammett's operative didn't have a name. He worked for the Continental Detective Agency, so he was the Continental operative—the Op. The Continental Op explained his approach to detecting:

> I like being a detective, like the work. And liking work makes you want to do it as well as you can. Otherwise there'd be no sense to it. . . . I don't know anything else, don't enjoy anything else, don't want to know or enjoy anything else. You can't weigh that against any sum of money. Money is good stuff. I haven't anything against it. But in the past eighteen years I've been getting my fun out of chasing crooks and solving riddles. . . . I can't imagine a pleasanter future than twenty-some years more of it.[20]

This seemed to Hammett the way people should do any kind of job. In March of 1923 he contributed to *Smart Set* some inside stories on detecting to enhance his own image as ex-detective.

FROM THE MEMOIRS OF A PRIVATE DETECTIVE
BY DASHIELL HAMMETT

I

Wishing to get some information from members of the W.C.T.U. in an Oregon city, I introduced myself as the secretary of the Butte Civic Purity League. One of them read me a long discourse on the erotic effects of cigarettes upon young girls. Subsequent experiments proved this tip worthless.

2

A man whom I was shadowing went out into the country for a walk one Sunday afternoon and lost his bearings completely. I had to direct him back to the city.

3

House burglary is probably the poorest paid trade in the world; I have never known anyone to make a living at it. But for that matter few criminals of any class are self-supporting unless they toil at something legitimate between times. Most of them, however, live on their women.

4

I know an operative who while looking for pickpockets at the Havre de Grace race track had his wallet stolen. He later became an official in an Eastern detective agency.

5

Three times I have been mistaken for a Prohibition agent, but never had any trouble clearing myself.

6

Taking a prisoner from a ranch near Gilt Edge, Mont., to Lewistown one night, my machine broke down and we had to sit there until daylight. The prisoner, who stoutly affirmed his innocence, was clothed only in overalls and shirt. After shivering all night on the front seat his morale was low, and I had no difficulty in getting a complete confession from him while walking to the nearest ranch early the following morning.

7

Of all the men embezzling from their employers with whom I have had contact, I can't remember a dozen who smoked, drank, or had any of the vices in which bonding companies are so interested.

8

I was once falsely accused of perjury and had to perjure myself to escape arrest.

9

A detective agency official in San Francisco once substituted "truthful" for "voracious" in one of my reports on the grounds that the client might not understand the latter. A few days later in another report "simulate" became "quicken" for the same reason.

10

Of all the nationalities hauled into the criminal courts, the Greek is the most difficult to convict. He simply denies everything, no matter how conclusive the proof may be; and nothing so impresses a jury as a bare statement of fact, regardless of the fact's inherent improbability or obvious absurdity in the face of overwhelming contrary evidence.

11

I know a man who will forge the impressions of any set of fingers in the world for $50.

12

I have never known a man capable of turning out first-rate work in a trade, a profession or an art, who was a professional criminal.

13

I know a detective who once attempted to disguise himself thoroughly. The first policeman he met took him into custody.

14

I know a deputy sheriff in Montana who, approaching the cabin of a homesteader for whose arrest he had a warrant, was confronted by the homesteader with a rifle in his hands. The deputy sheriff drew his revolver and tried to shoot over the home-steader's head to frighten him. The range was long and a strong wind was blowing. The bullet knocked the rifle from the home-steader's hands. As time went by the deputy sheriff came to accept as the truth the reputation for expertness that this incident gave him, and he not only let his friends enter him in a shooting contest, but wagered everything he owned upon his skill. When the contest was held he missed the target completely with all six shots.

15

Once in Seattle the wife of a fugitive swindler offered to sell me a photograph of her husband for $15. I knew where I could get one free, so I didn't buy it.

16

I was once engaged to discharge a woman's housekeeper.

17

The slang in use among criminals is for the most part a con-scious, artificial growth, designed more to confuse outsiders than for any other purpose, but sometimes it is singularly expressive; for instance, *two-time loser*—one who has been convicted twice; and the older *gone to read and write*—found it advisable to go away for a while.

18

Pocket-picking is the easiest to master of all the criminal trades. Anyone who is not crippled can become an adept in a day.

19

In 1917, in Washington, D.C., I met a young lady who did not remark that my work must be very interesting.

20

Even where the criminal makes no attempt to efface the prints of his fingers, but leaves them all over the scene of the crime, the chances are about one in ten of finding a print that is sufficiently clear to be of any value.

21

The chief of police of a Southern city once gave me a description of a man, complete even to a mole on his neck, but neglected to mention that he had only one arm.

22

I know a forger who left his wife because she had learned to smoke cigarettes while he was serving a term in prison.

23

Second only to "Dr. Jekyll and Mr. Hyde" is "Raffles" in the affections of the daily press. The phrase "gentleman crook" is used on the slightest provocation. A composite portrait of the gentry upon whom the newspapers have bestowed this title would show a laudanum-drinker, with a large rhinestone horseshoe aglow in the soiled bosom of his shirt below a bow tie, leering at his victim, and saying: "Now don't get scared, lady, I ain't gonna crack you on the bean. I ain't a rough-neck!"

24

The cleverest and most uniformly successful detective I have ever known is extremely myopic.

25

Going from the larger cities out into the remote rural communities one finds a steadily decreasing percentage of crimes that have to do with money and a proportionate increase in the frequency of sex as a criminal motive.

26

While trying to peer into the upper story of a roadhouse in northern California one night—and the man I was looking for was in Seattle at the time—part of the porch crumbled under me and I fell, spraining an ankle. The proprietor of the roadhouse gave me water to bathe it in.

27

The chief difference between the exceptionally knotty problem confronting the detective of fiction and that facing the real detective is that in the former there is usually a paucity of clues, and in the latter altogether too many.

28

I know a man who once stole a Ferris-wheel.

29

That the law-breaker is invariably sooner or later apprehended is probably the least challenged of extant myths. And yet the files of every detective bureau bulge with the records of unsolved mysteries and uncaught criminals.[21]

On October 1, 1923, the first of his Op stories was published in *Black Mask*, and people took to "the little man going forward day after day through mud and blood and death and deceit—as callous and brutal and cynical as necessary—towards a dim goal, with nothing to push or pull him towards it except he's been hired to reach it." Hammett understood the Op very well. He wrote about him in twenty-six stories and short novels and in two novels.

In them the fat little detective finds nothing to surprise him. There are crooks, and then there are upper-class people who are more sinister—their interest in power and money will make them do anything. And there are foreigners who are as bad. The women are never as nice as they look, but deeply unprincipled, with the morals of cats.

He also tried to write stories about real life, things between men and women, or about how it had been to be an ex-soldier in a hospital, young, ill, without hope. These were not often published. Either people did not want these stories or he felt a shyness about sending them out.

Though he wasn't excited about his detective stories—he called them Blackmasking or junk—he was excited about writing itself, about the idea that there were people noticing and approving of him. He felt tenderness and friendship for them, felt himself to be a part of some larger network of toilers in this excellent craft to which he belonged more than he belonged to Samuels' or had belonged to Pinkerton's, though he had belonged to them too. Writing was his secret life. He placed the greatest value on his witty little urbane poems, which were usually about seduction if

Courtesy of Lilian Hellman

Hammett, sometime in the 1920s.

signed by his own name, or about something prettier and more
abstract if signed by the name of the baby, Mary Jane Hammett.

It is not easy to decide to become a writer. It is a risky decision
by which you almost surely doom yourself to disappointment and
failure, for it is a pursuit alluring at one time or another to many
people but one in which only a few succeed—a matter of temperament, perhaps, or of perseverance. Hammett sent out stories
and poems like notes in bottles, from the literary desert island of
San Francisco. He had no writer friends, no one to talk to about
books. He worked at the kitchen table, industrious, determined,
driven.

1924–1926

ARTISTIC NOTIONS

Of course Jose wanted him to succeed as a writer, but she did not understand how much it meant to him. In her heart she wished he were something steady—perhaps a clerk in the store—and when he reproached her with this secret wish of hers, for he saw, it seemed, into her heart, she was ashamed that it was true. She did not think highly of the occupation of writer, the way he had to struggle, and the hours he kept.

But Josephine thought Hammett was a wonderful husband, so intelligent and kindly, so helpful with the baby and so fond of her, and so brave about his health—for he wasn't well—and he knew so many things! And when the mailman brought a favorable letter or check from a magazine, he was happy, so everybody was happy and asked him how he was doing, and he knew all about writing and was so full of ideas, and he'd talk to anyone—the mailman or the people down at Samuels'. He didn't talk much to her about his writing, but she was happy when he was happy, and she liked to hear about the doings down at Samuels' or about things he read at the library. In the park, where she went in the afternoons, there were many other women with their babies; one in particular from Mexico and another from China made an impression because the husbands in Mexico and the ones in China, you would have to conclude, were awfully bad, and she felt very happy and lucky to have Dash.[1]

It was a hard time in 1924 when Dash got sick again, and the public health nurse and the doctors didn't think she and the baby should stay with him and made them move across the bay to the country, to a little house in Fairfax, California. He was so sick that he could creep across the room to the bathroom only by holding on to a row of chairs that he had lined up for the purpose. But he kept writing. He wrote a story, "Ruffian's Wife," in which a pretty, honest, adoring little wife keeps a perfect little house across the bay from San Francisco, where the worldly, roistering husband comes on the ferry, and between his visits she cleans the little house obsessively and thinks only of him.[2]

He became thirty. How did he regard this birthday? His health was bad, but he may no longer have been afraid of dying. He knew now that he could beat these sessions of illness. His writing was going better. At thirty it was time to settle down, and he had settled down, had a wife, a daughter and debts, like the men who bought diamonds at Samuels', even if Hammett's living arrangements weren't so regular. He liked the West—the East was a place with "square houses, circle lives." He felt in himself the first signs of respectable stability, in the form of nostalgia for the old days before the War—B.C. he called it: before credit and the crisis of 1918. He saw the modern world of 1924 as characterized by exciting forms of progress (to which advertising could contribute) based on science and on reason. He had the romantic's regard for human possibilities, and a trust in the verifiable, and a mistrust of human personality, and doubted that it could be analyzed and quantified.[3]

It was very much a time in America when a man thought in terms of Getting Someplace. A likely young man could get someplace and Hammett himself, being ambitious, smart, interested in and good at a lot of things, might get someplace too. When writing advertising copy, he assumed that other people had certain aspirations: to own a house, a fine car, diamonds, nice clothes. But he had his eye on a more elusive good—Art. He had ideas about Art (and, probably, Fame), and entered into a brief exchange, in *Writer's Digest*, with one H. Bedford-Jones, who disapproved of sex stories: "Literature, as I see it, is good to the extent that it is art, and bad to the extent that it isn't, and I know of no other standard by which it may be judged." He quotes a Mr. Tully, who said that "art knows no morals—art being a genuine something— while morals differ in all lands." "Sex has never made a poor story good," Hammett goes on, "or a good one poor; but if Mr. Bedford-Jones will make a list of the stories that are still alive after several centuries, he'll find that many of the heartiest survivors have much to do with the relations between the sexes, and treat those relations with little of the proper Victorian delicacy."[4]

About this time Hammett wrote in a review in the *Forum*, about a book dealing with the creative mind—*Everyman's Genius*, by Mary Austin:

> The eternal problem of the creative worker in whatever field is to bring his whole mind, his every faculty, to bear on the task under his hand. To the extent that he succeeds, granted adequate equipment, he produces what we ordinarily call a work of genius. As he fails he has to rely on his talent, his craftsman's skill. . . . Mrs. Austin has some sound things to say on the mechanics of the creative mind, on autosuggestion, auto-prayer, and meditation. These things, consciously or not, are the accustomed tools of him who tries to focus his mind in its entirety on any subject.[5]

Once when he had cut corners, for he was sick and they needed the money, *Black Mask* rejected two stories; and he wrote to them so remorsefully that they printed his remorseful letter:

> The trouble is that this sleuth of mine has degenerated into a meal-ticket. I liked him at first and used to enjoy putting him through his tricks; but recently I've fallen into the habit of bringing him out and running him around whenever the landlord, or the butcher, or the grocer shows signs of nervousness.
>
> There are men who can write like that, but I am not one of them. If I stick to the stuff that I want to write—the stuff I enjoy writing—I can make a go of it, but when I try to grind out a yarn because I think there is a market for it, then I flop.
>
> Whenever, from now on, I get hold of a story that fits my sleuth, I shall put him to work, but I'm through with trying to run him on a schedule.
>
> Possibly I could patch up "The Question's One Answer," and "Women, Politics, and Murder" enough to get by with them, but my frank opinion of them is that neither of them is worth the trouble. I have a liking for honest work, and honest work as I see it is work that is done for the worker's enjoyment as much as for the profit it will bring him. And henceforth that's my work.
>
> I want to thank both you [Harry North, assistant editor of BM] and Mr. Cody [Phil Cody] for jolting me into wakefulness. There's no telling how much good this will do me. And you may be sure that whenever you get a story from me hereafter,—frequently, I hope,—it will be one that I enjoyed writing.[6]

He wrote a high-minded essay on style for *Western Advertising*:

To write of washing machines in terms of yachts is not to be too literary. It is to be not sufficiently literary. The disproportionately florid, the gaudy, have worse reputation in literature than ever they have had in advertising. There are few literary points on which there is general agreement, but I know of no first-rate writer or critic who does not call that style most perfect which clothes ideas in the most appropriate words.

Another—perhaps the only other—point on which there is agreement is that clarity is the first and greatest of literary virtues. The needlessly involved sentence, the clouded image, are not literary. They are anti-literary. Joseph Conrad, whose work John Galsworthy pronounced "the only writing of the last twelve years that will enrich the English language to any extent," defined the writer's purpose as "above all else, to make you see." Anatole France, probably the tallest figure modern literature has raised, and the most bookish of men in the bargain, said: "The most beautiful sentence? The shortest!" He condemned the semicolon, a hangover from the days of lengthy sentences, as not suited to an age of telephones and airplanes. He insisted that all unnecessary "which's" and "that's" must be carefully weeded out, as they would spoil the finest style.

. . . The language of the man in the street is seldom either clear or simple. If you think I exaggerate, have your stenographer eavesdrop a bit with notebook and pencil. You will find this common language, divorced from gesture and facial expression, not only excessively complicated and repetitious, but almost purposeless in its lack of coherence. Perhaps the plain man's written speech is a little better. If you wish to learn how little, pick out half a dozen men at random, men whose daily work is not with words, and give them a piece of copy to write. The result will be interesting and instructive. It will be neither clear nor simple.

The favorite words of the plain man are those which enable him to talk without thinking. . . .

You may read tons of books and magazines without finding, even in fiction dialogue, any attempt faithfully to reproduce common speech. There are writers who do try it, but they seldom see print. Even such a specialist in the vernacular as Ring Lardner gets his effect of naturalness by skillfully editing, distorting, simplifying, coloring the national tongue, and not by reporting it verbatim.

Simplicity and clarity are not to be got from the man in the street. They are the most elusive and difficult of literary accomplishments, and a high degree of skill is necessary to any writer who would win them. They are the most important qualities in securing the maximum desired effect on the reader. To secure that maximum desired effect is literature's chief goal. . . .[7]

This appeared in a magazine called *Western Advertising* in 1926. In December 1925 *Western Advertising* announced that it had made arrangements with a "careful reading, deep thinking advertising man to write the reviews on new books of advertising, selling, merchandising and allied subjects."[8] This was "S.H." "Dashiell Hammett" was also to write several short articles for them over the next year, and in 1926 the book reviews, too, were signed by "Dashiell Hammett."

"S.H." approached the books on advertising with interest, calm and thoroughness, yielding only occasionally to a facetious impulse.

PSYCHOLOGY IN ADVERTISING
by Albert T. Poffenberger, Ph.D.,
associate professor of psychology, Columbia University

. . . 'Way back East, up above the roarin' Forties and the sharp-shootin' corner of 42 Broadway, where swirl the high-ticklers and tickled; away, far up in the spinster environment of Morningside, near a certain great cathedral, there is a university called Columbia where many a teacher has pried "dawta" outa books and returned to Keokuk, Iowa, and never seen Times Square.

It is a place of serious thoughts, cool, calm, steady, unflustered movement of purple-deep thoughts. Read the preface to this book —read its introduction (the book's) by H. L. Hollingworth. We read it to our red-headed secretary (the introduction) then "us" went out for a pot of giggle tea and the wiff [wife?], later, rang up the office all evening and only the janitor answered.

Seriously—and you have to be serious to get *enrapport* of the author's motive thought back of this tome—it is a fine book, filled with tables and "dawta" and an inventory of human desires and measurements and psychology of appeal and the weighing of those appeals and everything. Oh, Brother!

But our red-headed secretary! The author of the book never pigeon-holed HER psychology at all, at all! And she is embued with the new Los Angeles spirit of "movie" youth that thinks a New York Night Club a "dumb dully," as she calls it, "a bow-legged Charleston!"

Some day . . . some day . . . when we gotta big bank account and *lezhure*—and if the world ain't changed *too much*, as Bergson's "evolution" suggests the world MAY change—we'll go up to Morningside, hire a room next to the suite of some lonely, rich widow, and go out on Columbia campus mornings and read the book from ten until eleven—then take our cane to one of them tea rooms around the corner, for a salad and hot English muffins, maybe meet-up with some lonely gal from Keokuk for the uplift purpose of showing her Times Square and the barbarian lands below 110th Street—perhaps the *raison d'être* of Club Mirador, or Club Lido.[9]

ADVERTISING, ITS PROBLEMS AND METHODS
by John H. Cover

Oh, the book by Cover! Get it by all means—at least look it over at the book store, or have it sent on approval. You'll like it, want it, read it—and this will help John establish himself in the University of Denver as a national authority on advertising.[10]

WHEN JAMES GORDON BENNETT WAS CALIPH OF BAGDAD
by Albert Stevens Crockett

Read how he smashed up Maxim's, or some such resort, and his wild Babylonian parties, how he nearly killed himself in a drunken drive through the archway to his home—and how Madame A ruled him. Crockett is a glorious writer—spinner of life.

Yes, perhaps his life was one continuous Arabian Night, and all that sort of thing—daring, profligate, arrogant, impulsive. His satanic delight in abashing and tantalizing workers. And no doubt he has served as an example for others to ape in their little way.

He makes me think of a passage in *Salammbo*.[11]

In a few years he would tell a friend that he himself meant to live flamboyantly. He himself would be living in the rooms of the King of Siam. Now he lived in ugly furnished places, and read Flaubert and Conrad and Aristotle and thought about Art and tried to write a novel—"The Secret Emperor"—about a dashing man in his thirties called Elfinstone.

Among his tries, this one was to linger in his imagination.

The hero is Elfinstone, 35, tall, gaunt, powerful flat muscles, copper hair and eyes, lean, bony mouth and chin, nose like a knife. The foremost intelligence man of his time, a detective who is above the ordinary detective as Napoleon was above a private. A record that covers several continents, including the World

War. He is now engaged in organizing a secret service in a Latin American country. He is a ruthless man, without manners, impatient of stupidity of people with whom he comes in contact, with little love for his fellows. Driven into work by some burning restlessness within him.

[The villain is] Seth Gutman, 50, black-haired, ivory skin, no lines in his suavely strong face, hawk nose, smooth-shaven, broad sloping forehead, hair thick and curly, oval face with something suggesting an Egyptian drawing in it, fairly plump but in perfect shape, except perhaps a bit soft. Dark, large and intelligent eyes. Low, musical voice, charming personality. Since, being a Jew, he may not be president, he decides to be secret emperor of the U.S. He does not depend on money. For fifteen years now he has been patiently collecting information about political moguls, so that he may make them his tools. He has a chain of private detective agencies, a scandal sheet, hirelings in banks, in hotels and apartments, most of these working for scandal sheets. This sheet, Capital Whispers, sometimes may be bought off, sometimes not, as in one case where it ruined a presidential aspirant who had millions to offer it. Gutman's usual way of getting hold of a politician, is to get something on his secretary or other intimate who will know secrets, and use that as wedge into those secrets.

He has also employed adventuresses.[12]

The heroine, Tamar Gutman, is ravishingly exotic. Hammett liked the idea of Jewish women, and women who were hot-blooded and foreign.

Congratulations. May health, wealth and beauty—in short, may all the blessings which the human heart enjoys, shine brightly for both mother and baby. May the strength and sanctity of their love continue to grow and flourish—may happiness always crown them both—such are our hopes and wishes in this wonder hour of their lives.

Cordially,
The White House, Raphael Weill & Co.
San Francisco

The new baby was Josephine Rebecca, to be called Jo. She was supposed to be a boy, Richard Thomas. She was born at St. Francis Hospital on May 24, 1926, to Mr. and Mrs. D. Hammett, who had rushed there in a taxi. On the title page of the little brochure that came from the department store, on the lines reserved for the autographs of Parents, Josephine signed her name, on the second line, leaving the first line blank for Hammett's signature, but he never signed. But seeing his new baby a few minutes after her birth, his heart swelled with love.[13]

In July 1926, at Samuels' one day, they found Hammett lying in a pool of blood, unconscious, bleeding from his lungs. This is one way you can die from tuberculosis—the lungs fill up with blood, and you drown, or you bleed to death. Unconscious from loss of blood and shock, he was near death. He had to stay home and rest and try to keep alive.

He continued sick, and Josephine took the new baby and Mary Jane to Montana at the doctor's orders to make sure that they, and especially the baby, would be safe from the infection, tuberculosis, that seemed to be worsening again.[14] Alone and sick in San Francisco, Hammett wrote to the Veterans Bureau that hemorrhages, weakness and the rest of the symptoms that go with tuberculosis had forced him to give up his work, and, knowing by this time the ways of the VA, enclosed an affidavit from Albert Samuels. This time the Board of Three agreed that his disability was total, if temporary, and awarded him $90 a month.

His writing was going better. The same year *Black Mask* had gotten a new editor, Captain Joseph T. Shaw, a former bayonet instructor and dashing character. He was also an exacting and exciting visionary of the detective story. Shaw admired Hammett's work tremendously, even came to see him and brought a doll for Mary Jane. "You are what we want," he told Hammett. He wanted stories with a simple, clear style, plausible action, "recognizeable human character in three-dimensional form." Hammett was flattered but not swept off his feet. He had a tendency to despise or suspect people who admired him for what he could do easily, and he still wanted to be one of the smart set instead of the head boy of the *Black Mask* school. Shaw was "Hammettizing" the *Black Mask*, Erle Stanley Gardner complained,[15] and it was true. Hammett's views on art were in truth similar to Shaw's belief in "simplicity for the sake of clarity, plausibility, and belief." The most important thing that Shaw now did for Hammett was to encourage him to revive the Continental Op and put him in a novel. Shaw saw that novels were where fame and money were. Writing for the pulps paid two cents a word.

Mary Jane hated being in Montana away from her father. He was her wonderful papa, and Mary Jane loved him terribly. When he was with them, he would take her on his lap and read to her. When he was away—but it was she and Mama and the baby who were away—he would send her little pictures, one each week, only for her, of elephants or turtles or bunnies, and sometimes of himself, which he had drawn, showing how he sat at his desk writing and drawing. Mary Jane had seen the room on Turk Street where Papa went to draw and write, and he had a pot of India ink there. She always kept the pictures her father had sent her. She said she would keep them forever.[16]

6

1927–1928

THE NOVELS

It was the view of doctors in April 1927 that Hammett's tuberculosis had totally disabled him; but he continued to write and had returned to work at Samuels' on a part-time basis. Jose and the children came back from Montana and got a place in Fairfax again. Hammett lived alone on Post Street and visited them weekends. The miseries of his life were two: his teeth, for which he was now seeing a government dentist, and his drinking. His drinking also worried Jose, whom he tried to reassure in unconvincingly jocular tones:

891 Post Street, San Francisco, May 24, 1927

Dear Jose,

I got back home safe and practically sober, which made me very nearly the only sober passenger. What a gang of riff-raff travels over that line on Sundays!

Al and I went out to Foster and Kleiser's joint yesterday and let them try to high-pressure us into buying some of their damned signs again.

The weather has warmed up here, so I suppose you are baking prettily over there.

In the good old government fashion, my dentist was off on his vacation when I reported for punishment yesterday, so I'll have to wait until late next month to get a crack at him again. Lucky my teeth have stopped bothering me!

Kiss the animals for me.

Love,
H

He was not faithful to Jose during these long separations. She was regretful, but she knew how men are. A drinking and phi-landering husband, though a disappointment, was not beyond the bounds of what you expected—and Hammett was at least a kindly, loving father.

He wrote little poems, always about love, which did not seem to refer to her. Women telephoned him.

YES

All complaisant in love was she,
With never a can't or no for me:
  A smiling yes, a beguiling yes,
  A you-must-wait-a-whiling yes.
But always a yes; to every plea
She'll acquiesce most readily.
  Her sole defect in love is this:
  She's seldom kept these promises.[1]

CURSE IN THE OLD MANNER

A plague on these women who, lengthily wooed,
Are not to be won till one's out of the mood,
And who then discerning one's temperateness
Accuse one of cooling because they said yes![2]

He began to write book reviews for the *Saturday Review of Literature*, usually of detective stories. His judgments, incisive and severe, reveal the development in his own mind of standards of form, plausibility and naturalness. A book's plan is "ironical. Its execution is not. The result is confusing. Rann McCloud is not adventurous. He is a sullen young man of no great intelligence. His interests, like his hatreds, are picayune. Had he accomplished all the few things he attempted he still would have been a man of no importance. The greatest height he can achieve is an exhibition of that senseless obstinancy which is the courage of the very weak."[3]

Of *The Clever One*, by Edgar Wallace, "We are not one of those who think that Mr. Wallace's inventions are sometimes a bit childish, and that his eventual solutions are too often more the result of chance than of honest detective work."[4]

About *The Daughter of the Hawk*, by C. S. Forester: "Then he sought the Hawk's daughter, found her; and at that point—page 97—the book goes blooey! From top-hole melodrama it degenerates into a nasty little idyl, a gooey affair that might have been written by Louisa May Alcott."[5]

Of *The Tannahill Tangle*, by Carolyn Wells, "Most of the people in the book are detective-story readers and they spend a lot of time talking about detective stories, which is bad enough, but their dialogue reaches its real depths when they indulge in what is supposed to be sophisticated banter. Toward the end, as usual, Fleming Stone is brought in, and clears things up by means of new developments and of clues that the reader hasn't been told about. It is all quite fourth rate."[6]

Hooch, by Charles Francis Coe, "is too trite and formless to be good fiction, too stiff and too general and too thoroughly bowdlerized to be good reporting. It is as if it had been rewritten without imagination or insight from newspaper clippings. . . . Never were crooked police officials and politicians so ignorant of the ways of the crooked, and never was a large-scale illegal enterprise conducted along such simple, trusting lines."[7]

Murder Mansion, by Herman Landon, "is one of those stories in which the author, determined that something startling shall happen in every chapter, lets nothing come between him and his purpose. If it is unreasonable for a character to have said this, done that, or suppressed the other, and if such unreasonableness will hatch out the desired chapteral surprise, then overboard with the character's sanity."[8]

The Benson Murder Case, by S. S. Van Dine: "This Philo Vance is in the Sherlock Holmes tradition and his conversational manner is that of a high-school girl who has been studying the foreign words and phrases in the back of her dictionary. He is a bore when he discusses art and philosophy, but when he switches to criminal psychology he is delightful. There is a theory that any one who talks enough on any subject must, if only by chance, finally say something not altogether incorrect. Vance disproves this theory: he manages always, and usually ridiculously, to be wrong."[9]

A librarian, Leslie T. Little, wrote to the *Saturday Review* from Waltham, Massachusetts: "We take all the *Reviews* and I have often had occasion to criticize them adversely for their tendency toward praising mediocre books. Dashiell Hammett's review of five mystery stories in your January 15th number is so honest and efficient that I am moved to commend it highly and to ask for more of the same kind. . . . If all the books in this class were given to honest, conservative, experienced readers who would do as good a job as Mr. Hammett has done, the reviews would win the appreciation of hundreds of librarians to say nothing of other readers."[10]

Sometimes it seemed to Mary Jane that Papa loved the baby more than he loved her. When he came to visit, Papa made pictures on the mirror in Bon Ami for the baby. She, Mary Jane, had to go to the movies with Mama, when she wanted to stay home and play with Papa and hear stories and make Bon Ami pictures. Papa wasn't home very much. Sometimes he gave her a sip of his drink.

This is a book by Dostoevsky, Hammett would say, taking Mary on his knee and turning over the pages. She would listen, but she liked the other stories better, especially *Winnie the Pooh*. But she listened to Hammett read the story by Dostoevsky, as she did all the stories Papa read, and so did Jo, when she was big enough.

Early August of 1927. Hammett is having lunch at the St. Germaine Cafe on Ellis Street in San Francisco with Al Samuels and his son, Albert Junior, Harry Sloss and Chipman, a rival—a high-class business expert making a thousand dollars a month, who has come to shape things up at Samuels'. Chipman doesn't like Hammett, who seems to think he also knows a thing or two about advertising. Hammett no doubt does not know, and would not have liked to think, that this is a kind of high or mid point in his life, a moment when all is success or possibility.

He is thirty-three, has a family, is employed, and works as a free-lance writer. His job is in advertising at Al Samuels' jewelry store, a job he's good at and likes. Advertising itself interests him; it requires the very skills he has—a knowledge of human nature, powers of rational analysis and the ability to write. It's wide-open and challenging, too. Hammett still reads all books on advertising, and reviews them for *Western Advertising*, whose editor is a friend of his. He also writes for the *Saturday Review*, and little poems and stories in the *Forum*, *Stratford Magazine* and others. He's fond of reading and of airing his views, and, moreover, needs the extra money that reviewing brings in. He is about to begin his own major works. His life is half over.

He still lives on Post Street while Jose still lives in Fairfax, across the bay, accessible by train, with the two girls, Mary Jane, now nearly six, and the baby, Jo, a young hippo of a baby just over a year old. Mrs. Hammett and the girls live separately from Hammett because of his tuberculosis, which, however, miraculously is better now, when as recently as last year it looked as if he would die from it. They live apart also because it has begun to suit him not to be with them. Hammett visits his family once or twice a week, writes them letters in between, but the rest of the time he enjoys his routine of writing in the morning and evening, going down to the jewelry store in the afternoon, having occasional nights on the town or stolen moments with his secretary. He considers infidelity a fact of his nature if not a fact of nature itself.

Another fact of his nature, more troublesome, is his liking for booze, but today, at this lunch, he isn't drinking. He has only had one drink since Friday and is proud of his temperance. Drinking may go along with the slow off-days of a detective, or with the low life of a soldier, and pass the time for a convalescent and even —so he thinks—improve the condition of the tubercular, but drink-

Courtesy of Josephine Hammett Marshall

Jose Hammett with Mary and baby Josephine, 1925.

ing gets in the way of writing. Whiskey might keep tuberculosis at bay but it makes you sick in another way, and there is no crawling to the typewriter after a few days' drinking. Hammett drinks all day when he drinks, pacing himself along.

But not today. At the table young Albert Samuels, fourteen, wonders about Mr. Hammett's suit, sort of bright and checkered. His dad doesn't wear suits like that. Mr. Hammett is skinny and smokes all the time.[11]

The men quarrel. They don't seem truly angry, but they are quarreling about the business. Hammett does most of the talking, and Mr. Chipman talks back, but less and less, and finally falls silent with a sort of aggrieved glint in his eye and a red and indignant face. Hammett tells Samuels and Sloss about the experience of other companies, he tells them about things that corporations do—he knows all kinds of facts and figures about business. He puts the other men in a whirl.

Hammett is fond of old Al Samuels, the more because Samuels is interested in him and in his writing, and asks after each new publication and predicts great things for him. Samuels lends him money and is as close to a patron as Hammett ever had, and in return Hammett gives his best to the advertising matters at the store. And now he has thrown himself into a rivalry with the new advertising expert, Chipman, of whom he is a little in awe because of the thousand a month, and of whom the pretty co-worker, Miss O'Toole, has complained.

Hammett takes pleasure in his combat with Chipman. They have "swell arguments" for an hour and a half after lunch. "I was in good shape for battling," he reports proudly to Jose, "I had a hell of a lot of fun: I hit him with statistics and flourished percentages and the like in his face and quoted all the authorities from Moses to Babson and smothered him with incidents from the experience of the National Biscuit Company and General Motors and sent up assorted facts like fireworks. Some of all this had something to do with the case and some didn't, but it was all amusing. Finally I got him indignant, peevish, and then to save his face he had to admit that he wasn't as sure of his side as he had seemed."[12]

Hammett is surprised and elated to win a case against Chipman. Chipman's doings form a part of his letters to Jose from this afternoon on: "Miss O'Toole told me he had been busy all morning prying into the advertising—so I reckon the fight is still on. . . . Not being able to fight with Chipman the last two or three days,

I've been carrying on a war with Sloss—over the credit department, which he thinks, or pretends he thinks, a good department,
though it's really the bunk. I think I'll prove that it's lost us more
business than we've ever had."

Hammett's advertising career was moving along as smoothly as
his writing career. Wherever he turned, he seemed to have something people wanted. The publisher of the Oakland *Post-Enquirer*
sent word that his ads were "the best advertising his paper had
ever carried," praise that Hammett suspected was "applesauce,
since he knows I'm thinking about cutting down the space used
in the Oakland papers."[13]

Similarly, Joseph Shaw's letters from *Black Mask* magazine were
getting more and more enthusiastic, "telling me how good I am,
one from Cody telling me the same thing with further trimmings,
and one from Gardner telling me the last dingus he read of mine
was not only the best ever printed in the *Black Mask*, but the best
he ever read anywhere, and so on and so on and so on." He suspected this was applesauce too, but, "overwhelmed by this applesauce I'm wiring them to shoot me some dough and I'll do them
some more of the shots-in-the-dark. On the strength of that I'm
putting in an order for an Encyclopaedia Britannica and some
gin."[14]

He'd been batting out this junk, as he thought of it, for *Black
Mask* since 1923. He amused himself by putting in shocking words
(such as "gunsel," which the editors wouldn't notice) or innocent
ones that had a racy ring ("gooseberry lay"), which editors took
out in a flash.[15] He got sick even of these games at one point and
thought they ought to pay him more. When they wouldn't, he
quit writing for them, but Shaw wooed him back. Hammett was
actually more pleased that his verse continued to appear here and
there. Just last month, in the *Stratford Magazine*: "Had a letter
from Stratford saying that copies of the issue containing my verse
were being sent me. Thank God, he didn't embarrass me by asking
about the book I was to have reviewed."

GOODBYE TO A LADY

> Ink is a stain, however gay
>   It sing.
> However saintlily it say
>   Some holy thing.

Consummate sanctity, utter grayness
   Neither'd requite
You for the loss of the dilute grayness
   Called white.

No word the hovering pen had learned
   Was ever traced
On a page that now is turned—
   Emptily chaste.[16]

                          Sunday afternoon

Dear Jose,

I've been Blackmasking all day and expect to put in a couple of hours more at it before I knock off.

I've even been too busy to go to mass—the first Sunday I've missed church since the last part of June, 1927.

Here's something for the yellow-head.

Tomorrow afternoon I start playing with the dentist again. A couple of more weeks should clean me up.

I left a library book behind me. Hold it for me. . . .

How did you like today's tricky advertising?

Kiss the germs for me. I hope all your colds are gone.[17]

Best of all, his novel was going well. He wrote to Jose that "the story goeth along slowly but nicely. I got a good hunk of it done this day of our Lord."[18]

Shaw wanted his writers to publish book-length fiction and thereby become famous and established; famous writers were what he wanted for his magazine. With Shaw's encouragement, Hammett had set to work on a novel that Shaw was going to publish serially in *Black Mask*. Hammett worked in the mornings and into the night and tried to stay off drinking. Shaw was all encouragement, and a colorful encourager at that:[19]

                              July 22, 1927

Dear Mr. Hammett:

Just a line to accompany enclosed check in an early mail.

I have nothing but praise for POISONVILLE. In one of your recent letters you spoke of keeping your feet on the ground; the sense of reality which this tale gives is gripping. You can see the place, the scenes, the action, the faces and the character of the actors. Some of the parts are raw meat: but it is not thrown out in ragged chunks. It is served with skill that preserves the virile strengths of it and obliterates any suggestion of coarseness. I am going to say that I like this and, anticipating that the balance will be moulded in the same spirit, I believe it will be a series to conjure with.

I am well aware that this sounds like enthusiasm. Reading your note that accompanied the story, I have been casting through my impression from first consideration, and I really do not see any important element to shun. This, of course, is the set-up. Naturally, as I wired, the following episodes will swing into quicker action. I suppose this would be more helpful if I should pick out one or two slants for constructive criticism. I shall read it over again more carefully in a few days and may then have something more to say. Just now I am satisfied that it holds well to the middle of the road.

I shall hope to hear from you when you find opportunity and inclination to write.

With very best wishes, I am,

Sincerely yours,
Joseph Shaw
Editor

Dear Jose,

A telegram from Shaw woke me up this morning. It was all about how glad he was to have me back in the flock and so on. The only important thing in it was that he's sending me $300. That's what the fight was about in the first place, so I won after all.

I wrote Dick a little while ago, sending him one of the pictures of the little hippo.

Tomorrow morning I'm going to start in on the Black Mask junk, putting my mornings in on that and my evenings on the novel. So you won't have to be economical any more. We'll pay off the debts gradually and everything will be great until I decide to quit again.

But I really think this time I'll do enough of the murder-and-so-on to make a book. It's time we were trying prosperity for a while. Pray God I can keep my thoughts on it!

See you Sunday. Kiss the little ladies for me.[20]

Hammett was learning the game of getting advances from eager publishers.

He enjoyed writing "Poisonville." It was about the days in Montana, the corrupt owners, the town bosses, the things he had seen, and it was farcical in a way. The cops go in one direction, the crooks in the other; things explode. It was funny the way in real life the horrible things are funny later, even funny at the time, though the deaths are real, the blood running. In "Poisonville," as in the other stories, the Op has lost faith in the values of his society, or society has lost its values or both, in a way Hammett understood. He put in bits of things that had happened to him. Personville had had a miners' strike: "Both sides bled plenty. The Wobblies had to do their own bleeding. Old Elihu hired gunmen, strike-breakers, national guardsmen and even parts of the regular army, to do this. When the last skull had been cracked, the last rib kicked in, organized labor in Personville was a used firecracker."

"The Cleansing of Poisonville," the first installment of the novel, was published in the November 1927 *Black Mask*, and "Crime Wanted—Male or Female" in December; in January 1928 "Dynamite" appeared, and in February "19th Murder." In February, too, Hammett sent the four parts off to the publishing house of Alfred A. Knopf.

891 Post Street, San Francisco, February 11

Editorial Department
Alfred A. Knopf
730 Fifth Avenue
New York City

Gentlemen,

Herewith an action-detective novel for your consideration. If you don't care to publish it, will you kindly return it by express, collect.

By way of introducing myself: I was a Pinkerton's National Detective Agency operative for a number of years; and, more recently, have published fiction, book reviews, verse, sketches, and so on, in twenty or twenty-five magazines, including the old Smart Set (when your Messrs. Mencken and Nathan ran it), Forum, Bookman, Saturday Review, Life, Judge, Sunset, Argosy-Allstory, True Detective Mysteries, Black Mask (where "Poisonville" ran as a serial), Mystery Stories, Stratford, and Western Advertising.

March 12th, 1928.

Dear Mr. Hammett:

We have read POISONVILLE with a great deal of interest.

I would like to suggest some revisions, and I hope you won't object to them. Towards the middle of the book, the violence seems piled on too heavily; so many killings on a page I believe make the reader doubt the story, and instead of the continued suspense and feeling of horror, the interest slackens. One of our readers writes:

> "I think that the best way to cut this would be to take Lew Yard out of the story entirely. He never figures personally, but even so, he is responsible for a good deal of violence that could be left out. This chiefly takes place in the shooting up of a roadhouse (beginning on page 141) and the blowing up of the Yard's house (page 149). Some re-writing would be necessary, but it seems to me that it could be very easily done by making Reno the head of this particular gang from the beginning. The roadhouse shooting is quite similar to several others that take place both before and after.
>
> "Another episode that could be entirely cut is the dynamiting of the Police Station (page 134). If the Lew Yard material is cut, I should advise leaving this in. The brief shooting episode on page 176 could be cut profitably.
>
> "It should be possible to dispose of Pete in a less wholesale way than bombing him (page 209) although this is an exciting moment."

Of course you may have some ideas of your own regarding all this, and I certainly hope that you will not in any way resent our suggestions. There is no question whatever that we are keen about the mss, and with the necessary changes, I think that it would have a good chance. Won't you tell me something about your ideas for detective stories, and whether you have any more under way?

Hoping that we will be able to get together on POISONVILLE (a hopeless title by the way) I am,

Yours faithfully,
Mrs. Alfred A. Knopf

891 Post Street, San Francisco, California, March 20, 1928

Dear Mrs. Knopf,

Many thanks for your kind letter and its suggestions for POISONVILLE'S improvement.

The middle of the book, as it now stands, undoubtedly is more than somewhat cluttered up with violence, and I am thoroughly willing to make whatever changes you consider necessary. But, if possible, I'd like to keep Lew Yard in the story, as most of the second half of the book hinges on Reno's break with him.

In the enclosed revised pages I have cut out the dynamiting of police headquarters (page 134); have cut out the attack on Reno's house (page 176), which shouldn't have been put in in the first place; and have changed the dynamiting of Yard's house (page 149) to a simple shooting off-stage. These changes will, I think, relieve the congestion quite a bit. If you think additional revision adviseable, please let me know.

In connection with these cuts, the following chapter titles should be changed:

Chapter XVI to "Exit Jerry"
Chapter XVIII, page 149, to "Painter Street"
Chapter XXI, page 169, to "The Seventeenth Murder"

You will notice that I have left the bombing of Pete the Finn's establishment (page 209) as it was. Since both of the other dynamiting episodes have been removed, I think this one might be retained, especially as it is further along in the story, not in the congested area. But it can be easily enough deleted if you so desire.

Somehow I had got the idea that POISONVILLE was a pretty good title, and I was surprised at your considering it hopeless— sufficiently surprised to ask a couple of retail book sellers what they thought of it. They agreed with you, so I'm beginning to suspect which one of us is wrong. Here are the only new titles I've been able to think up so far:

THE POISONVILLE MURDERS,

THE SEVENTEENTH MURDER,

MURDER PLUS,

THE WILLSSON MATTER,

THE CITY OF DEATH,

THE CLEANSING OF POISONVILLE,

THE BLACK CITY,

RED HARVEST

Maybe I'll be able to do better later, or maybe you can help me. The only prejudice I have in this connection is against the word "case" used where my sleuth would use "job" and, more officially, "matter" or "operation."

I've another book-length detective story—tentatively entitled THE DAIN CURSE—under way, using the same detective I used in this book, but not using him so violently. I hope to finish that next month. The first serial rights have been sold to The Black Mask.

Then I want to try adapting the stream-of-consciousness method, conveniently modified, to a detective story, carrying the reader along with the detective, showing him everything as it is found, giving him the detective's conclusions as they are reached, letting the solution break on both of them together. I don't know whether I've made that very clear, but it's something altogether different from the method employed in POISON-VILLE, for instance, where, though the reader goes along with the detective, he seldom sees deeper into the detective's mind than dialogue and action let him. If I can manage it, I want to do this one without any regard for magazines' thou-shalts and thou-shalt-nots. I hope to get it finished by late summer, in time to do another—a plot I've been waiting to get at for two years—before 1928 is dead.

I'm one of the few—if there are any more—people moderately literate who take the detective story seriously. I don't mean that I necessarily take my own or anybody else's seriously—but the detective story as a form. Some day somebody's going to make "literature" of it (Ford's GOOD SOLDIER wouldn't have needed much altering to have been a detective story), and I'm selfish enough to have my hopes, however slight the evident justification may be. I have a long speech I usually make on the subject, all about the ground not having been scratched yet, and so on, but I won't bore you with it now.

I want to thank you again for your interest in POISONVILLE. I hope you'll find the changes I have made sufficient, but if they aren't I'll appreciate any further suggestions you may make.

Sincerely Yours,
Dashiell Hammett

891 Post Street, San Francisco, April 9th, 1928

Dear Mrs. Knopf,

I am returning the RED HARVEST contract, signed and witnessed.

This new title is, I think, a satisfactory one; though my first choice probably disqualifies me as a competent judge.

Many thanks for the acceptance, and also for your wire concerning the motion picture dickering.

I included RED HARVEST in the half a dozen stories sumbitted [*sic*] to the Fox Studio, and have hopes that something will come of it.

In accordance with the terms of the contract, I shall, of course, pass on to you any offer Fox may make for RED HARVEST.

If, as seems quite likely just now, I make a more than transient connection with Fox, I'll probably let the stream-of-consciousness experiment wait awhile, sticking to the more objective and filmable forms.

Meanwhile, I'll have at you with another book next month.

Will you kindly put this dedication in RED HARVEST:
"To Joseph Thompson Shaw"

Sincerely yours,
Dashiell Hammett

Blanche Knopf had a cool, knowledgeable eye and was to influence the careers of the best of the hard-boiled writers—Raoul Whitfield, Raymond Chandler, James M. Cain. She had also been instrumental in bringing many of the best and most interesting of the European writers to Knopf; and both she and Alfred Knopf had a certain role as liaison between American and European letters. She must have known that in Hammett she had discovered something, the genuine article, a writer who wrote prose clean and spare as Hemingway did, with whom he would most often be compared, and with a voice that similarly spoke of a personal code in a modern world whose institutions were corrupt. The Knopfs must have sensed, as Hammett himself did, his growing mastery, the flood of his energy and power, his promising momentum. He was on the edge of a change in his life.

891 Post St., San Francisco, June 25

Dear Mrs. Knopf,

Here's the second detective novel. I hope you'll like it.

My Hollywood trip didn't carry the Fox negotiations much ahead. So far I haven't managed to trade them any of my published stuff for money, and a tentative agreement concerning some original photoplays is still very tentative.

Sincerely yours,
Dashiell Hammett

He had finished the four episodes of *The Dain Curse* in June 1928 and tried to peddle it to Hollywood as well as to Knopf. Hollywood wasn't interested, but Knopf was sure it would want to publish it, with, again, some changes, in particular because it was too complex and fell "too definitely into three sections, in the intervals of which the interest of the reader lags considerably. . . . If you could contrive to make the connecting thread between the murders at Leggett's, the murders at the Temple and the murders at Quesada a little stronger, I am very sure that the book would profit. We have thought too that the violence is piled on a bit thick and that cutting out one or two of the less imporant killings would do away with the danger of surfeiting the reader. The same thing holds true for the immense number of characters, which is so great as to create confusion."[21]

Knopf editor Harry Block—Blanche Knopf was in Europe—adds about Gabrielle, the heroine, "that for anyone so attractive Gabrielle is singularly repulsive. I realize that for the purposes of the plot her physical peculiarities must be stressed to a certain extent but, as someone has said, she does sound exactly like a monkey. It seems to me that if she could be made to have a more definite charm, her allure might be more plausible. This isn't a very important matter, however, and I hope you will do as you think best."

Hammett delayed making the corrections, but profiting either from Block's remarks or from his own discoveries, in the work at which he was now busy he did not repeat the mistakes. The perfectly controlled *Maltese Falcon* was probably already under way. In it the heroine would be unequivocably beautiful and all the violence would be offstage.

August 6, 1928

Dashiell Hammett, Esq.
891 Post Street
San Francisco, California

Dear Mr. Hammett:

Many thanks for your letter of July 29th and also for your earlier letter of July 15th, which has just been discovered on someone's desk where it had lain undisturbed for two weeks. I can't think of anything to suggest about the revisions of THE

DAIN CURSE other than the points I have already made. Your own very clear analysis of the difficulties in these two letters would seem to indicate pretty clearly that you know precisely what is to be done and that it is simply a matter of time for you to find the solution. In the meantime, I should not worry about it. The book is already so good that we are certain the revisions will work themselves out in your mind if you give them a chance to.

THE MALTESE FALCON is a swell title and I am already very eager to read the book.

Sincerely yours,
[Harry C. Block]
ALFRED A. KNOPF, Inc.
Editorial Department

November 22, 1928

Dear Mr. Hammett:

I should have written you long before this about the revised manuscript of THE DAIN CURSE. I have read it again very carefully and it seems to me you can still improve the book by working some more along the lines of revision that we discussed in our last correspondence. We want the book, certainly, and you can take this letter as our definite acceptance of it under the terms of the option in our contract for RED HARVEST. We want to publish it in the fall season of 1929 which still leaves you several months if necessary in which to work on the manuscript. I am sending it back to you now in the hope that having been away from it for sometime, you will be able to read it with a greater perspective than the last time. Please go over it again and see if it isn't possible to make some of these revisions. The book is an excellent one as it stands but while there is any chance to make it still better, I don't think we can disregard it. I am having the manuscript returned to you, under separate cover. With best regards.

Sincerely yours,
[Harry C. Block]
ALFRED A. KNOPF, Inc.
Editorial Department

December 14, 1928

Dear Mr. Hammett,

Thank you for your letter of December 8th. You will have until April 1st to deliver the manuscript in time for the fall publication and the next book can be either THE DAIN CURSE or THE MALTESE FALCON. I suggest that you let me see THE MALTESE FALCON as soon as you have it finished and perhaps it may be wiser to publish that one before the other.

Sincerely yours,
[Harry C. Block]
ALFRED A. KNOPF, Inc.
Editorial Department

The Dain Curse was published six months later, in July 1929. By publication day Hammett had already sent Harry Block the manuscript of The Maltese Falcon, "fairly confident that it is by far the best thing I've done so far, and I hope you'll think so too."

Hammett may have resisted revising The Dain Curse because he knew it was not the equal of his work in progress; The Maltese Falcon had taken his interest and it must have been hard to return to the earlier story. Nonetheless, the revisions were finally done, and the result pleased both Knopf and the public; The Dain Curse sold out three printings of the first edition and was speedily sold to Grosset and Dunlap, the reprint house. The critics were generally kind, and felt that it marked an advance over Red Harvest, though one, John Bartlow Martin in Harper's Magazine, may have echoed Hammett's own sentiments about what he later called his "silly story": "In this single Hammett novel the detective shot and stabbed one man to death, helped shoot another dead, was himself attacked with dagger, gun, chloroform and bomb, fought off a ghostly manifestation barehanded, wrestled with five women, cured a girl of narcotic addiction—and . . . was obliged to deal with one seduction, eight murders, a jewel burglary, and a family curse."[22]

The Dain Curse was dedicated to Albert S. Samuels, the names of the characters were those of employees at Samuels' jewelry store, and the villain was a novelist who resembled Hammett, "a long, lean sorrel-haired man of thirty-two . . . who pretended to be lazier than he was, would rather talk than do anything else and had a lot of what seemed to be accurate information and original ideas on any subject that happened to come up. . . ."²³ The Op himself, in this the last novel in which he appears, has grown from the taciturn factotum of the earliest stories into a wistfully compassionate man, feeling his age, half in love, or so he hints, with the intriguing Gabrielle. If the plot and the structure were the weaknesses of the book, the characterization was its strength and pointed the direction in which Hammett's talent was rapidly developing.

When Hammett submitted the manuscript of *The Maltese Falcon*, a month before the publication of *The Dain Curse*, his mood was excited, confident. He could hardly control the flood of ideas and plans with which he regarded his future. The *Falcon* might for instance be a play. He was already interested in plays:

> Will you let me know if you agree with me? I wouldn't take a chance on trying to adapt it myself, but will try to get the help of somebody who knows the theatre.
>
> Another thing: if you use THE FALCON will you go a little easy on the editing? While I wouldn't go the [*sic*] the stake in defense of my system of punctuation, I do rather like it and I think it goes with my sort of sentence-structure. The first forty pages of THE DAIN CURSE were edited to beat hell (hurriedly for the dummy?) and the rest hardly at all. The result was that, having amiably accepted most of your changes in the first part, I had my hands full carrying them out in the remainder, trying to make it look like all the work of the same writer.
>
> Like most of the world most of the time I am just now rather desperately in need of all the money I can scrape up. If there is any truth in these rumors that one hears about advances against royalties, will you do the best you can for me? If my appreciation equals my need I can promise to quite overwhelm you with gratitude.
>
> How soon will you want, or can you use, another book? I've quite a flock of them outlined or begun, and I've a couple of groups of connected stories that can be joined in a whole just as I did with RED HARVEST and the DAIN CURSE. The best of them were written just before RED HARVEST, a group that would make a book as exciting as RED HARVEST, though less complicated, with THE BIG KNOCK-OVER as title.²⁴

This was eventually to appear as a collection of short stories, but that was not, apparently, what Hammett had in mind here, as he goes on to propose a group of stories, "by the pound, as it were"—

an idea he thought better of in his next letter, after, apparently,
rereading the stories, which he thought would make up a book
called "The Continental Op."

> Also I've a horror-story I'd like to get to work on—a variant
> of the Frankenstein idea—tentatively entitled AEAEA; a pure
> plot detective story, TWO TWO'S ARE TWENTY-TWO; a
> political murder mystery, THE SECRET EMPEROR; one some-
> thing on the order of THE MALTESE FALCON, THAT
> NIGHT IN SINGAPORE; and an underworld mystery, DEAD
> MAN'S FRIDAY. (All these titles are tentative, of course.)
> I had intended the story of a gunman next, but according to
> Asbury, LITTLE CAESAR was *that*. So, until I've read it I'm
> holding off. I'm a little afraid anyhow that gunmen and racket-
> eers, as such, are going to be rather sour literary material by
> this time next year.

This perception may have affected his treatment of Ned Beaumont,
Madvig and the others in *The Glass Key*, who are no longer gunmen and racketers "as such," but may well have begun as such.

Harry Block liked *The Maltese Falcon*, but wanted Hammett
to modify what Hammett called the "to-bed and the homosexual
parts." Hammett replied: "I should like to leave them as they are,
especially since you say they 'would be all right perhaps in an
ordinary novel.' It seems to me that the only thing that can be said
against their use in a detective novel is that nobody has tried it yet.
I'd like to try it."[25]

In *The Maltese Falcon* he had written a little story within a
story, about a man named Flitcraft, who, despite or because of a
wife and children, decided to take up a new life. He had narrowly
missed being killed by a falling beam in the street, and the close
call had brought him to a consciousness of the brevity of life, and
the necessity of leading it in the right way. Now, with the book
finished and off to Knopf, Hammett planned to do exactly the
same thing—leave his wife and children and go to New York, the
center of publishing and culture and literary life. He was a successful author at work on his fourth novel. The future expanded
before him.

He had also, at this time, fallen in love, if that was the name he
gave the emotion. He had found a woman full of brains and energy
who understood him, excited him, and whom he respected. Her

name was Nell Martin. She was a writer who'd been an actress, a law student, a migrant worker—like him, a restless wanderer.

Nell described herself: "Soldier, sailor, oh what a plight I am, tinker, tailor, oh what a sight I am." She'd been a newspaperwoman in Chicago and in San Francisco and Los Angeles, a musical-comedy soubrette, vaudeville singer, strawberry picker, store clerk, piano player, press agent, taxi driver, movie actress, cabaret entertainer, proofreader, and erstwhile operator of a laundry mangle. Her novel *Lovers Should Marry* was dedicated to Hammett,[26] and his, *The Glass Key*, was dedicated to her.

They talked about writing, had a lot of laughs. Her books weren't very good—his private thought—but they were cute and sparkling, and they dealt with issues that interested both of them.

It interested them to question old ideas and old-hat notions: Which was the higher imperative—marriage vows or sexual attraction, not to mention love? What was the moral position of an Other Woman? If a woman and a man were business partners, shouldn't they split the check? What are the duties of a man to a wife he no longer loves? Virginity—that was old hat.

Jose tried not to be censorious. She knew that Hammett loved her in his way. She wished she were cleverer. She had a lot to do, with the two girls and trying to make ends meet. She knew she was lucky in a lot of ways and ought not to complain. He had never made a secret of his nature.

They decided, or he decided, that she and the girls should move to Los Angeles, where Jose had some relatives and where Hammett hoped eventually to get movie work. "You'll like Los Angeles," he told them before he left for New York in late 1929. Mary Jane and Mama and Jo packed their suitcases and boxes once again, and Papa took them to the train. "I'll be there before you know it," he said, but Mary Jane had a feeling they would never see him again. Mama didn't seem to know this—she didn't seem sad—and Jo was too little to feel what Mary Jane felt. "We'll see Papa soon again," they said, so Mary Jane let them think they were right and kept her tears to herself.

1929-1930

THE GLASS KEY

Life, then, was reversible. You were forlorn, ambitious, deserving but despised, sick unto death, unnoticed, strapped down with a wife and kids, coughing your insides out, poor, a nobody. But things implied in the literature of advertising and in the mind of the twenties about hard work and good ideas and talent had paid off. He had left the East a bum and a Pinkerton man and now was warmly welcomed back ten years later a famous writer—in a minor way. He met Erle Stanley Gardner and Raoul Whitfield and other writers of the *Black Mask* school, with whom he had long discussions about the craft of mystery writing; the Alfred Knopfs were happy to meet him; people thought him handsome and funny. He was a hit in New York, he seldom wrote home, and went to parties where people talked about books and writing and he found he could talk about them too. His stored-up lonely thoughts came out, and a drink or two helped overcome his shyness. Nell got in with show-business people, who interested him too, and no one thought much about his and Nell's irregular situation. If you were a famous writer, you had some latitude in your domestic arrangements—in fact, you couldn't afford to live a plain life. You had to be lost and crazy—it was the smart affectation of the time. Life had begun for him at last, rather late, to be sure, for he was now thirty-six; but better late than never.

Good fortune had set in for him at the time it ran out for many other people, with the crash of the stock market. In the spring of 1930 *The Maltese Falcon*, dedicated to Jose, was published by Knopf. Its success was immediate—the consensus was that it was the best American detective story yet written, and it was reprinted

Hammett, Scarsdale, N.Y., 1929.

seven times in the first year. Moreover, readers and reviewers were conscious of the writer himself; he at last had an intimation of what it was like to be famous.

He copied out the parts of reviews that particularly pleased him and, in a mood of exultant self-justification, sent them to Jose. "More hooey from the press":

> The detectives of fiction have been knocked into a cocked hat—which is where most of them belong—by the appearance of Sam Spade in a book called The Maltese Falcon. It is the work of Dashiell Hammett; it is a novel and it is also a mystery story— the combination is so rare that probably not half a dozen good examples exist between The Moonstone and the present one.
>
> The central mystery is not an especial good one; three groups of people are after an object of enormous value. But everything else, characters, plot, and the general attitude of the author, are fresh and novel and brilliant. Spade himself is hard-boiled, immoral, with a free fist and a free tongue. After the high-minded detective heroes, with their effeminate manners, their artistic leanings, and their elaborate deductions, he is as startling as a real man in a show-window of dummies. His actions and his language will shock old ladies.
>
> . . . the romance in the story is blown to bits by bitter realism.
>
> This book is far better written than most detective stories. . . . you read it with amazement and with wonder. Because this is the real thing and everything else has been phony. The publishers quote someone as saying that Mr. Hammett has done for the mystery story what Dumas did for the historical romance. I consider that an enthusiastic, but not unjustifiable, comparison.
>
> —Gilbert Seldes in the New York *Graphic*

HAMMETT BOOK SO GOOD IT STUMPS CRITIC
THE MALTESE FALCON IS BEST DETECTIVE STORY
BY LEADER IN THRILLER FIELD

There are detective-story writers, and then there is Dashiell Hammett. I can think of no one in the world who is his match. . . . I find it hard to figure out a way to tell you how good a book The Maltese Falcon is. . . . the blood of everyone I know who has read it has pounded in plunging jets through every vein during all the reading. . . . And what an underworld story! We've had a flood of them lately, between boards and in the magazines and in the movies, but nothing to touch this . . . it is made of reality. . . . The book is written with the snap and bite of a whiplash. . . . has a thousand virtues, of observation, of detail, of nuance, and of effect.

—Elrick B. Davis in the Cleveland *Press*

This department announces a new and pretty huge enthusiasm, to wit: Dashiell Hammett. Moreover, it would not surprise us one whit if Mr. Hammett should turn out to be the Great American Mystery Writer. (The fact is, he may be that right now, and this department is merely hopping aboard the Hammett band-wagon ere it be too late—Herbert Asbury, Walter Brooks and Joseph Shaw have already discovered him.). . . . The Horse-power of Mr. Hammett's pen . . . must be sampled to be believed. . . . In short, "The Maltese Falcon" is the best one . . . in Lord knows when. Read it and see.

—Will Cuppy in the *Herald Tribune*

If the locution "hard-boiled" had not already been coined it would be necessary to coin it now to describe the characters of Dashiell Hammett's latest detective story.

—New York *Times*

Until Mr. Hammett appeared, however, no American writer has taken the detective novel seriously enough to do more than ape the outstanding characteristics of the British school. . . . If you were to consider an amalgamation of Mr. Hemingway, the Mr. Burnett who wrote "Little Caesar" and "Iron Man," that other disciple of Hemingway, Morley Callaghan, and Ring Lardner in his prizefighting aspect, you would have a fair idea of the style and technique. I think Mr. Hammett has something quite as definite to say, quite as decided an impetus to give the course of newness in the development of the American tongue, as any man now writing.

—William Curtis in *Town & Country*

In *The Maltese Falcon* Hammett returned to a third-person narrative, probably the form in which he had begun his first at-tempt at a novel, "The Secret Emperor," and a form that, because it was better adapted for the use of dialogue, was better suited to his gifts, which were dramatic. The first person depends on self-explanation, never his strong suit, but is also useful for describing violent action, as it lends credibility to what might otherwise be incredible. *The Maltese Falcon* did not strain credibility, was not overly violent; indeed, he later said, the plot came in part from Henry James' *Wings of the Dove*. Perhaps in reaction to criticism of the violence of the Op stories, he carefully set the murders—only four in number—offstage.

The Op, though an "I," was short, fat, old, and safely not Hammett. To the third-person hero he now gave his own name, Sam, and though he would specifically disclaim an autobiographical connection, he made one. Afterward, when people asked him where the characters came from, he subtly identified himself with Spade.

I followed Gutman's original in Washington, and I never remember shadowing a man who bored me so much. He was not after a jeweled falcon, of course; but he *was* suspected of being a German spy. . . . I worked with Dundy's prototype in a North Carolina railroad yard. The Cairo character I picked up on a forgery charge in 1920. Effie, the good girl, once asked me to go into the narcotic smuggling business with her in San Diego. Wilmer, the gunman, was picked up in Stockton, California, a neat small smooth-faced quiet boy of perhaps twenty-one. He was serenely proud of the name the papers gave him—The Midget Bandit. He'd robbed a Stockton filling station the previous week—and had been annoyed by the description the station proprietor had given of him and by the proprietor's statement of what he would do to that little runt if he ever laid eyes on him again and see what he wanted to do about it. That's when we nabbed him.[1]

Brigid, he says, was partly based on a woman who engaged him to discharge her housekeeper. She would also have been familiar to any close reader of Hammett's other fiction, a *femme fatale* who strongly attracts the hero but whom the hero resists (in Spade's case after he has slept with her) when he is forced to choose between having her and turning her in for her crimes. Sexuality and crime or gain are thus associated: the "good" girls are rather asexual or turn sexual, like Janet Henry in *The Glass Key*, in response to disillusion. The view of women in the main is of amoral, untrustworthy and tempting creatures, and it is to these the hero is drawn.

Hammett relished being a New York man-about-town, perhaps too much to do justice to his new project, *The Glass Key*. He wrote to Herbert Asbury, who had admired *Red Harvest* and now approved enthusiastically of *The Maltese Falcon*:

I can't tell you how pleased I am with your verdict. . . . It's the first thing I've done that was—regardless of what faults it has—the best work I was capable of at the time I was doing it, and well. . . .

THE GLASS KEY, held back thus far by laziness, drunkenness, and illness, promises to get itself finished somehow by the latter part of next week. As soon as it's out of the mill I think we ought to get together and celebrate whatever there happens to be to celebrate.[2]

Whatever the obstacles, Hammett did finish *The Glass Key*, and he was pleased with it. He thought it was his best work so far. He had written four novels in three years, as well as book reviews, short stories and a novella, and he knew he was getting better all the time.

He now began a fifth novel, *The Thin Man*, but laid it aside. He would later attribute this to exhaustion, to having ruined himself in the sustained creative exertion of one marathon thirty-hour writing session on *The Glass Key*. But it is more likely that the exhaustion was the cumulative effect of the remarkable achievements of these thirty-six months. Exhausted or not, he must have felt himself almost secure in the mastery he had achieved, not only of the genre in which he had established himself as an important innovator, but of novelistic gifts he now planned to use on future novels that would be, in his view, more serious. *The Glass Key*, as elegant and controlled in style as anything he ever wrote, was also richer in emotional probabilities, and the subject was more ambitious. He had learned to plot, to make characters talk and sound like real people, to describe the most elaborate and sustained action so that the reader could almost see it before his very eyes. And he knew how, within the limits he set himself, to suggest through the use of dialogue the complex psychological makeup of his characters—for instance, the following passage shows Ned Beaumont's understanding of Paul Madvig's social ambitions and Ned Beaumont's own feelings about them, his understanding of the implications of gift-giving, of female and class psychology and much else:

Madvig yawned. "You didn't understand me right, Ned," he said. "I didn't ask for all this. I just asked you what kind of present I ought to give Miss Henry [the senator's daughter]."

Ned Beaumont's face lost its animation, became a slightly sullen mask. "How far have you got with her?" he asked in a voice that expressed nothing of what he might have been thinking.

"Nowhere. I've been there maybe half a dozen times to talk to the Senator. Sometimes I see her and sometimes I don't, but only to say 'How do you do' or something with other people around. You know, I haven't had a chance to say anything to her yet."

Amusement glinted for a moment in Ned Beaumont's eyes and vanished. He brushed back one side of his mustache with a thumbnail and asked: "Tomorrow's your first dinner there?"

"Yes, though I don't expect it to be the last."

"And you didn't get a bid to the birthday party?"

"No." Madvig hesitated. "Not yet."

"Then the answer's one you won't like."

Madvig's face was impassive. "Such as?" he asked.

"Don't give her anything."

"Oh, hell, Ned!"

Ned Beaumont shrugged. "Do whatever you like. You asked me."

"But why?"

"You're not supposed to give people things unless you're sure they'd like to get them from you."

"But everybody likes to—"

"Maybe, but it goes deeper than that. When you give somebody something, you're saying out loud that you know they'd like to have you give—"

"I got you," Madvig said.[3]

Readers of the *Black Mask*, its editors, Hammett's colleagues—the other writers of hard-boiled stories—had admired the nameless, dogged Op, at first simply the loyal and consummate professional, who by the end of *The Dain Curse* had become a more complex and human character. Sam Spade, in *The Maltese Falcon*, who combined the Op's professionalism with the more traditional qualities of a romantic hero—good looks and sexuality—had been even more satisfactory. Now, in *The Glass Key*, with Ned Beaumont he had drawn his most plausible and fallible hero yet.

In all these stories he had become more skillful in translating traditional fiction romantic motifs into the terms and tones of the modern city. In *Red Harvest* the Op arrives to clean up the Western town. *The Dain Curse* is a fairy tale of an enchanted damsel in distress, and *The Maltese Falcon* is a treasure hunt. Now his subject was loyalty among men (a theme occurring in some of the earlier tales as well), but where the Op and Sam Spade were confronted with tests of loyalty in conventional situations and had to choose between doing their job and succumbing to the temptation of making money or seducing beautiful women, *The Glass Key* spins a more ambitious and unusual web whose threads are male friendship, male loyalty and male betrayal, and considers the ultimate treachery—the murder of a son by his father.

Hammett liked male society, whether of Pinkerton agents or hospital inmates or men in the army and even prison. He liked the situation of solidarity with other men against the lower representatives of higher authority—against the unreasonable sergeant or supervisor, the officious orderly. (But above the odious functionary was a higher authority whose basic power and fairness he respected, as the Op respects the Old Man's.) Hammett also liked his protagonists, especially the heroes, and he understood them. He identified with them, and sometimes signed his letters with their names: Spade, Nicky, Whitey and even Elfinstone.[4] His heroes were getting to be more and more like himself. In the way of a beginning writer, he had disguised the Op by making him the opposite of himself, short and fat and fortyish and impervious to women. The assertive and attractive Spade is an idealized figure who is closer to himself. In Ned Beaumont—principled, forlorn, afflicted with an uneasy worldliness and the ability to understand the meaner motives and ambitions of his friends, and tubercular—Hammett produced his nearest self-portrait.

The Op had been good at his job, committed to the agency and to the idea of a job well done. Spade, reflecting the increasingly wary Hammett's developing view of life, plays his own game just a bit. The Op takes matters into his own hands only when the orders don't come through or when (as often) it is his client who is behind the sinister events, whereas Spade is in charge all the time. But Ned Beaumont still searches for value in values, for merit in authority. His boss and friend, Madvig, is a corrupt politician, but Beaumont is loyal and mindful of the good qualities Madvig has— friendliness and a certain kind of honesty. The people who most pretend to rectitude—here, Senator Henry—are murderers. Like Spade, like Nick Charles, Ned will sleep with the woman from a higher social class—pleasure but also a kind of revenge.

Hammett was himself now moving out of the world where he had begun.

But he kept his detective image polished up with an occasional reminder that he was himself an ex-detective:

It would be silly to insist that nobody who has not been a detective should write detective stories, but it is certainly not unreasonable to ask any one who is going to write a book of any sort to make some effort at least to learn something about his subject. Most writers do. Only detective story writers seem to be free from a sense of obligation in this direction, and, curiously, the more established and prolific detective story writers seem to be the worst offenders. Nearly all writers of Western tales at least get an occasional glimpse of their chosen territory from a car-window while en route to Hollywood; writers of sea stories have been seen on the waterfront; surely detective story writers could afford to speak to policemen now and then.

Meanwhile, a couple of months' labor in this arena has convinced me that the following suggestions might be of value to somebody:

1. There was an automatic revolver, the Webley-Fosbery, made in England some years ago. The ordinary automatic pistol, however, is not a revolver. A pistol, to be a revolver, must have something on it that revolves.

2. The Colt's .45 automatic pistol has no chambers. The cartridges are put in a magazine.

3. A silencer may be attached to a revolver, but the effect will be altogether negligible. I have never seen a silencer used on an automatic pistol, but am told it would cause the pistol to jam. A silencer may be used on a single-shot target pistol or on a rifle, but both would still make quite a bit of noise. "Silencer" is a rather optimistic name for this device which has generally fallen into disuse.

4. When a bullet from a Colt's .45, or any firearm of approximately the same size and power, hits you, even if not in a fatal spot, it usually knocks you over. It is quite upsetting at any reasonable range.

5. A shot or stab wound is simply felt as a blow or push at first. It is some little time before any burning or other painful sensation begins.

6. When you are knocked unconscious you do not feel the blow that does it.

7. A wound made after the death of the wounded is usually recognizable as such.

8. Finger-prints of any value to the police are seldom found on anybody's skin.

9. The pupils of many drug-addicts' eyes are apparently normal.

10. It is impossible to see anything by the flash of an ordinary gun, though it is easy to imagine you have seen things.

11. Not nearly so much can be seen by moonlight as you imagine. This is especially true of colors.

12. All Federal snoopers are not members of the Secret Service. That branch is chiefly occupied with pursuing counterfeiters and guarding Presidents and prominent visitors to our shores.

13. A sheriff is a county officer who usually has no official connection with city, town or state police.

14. Federal prisoners convicted in Washington, D.C., are usually sent to the Atlanta prison and not to Leavenworth.

15. The California State prison at San Quentin is used for convicts serving first terms. Two-time losers are usually sent to Folsom. . . .

16. Ventriloquists do not actually "throw" their voices and such doubtful illusions as they manage depend on their gestures. Nothing at all could be done by a ventriloquist standing behind his audience.

17. Even detectives who drop their final g's should not be made to say "anythin' "—an oddity that calls for vocal acrobatics.

18. "Youse" is the plural of "you."

19. A trained detective shadowing a subject does not ordinarily leap from doorway to doorway and does not hide behind trees and poles. He knows no harm is done if the subject sees him now and then.

20. The current practice in most places in the United States is to make the coroner's inquest an empty formality in which nothing much is brought out except that somebody has died.

21. Fingerprints are fragile affairs. Wrapping a pistol or other small object up in a handkerchief is much more likely to obliterate than to preserve any prints it may have.

22. When an automatic pistol is fired the empty cartridge-shell flies out the right-hand side. The empty cartridge-case remains in a revolver until ejected by hand.

23. A lawyer cannot impeach his own witness.

24. The length of time a corpse has been a corpse can be approximated by an experienced physician, but only approximated, and the longer it has been a corpse, the less accurate the approximation is likely to be.[5]

Jose and the girls were settled in Los Angeles, where some of the Kellys lived. It wasn't an easy thing bringing up the girls without Dash; but he'd never been around much anyway, and he sent money. She thought she'd be all right as long as he kept sending the money. They lived near some railroad tracks, and the girls went to a Catholic school.

Jo wanted to be an angel in the church Christmas pageant; Mary got to be the Virgin Mary even though she was naughty and was accused of hitting one of the nuns, which didn't seem fair to Jo.

Mary and Jo did not feel alone in the world. There were the Kellys, related to Mama, and far away were Aunt Reba and Uncle Dick, Hammett's sister and brother. Papa called Dick the kid and thought he was silly. He liked Aunt Reba. So did Mary and Jo. Aunt Reba sent them little outfits she had sewed for their storybook dolls, bridal dresses, and underwear and hats and cloaks. Once Aunt Reba sent them little stone crosses from an especially holy mountain. It was nice having an aunt. Papa said Aunt Reba was an old maid.

8

1931

HOLLYWOOD

Jo, playing in the L.A. street, heard Mary screaming "Papa's back! Papa's back!" Jo's stomach curled with fear and happiness. Her face alight, Mary came running and took her by the hand. There was Mama standing by the door, and Papa's embraces. Maybe things would be all right. With Papa there, they thought, things might take a turn for the good. The neighbors beamed with pleasure at the excitement of the little girls and the nice little Mrs. Hammett now that the father had come home. He did not stay long on this visit.

From the West, in the wake of the success of *The Maltese Falcon* came the beckoning and blandishments of high-paying Hollywood, which Hammett had unsuccessfully tried before to interest. Hollywood, not only the haven of writers but a place where they could get rich. With his family already in California, when he received an offer, Hammett decided to go back there in the late summer of 1930. He paid a short visit to his sister Reba and his father and old friends in Baltimore and then made his way West.

At first it cannot have seemed a mistake. The best writers were in Hollywood, putting in their time and collecting the huge sums of money, all affecting to despise the work but spending the money. That the world was falling deeper into the depression all around them lent a certain piquancy to this situation. Going to Hollywood was as much a mark of arrival as going to New York had been—maybe more, because Hollywood had the acceptance, even the respect, of New York.

"A comic time," Lillian Hellman wrote of it, "with its over-perfect English antiques that were replacing the overcarved Spanish furniture and hanging shawls; the flutey, refined language—one producer spoke often of his daughter's 'perberty,' and Hammett phoned me one night from Jean Harlow's house to tell me that she had rung the bell for the butler and said, 'Open the window, James, and leave in a tiny air'—and the attempt, running side by side with the new life, to stand by the old roots: Jewish mama stories and Jewish mamas proudly imported from the East; French cooks and stuffed derma; and one studio executive who lived in a Colonial house with early American furniture and a mezuzah above the door encased in pickled pine. And there was the wife of a composer who had two ermine coats exactly alike in case one should burn, and the ex-star, our neighbor, who often came calling to show me the knife cuts on her body put there the night before by a very religious movie director."[1]

The writers thought of the studio execs as preposterous little men, but of themselves as smart and witty people and great boozers who knew how to live. They eyed one another's style—style now expanded to mean something more than the classy arrangement of words. It had broad application—clothes and what you ate and drank, the house, the works. Hammett knew, and knew he knew, what to wear and eat and drink. Nothing was lost on him. He noticed that silk socks did not go with tweeds, that tweeds were classy, he noticed what expensive women wore and what the other ones wore. He never wore silk socks with tweeds. He lived in swell hotels and hired a couple—two black men, Jones and his lover. The lover cooked, and Jones was the valet and also drove Hammett around. Hammett made friends with writers—Ben Hecht and Charles MacArthur, S. J. Perelman, Dorothy Parker.

It was David O. Selznick who had cast covetous eyes on Hammett. Selznick believed that books were not written but "created" and had a nose for who was hot:

> Hammet has recently created quite a stir in literary circles by his creation of two books for Knopf, *The Maltese Falcon* and *Red Harvest*. . . . Hammett is unspoiled as to money, but on the other hand anxious not to tie himself up with a long-term contract. I was in hopes that we could get him for about $400 weekly, but he claims that this is only about half of his present earning capacity between books and magazine stories, and I am inclined to believe him inasmuch as his vogue is on the rise.[2]

Hammett, 1933.

So Hammett took on the job, for Paramount, of writing some-thing which Selznick hoped would be "new and startlingly orig-inal" and which turned out to be *City Streets*, directed by Rouben Mamoulian and released in 1931, starring Gary Cooper and Sylvia Sidney. Sidney played the pretty daughter of a mobster. Cooper was the handsome carnival yokel who gets roped in by the mob, only to end up running it. She sees that crime doesn't pay and tries to get him to be the straight Gary Cooper she had loved. The dia-

Lillian Hellman, c. 1930.

logue is snappy and witty, in an arch mode to which Hammett would return. The film was a success. Meantime Hammett lived first at the Roosevelt Hotel and then at the Hollywood Knicker-bocker. Here he corrected the proofs of *The Glass Key*, did some wheeling and dealing about the movie rights to it, and interested himself a little in the movie fortunes of *The Maltese Falcon*.

Hammett had been shocked at the heavily corrected and altered proofs of *The Glass Key*. It took him a while to set them straight again, and when, in November, he got Knopf's bill for the cor-rections, he refused to pay it. "If you take a look at the MS, which I think is still in your hands, you'll see you're very lucky I haven't billed you for the trouble I was put to unediting it,"[3] he wrote stiffly not to Alfred himself or Harry Block but to "gentlemen."

This same autumn—they were later to pick November 25, 1930, arbitrarily, as their anniversary—Hammett met a woman, tempera-mental and literary, a combination that had always appealed to one side of his imagination: Lillian Kober, a script reader for MGM who had New York publishing and theatrical connections and

wanted to be a writer. They began an affair, which escalated into a
love affair. They hardly knew how it began. He was coming off
a bad drunk, someone had introduced them at Musso and Frank's,
a restaurant. As nearly as they could remember afterward, they
sat in his car and talked about books. She was Jewish and little
and lively and tough as nails. She had advanced ideas, a salty vo-
cabulary and a compliant husband. They were in love before they
could account for it.

"When I first met Dash he had written four of the five novels
and was the hottest thing in Hollywood and New York," she
wrote of this beginning. "It is not remarkable to be the hottest
thing in either city—the hottest kid changes for each winter season—but in his case it was of extra interest to those who collect
people that the ex-detective who had bad cuts on his legs and an
indentation in his head from being scrappy with criminals was
gentle in manner—well-educated, elegant to look at, born of early
settlers, was eccentric, witty, and spent so much money on women
that they would have liked him even if he had been none of the
good things."[4]

She had reddish hair, was funny and full of ambition. He approved of that, though not of the way she was always restless,
wanting to be off someplace. She was a traveler by nature—it
wasn't a quality you'd want in a wife. She'd go to Spain, to Russia
at the drop of a hat—she'd sell out her own country, was his opinion, if somebody offered her a free trip, and it wouldn't have to
be to Spain—Jersey City would do.

He liked her beautiful clothes; she was stylish and educated and
a hell of a writer, or could be if she wasn't insecure and lazy. She
had ideas about writing and laughed at Nell's books, which made
Hammett angry; at least Nell wrote them and got them published,
and Lillian ought to apply herself. His letters to Nell grew in-
frequent; they remained friends but grew apart.[5]

There were things about Lillian he didn't like, besides her independence, which he did like and didn't. He didn't like her friends
sometimes, and he didn't like the scenes she made about his women,
though they amused him at first. He had explained his womanizing
to her: it was the way he was. But she would forget and yield to
emotion and throw tantrums. These were complimentary in a way,
but a nuisance, too. He almost preferred Jose's mode of quiet
resignation. Jose knew how men are; Lillian knew but refused to
accept it. That was her attitude about a number of facts of human

nature. She thought not so much about how things were and weren't but of whether they were Right or Wrong, according to her code. She thought he ought to have a code too. Well, he did, in a way, but not her way, and anyway he was a realist, a pragmatist up to a point, or so he thought. Their codes often conflicted. But they had a lot of fun.

These are my daughters Mary and Josephine, he would tell the men and women who visited him. The people would laugh and chatter. Sometimes one blond lady, sometimes another, would take the girls by the hand. Mary remembered Lillian, who had such beautiful clothes, and the ravishing but silent Miss De Viane—Elise. Papa had a lot of ladies and they all had lovely names like Lillian or Elise, not plain names like Mary or Josephine, which went with Jesus. None of Papa's ladies were like Mama, who made sure the girls went to Sunday School.

The ladies Papa knew laughed and laughed and didn't mind what they said. Sometimes Mary and Jo told Mama what the ladies said. "Don't tell Mama about Elise," Mary told Jo. But of course Mama knew. At Papa's, if you cried or wet your pants, you were a nuisance and were put to bed without a fuss. He liked to have Mary and Jo there, but not too often. Sometimes he took them to a toy store and bought them every toy in the world.

Elise was, as events proved, a real old-fashioned girl. One night after dinner at his place, he knocked her around a little. Sober, later, this scared him. And now she was charging him with assault and asking for damages.[6] He thought he should quit drinking. He fell to bickering with Alfred Knopf, too. Alfred said he thought "we," meaning "you," "ought to give a little more thought and worry to your titles,"[7] which irritated Hammett, who gave plenty of thought and worry to them and was damned if he could see anything wrong with them, especially *The Maltese Falcon* and *The Glass Key*. To Alfred the trouble with *Maltese Falcon* was as plain as the nose on his face ("very plain that is, you may remember," he said). "Whenever people can't pronounce a title or an author's name, they are, more than you would think, too shy to go into a book store and try." Knopf believed that people didn't know how to pronounce "falcon"; he didn't add they probably didn't know how to pronounce "Dashiell Hammett" either. As to *The Glass Key*, there were two opinions, of course, but in general

Courtesy of Josephine Hammett Marshall

Santa Monica birthday party: Jo (*at extreme right*) and Mary (*second from left*) c. 1930.

Mary's first communion,
c. 1930.

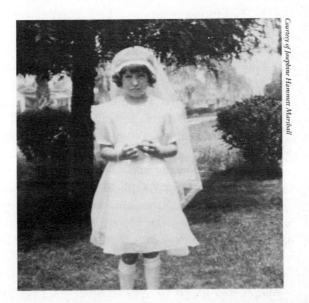

Courtesy of Josephine Hammett Marshall

Jo (*left*) and Mary, c. 1930.

at Knopf they had heard a lot of unfavorable opinion about Hammett's titles not having enough to do with the book.

In California Hammett had heard mostly favorable opinion about his title. "It doesn't matter what they think in the provinces," said Knopf.

Hammett asked if he could please see the jacket of his next book before publication. He'd hated the jacket for *The Glass Key*. The girl on it looked like Clara Bow. And "since this seems to have become an argumentative letter, I may as well go ahead and whine that there are things wrong with the front flap blurb too, several things, beginning with the incomprehensible thinness and fatness attributed to Madvig and O'Rory respectively."[8]

"I think it a wow," replied Alfred. "So does everyone else in the place and we had marvellous reactions from the booksellers regarding it." And as for the flap copy, "Send me in a couple of hundred words about *The Thin Man* and I'll put it in type."[9] This taunt was not met.

In March of 1931, when they had been together four months, Lillian had to go to New York, and Hammett stayed in Hollywood, taking time out to drive up to see old friends in San Francisco and repay Albert Samuels the $500 he had borrowed. He had Jones drive him in high style, rented a suite of rooms at the Fairmont Hotel, threw a big party in San Francisco, and played the prodigal son so well that he had to borrow more cash from Samuels to get back to Hollywood again.[10]

The Glass Key was scheduled for publication April 24, 1931, and he had high hopes for it. So did Alfred Knopf, who wrote him that they believed it would "smash through in spite of some bad times to the sort of market you deserve. . . . After much searching of the heart I ruthlessly cut the price to two dollars to remove the last possible obstacle to the circulating libraries who could use considerable quantities of a book like yours." He hoped, he added, to publish *The Thin Man*, which Hammett said was almost finished, within the year.

"Your hopes for the Glass Key aren't any more ardent than mine," Hammett said. He had already gotten $25,000 for the movie rights to it, and had even higher hopes for *The Thin Man*, which he was already showing bits of to magazines. His problem, which accounted for the burst of huckstering, was money, as usual. He was required to live grandly, with chauffeur and cook, and he liked to buy presents for Lillian and the girls. IN DESPERATE NEED OF ALL THE MONEY I CAN FIND STOP CAN YOU DEPOSIT THOUSAND DOLLARS IN MY ACCOUNT IRVING TRUST COMPANY FIFTYNINTH STREET BRANCH AND DEDUCT FROM MONTHLY PAYMENTS STOP.[11] The patient Alfred Knopf was to receive a number of these imperative requests. He complied with this one, April 28, 1931, and added to reassure the hopeful author, GLASS KEY OFF TO GOOD START.

The Thin Man didn't yet exist; it had only been started. This was the beginning of Hammett's tendency to live on books not yet finished, with plans running ahead, ideas and dreams put forward as *faits accomplis*.

He later explained that he had begun to write *The Thin Man* in 1930 in New York, but when Alfred decided not to bring out *The Glass Key* until the spring of 1931 and Hammett saw that the new book couldn't come out until fall, he had put it aside. "One thing and/or another intervening after that," he didn't get back to work on it. When he did, eventually, it didn't interest him much. Nevertheless he kept the basic idea, and the names Guild and Wynant. In the first *Thin Man* the detective, John Guild, is a dark man with very blue eyes, a taciturn Spade type. It is Wynant—tall, well over six feet, and thin and tubercular—who, like the villain of *The Dain Curse*, recalls Hammett himself. Wynant is an eccentric intellectual with Hammett's interests: "Definitions of science must be philosophical definitions," he says. "Science cannot know what it cannot know. Science cannot know there is anything it does not know. Science deals with percepts and not with non-percepts. Thus, Einstein's theory of relativity—that the phenomena of nature will be the same, that is not different, to two observers who move with any uniform velocity whatever relative to one another—is a philosophical, and not a scientific, hypothesis." To which Guild says, "That'll be enough of that."[12]

Now, in 1931, in Hollywood with a thousand in the bank and the fragment of *The Thin Man* making the rounds, Hammett had settled into a routine—the Brown Derby, the Clover Club, hobnobbing with the funny set of writers and starlets and aspiring people. He worked on the scripts he was assigned, for William Powell, Marlene Dietrich and others, forms of piecework, lucrative but anonymous, sometimes altering dialogue on the sets, sometimes redrafting scenes or working on story lines alone or in collaboration. He was a man of all work, a kind of Pinkerton of film. He wrote gossipy letters to Lillian, who remained in the East:

> Your rival, Marlene [Dietrich], is back in town with her offspring and reputedly living in sin with that great, if somewhat stunted, genius of the flickers and lisps, Joe Stoinboig.
> People like Harpo Marx and Dudley Digg[e]s have been telling me about a swell review Hansen gave me in the World-Tel. Did you by any chance see it? Maybe I ought to subscribe to a clipping bureau again. Will you do it for me? Whichever one you think best. If I remember when I get through I'll enclose a check. Otherwise just hock something.[13]

> So you're not coming home, eh? I suppose it doesn't make any difference if I have to go on practically masturbating![14]

By which he meant sleeping with other women. Love was real love, and sleeping around was "practically masturbating."

In consequence of this virtual masturbation he got another case of the clap, an affliction he was still philosophical about.

> Last night I ran into Sid [Perelman] in the Brown Derby, brought him home with me, gave him some Bourbon, and wound up by

doing a little pimping for him. God knows I'm doing my best to keep celibacy from rearing its ugly head in Hollywood! But something's got to be done to keep the gals moderately content while I'm out of order.[15]

It cannot have been easy for Lillian to receive letters that contained the muted taunt: "I have been more or less faithful to you," meaning he had not been faithful at all, except perhaps in his affections. These were the terms of their love, but she must have hated to be reminded, especially from afar when all she could do was bite her lip; but maybe it was better to be afar, where she wasn't likely to run into one of these chance casual ladies who would look at her with triumphant hostility and rouse the emotions of an outraged wife. Though she had not the legitimacy of an outraged wife, nor the responsibilities.

It was difficult being around Hammett sometimes. The fun was frenetic and drunken; it could wear thin.

The Glass Key was published January 20, 1931, in England, and April 24, 1931, in the United States. The enthusiastic reception of *The Maltese Falcon* had exceeded that of his previous novels, and that of *The Glass Key* now exceeded that of *The Maltese Falcon*—five printings in the first two months, at $2.50 a copy, and enthusiastic reviews: Will Cuppy of the New York *Herald Tribune*, who had thought *The Maltese Falcon* the best mystery in Lord knows when, felt that *The Glass Key* was "about twice as good," and other critics were torn between the two.

From New York Lillian sent him clippings. He wondered what she was up to. "I ran into Arthur, Sid and Laura [Perelman] in the Brown Doiby night before last and . . . tried to pump Laura about your conduct in New York, but she was so circumspect, gave you such a respectable tint, that I'd have suspected you of the loosest sort of conduct even if I hadn't previously received reports about you. Ts! Ts! Ts! Just a she-Hammett!"

His projects prospered. His movie *City Streets* was successful, and though he claimed to find it pretty lousy, he probably thought it wasn't bad; he liked Sylvia Sidney in it—she was really good—and Gary Cooper wasn't bad. Alfred Knopf wrote that *The Glass Key* had sold eleven thousand copies in the first couple of weeks. This was welcome news: "My ambition now is to collect enough money to be able to finish 'The Thin Man,' which God willing, will be my last detective novel. (So I'm being intimidated by Mrs. Parker, eh?)"[16]

This prayer would be answered in a way he did not intend, for *The Thin Man* would be both his last detective novel and his last novel.

He had read with great attention the daunting Dorothy Parker's review of *The Glass Key*, which interested him on a number of points. She agreed with Alfred that he showed a "touch of rare genius in his selection of undistinguished titles for his mystery stories—*The Maltese Falcon* and *The Glass Key*, his new one, sounds like something by Carolyn Wells." The plots were "so many nuisances; confusing to madness, as in *Red Harvest*: fanciful to nausea, as in *The Maltese Falcon*," or, in the present case, tired. "His new book . . . seems to me nowhere to touch its predecessor. Surely it is that Beaumont, the amateur detective of the later story, a man given perhaps a shade too much to stroking his moustache with a thumbnail, can in no way stack up against the magnificent Spade, with whom, after reading *The Maltese Falcon*, I went mooning about in a daze of love such as I had not known for any character in literature since I encountered Sir Launcelot at the age of nine." Here Hammett seems "a little weary, a little short of spontaneous, a little dogged about his simplicity of style, a little determined to make startling the ordering of his brief sentences, a little concerned with having his conclusion approach the toughness of the superb last scene of *The Maltese Falcon*."

He approved of her approval "that he is so hard-boiled you could roll him on the White House lawn. And it is also true that he is a good, hell-bent, cold-hearted writer, with a clear eye for the ways of hard women and a fine ear for the words of hard men, and his books are exciting and powerful and—if I may filch the word from the booksy ones—pulsing. It is difficult to conclude an outburst like this. All I can say is that anybody who doesn't read him misses much of modern America. And hot that sounds!"[17] All the same, he was eager to leave the detective story behind and do the work that lay ahead, which he felt would be his finest.

He had been drinking heavily since April, and tried intermittently to stop. He had begun to feel ill, anxious and depressed, and even thought unaccountably of suicide. He thought things might go better if he went back to New York, but Warner was demanding the return of money they had advanced him on a story,

"On the Make," which they had rejected. He had other debts. WANT TO RETURN TO NEW YORK NEXT WEEK BUT AM IN TERRIFIC FINANCIAL DIFFICULTY STOP, he wired to Alfred in August. CAN YOU DEPOSIT TWENTYFIVE HUNDRED DOLLARS TO MY ACCOUNT IRVING TRUST COMPANY FIFTYNINTH STREET OFFICE. Alfred wired back that he'd done it, but could not forbear adding that he was LOOKING FORWARD EAGERLY SEEING YOU AND RECEIVING THIN MAN.

By September 1931 Hammett still hadn't left Hollywood. He wired Alfred by way of a friendly gesture that the last chapter of Alfred Neumann's *The Hero*, which Knopf had just published, was unique in literature "for beautiful sheer brutality": "IT MAKES ME FEEL LIKE A PANSY."[18]

To Lillian: "This is my seventh day on the wagon. When are you coming home?"[19]

It wasn't enough just to quit drinking; he had begun to feel bad in other ways too—to have headaches and symptoms of TB. He tried serious reading, he read Gorky, Faulkner's *Sanctuary*, of which he wrote: "Without actually disliking it, am of the opinion that Mr. Faulkner is rather overrated by such people as have heard of him at all. He has a nice taste in the morbid and gruesome, but doesn't seem to do much with it." It drove him crazy that Faulkner could just knock these things out and was as big a drunk as he, Hammett. Hammett went on the wagon a few days at a time, tried to get hold of things. Abruptly he descended into a suicidal gloom, the gloom of success, when all struggle is behind, and is found to have been for naught.

Lillian had come back. Herself full of life, she paid little attention to his mood. He planned to kill himself. He went to another hotel; they'd been fairly decent to him at the Knickerbocker, no point in complicating things for them.

Why, for heaven's sake? Lillian asked. There wasn't any answer, except for the feeling that everything was over. He went to the Roosevelt, got a room. You could take poison or slit your wrists or hang yourself or shoot yourself; what he did is not known.

Jose got word that he was going to kill himself. She and the girls went over to the hotel. After a while someone came and told them he was all right.

Later someone else knocked on his door. It was Lillian, looking more curious than anything else, and what he felt, seeing her, was shame more than anything else. "I'm a clown," he said, and chose slower forms of self-destruction instead.[20]

9

1932–1934

THE THIN MAN

The world, worsening, had some hopes of political change in the fall elections of 1932, Roosevelt against Hoover. Hammett, who left Hollywood in the fall of 1931 for New York, had hopes too of things picking up but somehow they didn't. Like everybody else, he needed money, and he contracted desultorily to do little tasks—to write a preface for a book Knopf was publishing called *Freddy the Detective* (a parody of detective stories, by Walter Brooks), to go on a lecture tour, to write a story or two. He got a literary agent, Ben Wasson of the American Play Company,[1] and Wasson goaded him.

He preferred the literary company in New York. Bill Faulkner was there, a hell of a nice guy as it turned out and a good drinking buddy with nice Southern manners and a loyal attitude to fellow writers. He and Bill went to the Knopfs' after a day of drinking to meet Willa Cather, and Hammett passed out; when Knopf wanted to throw him out, Faulkner denounced Knopf, which Hammett appreciated when he was told of it later.

In a letter to Lillian, Hammett wrote:

STATEMENT
Too many have lived
As we live
For our lives to be
Proof of our living.

Too many have died
As we die

For their deaths to be
Proof of our dying.[2]

In May of 1932 Hammett and Lillian are living at the Biltmore, Hammett's third address since his return. Hammett is working on something or says he's working. Lillian has gone to New Orleans to visit her family. She is divorcing Arthur Kober, amiably enough, and will go back to being called Hellman. Hammett is luckily or unluckily too broke to join the games of bagatelle at Moriarity's with Buck Crouse or eat dinner at "21," which has taken the place of the Brown Derby in his life. Alfred Knopf, with whom his relations have become a little strained, sends him wistful notes of inquiry:

April 2, 1932: . . . we have to have that introduction of yours immediately . . . do you think you can manage this?

Also, I am expecting the THIN MAN next week [as he had for more than a year].

April 5: Just to remind you again that I need the introduction to FREDDY THE DETECTIVE badly. . . . I rather expected it at the end of last week.

Also I rather expected to see THE THIN MAN in today as per your own schedule. Is there a chance of its coming?

April 12: I have been trying to get you on the telephone as you had promised me the manuscript as well as the introduction to FREDDY THE DETECTIVE last week. . . . Do you think you could manage it for me?

May 4, 1932, and a
pretty black day in
the annals of America

Sweetheart,

So after you left me I walked over to Broadway and presently found myself watching "The Mouthpiece," and my lawyers will have something to say to your father about that later.

Then I sent you a wire—supposed to reach you at Washington, D.C., either as a good-night message or a good-morning one —bought a comb and brush, took on food at Childs, and came home expecting to find some such message as "Mrs. Kober, who missed her train, phoned." It wasn't here, though—there wasn't anything here but a bed you'd never slept in.

I love you, mugg!

1555 Ellesmere Ave.
Los Angeles, Calif.
Mrs. D. Hammett
[1932?]

Alfred A. Knopf—

Dear Sir:

Am doing this after all other things have failed.

For past seven months Mr. Hammett has sent me only one hundred dollars and has failed to write & explain his troubles—right now I am desperate—the children need clothing & are not getting right food—& I am unable to find work—living with my parents who are growing old & cant offer us any more help.

If it were possible to get in touch with Mr. Hammett & get any information—if he should be sick—or his financial condition.

I feel as thou he is not getting my letters—someone is holding them back—I know he loves his family—would hate to hear they are in this condition. I can't tell you how grateful I would be if it is possible for you to do this as early as you can find time—

I remain—
Mrs. Dashiell Hammett[3]

May 4, 1932

Dear Madam,

I am in receipt of your letter but unfortunately have no more idea than you have where Dashiell is at the present time.

Not long ago he checked out of his New York apartment, left no forwarding address there and has not been in touch with us in any way.

As soon as he does get in touch with us we will let him know about your letter.

Yours faithfully,
Alfred A. Knopf

TO: ALFRED A. KNOPF, PERSONAL
I AM IN RECEIPT OF YOUR BANK CHECKS TO DASHIELL CAN YOU MAKE
IT POSSIBLE FOR ME TO CASH THEM HERE AS I AND THE CHILDREN ARE
BADLY IN NEED OF MONEY PLEASE ADVISE WHAT TO DO THANKING
YOU FOR PROMPT REPLY TO MY LETTER—

MRS. DASHIELL HAMMETT

MAY 11, 1932

MRS. DASHIELL HAMMETT
1555 ELLSMERE AVENUE
LOS ANGELES, CALIFORNIA

YOUR BANK WILL HONOR OUR DOLLAR CHECK PROMPTLY IF ENDORSED
BY MR HAMMETT OR BY YOURSELF PROVIDED YOU HAVE PROPER
POWER OF ATTORNEY STOP RETURN POUND CHECK TO US PROPERLY
ENDORSED AND WE WILL CONVERT IT FOR YOU TO DOLLARS

ALFRED A. KNOPF

ACTRESS GETS DAMAGES FROM WRITER

Los Angeles, June 30 (AP)—Miss Elise De Viane, actress, bruised and battered in resisting the asserted fervid love makings of Dashiell Hammett, motion picture writer, yesterday was awarded $2500 damages by Superior Court Judge Call. The case was heard Tuesday, Miss De Viane describing the fracas to the court. Hammett did not appear to contest the suit. It was reported that he is in New York. The actress asked, through her attorney, Reuben Licker, for $35,000 damages.[4]

Broke, he had to leave the Biltmore, so he moved to the Pierre. He couldn't pay his bill of $1,000 at the Pierre and had to sneak out, wearing his clothes in layers, cheeks puffed out to alter his face. In such straits a writer could always put up at the hotel Nathanael ("Pep") West, Sid Perelman's brother-in-law, ran, the Sutton Club Hotel on East Fifty-sixth Street. He was a writer himself, and liked to have other writers around. His sister was Laura Perelman, whom Hammett found attractive. Hammett and Lillian had known Pep a little in Hollywood. Now Pep rented them the "diplomat suite,"[5] cheap. James T. Farrell and Erskine Caldwell and other writers were there. The food wasn't good and the furniture was sordid, "a bureau, a stiff wing chair, a lamp with a false pewter base, and an end table, each chamber contained a bed narrow enough to discourage any thoughts of venery, [in] a myriad of rooms so tiny that their walls almost impinged on each other, a honeycomb full of workers and drones in the minimum cubic footage required to avert strangulation."[6]

Hammett had in fact been working himself up to write, had begun with lazily redoing some Sam Spade stories—"A Man Called Spade,"[7] reworked from "The Tenth Clew," which had been published in July; "Too Many Have Lived";[8] and "They Can Only Hang You Once," rewritten from "Night Shots," which had earlier appeared in *Black Mask*, and now sold to the higher-paying *Collier's*.[9] This rewriting—reworking or recombining of old ideas—was in fact essential to Hammett's method; he seemed to need to do things twice, and would achieve the final possibilities of an idea only after trying it in some initial form. The rewriting served now to get him going. He next produced two good stories, "Night Shade" (in which a young black man rescues a white girl, daughter of a judge; his awareness of racism makes him reluctant to take her home in person, so he puts her in a cab)[10] and "Albert Paston at Home,"[11] as well as the very good novella *Woman in the Dark*, which was published in early 1933 in *Liberty* magazine and sold to Select, a minor film company, for $500 against $5,000.[12]

Once settled at the Sutton, Hammett locked himself in and worked seriously. Lillian had never seen him work like this, with dedication and fanatic pride, eschewing company and diversion. This novel, based on the early version of *The Thin Man*, took only the core idea of it. Now all the women in it talked a little like Lillian, the banter of the hero and heroine was a little like talk between Lillian and Hammett, the drinking a little like their drinking, and the hero's cynical and depressed attitude toward society quite a lot like Hammett's own. Ben Wasson sold the first serial rights to *Redbook*, Knopf accepted it, and it appeared that everything was back on track.

Hammett finished the manuscript of *The Thin Man* in May of 1933. About the same time he suggested to Lillian that she read William Roughead's *Bad Companions*, a compendium of criminal case histories, particularly "Closed Doors, or The Great Drumsheugh Case," which he thought would make a good play. It concerned a Scottish girls' school that had to close because of a lesbian scandal surrounding the owners.[13] He had earlier said in an interview that he himself had thought of writing a play—perhaps based on this case. But Lillian could do a wonderful job on it, and the subjects—guilt, passion, commitment, lesbian love—were suited to her strong style and to the times. And since she was now working for Herman Shumlin, if she wrote it she could possibly get it produced. She set enthusiastically to work.

Lillian and Hammett left New York for Florida, first Miami and then Key Largo to rest, read, talk, work. "We got drunk for a few weeks in Miami," Lillian wrote, "then moved on to a primitive fishing camp in the Keys where we stayed through the spring and summer, fishing every day, reading every night. It was a fine year: we found out that we got along best without people, in the country. Hammett, like many Southerners, had a deep feeling for isolated places where there were animals, birds, bugs and sounds. He was easy in the woods, an excellent shot. . . ."[14] It was good for them to be away from Hollywood and New York, to be together in the countryside, and they found themselves happier than they had ever been.

Lillian worked on her play, Hammett helped her, encouraged her, read and criticized drafts, corrected, suggested—and found that he quite enjoyed his role as mentor.[15] There were a few disruptive incidents—in Miami, Hammett got drunk with Nunnally Johnson and broke the window of Burdine's Department Store with a rock and said when arrested, "I don't like Burdine's." Mostly things were calm. Lillian and Hammett put some money down on a little lot and planned to build a house there and come back often. Then they went back to New York and Hollywood.

It was clear *The Thin Man* would be a hit. MGM bought the movie rights for $21,000 even before publication, *Redbook* published an expurgated version in December 1933, and Knopf published the complete version in January 1934. Twenty thousand copies of the book sold within the first three weeks, and more than thirty thousand in the first year.[16] Knopf capitalized in its advertising on the few lines of risqué dialogue that had been censored in *Redbook*. An ad in the *New York Times* (January 30, 1934) had Alfred Knopf saying, "I don't believe the question on page 192 of Dashiell Hammett's *The Thin Man* has had the slightest influence upon the sale of the book. It takes more than that to make a best seller these days. Twenty-thousand people don't buy a book within three weeks to read a five-word question." This arch come-on had more of the tone of Albert Samuels' advertising manager than of Alfred Knopf; in any case, it did the trick. Nora's five-word question to Nick was, in its entirety: "Tell me something, Nick. Tell me the truth: when you were wrestling with Mimi, didn't you have an erection?"[17] Nick's reply: "Oh, a little." Elsewhere an outraged wife wonders what people think of her for staying with a husband who is "chasing everything that's hot and hollow." Words like "bitch" appear—it was all very daring and exciting. The book aroused interest in the handsome author as well. A photo of Ham-

The Granger Collection, New York

Hammett, publicity photo for *The Thin Man*, 1934.

mett was featured on the jacket, and in interviews he presented himself as urbane, sophisticated, fond of dogs and music, a great reader whose favorite book was *Decline of the West*, and who smoked enormously." Hobbies? "Let's see, I drink a lot. Also play poker." He liked to loaf, he said, and was a married man with two children. "I was a sergeant during the war, but—please get this straight—not in the war. The war and my service in the army were contemporary, that's all you can say about it." This was a matter that continued to rankle.[18]

The fast-talking, amusing Nick and Nora Charles fascinated readers. They seemed to epitomize sophistication and a charming modern kind of freedom. Hammett kept one letter in particular:

Dear Mr. Hammett,

The result of three people reading "The Thin Man" has brought on the question: to wit—How old is Nora—or how old was she?[19] We are having much much discussion about WOMEN, all on account of her. We think she's a swell type if she could exist but we say this and we say that and we're not getting ANY-WHERE. What age did you have in mind for her?

Thanking you 'way 'way in advance for an answer,

Sincerely,
Dorothy Mackaill
23 West 68th St. NYC

Lillian would write later:

It was a happy day when I was given half the manuscript to read and was told that I was Nora. It was nice to be Nora, married to Nick Charles, maybe one of the few marriages in modern literature where the man and woman like each other and have a fine time together. But I was soon put back in place—Hammett said I was also the silly girl in the book and the villainess. I don't know now if he was joking, but in those days it worried me; I was very anxious that he think well of me. Most people wanted that from him.[20]

The problem is to think well of yourself; Nick Charles doesn't seem to. The Op, Spade, Ned Beaumont, struggling in worlds they don't like or approve of, devise for themselves their own codes of behavior, but Nick, an alcoholic ex-detective, leads a social life he seems to despise, drinks before or instead of breakfast, has changed his name to Charles from his real Greek name the better to fit into Nora's sophisticated world, and is in some sense a visitor or an impostor.

> Nora and I went to the opening of *Honeymoon* at the Little Theatre that night and then to a party given by some people named Freeman or Fielding or something. I felt pretty low when she called me the next morning. She gave me a newspaper and a cup of coffee and said: "Read that."
> I patiently read a paragraph or two, then put the paper down and took a sip of coffee. "Fun's fun," I said, "but right now I'd swap you all the interviews with Mayor-elect O'Brien ever printed—and throw in the Indian picture—for a slug of whis—"
> "Not that, stupid." She put a finger on the paper. "That." . . .
> "What was she like?"
> "Not bad," I said. "She wasn't bad-looking and she had a lot of sense and a lot of nerve—and it took both to live with that guy."
> "She lived with him?"
> "Yes. I want a drink, please. That is, it was like that when I knew them."
> "Why don't you have some breakfast first? Was she in love with him or was it just business?"
> "I don't know. It's too early for breakfast."[21]

THE LOMBARDY
111 EAST 56TH STREET
NEW YORK CITY

January 22, 1934

Dear Jose,

At last—and I hope forever—our financial troubles seem to be over. Barring acts of God, this week should see us out of debt and well on the road to some decent sort of security.

First, the book is going well. It got very fine reviews—as you can see from the enclosed clippings—and last week sold better than any other book in New York, Philadelphia, and San Francisco, besides being near the the top of the list in most other cities.

Second, M-G-M is buying the movie rights for $21,000, which is four thousand less than Paramount paid for The Glass Key, but a pretty good price this year at that. I ought to have the check in a day or two and will send you a thousand at once and then some each week regularly thereafter.

Third, I'm writing a story for a cartoon strip for Hearst's syndicate, which will bring me a regular and, I hope, growing income perhaps forever. If it goes over well it can make me a lot of money.

So it looks as if we were out of the woods, and this time I mean to stay out. No more nonsense. If I can get away I may go down to Florida for a while to try to finish my next book.

I didn't thank you all for the swell Christmas gifts. Thanks a million. Tell Mary I'm blowing my nose on one of her handker-chiefs now, and tell Josephine I shaved with her shaving soap this morning. Also if the three of you will write me right away and tell me what kind of gift you'd each *most* like to have, I'll send them.

I know how you feel about having the Kelleys on your hands, and I don't envy you. Can't you tell them you haven't room?

Sis is still with me and, of course, all excited over the book. I'm feeling pretty well and hard at work. I've got to run now.

> Love to all,
> D.

I'm on the radio—NBC—at 2 Friday afternoon, Los Angeles time.

Later in the spring, Hammett and Lillian went back for a few months to their retreat in Florida. MGM meantime hurried a film of *The Thin Man* into production. The screenplay was written in three weeks by Albert Hackett and Frances Goodrich.[22] W. S. ("Woody") Van Dyke, the director, shot it in eighteen days. Myrna Loy played Nora, William Powell Nick, and Maureen O'Sullivan Dorothy Wynant, and the venture was so great a success that five more *Thin Man* films would ensue (two of these also by the Hacketts). When Hammett emerged from seclusion in Florida, about the time the film came out in June, he was more famous than ever. He had just had his fortieth birthday. Lillian would soon be thirty.

The daily comic strip *Secret Agent X-9* was the Hearst rival to *Dick Tracy*, but *X-9* was better-looking and funnier—maybe too urbane to last. Doing *Secret Agent X-9* was fun and not too much trouble. The artist, Alex Raymond, was also doing *Flash Gordon.* At times he felt himself in over his head and Hammett sometimes thought of a way to relieve him—X-9 finds himself in a trap and shoots out the light. Days would elapse with X-9 in the dark room, until the editors would begin to get suspicious and X-9 would find his way out. Hammett and X-9 didn't last long because Hammett never met the deadlines.[23]

It was now that Hammett came to the attention of the FBI for the first time:

May 2, 1934

Mr. R. E. Vetterli,
Division of Investigation,
U.S. Department of Justice,
318 Hewes Building,
San Francisco, California

Dear Mr. Vetterli:

The Division has been advised that a series of illustrated stories is running in several papers on the West Coast dealing with the activities of Special Agent K-9 [*sic*], who is reported in connection with such stories to be a former operative of the Department of Justice. No articles of this kind have been forwarded to the Division and it is desired to receive advice from you as to whether such a series is being published in papers available to you on the West Coast. In the event such a series is running in the papers, please submit such information as may be available as to the identity of the person preparing the stories and the statement made by him indicating a previous connection with the Department of Justice.

Very truly yours,
Director

May 5, 1934

Director
Division of Investigation
U.S. Department of Justice
Washington, D.C.

Dear Sir:

In response to your letter of May 2, 1934 concerning a series of illustrated stories which is currently appearing in several papers on the West Coast dealing with the activities of Special Agent K-9.

Please be advised that undoubtedly the series of articles referred to is an illustrated story written by Dashiell Hammett, captioned "Secret Agent X-9." Attached hereto is today's illustration appearing in today's San Francisco Call-Bulletin and which, I am advised, appears in other affiliated Hearst papers on the West Coast. I am also attaching hereto a memorandum submitted by Special Agent H. R. Philbrick in this matter.[24]

Discussing the matter with Agent Philbrick, it does not appear that Hammett has made any representation to the effect that he is a former Special Agent of the Division of Investigation, or the Department of Justice.

Very truly yours,
R. E. Vetterli
Special Agent in Charge

May 5, 1934

MEMORANDUM FOR THE SPECIAL AGENT IN CHARGE

With reference to Division letter of May 2, 1934 setting out that there is currently appearing in West Coast papers a series of illustrated articles captioned, "Secret Agent K-9", who is reported to the Division as being a former operative of the Department of Justice, please be advised that investigation develops the following facts.

Beginning on Jan. 26, 1934, an illustrated series of articles was publicized in the San Francisco Call-Bulletin. After the first few days this illustration became a regular feature of their comic page. The caption of the article is, "Secret Agent X-9", by Dashiell Hammett.

During the month of February a continued story was commenced in the magazine section of the San Francisco Examiner, appearing daily, captioned "The Thin Man", by Dashiell Hammett. I am advised that this story has also appeared serially in the Cosmopolitan, a Heart [sic] publication. I am further advised that the matter is at the present time in the process of being screened at Hollywood, Calif. ... .

At the commencement of the illustrated serial which is now appearing in the Call-Bulletin, considerable publicity was given to Hammett to build up interest in the serial. I quote from a front page article of the San Francisco Call-Bulletin of January 26, 1934: "Hammet traps gem holdup suspect".

Thereafter, appears a narative [sic] of the capture of "Gloomy Gus" Shaeffer and bringing up to date the activities of Shaeffer, i.e., his implication in the Hamm case and in the kidnaping of Jake, the Barber.

In the San Francisco Examiner morgue I discovered a news item under date of June 29, 1932, indicating that Hammett was sued for breach of promise and battery in the Superior Court of Los Angeles, wherein one Elise De Viane, an actress, recovered judgment for $2,500. From various news articles and press publicity I ascertained that an actor by the name of William Powell recently appeared in a picture captioned, "Private Detective". The scenario for this project was apparently written by Hammett for First National Pictures.[25] I further developed that the most recent work of Hammett's, "The Thin Man", is being screened by Metro-Goldwyn-Mayer at the present time and that Hammett is in connection therewith living at Hollywood, Calif. "The Thin Man", the book referred to, was published by Alfred A. Knopf & Co.

I carefully scanned all of the publicity given to Hammett at the commencement of his various stories and articles in the local papers, but at no time did I discover any mention of the fact that he had been a government operative or an employee of the Department of Justice. He very conspicuously advertises the fact that he was, however, an operative for Pinkerton's Detective Agency.

From casual inquiry I gathered the opinion that Hammett's very successful in his field. He is well known to several of the local newspaper talent and they advise he has made considerable money from his detective yarns.

Respectfully submitted,
H. R. Phibrick
Special Agent

There is another letter from an informant, about her boss, which mentions Hammett, but the FBI concluded that "in view of the ambiguity of that letter as to whether the 'boss' of Dashiell Hammett is a 'red,'" no further action was contemplated by the FBI. Hammett, for now, was put in "closed status."

He took a job for $2,000 to write a film sequel to *The Thin Man*. Universal bought his story "On the Make," eventually to become *Mister Dynamite*; they'd need him to work on that.[26] Hollywood was already wary of Hammett: studio heads confided to each other that he was unreliable and it was hard to get any work out of him. But they didn't know what else to do but hire him, for his talent was still unlike anyone else's.

He went back to Hollywood by train on October 26, 1934, and wired Lillian from Kansas City, SO FAR SO GOOD ONLY AM MISSING OF YOU PLENTY LOVE NICKY, and from Albuquerque, HAVE NOT GOT USED TO BEING WITHOUT YOU YET WHAT SHALL I DO LOVE.

From the Beverly Wilshire: "Dear Alfred—So I'm a bum—so what's done of the book looks terrible—so I'm out here drowning my shame in M-G-M money for 10 weeks. Abjectly, Dash."

He started to work at the studios. "I think it's going to be all right. I like the people thus far and have a comfortable office," he wrote to Lillian. "We're going to make a picture with all the surviving members of the first cast—which won't be silly if I can devise a murder that grows with some logic out of the set-up we left everybody in at the end of the T.M.—and I think I can. We may title it 'After the Thin Man.'"[27]

Then he got drunk for a week.

I haven't written to you for a few days because I'm too ashamed of myself. I've been faithful to you, but I went back on the booze pretty heavily until Saturday night—neglecting studio, dignity, and so on. And was I sick Sunday and today! This morning I showed up at M.G.M. for the first time since last Tuesday and squared myself, but didn't get much work done, since the publicity department took up most of my time, what with photographs, interviews and the like.

I'm still surprised at the fuss the "Thin Man" made out here. People bring the Joan Crawfords and Gables over to meet me instead of the usual vice versa! Hot-cha!

Miss Elise De Viane was attaching his pay. He was philosophical: "I'm stuck for it, so I suppose there's no use bellyaching."

Angel—

And so I took Thyra to dinner each night and so I got very—
not to say disgracefully—drunk and so I saw Ben and Ad—who
are back together again—and Rouben and Marlene and the
Tuttles and the Dick Wallaces and nine tenths of Hollywood and
lost a lot of money betting Ben was right in a crap-game where
he was always wrong—and so home at what hour I don't know
and too hangovery to go to the studio today and god help me
you'd better come on out and take care of me.
  BUT ALL THE TIME I'M LOVING YOU VERY MUCH
PLEASE.
p.s. And so this afternoon I'm going to the Eddie Robinson's for
cocktails and to Nunnally's to see 'em off for N.Y. and then to
my folks' for dinner and I.L.Y.V.M.[28]

Lillian's play was to open in about three weeks—hardly the time
for her to come look after anyone. She stayed in New York, where
on November 20 *The Children's Hour* opened at the Maxine Elliott
Theatre to great acclaim. But in Boston and Chicago it was banned,
and in London it was performed privately. The New York drama
critics, indignant that the Pulitzer Committee didn't name it the
best play of the year, formed the New York Drama Critics Circle
and gave it their prize. The twenty-nine-year-old playwright was
praised and courted, and Sam Goldwyn wooed her back to Hollywood at $2,500 a week. A star on the rise.

The year 1934 wore on to Christmas. Hammett's income for the
year had been enormous, more than $80,000. He was done with
writing. He would live another twenty-six years.

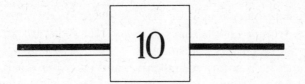

10

1935–1936

STRUGGLING UPWARD

325 Bel Air Road. A beautiful house, huge and empty except for the two black men, Jones and his lover, whose name nobody can now remember for sure, Winston or Winfield. They keep to themselves in the kitchen and garages and have Thursdays off and Sunday half-days. And Mr. Hammett himself is at home alone. It's afternoon, but Mr. Hammett isn't up yet. Nothing unsual in that. Mildred Lewis sits on the sofa, her back to the stairs, her notebook on her knees, waiting.

She comes every day and sits like this. Sometimes he comes down, some days he never does. If he hasn't come down by five, the limousine is waiting to take her home; if he does and it's Thursday he may ask her to cook something, though she can't cook. Mr. Hammett can cook better than she can. She's twenty. She's the secretary sent by the studio and she isn't a very good secretary either, as it's her first job. But she's the cousin of an important studio executive.

Sometimes he comes down, but he doesn't speak, doesn't say a word to her for hours on end. Sometimes they just sit there and do the crossword puzzles, and ask each other words. Mildred is uneasy, even a little scared of him. But he is always kind, and he makes her know that his silence has nothing to do with her. If it's caused by a hangover, that does not occur to her.

Sometimes he calls her to come upstairs. He is lying in bed. Come here, he says, and lie with me on the bed—nothing will happen. She does as she is told, and nothing happens, he just puts his arms around her and quietly holds her. It is strange. She wishes he wouldn't. She lies there stiffly and would rather do crossword puzzles.

Yet she cares very much for Mr. Hammett too, because whereas she comes from a family that made her feel awkward and dumb, he makes her feel pretty and smart.

Sometimes he is animated, talkative, and takes her out to dinner. He makes her eat funny things—snails—or try new drinks—champagne cocktail or British Cream. Sometimes they go to a club, usually the Clover Club, and he gambles a lot, and gives her chips to gamble with. His friends ask him for handfuls of chips and he obliges. He gives chips to the Marx Brothers' wives. It doesn't seem to Mildred that Mr. Hammett is very practical or has much sense of money.

They do no work. Mr. Hammet is supposed to be writing a sequel to *The Thin Man*, and that's why the studio has sent her there, but how can she help when Mr. Hammett refuses to do anything, day after day, even on the days he gets up? He reads a lot.

Sometimes, sitting on the sofa in the morning, Mildred can hear footsteps coming down the stairs—women, often black or Oriental, prostitutes from Madame Lee Francis's. Everyone knows about Madame Francis. It used to embarrass Mildred to meet the eyes of these girls who came down in the morning. Did they think she was waiting her turn? They were never seen again, just different ones each time, but Mildred felt embarrassed just the same, and had taken to sitting on the sofa with her back to the staircase in order to pretend that she neither saw nor heard them. She could hear but not see them, though sometimes she peeked around.

What he does and doesn't do is no affair of hers, is Mildred's opinion, but she happens to know that Mr. Hammett has both a girlfriend named Lil, whose picture is on the piano but who seems to live somewhere else, and also a wife and two daughters. They live nearby but send letters. They never come here when Mildred is here, but she has seen letters to and from them lying on the table. Mr. Hammett has a phonograph; one record he plays again and again: Lucienne Boyer singing "Parlez-Moi d'Amour."

People from the studio call Mr. Hammett up. Hunt Stromberg, the producer, calls often, wistfully asking how the thing is going. He is not allowed to call on Thursday, when Jones is out. "You know I have no help here on Thursdays," Mr. Hammett will snarl into the phone. His friends call, though, whatever the day. Dorothy Parker is one. They see her at the Clover Club. Once Mrs. Parker borrows $200 from Mr. Hammett at the Clover Club, which Mildred Lewis thinks a bit much.

A new bride, Mrs. Lewis is learning the value of money, and Mr. Hammett throws it around unbelievably. Once he stops the cab they are riding in, goes into a florist's and sends all the flowers in the shop to her flat, where they puzzle and annoy her husband, who does not say, luckily, what he probably thinks. On her days off Mildred wonders if Mr. Hammett has got up. She thinks of him lying there, just lying there, in his darkened room.[1]

Blanche Knopf, in California early in 1935, reported to Alfred Knopf that Hammett was looking "simply superb," and this "elegant news" animated Alfred's hopes for a new book—hopes somewhat qualified by news from Leland Hayward that Hammett had been made some sort of high-up at MGM.[2] "Well, good luck to you," Alfred grumbled, "and pray God as an executive you take a little time off every other day or so and complete a book for us. Otherwise I'm damned if one of these days I don't wire you to deposit X dollars for me in my bank account as an advance against the profits that ought to accrue to me and would if you'd do your duty by us."[3]

Instead, Hammett, lavishly installed in Bel Air, wired Alfred for money a few months later: WILL YOU DEPOSIT MY ACCOUNT GUARANTY TRUST SIXTIETH AND MADISON ONE THOUSAND DOLLARS AND WIRE ME THREE TWO FIVE BELAIR ROAD WEST LOS ANGELES STOP THANKS AND BEST REGARDS AND DONT BE SURPRISED IF YOU GET A BOOK BEFORE SNOW FLIES.[4]

Alfred by this time would have been surprised, but hoped cautiously, and sent only $500.

Jo wanted to learn to ride. Hammett took her to the store for an equestrienne outfit. Once he brought his friend Lillian. She was wearing beautiful clothes—she always did—and her bored eyes slid off toward the exit and she snapped at the clerks so that Jo could die of shame. Either Papa didn't notice Lillian's manner, so cruel to the clerks, Jo thought, or he just laughed. He loved Lillian. Mama hated Lillian, and thought that Lillian had ruined their lives. Papa bought Jo a riding coat and boots and a hat. Jo was going to learn to ride English.

The Kellys thought it was awful how Josephine's husband was treating her, not that they were surprised. But the man could afford to treat her decent. She ought to bring an action, let the judge decide. Look at the way he lived; look at the way she lived. Jose didn't know what to do; maybe the Kelly relatives were right that her taking him to court would bring him to his senses. For the moment she did nothing.

Parties! A congested cocktail party at Dorothy Parker's. Hammett, Marc Connelly, Alexander Woollcott. Hammett has dinner with Woollcott, Chaplin, Disney. A party at Hammett's which Pep West remembered unpleasantly: "He made me eat plenty of dirt." Hammett "had some kind of party and I sneaked out early and spit all the way home to get the taste of arse out of my mouth. I couldn't drink and had a miserable time of course, drinking wouldn't have helped and he did his best to rub it in. One of the girls there tried to make up to me and for some reason or other he said, 'leave him alone he hasn't got a pot to piss in.' Another time when I tried to talk to him about Stromberg and a job, he made believe he didn't understand what I was saying and called out in a loud voice so that everyone could hear, 'I haven't any money to lend you now, but call me next week and I'll lend you some.' "[5]

Hammett's friends remembering:

[FRANCES GOODRICH:] Remember the time Hammett took that cat's-eye ring away from Hunt Stromberg, and Hunt was so upset —he thought that ring was his good luck—and Hammett said *Let me see that, Hunt*, and then wouldn't give it back, and Hunt pretended not to care but when he was back in California he was always calling, to find out how he could get that ring back—he thought it was his good luck. Of course Hammett gave it back eventually. Oh, he was so naughty.[6]

[DOROTHY NEBEL:] I liked Dash, as I presume most women did, for he could be very charming and wonderful company. But I was often a bit uneasy when he was drinking heavily for he could be completely unpredictable. I recall one evening when Fred and I were having an early dinner at the Basque—a favorite speakeasy that served excellent food. We looked across the room and Dash was standing there beside a serving table but suddenly he started scooping up handfuls of knives, forks and spoons from the table and throwing them across the room at us; they flew all around the room before the waiters could reach him, but the place wasn't crowded so fortunately no one was hurt.[7]

[ALBERT HACKETT:] Remember the time there was this hooker in his bathroom, a call girl altogether nude up there—it was a practical joke against Sid Perelman, remember, and Sid went to the bathroom and gee, he was gone a long time, and then Laura Perelman and whoever went up there and caught them flagrante delicto. That was a story. It ended with Laura going off to San Francisco with Hammett, I remember that, they were gone for days, and there was hell to pay all around.[8]

[MILDRED LE VAUX:] Flat on his face in the Trocadero, I remember. He fell flat on his face. Sometimes in gutters, too. He was a shy man, but when he'd had a few, he got talkative, you know? Then he was very funny. Sober, he was kind of quiet.[9]

[ALBERT HACKETT:] He was chasing some girl called Sis, then. But he said if you wanted to get anywhere with Sis, you had to sleep with her mama first. They shared men—Sis and her mama. Oh, I don't know whether he did or not, but he was a guy who would always go to certain lengths, no farther. He never really cared one way or another.[10]

[LILLIAN:] Sis was always too doped to talk much, and as she sat in a chair holding a small dog on her lap, silent, waited upon by her vigorous green-blonde mother, she seemed to me an interesting girl, but the one time I tried talking to her she suddenly slapped my face. She died a few months later when, according to her mother, she was so drunk that she fell to the floor and hit her head on a radiator. Hammett said he didn't believe that because he had never known anybody who doped heavily to drink heavily, and evidently somebody agreed with him because there were a few days of excitement when the mother was arrested and charged with throwing Sis against the radiator during a fight. Nothing ever came of that except a party the mother gave when the police could prove nothing, or didn't want to.[11]

[ALBERT HACKETT:] He had a house. There was a little dog named Flic. And I was going to send some money to a girl in trouble for him—you get me—but I wondered if it was on the level, and Dash said ask her to describe the chandelier.[12]

[HANNAH WEINSTEIN:] A friend of mine had a little fling with Hammett—oh, not serious, but maybe a dozen times—but them she broke it off because of all the whores around. That was when he lived at the Beverly Wilshire. She said she couldn't take all the whores. It was so insulting. . . .[13]

[NUNNALLY JOHNSON:] From the day I met Hammett, in the late twenties, his behavior could be accounted for only by an assumption that he had no expectation of being alive much beyond Thursday. . . .[14]

Plenty of people disapproved of Hammett. "One of the many guys who couldn't take Hollywood without trying to push God out of the high seat," Raymond Chandler sniffed, though Chandler liked him. But Hammett made no effort to make people like him and stayed remote in his sumptuous rooms, dressed in a silk dressing gown and scarf, haughtily receiving supplicants who came to borrow money.

Elegant clothes make a taciturn or shy man seem haughty and dignified. The style suited him and it was expensive. Yet it made him feel uneasy to have money coming in, so he spent it or gave it away. Sometimes he gave money to Jose, or he gave it to causes and bought presents and gambled. He would tell people to pick out things that they liked. Buy yourself a dress, he would suggest to Lillian, meaning a dress by Adrian or Lanvin. Or he would buy the dress, or a jewel, or a case of finest leather like his own cases. He would in time buy Jose a little house. By gambling he kept track of how the stars were working for him—you were on a winning streak or a losing streak; your luck at the tables or the track was an index of everything.

"Listen, Paul," says Ned Beaumont in *The Glass Key*, "it's not only the money, though thirty-two hundred is a lot, but it would be the same if it was five bucks. I go two months without winning a bet and that gets me down. What good am I if my luck's gone? Then I cop, or think I do, and I'm all right again. I can take my tail out from between my legs and feel that I'm a person again and not just something that's being kicked around. The money's important enough, but it's not the real thing. It's what losing and losing and losing does to me."[15]

He bought Jo and Mary huge boxes of candy and stuffed Easter ducks as big as they were, and a crate of toys from F. A. O. Schwartz, and once when he had won at the track he gave Jo $50, and she was only nine, and $50 each for Jose and Mary. It was a fortune. He bought garnets for Jose, and a silver brush and mirror. He bought beautiful things always. It was his misfortune to understand the mechanism of gifts, by which the giver enhances his self-regard and forgives himself for lapses of affection. He liked

Lillian's unsentimental attitude to receiving presents: of a brooch, a pearl set in black metal, she asked, "Did it cost more than $500?" and he said, "Yes, but not as much as $600." He put her down as the $500 type.

His friends remembering:

> Hell, he'd give you the shirt off his back [Ed Rosenberg said]. Money meant nothing to him. Oh, he appreciated it if you paid him back, but he never asked you for it. Most people never paid him back. There came a time he could have used the money too. At the end of his life he didn't have a bean.[16]

> [LILLIAN WROTE:] One night Hammett and I were having dinner in the Brown Derby and the Indian came in, pushing his way past the headwaiter, to sit down next to Hammett. He said, "My grandfather was chief of the Sioux, my great-grandfather was killed by . . ."
> "How much do you want?" Hammett asked.
> "Nothing as a gift from you. You told me once you arrested an Indian for murder . . ."
> Hammett put his wallet on the table and said, "Take it any way you want, but don't tell me what you think."
> The Indian opened the wallet and took out five twenty-dollar bills. "Be sure I do not take it as a gift. I take it as a loan. You are better than most, but you . . ."
> Hammett said wearily, "Arrested an Indian for murder. That's right."
> The Indian said, "And thus it is impossible for me . . ."
> "Sure, sure," Hammett said. "Mail it to me someday." The Indian bowed, kissed my hand, and was gone.[17]

> I think Hammett was the only person I ever met who really didn't care about money, made no complaints and had no regrets when it was gone. Maybe money is unreal for most of us, easier to give away than things we want. (But I didn't know that then, maybe confused it with showing off.) . . . Hammett said, ". . . Things belong to people who want them most."[18]

He bought Lillian a mink coat and a broadtail coat, an enormous broadtail stole and a necklace, which she took back and had the money credited to his account. He endlessly bought her jewelry.

He bought Jose a Packard car. When he forgot about the payments, it was taken away. Jose didn't mind too much. She hated to drive.

I was a celebrity [wrote Gertrude Stein], and when I was at Pasadena Mrs. Ehrman whom I had met at Carl Van Vechten's in New York asked us to come over to Beverly Hills and dine with her. Whom did we want to meet. Anybody we liked, she said she would get Charlie Chaplin and the Emersons and some others not more than twelve in all would that do. . . . then suddenly the next day I said but I did want to meet Dashiell Hammett. . . .

I never was interested in cross word puzzles or any kind of puzzles but I do like detective stories. I never try to guess who has done the crime and if I did I would be sure to guess wrong but I like somebody being dead and how it moves along and Dashiell Hammett was all that and more. . . .

We went to dinner that evening and there was Dashiell Hammett and we had an interesting talk about autobiography, but first how did he get there I mean at Mrs. Ehrman's for dinner. Between them they told it.

Mrs. Ehrman called up an office he had at Hollywood and asked for his address, she was told he was in San Francisco, then she called up the producer of The Thin Man he said Hammett was in New York. So said Mrs. Ehrman to herself he must be in Hollywood. So she called up the man who had wanted to produce The Thin Man and had failed to get it and he gave Hammett's address. Mrs. Ehrman telegraphed to Hammett saying would he come that evening and dine with her to meet Gertrude Stein. It was April Fool's Day and he did nothing and then he looked up Ehrman and it was a furrier and no Mrs. Ehrman and then he asked everybody and heard that it was all true and telegraphed and said if he might bring who was to be his hostess [Lillian] he would come and Mrs. Ehrman said of course come and they came. . . .

Anything is an autobiography, but this was a conversation.

I said to Hammett there is something that is puzzling. In the nineteenth century the men when they were writing did invent all kinds and a great number of men. The women on the other hand never could invent women they always made the women be themselves seen splendidly or sadly or heroically or beautifully or despairingly or gently, and they never could make any other kind of woman. From Charlotte Brontë to George Eliot and many years later this was true. Now in the twentieth century it is the men who do it. The men all write about themselves, they are always themselves as strong or weak or mysterious or passionate or drunk or controlled but always themselves as the women used to do in the nineteenth century. Now you yourself always do it now why is it. He said it's simple. In the nineteenth century men were confident, the women were not but in the twentieth century the men have no confidence and so they have to make themselves as you say more beautiful more intriguing more everything and they cannot make any other man because they have to hold on to themselves not having any confidence.[19]

I

Arise, ye movie writers, and cast away your chains.
Executives are human after all!
Shall they still rewrite our scripts, the children of our brains?
And shall we be a supervisor's thrall?
No! No! No! No! A million, million no's!
Not in vain our fountain pens are filled!
The writers all will join
And executives will loin
To monkey with the Screen Writers Guild.

II

They pay us weekly salaries, a measly grand or two,
And think we ought to work because we're paid!
Shall we yield and do our job? Will you? Will you?
Defend the rights the tryrant would invade!
Up! Up! Up! Up! Attack them from the rear!
Never shall the voice of art be stilled!
Through gory battle scenes
Drive your gleaming limousines!
Ye heroes of the Screen Writers Guild!

III

Ye Gentlemen and Ladies that push the fervent pen,
The time has come and Freedom is in sight.
The cudgeled brain grows weary. When a bottle is your yen,
Have at it! And remember, write is write!
Drink! Drink! Drink! Drink! Write a masterpiece!
Till twenty thousand pages have been filled.
They'll all be thrown away
But the producers have to pay
To members of the Screen Writers Guild![20]

In 1934 and 1935 the economic situation in America continued to worsen. People lost or left their homes. The breadlines were long. In California, liberal Upton Sinclair decided to run for governor, and the studios worked to defeat him by faking newsreels showing bums flocking to California to support him. Studio employees were forced to contribute to the campaign of his opponent, the conservative incumbent Frank Merriam, though most of them opposed him.

Studios had extorted money from writers before. In March of 1933, Hollywood writers had been required to take a wage cut—the studios claimed it was necessary in the hard economic situation of the day, or they would have to close. The wage cut had given impetus to the formation of some sort of union or organization for screenwriters, not so much for the highly paid and relatively powerful writers like Hammett but for the scores of junior writers who felt both the cut and their powerlessness against the studios, for whom they were indistinguishable drones, "schmucks with Underwoods." The studios were determined to keep writers divided, anonymous, and, except for the few, underpaid. Thirty percent of Hollywood screenwriters earned less than $2,000 a year in 1934, and only 10 percent earned over $10,000.

Several existing groups might in theory have represented the writers—the Motion Picture Academy was one, but it was too closely associated with the interests of producers. "Like trying to get laid at your mother's house," Dorothy Parker is said to have said. The musicians and technicians, and the sound and lighting people, had unions, but their interests were not quite the same. Members of the Writers Club, a branch of the Authors League of America, were perhaps too prosperous to be motivated to organize in behalf of struggling writers. There was a moribund Dramatists Guild, which might have been revived. In April 1933 the Screen Writers Guild was reorganized out of the Writers Club and elements of other groups, but saw itself as a distinct entity with new rules.

The big studio bosses—Louis B. Mayer, Irving Thalberg, Harry Warner—were outraged, alarmed and resolutely opposed to the idea of a union for writers. A struggle began.

During 1934 the Guild, with Roosevelt's NIRA (National Industrial Recovery Act) backing, tried to negotiate a code of fair practice with the studios. The screenwriters asked for a number of regulations, which have since become accepted, which infuriated the studios even more:

1. that writers not be lent from studio to studio without their consent,

2. that writers not be asked to write on speculation,

3. that all notice of writer suspension or layoff be in writing,

4. that producers transport writers to and from locations where their presence was required and that producers pay for the writers' room and board while on location,

5. that writers receive screen credit according to their contribution to a picture and that no contract violate this,

6. that all writers working simultaneously on the same material be notified of this by the producer,

7. that agreements or understandings by producers, formal or informal, to blacklist writers be prohibited.[21]

Negotiations stretched into 1935, along with attempts to strengthen and enlarge the membership of the guild. In 1935, too, the League of American Writers, replacing the John Reed clubs, sought to involve a broad coalition of political forces on the left in actions against the rising Nazi threat. LAW held its first conference.

LAW and SWG were both to become important interests of Hammett's, and he was to assume leadership roles in each. Now, 1935, he was not yet a member of either, but his interest in unions had been rekindled by the San Francisco general strike the previous year. In San Francisco, Harry Bridges' striking dockworkers were joined by teamsters, and had been violently attacked by police. The bloodshed led to a general strike, evidence of the power of union action. Hammett remembered his strikebreaking Pinkerton days. Back then he had seen the frightened faces of the workers, and had seen that his might be one of them. Politics began to be important to him now, or, if not politics, principles.

1936 was a bad year from the start. At the end of January there was one pleasant social occasion—the *Black Mask* writers' dinner. The other writers either looked up to Hammett or resented him. One who looked up to him was Raymond Chandler. The two men never met after this night, but Chandler was impressed with the slightly younger Hammett, to whom he owed, he often said, a considerable artistic debt. "Hammett's all right. I give him everything. . . . Met him once only, very nice looking tall quiet gray-haired fearful capacity for Scotch, seemed quite unspoiled to me . . ."[22]

The New Year's festivities in Los Angeles were followed, after a suitable incubation period, by an unmistakable and disagreeable sensation: he'd got the clap again. He went on with his plans to go to New York, boozing considerably on the way, which eased the discomfort. Drunk at the Kansas City airport, he sent jocular wires. To Jo: AND AS FOR YOU MY FINE FEATHERED FRIEND I AM STILL ON THE WAY AND I LOVE YOU AND YOUR RELATIVE GUESS WHO

In New York a couple of days later he was really sick and checked into the hospital, spent a couple of weeks there and emerged somewhat better. Blanche Knopf sent him books for convalescent reading. By the way, how was his novel coming?[23]

Wherever his life was going, he felt he hadn't got there yet— he was still on the way. He moved into the Madison Hotel and tried to take up everyday routine, hoping that with a life pleasant and calm his writing would come. Killing time was the thing. He went to dog shows and collected matchbooks for Jo. To Jo: "Have you heard the little verse that goes something like this?"

> Yesterday, upon the stair
> I saw a man who wasn't there.
> He wasn't there again today.
> Oh, how I wish he'd go away![24]

He hung around in bars and missed Lillian, who was back in Hollywood. She was successful and well known there now. Her play was being made into a movie, to be called *These Three*, directed by William Wyler; and she had written another screen-play, *The Dark Angel*, with Mordaunt Sharp, and would soon write another play; and Hammett knew, if she did not, that she was and would be a great success from now on.

The hopeful Alfred Knopf wrote nagging little letters from time to time: "I haven't heard from you for a long time and I am curious to know how the book is coming. Do give me a ring and let me know when we can meet, as I would like to hear about it and see you" (April 2, 1936); "I am anxious to know how the book goes and whether you will have it ready in the summer. Will you give me a ring when you get this as I am sailing early in the week and should very much like to hear about it before I go. With my best regards and hopes that you are feeling much better. . . ." (May 5, 1936).

Hammet wasn't feeling better. Injections in May didn't work to clear up his gonorrhea, and he was obliged to stay in New York near doctors. Lillian came through and went on to Havana in June, then came back and lived pleasantly on Tavern Island, off Connecticut. He longed to be with her. In New York the world busied itself with producing, reprinting, praising, resurrecting and paying for his old works, something to which he had grown accustomed. He liked the money and hated the attention, which increased his sense of fraudulence and indolence. King Features was reprinting some of his short stories, and he tried to read one, "Flypaper," and could hardly bear it. *The Thin Man* was going to be done on the Lux Radio Theatre—he'd try to borrow a set to listen—it was Powell and Loy as in the film. Made little bunches of matchbooks for Jo: "The red ones taste best, I think, though the silver ones are more nourishing."[25]

To Lillian: "I'm missing you terribly. Last night I almost phoned Rhinelander 4-4108 just to hear it ring, but that seemed a little too silly."

Little decisions came easy: the decision not to go see Joe Louis fight Max Schmeling, the most highly touted match in decades; the decision not to spend a month with a friend in Connecticut. He went through the motions of working, aware of what it amounted to—blank paper. He devoted some thought to Lillian's play *Days to Come*, scheduled for production in December. He enjoyed play-doctoring and was good at it, and it provided the sensation of writing. He could always tell when other people's words went wrong and he had a sense of how to fix them, and from this he derived vicarious relief from the task of sitting blankly.[26]

His gonorrhea still didn't clear up, so he was out of commission in every respect. He tried sitz baths and rectal irrigations, boring and humiliating.[27] He saw specialists. In July he surrendered himself for a fever treatment against the gonococcus: they put you in an oxygen tent and heated you up until the germs died or you did. It was said to be a ghastly treatment, dire, extreme, excruciating.

He was put in at eight one morning, and they began to heat him up. By ten his temperature was 103.6, and by two 104 and finally 107, when he lay delirious. Doctors came at intervals and took samples of the sinister discharges that emitted from his inert body. By seven at night these contained fewer evil cells than before. The doctors continued, burning his leg horribly in the process. They began at eleven at night and continued through the next day and the next; and on the third of August all the organisms had died and Hammett had not, so they let him out, somewhat shaken by the wages of sin.[28]

. . .

About this time, in 1936, Francisco Franco joined forces with other Spanish generals in hopes of overthrowing the legitimate republican government of Spain. At first this distant military action didn't attract the notice it soon would among Americans.

July 20—from Alfred as usual: "I am just back from Europe and realize that you must be about finishing your book. How is it coming along and when will I be able to see it? I would like to see you, too, so let me know."

Hammett hung around New York the rest of the summer and then in the fall rented a house in Princeton at 10 Cleveland Lane, because he and Lillian thought it would be nice to be in a small pretty town somewhere, not too far from things but in the country, where they could be together peacefully and work. Instead he threw parties, wrecked the house and the owner sued him. He was used to being sued. Back in L.A., he owed a chauffeur, a secretary, a rental car agency, someone called Ruth Meyers and a company called Reliance Products.

He lived in the present, and he didn't like to talk about the past. "Tell me about the silly girl on Pine Street," Lillian Hellman would ask him.

"She lived on Pine Street and she was silly," he would say, and nothing more. He resisted reminiscences and confidences.

"When did you first know that you were handsome?" she would ask, and he would say he knew nothing of the kind, and then once admitted that his grandma had told him so. His grandma thought he looked like Wallace Reid.

"It's for when I write your biography," she said.

"That'll be a book about a girl named Hellman," he said, "with an occasional reference to a friend named Hammett."[29]

He intended to get to work on the novel, and told a kid reporter from the Princeton newspaper, "Yes, I'm working on a book here, but it's not a mystery, and it's not about Princeton. I don't really like detective stories, anyway. I get too tangled up in the plots. This one is just about a family of a dozen children out on an island. You see, all I do in a story is just get some characters together and then let them get in each other's way. And let me tell you, twelve kids can sure get in each other's way!"[30] This invention was more fanciful than most, but his invented plots would in fact often involve large familes, or fathers and sons, and the idea of an island had always drawn him.

From Alfred, September 14: "I am just back from various places and hear that you have been ill. I am very sorry about this and hope that you are much better now. Also it seems to me that your manuscript must be finished. Could you let me know? At any rate, I want to see you." And, November 13, 1936: what chance of your completing your book for spring publication anxious to know please wire.

> SCENE—The library of a
> rented house in
> New Jersey, U.S.A.
>
> TIME—Late at night late
> in December late in
> 1936 A.D.[31]

Hammett was writing Lillian a kind of play-letter. Lillian, smarting a little from the failure of her play *Days to Come*, which had opened on the fifteenth and run for only six performances, had gone on a cruise. He put her on the boat that afternoon and came back to Princeton. The weather was rainy and warm for the season. He was reading *Gil Blas*. His companions were two dogs named Baby and Pal.

He was trying to stop drinking. Lillian had been raising hell about his drinking, she could no longer stand drunken students lying around, and Hammett's debauchery, the spectacle of destruction. It was easier to quit in solitude this way, away from friends and New York bars, with a couple of dogs for companions. He tried rereading *Don Quixote*, which, sober, went better than the other times he'd tried. He tried to work, and wrote letters each day to Lillian and sent them seaward:

> Today is even warmer than yesterday, with a very bright sun and a nice breeze blowing. Do you suppose Winter is over? Do you want to discuss nature and the peculiarities of the seasons? And do you suppose I'm just running on like this because I've told myself I'll have to go to work as soon as I've finished this? Of course I could walk down to town first and get a haircut on the grounds that you told me to get one.[32]

Anyhow I hope you're having what you call fun.

Rather than get a haircut I went to work after I had finished writing you yesterday and rather than do what my more rabid fans would call creative work I spent most of my time rewriting most of what I had already written.[33]

It may have seemed to people that this was not exactly true. But even if true, he went on doing what he'd always done—the races and poker and whores. Real whores or just light ladies in a bar, or sometimes it would be someone he and Lillian knew. Sometimes he asked Lillian to make a threesome. It interested him to see how far she would go.

One thing Hammett knew about women: Do not confide your every thought, especially about them. "I love a girl like you," he would say to them, so glibly and sweetly that they could not quite believe it. There was something impenetrable as much in the sweetness of his smile as in his blacker silences.

The professional of vice has a certain sense of rectitude: Nobody is kidding anybody, nobody's hurt. A paying job, an honest understanding. If Hammett drank because he was confused by how people's actions and what they said had nothing to do with each other—an explanation he once gave—with a prostitute there was no such misunderstanding. And there was also this: that a respectable woman sometimes reminded you of a sister or a wife or mother, earnest, sweet and bound for disappointment, and just drained away passion.

Cooped up indoors by the rain, Baby and I are so full of animal spirits and physical energy that we'd be unbearable if there were anybody around who had to put up with us. I've even been thinking that I ought to provide myself with means for getting regular exercise. (See what four days without a drink does for the lug! He'll—two to one—have a hemorrhage tomorrow.)

He was reading he said, *Le Faucon de Malte*, a French translation of his work. "*Tu es un ange.*"[34] He knew that much French, at least.

So 1936 ended struggling upward, a year that had begun badly, and it seemed to him that he still had enough heart for endless struggle, and, ahead of him, plenty of time.

11

1937

ON THE WAGON

He relapsed after the New Year, of course. Lillian came back from her cruise and went to Hollywood to write a screen version of Sidney Kingsley's socialist-realist play *Dead End* to be directed by William Wyler. There would be real rats in real garbage cans. Hammett hung around Princeton awhile longer, but he didn't get anywhere on his novel. Hollywood was after him as usual, now with an offer of $50,000 from William Randolph Hearst to write a story for Marion Davies, another from Samuel Goldwyn to write an "original," and an idea was afoot to make a third Thin Man movie. He decided to sell Nick and Nora to MGM, and go back to Hollywood to oversee their fates:

> You now wish to arrange with me so that you can, without further authority or license from me, or further employment of my services, create or have written further stories containing any or all of the characters that were in your said pictures "THE THIN MAN" and "AFTER THE THIN MAN," including particularly but without limitation the characters "NICK" and "NORA" and the dog "ASTA," and own these stories outright, and, among other things, produce motion pictures which are based upon such stories . . . assured that no motion pictures, other than those produced by you, can hereafter be produced or exhibited, which contain the characters "THIN MAN" or "NICK," or "NORA" or the dog "ASTA," or any characters which are substantially similar thereto, and to grant you the above rights and all rights herein produced, all for the total consideration of Forty thousand ($40,000) Dollars. . . .[1]

On his last weekend in Princeton (March 13, 1937) he wondered if he'd made a mistake. There were friends around—Lillian's friend Lois Jacoby came for a couple of days, and André Malraux, who was going on to the Coast to raise money for Spain. Hammett wrote Lillian that he thought she'd like Malraux:

> Very intense, dogmatic, actorish, with a very interesting face, looking somewhat like a soft hawk. He lectured here yesterday afternoon. I didn't hear it, but met him last night. I don't think we understand one another very well. He insists that I'm the "technical link" between Dreiser and Hemingway and I don't exactly know what he means by that. On the other hand, when I suggested that he might be the French O'Flaherty he didn't seem to know what I meant by that. But we got along all right and I really liked him. Which is more than I can say for your friend MacLeish (or however you spell it) who is a stuffed shirt if I ever saw one.[2]

He adds that even Leland Hayward, who was now his agent, agreed ("against his pocketbook") that he had no business working in pictures at all. But his little dog Baby had died, and Princeton had not been the same for him since. He negotiated a separate contract with Metro that required him to do a story or treatment involving Nick and Nora, and made his way West.

In L.A. he moved into a grandiose six-bedroom suite at the Beverly Wilshire and threw a lot of parties, and then, a few weeks later, after reflecting upon the headaches, blank pages, lost weekends, lost weeks, and failures at making love, went on the wagon again and tried to get his life in order. People were beginning to catch on to him: he was a drunk, he spent too much money, he didn't turn up or turn things out on time. He protected himself against people's reproaches about lateness with smiles and jokes, with the excuse of his being dead drunk, or with sudden aggressive contempt: wasn't it stupid of them to be concerned with a deadline about something as low as a *movie*? As crass as *money*? His personal indiscipline attracted people at first; it was fashionable to burn yourself out, but not everyone had the courage to do it. He did—witness his behavior. He was a spectacle. "I mean to live flamboyantly," he said.[3]

Now, even on the wagon he was attractive, flamboyant, a spectacle. Guys like screenwriters Dudley Nichols and Sam Hoffenstein were proud of the ease with which former drinking com-

The Bettman Archive

Hammett arrives in Hollywood, c. 1940. A studio publicity photo.

panions—Hammett, Fitzgerald—could stay on the wagon, assurance that no one was really the slave of alcohol.[4] Anyone can stop drinking when the time comes! "Keep up the good work!" they would say.

Hammett was writing an extended treatment of a film to be called *Another Thin Man* with the Hacketts for Hunt Stromberg, and was making good progress on it.[5] A more important consequence of sobriety was that he began to think about political things. The world didn't seem to have improved much, and in fact was deteriorating fast, and people seemed to talk more nonsense than it had seemed to him when he was drunk that they did. Things went more slowly, much more slowly, and he still couldn't write. But his energy returned, and his concern for the world, and his conviction that an individual should get involved, and could make a difference.

In January of 1937, U.S. citizens had been warned by the State Department against serving in Spain, in a war toward which the American government was officially neutral. This, of course, made many people look very closely at Spain, and made some wish to go there, if they had not already decided to go, to help the valiant government against Franco's fascist armies. The virtue of the cause was proved for many by the U.S. government's opposition to it, or by Russia's support of the Loyalists.

Hammett, like other people he knew, became interested in Communism. For many it was no more than a rather chic thing to do. Hollywood was becoming political with typical enthusiasm: baby-talking starlets now discussed politics, and people boned up on big words. It was even wrong to be blond; a fashion for brunettes developed. And you should be seen reading the *Theory and Practice of Socialism*. Out there, somewhere beyond the ocean, there was a world and a war in Spain, a growing fascist menace in the world. People even noticed the problem in Japan. So you should not wear silk. Not even silk stockings. You shouldn't go to the department stores that still stocked goods from Germany—you ought to protest Hitler's non-Aryan policy. When Vittorio ("War Is Sport") Mussolini came to town, people snubbed him definitively.

For Hammett the interest in politics was sincere. He remembered Frank Little and the hungry miners kept down by soldiers and guards, remembered their ragged wives and children. He hoped, and even thought it possible, that a better system could right social wrongs. He was very American in his optimism and in his belief in equality, though he would never become, quite, an organization man in his heart and, having no love for meetings, skipped them, even when they involved causes he was for.

The Hollywood Section of the Communist Party (which Martin Berkeley later testified to the House Un-American Activities Committee had been founded at his house because he had a big living

Hammett with Dorothy Parker at a public meeting.

room and good parking) was said to contain so many famous people that they didn't issue cards. Berkeley claimed, though others denied, that Dorothy Parker, Alan Campbell, Hammett and Lillian, V. J. Jerome and Donald Ogden Stewart were among others at that first meeting.[6] Whoever did or didn't belong to it, the Hollywood Section of the Party grew quietly, with a certain amount of secrecy and a certain amount of general knowledge among members of who the other members were. It broke down its organization into sections, branches, fractions. The fractions were made up of writers or other special groups; the branches had weekly meetings and collected dues. "Once we were told that we could be communists and still support the New Deal and Roosevelt, and that the CP was simply a more advanced group going in the same general direction, it was pretty heady and convincing stuff to us," Budd Schulberg has since explained. "All these people knew that an awful lot was happening in the world and Hitler was growing stronger, and there they were, sort of fiddling while Rome burned, and I think the CP gave them a sense that they were doing something more serious and more socially useful, which would compensate for the waste of so much of their talent. Dialectical materialism by the pool. . . ."

"Most of the people I came to know as communists," Ring Lardner, Jr., said later, "were brighter and more admirable and more likable than other people. I once proposed the slogan 'The Most Beautiful Girls in Hollywood Belong to the Communist Party,' but it wasn't taken seriously, even by me."[7]

Martin Berkeley's CP meeting was in June of 1937. Also in June, on the eleventh, the Screen Writers Guild reappeared after a clandestine period, which had followed defeats and opposition by the producers. They had in some ways followed a plan of secrecy parallel to that of the Communist Party, but the plan now was to organize publicly, increase the membership, and present an appeal to the National Labor Relations Board on behalf of screenwriters, who meantime were being represented, poorly, by the weaker Screen Playwrights. A new SWG slate of officers was elected, including Hammett's *Thin Man* collaborator, Frances Goodrich. Hammett took up the cause of the screenwriters with renewed enthusiasm. He himself was elected chairman of the Motion Picture Artists Committee for 1938, with Sylvia Sidney as vice-chairman. The objective of this committee was to raise money for antifascist causes, particularly in Spain and China. Critics of the Screen Writers Guild made much of the fact that many members of the SWG were Communists or fellow travelers, associated now with a growing number of these antifascist organizations.

Hammett's Marxism was sincere, if not his allegiance to the Communist Party, and "when the Republican Party becomes more Marxist than the CP," he told his daughters, "then I'll become a Republican." He also told them it is better to die on your feet than live on your knees. So, for a time at least, he did what the Party told him.

He had been increasingly concerned about Spain. He wanted very much to go there, and for a while expected to be told by the Party to go. His lack of real participation in World War I still rankled, and now here was another chance. He harangued Jose and the girls about it. In the end the Party told him he could not go and he was disappointed. He was expected to be more useful here, and he tried to be.

The Spanish Civil War continued to concern Hollywood liberals, and indeed more and more thoughtful, farsighted people were beginning to see that if fascist forces could be stopped in

Spain, far worse events could be averted in the rest of Europe. The American government was still officially neutral despite valiant attempts by leading American public figures to create some public opinion pressure to gain support for the anti-Franco forces, and it was to this end that Hammett directed his efforts.

Lillian was the one who actually went to Spain. In the summer, after she had finished the first version of her play *The Little Foxes* and after *Dead End*, the movie for which she had written the screenplay, had opened in New York, Lillian sailed, on August 25, going first to Paris and Moscow, and wrote letters about the people she saw there—Hemingway, Dorothy Parker, the fabled Sara and Gerald Murphy, James Thurber, Otto Simon, Archibald MacLeish and John Dos Passos. Then in October she went to Spain, where she and Hemingway, MacLeish and Joris Ivens were making a movie about Spain. Hammett donated some money for it. He guessed she was having an interesting time—she hardly wrote. "My Lilly is a postage stamp miser"[8] was his view.

MRS. F.D.R. TO LUNCH
Burbank—Mrs. Franklin D. Roosevelt will be a special guest of Bette Davis when the Warner Bros. star acts as hostess at the weekly luncheon to be held this noon at the "It" Cafe. Among others at Miss Davis' table on this occasion will be Sylvia Sidney, Melvyn Douglas and Dashiell Hammett.[9]

While Lillian was away, Hammett thought of putting his life in order: perhaps he should be divorced so he could marry or Jose could—if it could be managed cheaply and quietly and without too much trouble. He didn't really care, neither did Jose; in fact, she demurred a little.

Without any sense of urgency, they sent off to Nogales, Mexico, where lawyers for a price entered routine pleas used for every couple from anywhere: "a disturbance in marital harmony had interrupted conjugal happiness." The statement mentioned unkindness without justification, threats and injury—grounds that doubtless actually applied to most of the cases that came through here. The decree was granted on the twenty-sixth of August, and Hammett got the news in early September, along with a heavy case of flu.

HAVE DIVORCE AND FLU STOP REMAINING HERE UNTIL TWENTIETH
STOP MUCH LOVE DASH

Jose went on thinking of herself as Mrs. Dashiell Hammett. That was how he thought of her too.

While laid up with the flu, he wrote letters to Lillian, who was still off on her travels. When he was sober, he found the Hollywood gossip more amusing than ever. Willy Wyler was giving a cocktail party for John Huston, Lou Holtz was taking a screen test for David Selznick, and there was a Gershwin concert on the radio. The Hacketts cabled from Stockholm that Hunt Stromberg had wired them from Biarritz to cable Hammett to ask about how his writing was going. *Life* magazine had pictures of Lillian: "One bad of you playing tennis, one good one of you knitting, so I guess you're more the domestic type." She was probably in the war zone by now. "Al Lichtman still says the chemin-de-fer's no good since you left town; my gambling has not been doing me any good financially; the Guild has been signing up an average of about twelve members a week, including a few from the Playwrights; and the weather remains pleasant, though I've been out only twice briefly in the past two weeks."[10]

In November:

Dear Lilishka,

Since you've never been to Hollywood, I suppose I should try to show you what kind of place it is. Perhaps you can get some idea from this: when Ethel Butterworth and her newest collaborator had a row the n. c. suggested that perhaps Ethel's lack of literary experience made her judgment of story values not too good, whereupon Ethel is quoted as having said, "That's silly! Why, I've criticized George Kaufman!"

Or maybe this will supply a better clue: Tommy Manville, Jr., is trying to get a picture job through Earl Carroll, with some idea that he might be connected with Paramount's "Bluebeard's Eighth Wife," as technical advisor, I hope.

Or there is the strange marriage of . . . whose bride is supposed to have said that the only reason [he] married her was that he was jealous of Charles Bennett (What! what!) who had a yen for her. She told Frances Goodrich that as soon as [he] gets a thousand dollars he wants her to have her breasts lifted (I think he means a boyish bob) and her nose fixed. [He], by the way, was given "The Foundry" to do some months ago and told the Hacketts he was very enthusiastic about it because he "had always wanted to take a crack at those labor unions."

But I don't suppose that's enough yet: well, the last time I saw Ogden Nash he was on his way to see an eye-doctor who guaranteed that after one half-hour treatment, that's all, anybody could throw his glasses away and never need them again. I haven't seen Ogden since: he's probably too busy walking into walls.

Then there was the radio announcer at the Stanford-California game who said into my ear personally: "We'll now go down to the field microphone and see if we can pick up some of the cheers and innuendo from the stands."

So you can see that, in spite of the Buddy Rogerses' preferring a cottage to Pickfair, life is not and cannot be simple out here. There is Morrie Ryskind writing a guest column for the Citizen-News in which he says that if Black's past is to be forgiven there is no reason why Al Capone can't some day be a member of the Supreme Court; there is Jane Withers to be given "a skating audition by Sol Wurtzel," according to the same paper; there is . . . but you'll think I'm exaggerating.

The Hacketts had a party last night, but I didn't get away from my groupie meeting in time to go. Bruce Lockwood, who has been borrowing money from me, sent me a dozen of his wife's horrible watercolors, from which I'm supposed to select a couple to be gifted with. Sidney Skolsky has had a fight with the Examiner and is shifting his column back to the Citizen-News. There's a poker game at Billy Wilkerson's tonight, but I'm still playing hookey from them. It is rumored that American Tel. & Tel. is thinking about backing a chain of ten-cent movie theatres. Want any more news today?[11]

Film Committee to Raise Funds for China

Dashiell Hammett, prominent screen writer and novelist, has been elected to serve as chairman of the Motion Picture Artists Committee, according to an announcement by Charles Page, executive secretary. Miss Sylvia Sidney was elected to the position of vice-chairman.

Among those chosen for the board of directors are Anna May Wong, Melvyn Douglas, Luise Rainer, Lewis Milestone, Dorothy Parker, Philip Dunne, Johnny Green, Dudley Nichols, Gale Sondergaard, Stella Adler and Donald Ogden Stewart.

The Motion Picture Artists Committee has been actively engaged during the past year in raising funds for aid to Loyalist Spain. It will inaugurate the second year of its existence by the extension of its activities to include aid for China, as well.[12]

ADDRESSES SLATED BY RALPH BATES

Ralph Bates, novelist and captain in the International Brigade
of the Spanish Loyalist forces, is due to arrive in Los Angeles
tomorrow afternoon via United Air Lines for a week's speaking
engagements in the Southland, to be climaxed with a Trinity
Auditorium mass meeting Wednesday night, December 8.

Monday night, December 6, the League of American Writers
will present a symposium on "Should Writers Mix in Politics?"
at the Hollywood Women's Club, 7078 Hollywood Boulevard,
with speakers including Bates, Dashiell Hammett, author of "The
Thin Man," and Cedric Belfrage, author of "Away From It All,"
a recent Book of the Month Club selection.

Bates' local itinerary also calls for his speaking before the Ad-
venturers Club, at 311 1/2 South Spring Street, tomorrow evening
at 8 o'clock, and at a mass meeting for the Santa Monica Bay
District, Sunday night, December 5, at Eagles Hall in Ocean
Park, with Assemblyman Ben Rosenthal as chairman.[13]

In December Hammett suggested to a symposium of the League
of American Writers that since left-wing ideas were proving more
and more popular, producers would soon convince themselves that
liberalism and radicalism had box-office potential and begin to go
for progressive-minded films.

Papa's coming over, Mary said. The news made Jo both happy
and miserable at the same time, as always, for it meant you couldn't
do the things you'd planned to, or maybe you could, but you
didn't. Maybe Papa didn't really like to have them all sitting there
watching him read.

Mama liked it when he came; she twittered in the kitchen, cooking things he liked, and it seemed as if he liked to be there, relaxing
in the living room or out in the backyard in his bathing suit in the
sun doing crossword puzzles, just as if he were often there. And if
you'd been planning to go to the movies or something and Papa
was coming over, you didn't go. Jo's friends thought it was strange.
Jo wished her family were like other families, with the father
home, or if they were divorced, then the father not home, but
not both divorced and home. Once when Papa was coming over
she went out anyway, and when she got home Papa wasn't even
mad.

But sometimes he would turn and yell at Mary to go take off
that lipstick, or he would look at Jo's fingernails, and if they were

dirty his stern and disapproving glance would send her into misery. When Papa wasn't home, Mary Jane and Mama would try to imagine what he would want them to do about this or that. Jo didn't think they should. If a father was to be heeded, then he should be there, that was her view.

Like those of many promiscuous men, his ideas about women were at bottom conventional—there were nice girls and bad girls. By being smart and independent like Lillian, you earned, maybe, the right to be a little bit bad. He wanted the girls to be smart, of course. But above all, he hoped they'd be nice.

Christmas Day, 1937, a nicely dull day, spent at home at the Beverly Wilshire brooding over nothing. Jo and Mary came for lunch and brought Hammett presents. Otherwise he saw nobody. A few people sent telegrams—people who wanted him to do something, or wanted to borrow money. They wished him an unbelievably happy future.

Outside, the California Christmas that he'd never been able to get used to—lit-up Santas on adobe walls, cactus trees with colored lights on them. He'd had Christmas Eve dinner with the Hacketts, playing pool. Henry Myers and his friends came in costumes to sing carols. They sounded awful, but they were sincere. It rained.

If it didn't rain next week, he guessed he'd go to Santa Anita. That would be better than more screaming fights with Hunt Stromberg about the script they were working on. Hunt was complaining that it wasn't like the other Nick and Noras, but as far as Hammett could see, Hunt had no idea what was good and what was bad about the others and shouldn't meddle in this one. The Hacketts trembled on the sidelines. These fights shouldn't lead to anything more serious than blows, Hammett said. Maybe, Christmas Day or not, he'd put in a little time on his "charming fable of how Nick loved Nora and Nora loved Nick and everything was just one great big laugh in the midst of other people's trials and tribulations. Maybe there are better writers in the world, but nobody ever invented a more insufferably smug pair of characters. They can't take that away from me, even for $40,000."[14]

Should they marry? They talked of it. Sometimes Lillian or sometimes he would say, "We should marry," but they never got together on it. Once, before they met, Hammett had written little poems. Lillian hadn't seen them.

CAUTION TO TRAVELERS

Hold it lightly if you'd carry it long,
Nor bind too tightly what you'd bind strong.
Heavy the thing mightily gripped,
The too-tight string is soonest slipped.[15]

Once they set a day, but when the wedding day approached,
Hammett disappeared for a while, with another woman.

A CLINCHER

By one decisive argument,
Giles gained his lovely Kate's consent
    To fix the bridal day.
"Why such haste, dear Giles, to wed?
I shall not change my mind," she said.
    "But, then," said he, "I may!"[16]

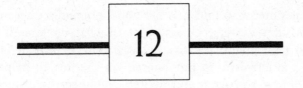

12

1938

CRACK-UP

January of 1938 was his tenth month without a drink. People were watching him as if he were some sort of wonder. He was still living luxuriously at the Beverly Wilshire, in the Royal Siamese Suite, whose name and décor amused him, whose splendor he rather enjoyed.[1] But he was not enjoying much else; he was beginning to feel sick and shaky, when without drinking he ought to be feeling better, ought to be writing, ought to be happy. He poked along at "Another Thin Man." He was sick of Nick and Nora—so were the Hacketts—and they all knew this would be the last Thin Man for them. (Others would carry on for three more scripts.) He was one of the thirteen highest-paid writers in Hollywood, but this in some ways made his life stranger and more difficult. If this was success, it did not please; he respected it no more than he had respected Blackmasking. The money came and went, barely noticeable. Sobriety conferred an extra dimension of falsity and foolishness on people and institutions that had seemed not so bad if you were drunk.

He forced himself to perform his political tasks. One was as a kind of enforcer, making sure people coughed up their weekly dues of $15 to the Party. He was active in a campaign to unseat Governor Frank F. Merriam in the elections. And he made endless efforts on behalf of the nascent Screen Writers Guild; he continued as chairman of the Motion Picture Artists Committee, and signed and drafted petitions against Franco and for Art. Sober, he was impatient with half efforts toward the right and good. He jeered at some nice old ladies whose idea of helping Communism was to buy the *Daily Worker* and tide it over a few days of financial trouble.[2] Politics were more serious than that at the "It" Cafe.

Most important to him was the non-Communist cause of unionizing the film writers. Uneasily aware that he himself was not going to gain much, because he was so well paid, he felt high-minded and altruistic to put himself on the line to help the rank and file. He gave parties and invited young screenwriters; Lillian, when she was there, or Dorothy Parker, or others well established would then talk them into joining up. Frances Goodrich remembered Lillian coming out of a room "where she'd been talking to a writer named Talbot Jennings, a big writer at MGM who did some additional dialogue for Shakespeare in *Romeo and Juliet*. And poor Lillian came out of the room and said, 'Well, if I get Talbot Jennings to join this thing, somebody's got to pay for the abortion.' "[3]

In February 1938 the Screen Writers Guild won its battle to incorporate, with Dudley Nichols as president. The directors included Hammett, Dorothy Parker and Ring Lardner, Jr. In March they held a mass meeting against the rival International Alliance of Theatrical Stage Employees, an organization widely felt to be in the pocket of the studio bosses, which wanted to include writers. Hammett addressed this meeting.

WRITERS ACT TO UNITE AGAINST STAGE ALLIANCE

The Screen Writers Guild today sought a mass meeting of actors, directors and other studio crafts to present a united front against any move by the International Alliance of Theatrical Stage Employees to control all studio labor.

The guild also studied a proposal to ask the screen actors' and directors' guilds to join in financing an industry-wide employment and economic survey, particularly in reference to creative crafts.

The proposals were outlined last night at a mass meeting of the writers' union at the Sunset Arbor where Dudley Nichols, guild president, conducted the session.

Dashiell Hammett and Boris Ingster outlined to fellow writers the background of the I.A.T.S.E. threatened move to extend its studio jurisidiction. The writers voted to invite other crafts not affiliated with the alliance to join in a "show of strength" mass meeting before April 1 when producer-labor annual conferences are scheduled to begin. It was pointed out that such a meeting would serve notice on producers of opposition to recognition of the alliance's expanded claims.

A report on writers' employment was made by E. E. Paramore who said approximately 431 persons were listed on studio payrolls. His report indicated a seeming steadying in employment after the recent slump.[4]

He also signed petitions against Franco's inhuman bomb attacks: "Brutal beyond words, this plague of death and destruction from the air has shocked the conscience of mankind." He wrote of these matters to Lillian, who had gone to Florida, and added: "Did I forget to tell you that the John Brights' Christmas card was a picture of a Spanish loyalist bayonet charge, with the greeting, 'Viva'?"[5]

But he felt more and more tired, and in February he began to lose weight. He stopped writing weekly letters to his daughter Jo, "the crazy princess of Santa Monica" after telling her: "Dear Ex-Princess—today I have abdicated so you won't have to worry about embroidering your coat-of-arms on your handkerchiefs any more. Your father the Ex-King."[6]

It was as if he had abdicated life: he wrote nothing, and was troubled by sexual impotence, that most dreaded symptom and punishment.[7] He left his hotel rooms less and less. His hotel bill grew huge, and was left unpaid. He looked gaunt and white. His absences were noticed, his friends grew worried. Where's Hammett? people would ask. "In his apartment at the Beverly Wilshire contemplating his novel," Dorothy Parker said. By May of 1938 he had lost twenty-five pounds, and finally did not get out of bed at all. People called Jose to see if she could do anything, but she couldn't.

All the while he wrote cheery-sounding letters to Lillian about little things:

> M-G-M and I are still at odds over the price on the new story, so I told my agent fellow to say bye-bye to Hunt for me and begin talking to Dave Selznick and maybe Sam the Good. Some little technicality about $5,000 I owe the studio on The Foundry deal a couple of years ago is holding up my get-away check. . . .
>
> Today I went book purchasing to the extent of Hope of Heaven, Reader's Digest of Books, Long Haul, the History of Motion Pictures, I Should Have Stayed Home, the Folklore of Capitalism, Dashiell Hammett Omnibus, and the People's Front. Rangey, eh?[8]

Two days after this chatty note, in despair after fourteen months of sobriety, he sent down to the hotel pharmacy for some bottles and began to drink again, first calling Lillian, then writing her, the even tone of his composure belying the desolation of his spirit. But any correspondent of Hammett's had long since learned to read between the lines.[9]

Darling,

So after I phoned you I took a shot of scotch, the first I've had since when was it? and it didn't seem to do me any good, but I suppose it hardly ever does anybody any good except those who sell it to get enough money to buy detective stories or tickets to Elliott (41st week) (D-929-83.30) and that damned barking bird is at work outside and if I don't look out I'll become a stream of consciousness writer and be discopered by Whit Burnett. (If you committed a crime and left an incriminating letter behind I Whit Burnett.) Want to see me do one with Martha Foley? In the screen version of The Children's Hour Karen says, "Martha, Foley we could make Mary tell the truth we . . ." Oberon could do that nicely: it's the way English actors talk normally. (I hear the editors of Story are no longer Whit Burnett Cerf.) I hope you can stop laughing long enough to read the rest of this letter: it gets better as it goes on.

That's what I'd like to think,
and like to have you
think, but I know
as well as you
do that just
about now
what lit-
tle im-
agin-
ati-
on
I
'
v
e
g
ot
i
s
u
s
e
d

u

P

a

n

d

s

o

.

.

.

Love,[10]

Albert Hackett got a note from Frances asking him to come to the Beverly Wilshire. A problem with Dash. She was already there. He hurried to the hotel and burst into the elegant suite, but at first he couldn't find Dash. Doors were open, with everything scattered around, and then he saw him lying across the bed in the bedroom. Hammett looked so pale and gray-skinned and thin lying there that Hackett thought he might be dead. He was not dead, though—his eyes were half open, and he managed a feeble smile of greeting. He couldn't say what was the matter, and he couldn't get up either. Hackett thought he should go to a doctor, but the hotel wouldn't let him leave until he paid the bill.

Frances downstairs was talking to the manager, who said, "If you're such a friend of his, why don't you pay the hotel bill," and when Albert came up to them and Frances was standing there looking dazed, Albert said, "For heavens' sake, why don't we?" and Frances whispered in a shocked voice, "Eight thousand dollars?" "We'll figure something out," Albert said.

They thought they should send him to Lillian somehow. Frances asked an airline if there was a berth or bed on the plane: "This man isn't feeling too well."

"Madam, if he isn't feeling too well, then he can't fly without a doctor's permission."

More difficulty to find a doctor, and when they finally did, the doctor shrugged and said, "He can die here as quickly as on a plane," but he signed the paper. Albert and Frances sneaked his belongings out separately, bit by bit, in briefcases and boxes. Hammett took some swigs of whiskey, which strengthened him a little, enough to totter through the lobby and be taken to the airport. They were going to airmail him to Lillian, and Hammett made no protest.

At the airport the plane was late, and his secretary, whom they were sending with him, was afraid when Hammett told her they were repairing it with rubber bands. He was not afraid of death, did not think he was going to die, but he was terrified of going crazy. He drank some more whiskey and then rallied a little on the plane. He must have supposed at last that his fortunes had reached bottom: to be sent in a hapless state to Lillian—in debt, unable to write, drunk, sick, sick of himself, frightened and disgusted.

A terrified Lillian met him in New York with an ambulance. It made the society columns. Sidney Skolsky told his public that Hammett had checked into Lenox Hill Hospital to avoid a nervous breakdown. Hammett was in fact having a nervous breakdown, whatever that was. He didn't know, but it felt good to lie there.

Lenox Hill Hospital   May 23, 1938

cc. Loss of weight—3 months. Breakdown 9 days.

Present illness—has lost 25 lbs. in past three months. He has been a chronic alcoholic but has not drunk: the past 14 months. 9 days ago felt weak, frightened and panicky. Began to drink again. Felt so fatigued that he took to bed. Had a definite fear of insanity. No cough, no pain, no headache.

Patient is emaciated. Hair prematurely grey. Has low blood pressure, low blood sugar, high cholesterol for his state of nutrition, low basal metabolism. Heart small. Patient is impotent.

Evidences of hypofunction of thyroid—adrenals, gonads are definite. While the case is not one of Simmonds' disease, is likely one of pituitary hypofunction.

	Diagnosis 1) Neurosis
Has gained 10 lbs and	2) Pituitary Hypofunction
made a splendid recovery	3) Pyorrhea

Irwin Sobel[11]

He was not permitted out of bed. Nurses washed his face, fed him. His teeth were infected, and his adrenal glands suspected. With care, in a few weeks he had gained weight, gained spirit again. Donald Ogden Stewart brought him a single lily.[12] The terrible fear and the terrible lassitude subsided. It was early June, but it snowed, and from the hospital window he could see hundreds of roofs covered with white. Jo and Jose wrote him worried letters. He made little plans. He announced that when he left he would not go to the Plaza because the service was too lousy. But when he was released, in mid-June, he did go to the Plaza, and then later in the summer went with Lillian to Tavern Island, which was restful and peaceful. He put on a little more weight, and did a little work on a story idea for a "sequel to *The Thin Man*," which the studios rejected.

August 1, 1938

Dear Princess,

I liked your letter, especially the suggestion that you might be willing to renounce your title and your claim to the throne and join the Communists. All the Communists I know would be very glad to have you; they feel that as a rule they don't get enough royalty.

Did you get the bales of match-covers and clippings I sent you by carrier pigeon and dog-sled a week or so ago? Here are a couple more of each. The dogs and pigeons are eating now, so I'll have to send this by Indian runner, which takes longer. . . .

I've got to go out now and wind up the sun dial. Give my love to any sisters or mothers you may have.

Love and kisses,
Big-belly Hammett

Marshall Maslin ("The Browser"), in his popular book column "All of Us," remarked that he had just had a pleasing experience: he tried to remember the name of a once popular author, Michael Arlen, and failed. This once popular author "made hunks of money out of his impudent, amusing books. Then he met, the Browser thinks, a countess in the Alps and settled down somewhere and wrote no more. . . . And the Browser, in unconscious revenge, has forgotten his name.

"There are other names the Browser has great difficulty remembering. It should be easy to remember a name like Dashiell Hammett, now, shouldn't it? He wrote 'The Thin Man' and that was the last of him. The Browser is very much annoyed at him and forgets his name frequently."[13] It was now five years since Hammett had published a novel.

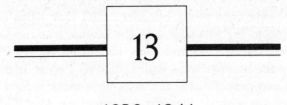

13

1939–1941

Recovered and back in New York after a lazy summer, Hammett, in the early weeks of 1939, turned to his novel. He told everyone that he was at work on it and let Random House announce it as forthcoming. Hammett and Knopf had parted company, and Bennett Cerf, the persistent president of Random House, had taken him on. Cerf had been warned about Hammett by Alfred Knopf, who had despaired of him, and Cerf would learn about Hammett in his turn; but in the meantime Hammett wrote to him disarmingly:

> Just a note of warning: the MS won't be in by February 1st.
> To answer your questions:—
> A. No, I'm not drunk.
> B. No, I'm not on my way to Hollywood.
> C. No, I haven't put it up to work on something else.
> D. Yes, I am plugging away at it.

"Just keep on plugging," replied the anxious Cerf.[1]

Hammett told some people that the new novel was going to be called "There Was a Young Man." And he told others it would be called "My Brother Felix." He may have thought that if you tell everyone you're doing something and say it often enough, and let your promise be printed in the paper, some sense of honor or urgency will get you going on it. Once, seeing an item in the newspaper about a forthcoming Hammett novel, Jo wrote to ask him about it, and he told her that it was a lie, that when people asked him what a book or story was about, he told them the first thing that popped into his head.[2]

He didn't kid himself. For a long time he kidded others, describing the fanciful plots and titles of his newest imaginary project. With his family and with Lillian he was more candid: "I know, I know that sounds like an alcoholic plan." With himself he was the most candid: he could not write.[3]

He could not write, it seemed to him, because he had nothing to write about. His life, in some sense, had ended when he left San Francisco and obscurity, and his work and family, and the social class to which he owned allegiance but was uncomfortable in. He could no longer make any sense of his life, but he also couldn't bring himself to put an end to it more directly than by drinking.

The praise, the admiration and the fame increased his sense of fraudulence while at the same time they reassured him. He became careful about clippings, would send them in wads to his daughter, "the crazy princess of Santa Monica," as they came from the clipping bureau.

Though he was doing nothing, his wealth increased. Ashamed, he erased his bank account as thoroughly as his paragraphs. He bought presents for people, gambled, handed out loans.[4] Of the million or two he was to make in his life—he never quite knew how much— he would die with nothing material left, and in debt.

For some tasks he had words: letters to Lillian—what a convenience that she was a frequent traveler and seldom nearby. And he wrote manifestos and earnest letters for political causes, and snippets of stories and helpful additions to other people's writings, and tinkered with bits of Lillian's plays. But ideas and words fled from his mind as soon as he sat down at the typewriter and were replaced by blank despair, and if he managed a paragraph or line, he suffered an almost compulsive destructive need to minimize, reduce, destroy it.

He would mention this, lightly: Did it happen to other people? "I spend most of my time rewriting most of what I had written. I bet if I worked hard enough on those few pages, I could whittle them down to a phrase."[5] And even the pages were likely to be old pages, old stories. New pages did not come. Nothing came. Though he appeared to others the very model of reckless abandon, Hammett maintained a secret and most painful discipline. He hinted of its rigors to Lillian but made light of them, and though she was sympathetic she could not really understand the extent of this self-torture, the almost unbearable physical agony, the spiritual discipline, because she was not troubled in this way.

His discipline was this: to sit down at the typewriter and put in his time. Unless he had a good excuse. He would try to contrive one: imperative good works, the service of his country or being dead drunk. But most days of life do not produce an excuse not to work, and usually he would sit down at the typewriter and wait.

He tried tricks on himself: a new typewriter, a different kind of paper, writing in longhand, beginning with letters, hoping that once the words began to come, he would slide into work on their slick. A drink of whiskey before working, no drink of whiskey until after a decent day's work, a walk, getting right out of bed in the morning, or promptly at six in the evening. No strategy sufficed.

Hammett was to do this for more than twenty more years; it was the organizing theme, the torture, the meaning to him of his life, that he should not abandon this fiction of his work.

It was true, as he wrote to Cerf, that he wasn't drinking—at least not heavily, because he was trying to watch it a little; but at night he made the regular rounds—"21" for dinner, the Stork Club or Billy Rose's after, and he had a new enthusiasm, the uptown nightclubs in Harlem—the sepian spots, people called them— where the shows were extravagant and the music wild.[6] He liked a wild show.

In the daytime, political matters continued to occupy him. In March 1939 Madrid fell to the fascists. In a fast-deteriorating world, MGM finished making *The Wizard of Oz*, and had complacently begun working on a film version of Sinclair Lewis' *It Can't Happen Here*.

Hammett associated himself with two magazines. In April appeared the first issue of *Equality*, a "monthly journal to defend democratic rights and combat anti-Semitism and racism," with an editorial council that included Hammett, Cerf, Moss Hart, Lillian, Arthur Kober, Louis Kronenberger, Dudley Nichols, Dorothy Parker and Donald Ogden Stewart. This first issue contained, among other things, an open letter to the Catholic hierarchy of America "to examine and stop the activities of those Catholics" who were spreading hate and prejudice against the American Jewish people and an article, "Anti-Semitism is Anti-Christian," by Harry Emerson Fosdick. Hammett was also on the editorial board of *Jewish Survey*, along with Albert Maltz, Rockwell Kent, Max Leiber and others.

Hammett interested himself also in the proposed New York

newspaper *PM*, and threw himself enthusiastically into its planning. *PM* was the brainchild of Ralph Ingersoll, who gathered around him a distinguished collection of idealistic journalists. It had long seemed to a lot of people that a good liberal afternoon newspaper was needed in New York—a fair, honest paper not loaded down with ads, where good writers could write and say what they wanted. Hammett took a suite in the Plaza and helped with the interviewing. According to a list compiled by the FBI agents watching him, he was inclined to hire Communists or people they believed to be Communists.[7]

After the staff was hired, a dummy issue was planned to attract a publisher. Hammett would write a review of Joyce's *Finnegans Wake*. He was among the few who thought it better than *Ulysses*— though God knew it was hard work reading it, he said. But Hammett liked writing that was hard work, he liked it to taste of Art. He thought and wondered about Joyce, whom he thought a great writer. Was he working on a new book? What would it be like? How did he live? In an apartment or a house? He would have liked a photograph of Joyce for his *PM* review, and wrote to Bennett Cerf for answers to his questions. Cerf wrote back that it had taken Joyce

seventeen years to finish FINNEGANS WAKE. I doubt that he will ever write another book. At least, when I saw him in October 1938 he had no plans for another one.

2. Joyce lives with his wife in an apartment in Paris at 7 Rue Edmond Valentin. He spends a great deal of his time at the home of his son Giorgio, who has a little house at 17 Villa Scheffer, Paris. Giorgio is married to an American girl whose name was Helen Kastor (Joosh). They have a little son whom Grandpa Joyce adores and drools over.[8]

He suggested that Mrs. Giorgio Joyce might have the photo Hammett wanted, but there is no record that Hammett wrote her.

In June he spoke at the Third American Writers Congress, a meeting sponsored by the League of American Writers, which convened in Carnegie Hall. A magazine report, which Hammett saved, noted that "the mean temperature of the Congress was well below the boiling point. Rare were such fighting words as: 'Writers have no base outside the labor movement.' Rare were such old battle cries as 'proletarian,' 'class-consciousness.' Delegates hurried through their mainly autobiographical speeches, subsided meekly on the chairman's time-signal, as polite fellow delegates rose politely to comment. From Communists, as such, came not a sheep-dog's bark."[9] The *New Republic* took a kinder view of the serious and subdued note that the worried group struck, the first occasion on which one could hear "a great many writers talking about their own problems without being boastful or snickering or self-conscious— simply talking because they had something to say . . . [which] will certainly encourage writers to think of one another not as rivals but as partners in the same undertaking and as human beings to be treated with consideration."[10] "It should . . . be noted," commented the *New Masses*, "that the expulsion of the disruptive Trotskyites—who tried to destroy the 1937 Congress by turning it into a political fight—cleared the decks this year for a truly literary conference."[11] Sobering times. The congress voted Steinbeck's *Grapes of Wrath* the best novel of the year.

Hammett spoke, mildly enough, on "Tempo in Fiction," in which he articulated principles that James Joyce might not have agreed with: "The contemporary novelist's job is to take pieces of life and arrange them on paper, and the more direct their passage from street to paper the more lifelike they should turn out."[12]

Despite temporary accord at the Writers Congress, writers and other groups with which Hammett was involved were to split into factions soon enough in the aftermath of the Hitler-Stalin non-aggression pact on August 23, 1939. Nine days before, Hammett and others, many of them members of the League of American Writers, had issued a statement denying the possibility of cooperation between Germany and Russia:

> With the aim of turning anti-fascist feeling against the Soviet Union they [right-wing forces] have encouraged the fantastic falsehood that the U.S.S.R. and the totalitarian states are basically alike. By this strategy they hope to create dissension among the progressive forces whose united strength is a first necessity for the defeat of fascism.[13]

One week after the pact was announced, Hitler invaded Poland, and England and France declared war on Germany. Two weeks after this, Russia also invaded Poland. It was a time of confusion and dismay, in particular for American Communists. One hundred of its eight hundred members left the League of American Writers formally; others drifted off because of its status as a front organization.

The choices of attitude were, roughly, to oppose the war utterly (and this was the choice of the American Communist Party, along with conservative isolationists like Charles Lindbergh); to support Russia's invasion of Poland but not Germany's invasion of Poland and pretend there was some moral or qualitative difference; or to urge, as some Communist Party members did, that despite the Party position America should support a war to stop fascism. When the American Communist Party took the first line, many left the Party, but others, including Hammett at this time, took the Party's view that America should skip this war, as the slogans put it, and concentrate on pressing for socialist reforms here at home.[14]

Some good things happened in 1939 to Hammett and Lillian. In February Hammett went down to Baltimore to attend the out-of-town opening of her new play, *The Little Foxes*, at the Ford Theater, and in mid-February it opened in New York, a great success. It would run for four hundred and ten performances. Mr. and Mrs. Henry Luce gave Lillian a fancy dinner after the opening. After a few weeks she and Hammett went to Havana and had a happy time together, and in May Lillian bought a large farm called Hardscrabble Farm, in Pleasantville, New York, a beautiful place where Hammett would spend the happiest days to come. Lillian wrote of it:

Even in those days, 1940, it was one of the last large places in that part of Westchester County. I had seen it on a Tuesday, bought it on Thursday with royalties from *The Little Foxes*, knowing and not caring that I didn't have enough money left to buy food for a week. It was called an estate, but the house was so disproportionately modest compared to the great formal nineteenth-century gardens that one was immediately interested in the family who had owned it for a hundred and twenty years but who had, according to the agent, disappeared. . . .

In the first weeks, I closed the two guesthouses, decided to forget about the boxwood and rare plants and bridle paths, and as soon as Hammett sold two short stories we painted the house, made a room for me to work in, and fixed up the barn. I wanted to use the land and would not listen to those who warned me against the caked, rock-filled soil. I hired Fred Herrmann, a young German farmer, because I had an immediate instinct that his nature was close to mine, and together, through the years, we drove ourselves to the ends of weariness by work that began at six in the morning and ended at night. Many of our plans failed, but some of them worked fine: we raised and sold poodles, very fashionable then, until we had enough profit to buy chickens; I took the money I got from the movie script of *The Little Foxes* and bought cattle and three thousand plants of asparagus we bleached white and sold at great prices. We crossbred ducks that nobody liked but me, stocked the lake with bass and pickerel, raised good pigs and made good money with them and lost that money on pheasants; made some of it back with the first giant tomatoes, the sale of young lambs and rich unpasteurized milk.[15]

Hammett and Hellman at Pleasantville, c. 1950.

Hammett's political sympathies had been animated in Montana against vigilantes and hired killers. It semed to him now, in 1939, that fascism, rampant in Europe and Poland, and, he believed, always latent in America, was becoming stronger. Supported by others who shared this fear, he promoted a "defense of the Bill of Rights," which outlined some of the worrying things that were happening. The House Un-American Activities Committee under Martin Dies, which had been investigating Hollywood, was now talking openly of suppressing dissident groups. Talk of vigilante activity against labor unions, minority radical groups, and ethnic and religious groups was increasing. Congress was passing discriminatory and repressive measures against aliens. The Communist Party was coming under particular scrutiny, and the general secretary, Earl Browder, was being prosecuted on data that the government had had for years. Communist meetings were disrupted in various cities and refused police protection. Harvard University broke a precedent of more than three hundred years and canceled a speaking engagement arranged for Browder. These activities, protofascistic and repressive, seemed to threaten widespread abridgments of the freedom of all Americans.

The "Defense of the Bill of Rights" said in part:

> We recognize particularly that serious efforts are being made to silence and suppress the Communist Party. . . . We have before us the example of many European countries, where suppression of the Communist Party was but a beginning, followed by a campaign against trade unions, cultural groups, Jews, Catholics, Masons, and ending with the destruction of all freedom. It is in our own interest, therefore, and in the interest of those rights for which America has struggled these many years that we raise our voices in solemn warning against denying to the Communists or to any other minority group the full freedom guaranteed by the Bill of Rights.[16]

Voting rights were an issue that exercised Hammett particularly, for there were states where legal challenges were presented to prevent Communist Party candidates from appearing on ballots. As chairman of a Committee on Election Rights, he organized meetings and speakers. The prosecution of Browder would continue to concern Hammett. Sentenced to two years, Browder went to prison in 1941, after court battles arising from his admission to

HUAC that he had traveled on false passports. Hammett, with others, formed a citizens' committee to free him.

FBI agents observed him signing a petition demanding the dismissal of charges against Sam Adams Darcy, the state chairman of the Communist Party in Pennsylvania, for a minor inaccuracy in his registration as a California voter in 1934. They saw Hammett obtaining a permit for a meeting to be held at the Municipal Fund Hall for the People's Forum, giving a speech entitled "The Case of the Mysterious Disappearance of the Free Ballot," and setting up a campaign office for the National Committee for People's Rights to protect minorities at the polls in November. The committee on election rights held another meeting at the Astor Hotel; Hammett was the chairman. The meeting was disrupted by a man named Hamilton who got up and said that where its own members were concerned the Communist Party protested the denial of civil liberties and election rights, but that it organized movements to deny those same liberties and rights to members of the Socialist Party. This man was hissed, and Hammett said that he had violated the spirit and purpose of the meeting, and that only antidemocratic elements would benefit by such signs of disunity.

In 1940 Hammett was happy at Hardscrabble Farm. It had been six years since he and Lillian had been to Florida, the trip being the last time they had spent any length of time away together, away from cities, away from work and other people. Now they threw themselves into the work of making Hardscrabble into a productive and, they hoped, self-supporting farm, kept chickens and puppies, cleared fields; they were helped in the enterprise by Gus Benson and his wife. And as in his boyhood, Hammett walked in the fields and the woods, fished in the pond, enjoyed his barn quarters and felt that this was his preferred life.

That spring, 1940, Josephine had no money again, and wasn't feeling well. She wondered if maybe she wasn't entitled to some of Dash's money from the VA. She wrote to the agency, but it was no use: the reply said that "A divorced wife of a veteran is not entitled to receive an apportioned share of his compensation in accordance with the law. However, your children will be entitled to receive an apportioned share of the veterans compensation up to the date that they reach eighteen years of age, or the date of their marriage, whichever is the earlier date," and she got a little money from then on for a while, which made a lot of difference to them.

. . .

Hammett liked restaurants he already knew, not new ones. He liked restaurants where people liked him. He liked the food and company at "2 1" and always had a good table. He gave a book to the proprietor with the inscription:

> For Bob Kriendler
> with best wishes—but
> this wouldn't still be
> my last book if
> I hadn't spent so
> much time in "2 1."[17]

Problems in Europe continued to trouble Hammett. He spoke at a meeting in protest against Nazi atrocities against Jews and Catholics in Germany and at a meeting of the Professionals Conference Against Nazi Persecution, of which he was president. He sent a letter to Lord Lothian, the British ambassador to the United States, protesting the treatment of seventeen hundred seventy-one Jewish refugees by Great Britain and "asking that the survivors of the refugees be permitted to remain in Palestine."[18] He was also chairman of the Exiled Writers Committee, which helped bring exiles to America and supported them while they established themselves. Some of these were Anna Seghers, Egon Rich, Paul Westhim, Ludwig Renn, Bruno Frei, Aladar Tarmas, Theo Balk; he solicited funds for them, and on behalf of others still imprisoned he signed petitions.

The first issue of *PM* appeared on June 18, 1940, a few days after the Nazis marched into Paris and a week after Italy declared war on France and Great Britain. There was an audience for a paper like *PM* and New Yorkers rushed to buy it. Hammett stayed up nights seeing the editorials through the press. But in July he walked out. Someone had circulated through other New York newspapers a list of *PM* staff who were reputedly Communists or fellow travelers, and Ralph Ingersoll, whatever his motives, had invited government scrutiny of this list: "Despite the fact that the government agencies are very busy—and we hate to bother them— we are sending a copy of this slanderous document to the FBI," Ingersoll wrote. Hammett and others had protested that this not only dignified an anonymous attack but could bring trouble upon people named on the list. When Ingersoll persisted, saying it was better to bring charges out in the open, Hammett left *PM*.[19]

In Hollywood, John Huston was making yet another *Maltese Falcon*,[20] with Humphrey Bogart, Mary Astor, Sydney Greenstreet, Peter Lorre, Elisha Cook, Jr.—a good cast—and the script following the book closely. It was a great success, but Hammett didn't see it when it was first shown.[21] *The Glass Key* was being remade, too, with Alan Ladd, Brian Donlevy, William Bendix and Veronica Lake. But it wasn't very much better than the first version had been.

It had been chic to be a Communist during the late thirties, but Hollywood liberals had begun to draw away from those, whether Communists or not, who stuck to the Party's antiwar line after the Hitler-Stalin pact. As Lester Pine, at meetings of front organizations, said, "You could always tell the Party people, because they were the four schmucks putting up the chairs and sweeping up and doing everything nobody else in Hollywood would deign to do."[22] Jews, European Jews in particular, were outraged at Russia's new association with Hitler, and with those who countenanced it.

In lieu of other political activities, Hammett began to devote more time to the League of American Writers (LAW), the front organization that had sponsored the three previous writers' conferences. He did not participate in the day-to-day running of the league, but left this to Franklin Folsom, the general secretary, who remembers that he "was not even present at many of the meetings of its governing body, but I consulted him whenever I could on matters worth bothering him about. My impression was that he trusted me and the other active League leaders and did not feel that he needed to be informed about every detail." But he donated generously. "I do remember one time when he came into the office to sign something he called my attention to how steady his hand was. He wanted me to see this, as he announced he had just been on a bender."[23]

In 1941 the League, of which Hammett now became president, took the official view of the Communist Party, which still regarded the war as a profascist imperialist effort by which "Britain and Germany hoped eventually to redivide a great deal of the earth's surface" and believed that America was interested only in getting in and getting its share. In a facetious talk to the fourth American Writers Congress June 6–8 that year at the Commodore Hotel in New York, he joked that to catch up with Hitler in suppressing civil liberties, the U.S. would have to suppress at an even faster rate than she was doing.

> But today government agents are going from door to door in certain states begging old rumors of sabotage and subversive activities from housewives.
> War-mongering is only just beginning; if it were pursued to the full we could probably double our hysteria as of today. Hardly any war industries are yet working three shifts outside of Winchell and Ralph Ingersoll. There has been no real increase in the serious pro-war content of our major publications—though God knows their fiction has increased enough. . . .

The view of the league-sponsored Writers Conference was that "AMERICA MUST BE DEFENDED NOT BY INVOLVEMENT IN THIS WAR, OR BY STEPS TOWARD DICTATORSHIP, OR BY PURSUING A COURSE OF IMPERIALIST EXPANSION, BUT BY PRESERVING PEACE AND EXPANDING DEMOCRACY ON THE ECONOMIC, POLITICAL AND CULTURAL LEVELS."

Nonetheless it came as a relief to many when later in the month, on June 22, Hitler invaded Russia, thus invalidating the Hitler-Stalin pact, and people on the two sides of the question of its morality spoke to each other once again.

In six months the Japanese would bomb Pearl Harbor, and the League of American Writers would do an abrupt about-face and

Billboard, c. 1941.

support the war, on December 10, 1941, three days after the day that was to live in infamy:

> The League of American Writers proudly supports the President and Congress in the Declaration of War on Fascist Japan. This treacherous malefactor is a part of a Fascist Axis and in collusion with Hitler has brought war to our country. America will resist aggression with a resolution and heroism equal to that of the Chinese, the British, and the Russian people. Japan's war upon us is a new phase of the world struggle between democracy and fascism. It would serve the Axis conspiracy which plotted this attack to limit our action to Japan. Our war is with the entire Fascist Axis, and not with one end of it. We therefore urge the immediate declaration of war against Germany and Italy and their satellites.[24]

In September of 1942 LAW urged Roosevelt to open a second front, and made the appeal: "The unswerving courage of the American people will be necessary, and the writers of America should resolve to put their talent and devotion at the service of their country." The Screen Writers Guild notified Roosevelt that it was at his service, and the day after Pearl Harbor LAW sent its members a message of support for Roosevelt and the war effort. Some of Hammett's friends who tried to do something for the war effort suspected they were on some government list of "premature antifascists" because they were denied the opportunity to help. Dorothy Parker, who hoped to be a war correspondent, couldn't get a passport; Ring Lardner found himself put into a safe stateside post in the signal corps. Hammett, forty-seven years old, volunteered for military service and was turned down because of his age and health.

In 1940 and 1941 Lillian had been working on a play "about nice, liberal Americans whose lives would be shaken up by Europeans," she explained, "by a world the new Fascists had won because the old values had long been dead. . . . I . . . placed it in the house of a rich, liberal family who were about to meet their anti-fascist son-in-law, a German, who had fought in Spain. . . .

"Many Europeans had moved here with the triumph of Hitler in the 1930s. Few of us asked questions about their past or present convictions because we took for granted that they had left either in fear of persecution or to make a brave protest. They were our kind of folks. It took me a long time to find out that many of them had strange histories and that their hosts, or the people who vouched for them, knew all about their past."[25]

"It was a pleasant experience, *Watch on the Rhine*. There are plays that, whatever their worth, come along at the right time, and the right time is the essence of the theatre and the cinema. From the first day of rehearsal things went well."[26] The play opened, and a special performance was given for Roosevelt; it was the first time he had appeared in public since war had been declared.

Hammett's father came to dinner and went to the opening with them. Hammett was proud of *Watch on the Rhine*. It won the New York Critics Circle Award for "a vital, eloquent and compassionate play about an American family suddenly awakening to the danger threatening its liberty," though the *Daily Worker* found it too severe upon the Nazis, who had just then signed their pact with Stalin.

Hammett believed passionately in the issue of conscience, and set about doing a screenplay that was very close to the play itself, though at the end Lillian wrote some additional dialogue. The film was praised for its patriotic anti-Nazi stance.

Jo and Mary were taking the train all the way East to visit their father. Jo was fifteen and Mary almost twenty. They packed their best clothes and were both excited and frightened. The train took four days and nights, and when they got there Hammett took them to stay with him at the Fifth Avenue hotel where he lived. It was very exciting. There were plays and shows. He took them to nightclubs too, which Mary liked and Jo found boring. She didn't know what her father saw in nightclubs, but he seemed to know a lot of people there, and laughed and talked a lot.

The best part was Hardscrabble Farm, which was more beautiful than anywhere they had ever been, with a lake and acres of lawn, and the house so charming and built, Lillian said, in part before the American Revolution. Alfalfa grew in fields, and there were birds and a magnolia tree. Hammett was happy walking around the acres and fishing and teaching them to fish and to respect and love nature. They hadn't had too much nature in their lives in L.A.

There were some bad times too. Mary and Hammett would drink and fight. Jo knew, but she couldn't talk about it with Lillian, that Mary had told Papa some of the things she did back in California. Jo knew about them—Mary would tell anyone about them and now had told Papa, and he had blacked her eyes. Jo was sorry that Papa had found out that Mary was so wild. She was afraid of Mary.

So now Hammett knew what he had pretended or hoped not to know about his child, that she had taken up his ways. "How long has your sister been like this?" he asked Jo. She was afraid to tell on Mary. But it seemed to her that Hammett had now guessed all.

Lillian remembers liking little Jo, a pleasant, docile girl, but Mary was a brat straight from hell. Obviously her mother had no control over her; Lillian felt thankful they were going back to California—things were becoming strained anyway between Hammett and her, with his drinking, the cold way he seemed sometimes, his moody silences, the visit of these daughters. Lillian was newly in analysis; her feelings were raw, irritable.

Hammett tried to enlist, but they practically laughed at him. They needed young, fit men. He would have to do what he could in other ways. In the summer of 1942 he taught an intensive course at the Writers School, 381 Fourth Avenue: six two-hour intensive sessions emphasizing writing techniques used by government propaganda agencies and in the "production of manuscripts that can aid and inspire America at war."[27]

Passing the time. He had figured out a way to photograph insects in color. Years later he wrote to Jo about how to do it. They had to be alive:

If you take a picture of a dead insect it looks—no matter how you fake it—like a dead insect. On the other hand if you try to take a live insect in its natural state you've got to use too much speed to get any sort of accuracy as far as color is concerned. So what you do is catch the critter and put it in the ice-box till it's frozen stiff. Then you take it out, put it against the background you want, and turn on your lights. To get true colors you have to use a pretty strong light, which, very soon, warms your model back to life and activity. And there's your chance! You've got a matter of seconds, maybe even a full minute, in which the insect is alive enough to look alive, but not yet frisky enough to start moving around too much. You either get your picture in that little time or you don't. If you don't he probably takes off and you chase him around the room till you catch him, and put him back in the ice-box till he's stiff enough to try the whole thing over again. It's a fine, fine way to spend your time. And then, as in the case of all color photography nowadays, if you've caught approximately true color values once out of twenty tries you're doing swell. But one bell-ringer more than makes up for any number of flops. After all, how many really good color photographs of insects has anybody seen so far?[28]

And it passed the time, the hot summer Pleasantville days, though there were farm things to do, and the turtle traps to set, and fish to catch—or drinking, walking in the forest at night or down by the pond, until morning.

Lillian wrote of this time:

> When I bought the farm, he would spend the autumn days in the woods, coming back with birds or rabbits, and then, when the shooting season was over, would spend many winter days sitting on a stool in the woods watching squirrels or beavers or deer, or ice fishing in the lake. (He was, as are most sportsmen, obsessively neat with instruments, and obsessively messy with rooms.) The interests of the day would carry into the nights when he would read *Bees: Their Vision and Language* or *German Gunmakers of the Eighteenth Century* or something on how to tie knots, or inland birds, and then leave such a book for another book on whatever he had decided to learn. It would be impossible now for me to remember all that he wanted to learn, but I remember a long year of study on the retina of the eye; how to play chess in your head; the Icelandic sagas; the history of the snapping tutle; Hegel; would a hearing aid—he bought a very good one—help in detecting bird sounds; then from Hegel, of course, to Marx and Engels straight through; the shore life of the Atlantic; and finally, and for the rest of his life, mathematics. He was more interested in mathematics than in any other subject except baseball.[29]

He was also spending more time in Harlem whorehouses. With a whore you know where you are. You can't hurt or shock her, she's not surprised at some things you wouldn't want a nice woman to know. And a whore understood that a man might have certain problems, and what to do about them. All was cheerful and unsurprising, and in the end successful, while with a respectable woman there was an element of combat, or exploitation, or sentiment, or restraint that altogether blighted or might blight what should be simple and pleasant. He liked an Oriental or a black woman. He liked whatever he liked, and seemed these days to need. Some days his body would not work at all, as if it belonged to someone else, as if his soul were imprisoned in the body of a ragman, a scarecrow, a burnt-out case. And in Harlem, in these whorehouses, they had amusing shows beforehand, and you could see amazing things.[30]

One night, as Lillian was driving into town, Hammett was plastered as usual and it all seemed too much to her. He was a disgusting drunk, pawing her and leering, and when he suggested making love, something borne of her deep exasperation, of her sense of his waste of his time, of his life, of the stupidity of all this, made her say no, she wouldn't sleep with him when he was like this. She had never said no before to any of his demands or sexual whims. Tonight, simply, no.

This surprised him, sobered him, shocked him. That was it, then.

Private Hammett reporting for duty, 1942.

N.Y. Daily News

He loved Lily, would always love her. But he decided he would never make love to her again, and he never did, and never spoke of it. But she did not know now that this would be the consequence of her refusing him.[31]

On September 17, 1942, reading that the army had relaxed its standards, he went around to the Whitehall Street Induction Center and got them to take him. He was anxious about the physical, but his X-rays showed that his TB had been arrested. They did think he was too thin. But he was most worried about the psychiatric examination: an alcoholic with a history of nervous breakdown. "You're not a nervous person, are you?" the medical officer asked trustfully. "A famous writer like you?"

"Oh, nooo," Hammett said as calmly as he could.

"You're a writer, I expect you know more about human nature than we do," the psychiatric officer said. He was a reader, he had heard of Hammett. He signed the form.

Lillian was stunned, appalled, he'd get killed, he was too frail, it was a silly stunt to escape from real-life problems. She railed as much as she dared.

"This is the happiest day of my life," Hammett said.[32]

14

1942–1943

SHIPPING OUT

He was happy to be in the army again, unhappy to be stationed once again near home doing a mild sort of service. He was in a signal corps unit at Fort Monmouth, Sea Girt, New Jersey.[1] It was not what he had wanted. He went to New York most weekends wearing a uniform, was a hit at his usual night spots. He got a kick out of getting a better table than the officers who tried to get into "21" and the other smart clubs: "Yessir, Private Hammett, sir, right this way."

Military service imposed a kind of order on his life: early to bed, early to rise, with dull and simple routine tasks during the day. Pfc. Ed Langley remembers him at another New Jersey post:

> Hammett made no friends, that I could see, a distant, largely unhappy man, I guessed, out of it, so far as the army was concerned. He marched badly, coughed a lot, and looked like a bookkeeper forced into uniform. We thought him terribly old, and when someone looked at his barracks bag they reported his serial number began with "1." Now, as you may know, a "one" serial number was a rare thing in WWII. It meant you enlisted. I had the same "one" number and I know the hazing I got for being a "went not a sent." It's an article of faith in the army to "never volunteer for anything, least of all the army." So Hammett and I were a pair of fools. I mentioned this to him and he nodded. That was all. My mates in the barracks thought he was a singular nut.
>
> I once shared a seat on a train with him, going into Manhattan for a weekend of hilarity and mirth. He never spoke, even when I congratulated him on the character of Sam Spade. He was a male Garbo.[2]

On Saturday he'd get one of the young soldiers to drive him to one of the whorehouses he liked in Harlem, where he'd spend the weekend; they'd collect him drunk and a hell of a lot poorer on Sunday night for the drive back.³ This dramatically dissolute weekend life made him a kind of hero at the base, even among those who didn't know—and most of them didn't—that he was a famous writer. They called him Sam and were amazed that he had volunteered at his great age for military service. He was liked because he was likable—pleasant, mild and frank.

The bookish found him out, of course: Sam Hammett was really Dashiell Hammett of *The Thin Man* and the terrific movie. Some of the kids on the base were not born when Hammett's first stories were published, and when his last story was published, most were too young to have read it. But he was famous nonetheless. He wrote to Lillian:

A couple of days ago I blossomed out as the camp celebrity—somebody got past that Samuel to the D.—so I have a great many dull conversations with people, and quite a few autograph requests, including one from my company commander. I had one rather nice talk with a lieutenant here, who, after bumbling uncomfortably for a long time, said what he really wanted to do was thank me for, through my books, having given him back his self-respect at a time when he had got himself in a very bad hole. I can't figure it out, but it was—as I told him—probably the nicest thing anybody could say to a writer.⁴

The bookish found him out, but the FBI, getting the news that he'd joined up, couldn't find him, for the simple reason that the army couldn't, either.

To:
Brigadier General Hayes A. Kroner
General Staff
Chief, Military Intelligence Service
War Department
10-6-42
Washington, D.C.
From: J. Edgar Hoover—Director Federal Bureau of Investigation
Subject : DASHIELL HAMMETT

This Bureau has been advised that the captioned individual, President of the League of American Writers, a Communist front

organization, enlisted in the United States Army as a private on
or around September 18, 1942. Hammett has been reported to this
Bureau as being a Communist Party sympathizer.

This information is being brought to your attention for your
appropriate consideration.

Lieut. Colonel J. Edgar Hoover
Director, Federal Bureau of Investigation   October 22, 1942
Department of Justice
Washington, D.C.

Dear Colonel Hoover:

A review of the files of the War Department does not indicate
that the person named below is a member of the military establishment or a civilian employee of the War department. Therefore, no investigation of this person is contemplated by this
Service.

John T. Bissell
Colonel, General Staff
Asst. Executive Officer, MIS

By October he'd been tapped for training as an instructor and
he thought he might take the job, for although it would mean
he'd have to stay in the U.S. for six months or more, it might
pave the way for combat duty—and if he didn't take it, he'd be
stuck as a "specialist" in public relations, which he most wanted to
avoid. "I'd like to teach for a while: it would give me the feeling
that I was actually having a hand in making an Army instead of
just drilling along preparing myself to be part of it."[5]

By December he could go through the day with his eyes shut:
up at 0530 hours, breakfast of a half grapefruit, cornflakes, two
fried eggs, a slice of toast and two cups of coffee. He'd put on a
little weight and felt well. He worked in the Army Organization
Office until coffee and doughnuts at 1030, lunch at noon (celery
soup, beef, potatoes, carrots, bread, butter, pumpkin pie and cocoa).
Cupcakes and coffee at 1530, class at 1830, and dinner with, say,
Privates Gottlieb, Stewart, Senecal and Fingatti,[6] in bed before
lights out, a good night's sleep. There were a few kindred spirits
around—Robert Boltwood was one.[7] Hammett introduced him to
the Kobers and met his wife, and gave him one of his books.
Hammett's day was not always the one organized for him by the

army: after meals he preferred rest to close-order drill, so he simply did not turn up for it.

All of this brings you up to about nine o'clock and you're a pretty tired old fellow who feels at least fifty-eight as you sit down to dash off a few lines to some sweet young thing on Eighty-second street whose life is some bed of roses, heh, kid? But you eat like a wolf and sleep like a log, so you know you're not tiring yourself out too much and you still think you'll—what with one thing and another, including chiefly the increasing bitterness of the war—be able to get past the rule that no men over forty-five can be fit for combat duty.[8]

Jose needed an operation. Hammett wired her $1,000.

By January 1943 he was still stationed in New Jersey, sending little missives to his friends and partying in New York on weekends:

In 21 early one night I met John O'Hara.
He: "Hello, Dash. Where are you stationed?"
D: "Fort Monmouth."
He: "I've got a brother down there."
D: "I didn't know you had any brothers."
He: "I've got five of them."
D: "What outfit is he in?"
He: "The Signal Corps."
D: "I know. But what company? Is he at sea unit, or the post proper, or at wood?"
He: "I don't know. He's about 28 years old."
That is the news for now.[9]

Lillian had begun on the script of a new play, *The Searching Wind*, and, as ever, was eager for Hammett's response, which was soothing and supportive:

Dear Cutie and good writer—

Last night I read the script and I kind of guess it's kind of all right. I like. Maybe you're going to have to cut the early parts a little—as who doesn't?—but you've done what you set out to do, and what's wrong with that? The desired documentary effect comes over nicely. It's nice and warm and [   ] and moving. And so are you. . . .[10]

He could become impatient. In a later letter:

> If you'd had any memory—or I'd saved such letters as you may
> have written me while you had previous work in progress—
> you'd know that your present dithers over the play are only the
> normal bellyaching of La Hellman at work. You still think you
> dashed those other plays off without a fear, a groan, or a sigh;
> but you didn't, sister: I haven't had a dry shoulder since your
> career began, and I was an amphibian long before the Army and
> Navy ever heard of combined operations.[11]

On May 18 he became a corporal and signed his letters "COR-
PORAL HAMMETT."

He had long been plagued with dental problems, and he was told
now that his teeth were infected and bad enough that he could not
go overseas even if there were no other difficulties. He suggested
that his teeth be pulled out, and over a couple of days in early May
the base dentist removed them. He wrote to Lillian: "The toothless
one has to report that he is now completely out of teeth, having
given up his jawbone. In return he has some stitches in his mouth
and a swollen jaw, none of which are much good for chewing with.
He'll probably be going around like this for three or four weeks,
gumming eggs and soft bread and looking like an English character actor."

He hadn't seen Lillian in a while, but one day he wrote her twice:

> I'm CQ at the school tonight and I'm depressed and I can't
> find anything to be depressed about and that makes me restless
> and it's no good being restless because I can't go anywhere. The
> CQ at the school on Sunday night hasn't anything to do but stay
> there and listen to the radio or read or write or lie down and
> sleep or, as in my case just now, be depressed.
> So I'm depressed. But I can't find anything to be depressed
> about. I feel all right. I can't think of anything disagreeable that's
> likely to happen to me in the near future. (I don't mean that
> nothing of the sort can happen, but I've no inkling of anything.)
> I'm not even bored: as a matter of fact I've had a pleasant evening.
> Maybe I'll listen to Winchell. . . .

That didn't help much.

> The war looks pretty good as of now, doesn't it? I guess maybe
> we picked the winning side again. Come to think of it, I've never

been on the losing side in a war yet. Suppose I'm just lucky? Or maybe the side that gets me is lucky? Write your answer in not more than twenty-five words.

There is a man in my barracks named Edward Extract, but I do not think that is what I am depressed about. What do I care what his name is? He is one of your people anyway. I wasn't depressed by Joe Purchase, was I? So what's this other guy's name to me? I tell you, it's not that.

I'll plan my tomorrow. I'll sleep until six-fifteen, then go back to my barracks and shave. Then I'll go to the PX and have grapefruit juice and fried eggs for breakfast before I show up in the tent area for my morning classes. In the afternoon—after I've gone to the infirmary to have the stitches taken out of my lower gums (he had to slice away some bone there too)—I'll take a shower before I show up for my afternoon classes. In the evening I will go out to Sea Girt to Ozzie's Bar and Grill, where they love me and will scout all New Jersey to find me soft delicacies for my dinner. I feel better now.[12]

A face without teeth is sunken and strange, like the face of death, and it is no wonder that the handsome Hammett was shocked by his face in the mirror. This was the nearest he could speak of it. By the weekend, when he met Lillian in "21" and ordered soft-boiled eggs, he seemed not to mind or care, but Lillian screamed when she saw him.

In June 1943 he was transferred, at last, for ten days to Company A, 12th Battalion, in Camp Shenango—as it happened, a kind of catch-all base for ideologues of every conviction[13]—in Transfer, Pennsylvania, and then on July 9 to Fort Lawton, in Fort Lewis, Washington, a jumping-off place for military personnel on the way to the Pacific. He felt now "in the pink and mighty glad to be stirring my brittling bones at long last. Peculiarly, those ten months in training camps now seem—for the first time—more like years."

Cooling the heels in Washington was an improvement, but it was still cooling the heels. He carefully didn't drink, wanting to appear combat-ready, and fretted when others were sent out before him. He thought Seattle dull, without flavor or chic, but the beautiful countryside made up for it. The young soldiers suddenly began to get on his nerves—not the endless horseplay but the endless capacity for it. He enjoyed the gambling—most of the men figured they were going places where they couldn't spend their money, so there was always a game.

After a few weeks he was attached to the 14th Signal Service Company, with headquarters at Fort Randall, and on July 31 left Seattle for the Aleutian Islands.

Here, in remotest Alaska, the new calm life suited him. He noticed that he was sleeping less but not missing the sleep, was stronger, and had gained weight. At the end of August he realized that he had had only one drink since the tenth of July. He lived in a Quonset with men he didn't much like; he worked at the post radio station and did book reviews, and was contented. He wrote of odds and ends to Lillian, and kept her spirits up about reviews of the film version of *Watch on the Rhine*, which were mixed,[14] or so they seemed to her, though they were generally favorable.

His sister Reba wrote that their father, now diabetic, and whose leg had been amputated, was getting an artificial leg. He rather admired this: "Jesus, those Hammetts! You can't say they give up without a struggle." He also wrote Jose, Jo and Mary and Maggie, Arthur Kober's wife, and business letters. His mail arrived only sporadically, so he had a sense of writing notes in bottles. He reported trivia: a seasick boy from Brooklyn said, "I'm as sick as a dead duck." Another one said, "Well, we're all in the same shoes."

"Life is very fine up here just now," he wrote Lillian, "and I'm sorry for who either can't go to war or who have to go off somewhere else for it. This feeling may not last long, but it's awful nice while it does."[15]

A. Notes for post-war lies.

(1) Remind we to tell you about the time I was in love with a volcano named Pavlov. That was in another part of Alaska many miles from here. Early on a clear morning—after it didn't rain until later in the day—I could go to the door of the hut I was living in and see Pavlov smoking against the sky. Its main crater was crusted over. The smoke came out in slow-spaced smallish dark puffs from a vent near one edge of the top and usually hung for awhile just atop the mountain before the wind blew it away.

I could walk from the door of my hut fifty yards to the crest of a hill and—on a very clear morning—see another volcano. It was larger than Pavlov and had a prettier name, Shishaldin. A lot of people say Shishaldin is second only to Fujiyana—or however you spell the Japanese showpiece—in perfection of form. It was a beauty all right, but—maybe because I could see Pavlov oftener, maybe because I liked the little dark smoke-puffs—Pavlov seemed cozier to me and I stayed pretty faithful to it.

At first it was dark, but, as the summer got along, snow appeared and each morning the snow would reach further down towards Pavlov's foot. Later I passed that way in a boat. It was a sunny morning and Pavlov was solid white against a luminous mirror-grey sky. Its base was hidden by mist that was a glowing white in the sun and two long thin cloud streaks cut shiny white cross-sections out of the volcano. The puffs of smoke were very dark against all this bright gray and white. It was lovely—two-dimensional and unreal as fairyland, as that part of Alaska often is—only I wouldn't be surprised if Pavlov that morning was lovelier than anything else ever was. See what I mean? I liked it.[16]

The Quonset huts were strung out down along both steep walls of a little valley and concealed by sod, tundra and mud spread over chicken wire. Electric light from a generator and a radio that might get San Francisco on shortwave or Radio Tokyo, which told each day of the sinking of the entire American navy. Bunk beds and plenty of blankets, but no pillows or sheets, a bulletin board full of Varga girls. The wind blew hard—how hard they couldn't say, their gauge registered only up to 109 mph. Three of the men in his hut ground their teeth in the night.[17]

But, as he wrote to Lillian, he loved Alaska:

I'm still having more or less a love affair with this country. Once on a boat with islands looming up half-real in fog and rain I suddenly thought how nice it would have been to have been born on one of them and to be coming home to it—and I'm a white-haired son-of-a-gun if I wasn't actually sorry for myself for a moment. . . . APO 944 had grander distant scenery than this place.

It will be nearly the middle of October when you get this letter. There will be leaves on the ground at Hardscrabble Farm, and fat and edible gray squirrels scampering through them.[18]

He hadn't seen a tree since July. He thought of Lillian burning apple wood, maybe roasting a chicken over it, and if he were home he'd be listening to the World Series and Lillian would be in her study, pretending to work so as not to have to listen to the radio, and that would be a lot more intimate than this endless letter writing.

In October, when he had been in the army for a year, he tried to sum it up.

A twenty-nine-year-old Texan sleeps in the bunk across from mine. He has four brothers in the Army and we talked about hunting and fishing a good deal. He used to call me "Corporal Sam" (it worries him that I'm not a Colonel) and once after that he said, "Here I am you're the only one I'd like to put a Mister in front of his name in the whole fucking army and I call you Sam." He was a semi-pro football player until he bunged up his back, then he coached high school teams.

The next bunk belongs to Willie, another Texan, a nice quiet boy with a foolish face. Then comes the Iowa boy we call Mouse Rip. Next to him is a radio repairman who has the only tommygun in our hut, and then a newcomer from the infantry whom I don't know very well. A blond sergeant, also attached to us from the infantry, sleeps in the corner. Across from him is another infantryman who is packing to go back to his outfit. Then comes John, a big young man with a face exactly like Eric's; then another blond, a messenger from Minnesota, a rather foolish smug lad who was trained for cryptography and considers less "intellectual" duties—especially carrying messages—beneath him. Then comes a collegiate—in the manner of a not very good college—Irish boy from somewhere around Chicago; and, next, his pal—Massachusetts cum University of North Carolina—who probably isn't as bad as he seems. He's not outgrown the hey-look-at-me-I-can-stand-on-my-hands stage yet. And, having completed the circuit, whom do we find in this corner of the hut but old futz-face Hammett!

Do you want me to tell you about Hammett? He's a strange, many-sided and incomparably tiresome character. The only thing that keeps me from going into greater detail about him is that I know—try as I might—I'd now and then make him seem for the moment less dull than he is. And I wouldn't want to do that. You may have to put up with him for many more years—it'll be thirteen in November—and I don't want you to have the comfort of too many illusions.

I puff steadily and, I hope, seductively at the thing of beauty in the shape of a meershaum pipe that you sent me, with intent to color it properly. It has now taken on a very pleasing deep bisque and I have many hopes for it. It's a nice pipe and nice things are valuable to me. I am big strong man who throw out the chest and laugh at war, "ha ha!" and stride over tundra baring upper plate to wind and rain and going "Pouf!" to such as sigh for him;

Military bunk, probably at
Fort Monmouth, N.J., 1942.

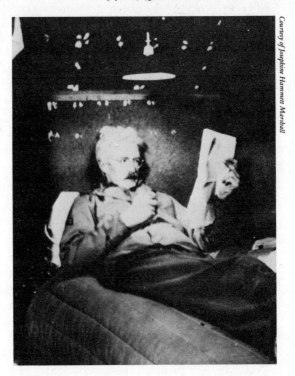

Courtesy of Josephine Hammett Marshall

only sometimes I am not like that and am unable to mistake myself
for D'Artagnan at all and then it is I-don't-know-how-to-tell-you
to have some very nice little thing to hold on to. You will understand this, not because I have made it clear, but because you will
understand it.[19]

In the previous month, September, in 1943, the mystery of Hammett's whereabouts continued to worry J. Edgar Hoover:

JOHN T. BISSELL
Colonel, General Staff
Asst. Executive Officer, MIS

Sept. 22, 1943

From: J. Edgar Hoover—Director, Federal Bureau of Investigation
Subject: DASHIELL HAMMETT
     INTERNAL SECURITY—C

With reference to the above captioned individual who is carried
on your key figure list the Bureau's files contain no report concerning him. Your attention is also called to the fact that the

Daily Worker of September 22, 1942, stated that Dashiell Hammett had enlisted in the Army as a Private and left for training camp. By letter dated October 22, 1942, the Military Intelligence Service in Washington advised the Bureau that the files of the War Department did not indicate that he was a member of the Military establishment or a civilian employee of the War Department.

It is desired that a report be submitted in this case in the near future.

Hammett didn't find it entirely easy being an elderly grouch living with a bunch of teenagers:

They sometimes do not make me love them. They sometimes get themselves onto the nerves. It is that I am in possession of whims tonight. It is also that irritation comes upon me with an easiness. In addition it is that they should cease the tapping of the foot in faulty concord with the dubious music on the radio of an inferior tone and go fuck themselves. What I mean is tonight I would not buy victory bonds.

Tell me about women. Are they still the same? (Don't just say, yes. Are they still the same as what?) I have seen four women since July, but not to speak to. The last one I spoke to was a girl in the PX at Fort Lawton, in Seattle. My conversation went like this, "Coffee and doughnuts, please." . . . Tell me about trees too.[20]

Looking at a picture of himself in *Yank*: "I look like God's older brother, the one that always stuck up for Him but never thought the Kid had enough gumption to make His mark in the world."[21]

Christmas 1943. Six months ago he had said good-bye to Lillian, a long time to be without seeing her. He guessed he must really hate fascism and such to have landed himself here like this. Now in the Aleutians he felt far away and changed. The men had turkey at noon and a few drinks in the afternoon, and Hammett made himself a cold supper of tidbits from Lillian's boxes—pâté de foie gras, caviar, anchovies and the like. He had had more exciting Christmases, but he couldn't remember any that were freer of any sort of irritation or small bothers—a nice, serene day, and, all in all, a good year, though he expected even better things of 1944. He'd see the old year out with beer and a packet of letters from home. Mary, never one for taking a job or sticking to things, now had a job in a defense plant and held it down too, and Jo was going to graduate from high school. She and Mary and Jose all wrote letters to him. Mary wrote that Jo had a new cat named Rabbit, things like that.

He had $882.66 in his pocket—it was payday—and though gambling had come to bore him after about twenty minutes, he thought he might look in on a game.[22]

To Lillian he sent a letter with detailed "Notes on the art of war."

> There's more to modern warfare than just going out to try to kill a man who's coming out to try to kill you. For instance:
> (1) Military Urination.
> To make civilian urination is a relatively simple matter. He simply walks into a readily recognized room, faces familiar white fixtures, unbuttons his fly, and gravity and either Crane or Kohler and Kohler takes care of the rest of it. But there's more to it than that in the Army.
> Here we ordinarily urinate out of doors, into oil drums that have been split lengthwise and mounted on two-foot lengths of pipe. The pipe is driven down into the ground, whence it is supposed to carry such urine as gets into it. On an average it may be estimated that sixty or more percent of urine does get into and run down through these pipes, though the percentage will vary widely with the weather, as we shall see.
> These urinals—they look like large unornamented bird baths—stand completely open to the elements—no walls, no shed, nothing—and there is usually a wind. Now it's pretty obvious that if you try to urinate facing the wind you're going to get wet. So what? Do you merely turn your back to the wind? That's not so good. A strong wind—and that's a mild way to describe the kind we have most of the time—then creates a vacuum in front of you, the process that propels sail boats forward. But this time it won't so much propel you forward as whip the urine back in a fine high spray. Face to the wind's no good, back to the wind's no good, so you try side to the wind. Now you're getting somewhere—but you've still got some delicate problems. If you turn your—say—left side directly to the wind, it's naturally going to spray your right side. You've got to shelter your front a little, inching your back diagonally into the wind, and as soon as you inch it the least bit too far you start creating that dangerous vacuum again. Then, too, the wind doesn't always blow steadily, but in gusts that upset the carefully calculated physics of the operation. You try regulating the flow of urine—on and off with

the gusts, and you learn to shift your stance to compensate for constant shifts in the wind, and you learn to work it out pretty well at times, but the results are seldom altogether happy.

Many men say it is better not to go out to urinate at all, but simply to wet your pants. Then you are at least sure of being dry above the waist. But I don't know anybody who practices this.[23]

The FBI, meantime, was still trying to figure out where Hammet was:

A Confidential Informant of the Chicago Field Division, whose identity is not known, advised on October 7, 1939 that subject was a sponsor of the "Friends of the Abraham Lincoln Brigade." It is also noted that subject's name appeared on a five-page bulletin entitled "Soviet-Nazi Non-Aggression Pact," which was issued by MAX BEDACHT, a General Secretary of the International Workers Order. This bulletin was written in the Polish language.

Special Employee [deleted] checked the records of the [deleted] and their files reflected that as of June 13, 1936 subject was married to JOSEPHINE HAMMETT and resided at the Hotel Plaza, 58th Street, New York City. His wife resided at 943 9th Street, Santa Monica, California. His business was stated to be that of a writer. It was noted that subject was rather slow in meeting his commitments. It was also noted that subject was said to be tubercular, and had been in a hospital. It was also noted that he spent some time in Hollywood writing for Metro-Goldwyn-Mayer. In addition it was noted that the Internal Revenue Department was maintaining suit against subject for delinquent taxes, but the exact year in question was not set forth.

[deleted] subject was last registered at the Hotel Plaza on March 18, 1943, and that [deleted] he registered as Corporal DASHIELL HAMMETT, Fort Monmouth, New Jersey, and it was also noted that subject received a 25% deduction by reason of his alleged service in the Armed Forces. Subject also registered at the Hotel Plaza on January 3, 1943 and received the same deduction. [deleted] stated that LILLIAN HELLMAN had lived at the Hotel Plaza at a time when subject was a permanent guest there and that she and the subject were obviously very close friends. [deleted] stated that LILLIAN HELLMAN had sent subject a pipe for Christmas, and that while it was impossible for him to secure the exact address, he knew that she had sent this pipe in care of the Postmaster, Seattle, Washington, and had

stated at the time she purchased the pipe that subject was serving with the Armed Forces in the Aleutian Islands.

In a reference letter from the Bureau dated September 22, 1943 the Bureau advised that . . . no record existed indicating that subject was a member of the Military establishment or a civilian employee of the War Department.

In view of the fact that subject is 49 years of age and is believed to be tubercular, and since no record was found in October, 1942 of his being in the Army, a further check is being made to ascertain whether he is actually in the Army.[24]

Corporal Hammett, c. 1942.

Courtesy of Lillian Hellman

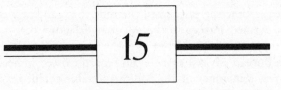

15

1944–1945

BRIEF HAPPINESS

My memory of civilian and continental US ways is certainly not too good most of the time, though things like snapshots bring it back sharply enough now and then. It may be that most of the time I don't want to think about the outer world: an Army station is, if not a fine safe place in actuality, at least as good a substitute as you're likely to find anywhere.[1]

If there were a happiest year for Hammett, it might have been this one, 1944, though it was notable for its lack of all the things he thought he loved or valued: people—Lillian, Jo, Mary, even Jose—comfort, smart society, booze and women, elegance and fame. He was only one small figure in a bleak landscape of austere beauty, involved in daily tasks of monotonous triviality, little writing tasks, and keeping odd and uncomfortable hours, but all this suited him—as being a Pinkerton man had suited him.

> Aleutians
> 19 Feb 44

Dear Lilishka,

Well, here I am again. Let's see, now, what's the burden of my song to be tonight? Shall I run on about life in the Army, the details of my work, one of the arts, folkways, the world after the war, the progress of science, current events, common friends, or the Adams family? I've got such a wealth of material at hand that to tell you the truth I don't know just where to start.

So I'll start right out by saying as usual that there is as usual not a god damned bit of news.

So what have I been doing all day? I could put it in a punctuation mark. Well, I got up. That was at four-fifteen this afternoon. Let me see what you can do with that juicy little news item. I got up at four-fifteen and got dressed. Now we're getting into the fascinating details. I had slept in my underwear, so that was already on. Remember that. So I put on a pair of lightweight woolen socks. Then I put on over them a pair of heavy woolen socks—grey with red tops as sent by you. OK, now we leave my feet for the moment, though we shall, as you'll see, come back to them later. Next I stood up and put on an OD (woolen) shirt which has a button off one pocket that I keep meaning to sew back on. It also has soot down one sleeve from fooling around with a stove, but, for god's sake are we going to spend all day talking about this lousy shirt? Over the shirt I put a field jacket. Then I put on a pair of jersey-lined pants, putting them over the tails of the shirt but not over the bottom of the field jacket. Is that clear? Good. Now I fastened the belt that was attached to the pants and buttoned the fly. That fixed me all up for—as soon as I had buttoned the field jacket: I didn't zip it because zippers sometimes stick—sitting down again. I forgot to tell you that when I am sitting down throughout this dressing I am sitting on the side of my bed. So I sit down and put on—remember, I've already got 2 pairs of socks, 1 light, 1 heavy, both wool, on my feet—a pair of rubber shoepacs, very like those I used to wear in the winter on the farm, except they are black instead of brown and come higher up on my legs, which are just as thin. Then— always a restless character—as soon as I've laced the pacs I stand up again and put on my parka, which is reversible, but you would not know it because the supposedly white side is too dirty to look much different from the tan side. I do not hear any elements pounding on the roof, so I put on my head a little knitted woolen cap of the kind we wear under helmets, but I do not put on any helmets because there is no reason to suppose that I am going to be shot at, and I do not want to give anybody any ideas. And then, thus togged out, I . . . go . . . to . . . breakfast.

Looking back on what I've written, I see that I've left out a good deal. There's that handkerchief I took from under my pillow and put in my pocket. And there's the pillow itself, a rigid little thing devised by rolling a suit of fatigue clothing up in a bath towel. And I didn't say anything about taking my cigarettes and lighter out of the inverted helmet on the floor beside the head of my bed. (The cigarettes were Chesterfields.)

I guess I'm getting to be a sloppy narrator. That comes from trying to hurry through things—trying to compress a whole volume into a paragraph. Don't tell Henry James or M. Proust. I'll rewrite the whole thing for you as soon as I can and show you that I didn't actually mean to hide anything from you. It was just carelessness.

A goodly batch of mail came today—mostly clippings from Nancy—but . . . there . . . was . . . nothing . . . from . . . a . . . slightly . . . jewish . . . she . . . playwright who forgets that Vice President Wallace said in Los Angeles no further back than February 4, "The common man means to get what he is entitled to."

And there is no commoner man than me, and I know what I am entitled to.

Think that over, sister,

Meanwhile, much love,

SDH

Month after next I'll be fifty, definitely a milestone, and between now and then I shall try to think up a gift with which you can mark the occasion—something fantastic enough to be appropriate for one who has chosen to spend his half-century anniversary as an enlisted man in the Aleutians.[2]

And to Mary he also wrote that it seemed incredible to him that in two weeks he would be fifty. He supposed it was always impossible to remember how long you've actually lived. "I've been thinking too much about my age the last couple of years. Maybe, once I'm past the half-century mark, I'll stop it. It's a foolish sort of occupation and can in the end lead only to thinking you're pretty good just because you're pretty old. And boy, oh, boy! can you go wrong on that!"[3]

To Lillian:

You may as well put away that Pinochet photograph and your memories now so that you will be in shape for my return on some distant day. You will not—unless you've developed a newer and higher order of idiocy—find me very beautiful—not even if I let my hair grow long and wavy. What the Army will be giving you back is definitely a scrawny—who shows plenty of signs of wear and tear and on whose face Father Time has left a footprint or two. The best I can say for myself is that I probably still look intelligent, though maybe a better fitting lower plate might help a little. But even at that I feel that I'm going to have to do business with little shop girls on the strength of my beautiful nature and my wealth and fame and low animal cunning. I can no longer count on dazzling the eye.[4]

Sex—and by that, up here, we seem to mean chiefly the absence of women—has been bothering me a good deal lately, and, while I'm not one who thinks he's too old to be bothered that way, still I feel that my age should have let me off more lightly. However, always the scientist, I have roughly traced it to the small streak of sunshine we had some time ago and shall certainly include the relation of sunshine to sex in my ecological studies. Some work has been done in that field, of course, but I don't think the surface has been scratched, except perhaps in the narrower field of biology, which by no means covers the whole subject. . . .[5]

There was a lot of time for reading. He declared a W. H. Auden week in the Aleutians. He reread Marx and also *Dracula* ("fine and scary—though the garlic always brought in a touch of comedy for me. . . . it's pretty difficult to make horror last throughout a whole book, which is why most good shock stuff has been either short story or novelette length)." He rather liked Dali's *Hidden Faces*, despite "a great deal of perversion and very little sex. But I guess most perversion is kind of like that. If you've got more in your mind than you've got in your glands I dare say you have to think up tricks."[6]

Sometimes he read things about himself: "I do not like your friend André Gide's comment on *Red Harvest* as quoted by *Time* and I wish the old fairy would keep his lecherous tongue to himself and his ilk."[7] And classics: "Today, wearing gloves, I picked up *Wuthering Heights*, which—remember me? I never could get into, and guess what? That's right . . . I'm having a good time reading it. You were right and I was wrong."

The war in the Aleutian theater was effectively over. The Japanese had withdrawn, and the danger that these islands would become, as the Japanese had hoped, a bridge to the mainland was now remote. The large Aleutian force, some fifty thousand men, was therefore apt to feel useless and out of touch. Morale was a considerable problem, and to improve the situation, Hammett was designated by the commanding officer, Brigadier General Harry F. Thompson, to start a newspaper that would inform, entertain and reflect the views of the lonely Aleutian troops. It was a task that appealed enormously to Hammett. It seemed to him that the news magazines and stateside newspapers, which they got only late, were themselves hopelessly late in reporting war developments, and, moreover, were so unrealistic as to represent a "college graduate dream world." Hammett wanted to tell the GI "what's cooking— why we got into this war and what we stand to get out of it, good or bad; how the war is progressing, and what people at home and any place abroad think of it; what's going on in the U.S. and else- where, what people think and do; what plans are being conducted at home and abroad for post-war life, and what people think of that: in short, we want to produce a soldier who, up here, knows more, not less, than he ever knew about his world in civilian life down there." He would have liked it that several of the little group he gathered went on in the postwar world to careers de- voted to these same ends.[8]

The paper was called the *Adakian*. He showed his commitment to it not by making speeches but by setting an example. They worked far into the night, producing the first issues on a sort of ditto machine. They also planned radio broadcasts, films, lectures, bulletin boards and weekly classes. He knew there was plenty wrong with the *Adakian* and supposed a year from then things would be still wrong with it, but he was having as much and maybe more fun than he had had with *PM*.

The first edition of the *Adakian* emerged not without difficulty on Wednesday, January 19, 1944, as a concise and agreeable little publication. Policy disputes with generals and intelligence people about what could and could not be published resulted sometimes in revelations and sometimes in suppressions. Hammett was philo- sophical: "Editing an Army newspaper in such a theater as this is often like walking an invisible tightrope between two moving towers while juggling hot stove-lids and trying to eat a sandwich."

For the first issue the staff consisted of Corporals Bernard Anastasia, Bill Glackin, Dashiell Hammett, Dick Jack, Bernard Kalb, Al Loeffler, and Hal Sykes and staff of the WXLB news- room; later additions were Sergeant John Miner, Private Bryant Stoudt and Corporal Claude Steel. Two black staff members—Don Miller, the artist, and Alva Morris—later joined, representing the first integration of troops on the island, which was evidently Hammett's innovation, one that was admired by the idealistic young staff members.

The boys in his group were in awe of him and liked him. They admired his self-containment and his trenchant ways of settling discussions: "Not having a woman will not make your teeth fall out. Now shut up and go to sleep." He'd also lend them money, advise them, tolerate them. They called him Pop, which he didn't exactly relish and didn't exactly mind. He didn't feel like Pop but looked, he knew, like Pop.

Sometimes he would turn on them, demand that they turn down their atrocious radios playing too-loud music he didn't like and to which they tapped their feet out of time. Booze was $45—the sailors smuggled it in; Hammett was the only one who could have afforded it, but he didn't seem to care about booze now.

One of the men later recalled:

> He was a super guy. He used to give two lectures a week on China. I think it was just super. It was like going to school. He had a lot of knowledge and was a wonderful man. He ran a newspaper called the Adakian. We were on the island of Adak in the Aleutians, of course, and he had this marvelous newspaper and he handled all the editorials. . . . I remember that he would favor the progress of the Russian forces, our allies, and rarely ever mentioned anything about the American forces. And, as I recall, the general of the Alaskan Command came down to see him about that. The general asked him why he didn't write of the progress of the American forces. Dashiell said, "Well, sir, this paper has a policy not to publish any ads."[9]

It amazed them that he was famous, since he was not off somewhere being famous and glamorous but was right there, among them, lying—he spent a lot of time being horizontal—in his sleeping sack reading, or walking through the wind and mud, seeming happy. From the things he did you could infer the things he cared about: giving the colored fellows jobs in the white unit, making the little newspaper the best source of reliable information available to them, and funny too. Rumor expanded the mystery and interest of his life: he got more cables, people said, than the general, and letters in every mail from famous people, practically the roster of *Who's Who in America*, stars and producers, and the famous playwright whose scripts he could be seen reading and criticizing when she sent them for his okay, and boxes of caviar arrived for him, and other strange stuff you wouldn't want to eat, and clothes from Abercrombie and Fitch. Rumors maintained that he was often offered commissions and refused them. These rumors had reached the mainland, too, and Hammett heard from a military outfitter in New York from whom he had ordered some gadget: "Dear Mr. Hammett— Glad to know where you are—you certainly sold out too low—when surely you could have made major, *at least.* We know guys who couldn't write within miles of your stuff, who sold the Army a bill for Major & *Lt. Col.* Write us if you need anything."

> I dreamed the other night I was in Abercrombie & Fitch. I had ordered three suits of tweeds and was trying on shoes when I woke up probably saving myself a lot of money, since the last pair I bought cost me forty dollars and I hope you won't let any of the puppies play with them.

People took seriously the injunctions to write to lonely GI's, and Hammett got letters from people he hadn't heard from in years—his brother, Dick, for example, or his old friend Nell Martin, who gave him "a great deal of very detailed information on the latest happenings to a great many people whom I no longer remember at all." Reading her letter, he said, was practically like having aphasia. He relayed tidbits of these letters back to Lillian. "My own old man, dissatisfied with the first artificial leg he got in Baltimore—it probably wasn't youthful enough in contour for him—has sent it back & is getting another. Maybe it didn't fit his dancing pumps."[10]

Lois Jacoby, Hammett and Lillian's friend, had decided to write a play. "Since I have been around here and seen the jerks who do it, I think I must be a sucker not even to try," she wrote Hammett, who passed the news to Lillian. Leland Hayward was back in New York. Bennett Cerf sent books, the Whitfields wrote, and, of course, so did Jo and Mary and Jose, and Hammett's sister, Reba, and Lillian's nice young secretary, Nancy Bragdon, and the theater people—Shumlin, the Kobers, especially Maggie Kober. Hammett spent a chunk of each day writing letters or reading the things that other writers and the many would-be writers around there brought to him for advice. His help, when he wanted to give it, was generous. He sent Sam Hakam's play to Herman Shumlin, with his opinion that though naïve it had something. He met a young writer, Jean Potter, who was in Alaska to write a book called *The Flying North* about the pioneering of Alaskan aviation and spent many hours with her, polishing the manuscript.[11] He tried to get the cartoons from the *Adakian* put together and published as a real book.

FEDERAL BUREAU OF INVESTIGATION

Synopsis of facts: subject on active duty with U.S. Army at Seattle, APO #980.

REFERENCE: Bureau File #100-14499,
Report of SA [deleted] New York City, dated 3/16/44

DETAILS: The title of instant case is being marked changed to reflect the additional names of Subject as ascertained from Confidential Informant T-1. It is noted that Subject's name on the Army records is reflected as SAMUEL DASHIER HAMMETT and it is further reflected in said records the additional name SAMUEL DASHIEL HAMMETT.

AT ANCHORAGE, ALASKA

On March 27, 1944, Confidential Informant T-1 advised that Subject is presently assigned to a Detachment, 14th Signal Service, located at Seattle, APO 980 and that the records of his office reflect Subject's name in the Service as Corporal SAMUEL DASHIER HAMMETT, Army Serial number 3118358.

Informant advised from the records that Subject was apparently inducted at Camp Upton, New York and from there was assigned to a Signal Corps School at Fort Monmouth, New Jersey, after which he was again transferred to Company G, First Signal Training Battalion. He was then transferred to the Shenango Personnel Replacement Depot, Transfer, Pennsylvania. In connection with this transfer informant stated that the Shenango Personnel Replacement Depot is one maintained for the potentially subversive. He was unable to furnish any information as to the reason for Subject's transfer thereto nor was he able to explain Subject's release therefrom, stating that said information was not available to him locally.

Thereafter Subject was transferred to Fort Lawton on July 10, 1943, to Seattle APO 944, July 31, 1943, and since September 8, 1943 has been on duty at Seattle, APO 980 as a Corporal in the 14th Signal Service Detachment.

The informant further advised that at the present time a casual surveillance is being maintained on Subject and that any information derived therefrom will be furnished to the Anchorage Office.

His records, however, fail to reflect a physical description of Subject.

Pursuant to the request Confidential Informant T-1 is being

furnished with two copies of the report of Special Agent [deleted]
dated at New York City March 16, 1944.

REFERRED UPON COMPLETION
TO OFFICE OF ORIGIN

Mary fell in love and didn't know much about it, so she wrote
to Papa: How do you know when you're in love? How much
love—in the romantic sense—is needed to make a marriage? How
much can one depend upon mutual respect, interest and understanding to carry the load? "How much difference in age is wise?"[12]

He replied as best he could, and wrote to Jo on her eighteenth
birthday:

So now you're eighteen and I'm all out of child daughters. My
family is cluttered up with grown women. There's nobody who
has to say "Sir," to me anymore and there are no more noses to
wipe. I feel old and caught-up with. But there's no use sulking
about it, I guess, and I might as well try to make the best of it and
welcome you into the ranks of the adult. I'm sure you'll like our
little club.

As you've probably found out by now, this world of grown-
ups into which you have been admitted is a very, very superior
world indeed, inhabited only by people of sound, mature and
mellow mentality—all of which they can of course prove simply
by showing the dates on their birth certificates.

But what you may not yet have noticed is that all these people
stand on their own feet as independently as all get-out, being
beholden to their fellows only for food, shelter, clothing, safety,
happiness, love, life and picture post cards.

Another thing you'll discover is that one of the chief differ-
ences—some cynics say it's the only difference—between a child
and an adult is a child is under some sort of obligation to grow,
while an adult doesn't have to if he doesn't want to. Isn't he
already grown up? What do you want 'im to do? Try to make
himself into God or something?

You'll *love* our little club.[13]

Lillian managed his finances; they were locked in a struggle
over his determination to spend money and hers to lay some by
for him. Knopf sent royalties for 1943 for $2,319.59, which re-
minded him that he needed to see to his income tax: "My very
vague notion was that soldiers overseas can postpone everything
until some four months after they get back home. That, and the
twenty per cent pay raise, were practically the only things I left

the states for." His offhandedness about income tax was to have serious consequences.[14]

Raoul Whitfield had been in the hospital and was broke, so Hammett sent him $500. To Lillian: "You are not to sulk about that, and you are not to mislead the bank with hints that my check may be a forgery. I know this is asking a lot of you, but you must be brave and kind and—mind your own business."[15]

But she was entrusted with errands:[16] a dozen wool-and-cotton-blend white or gray socks (size 11½), magazine subscriptions, the bulletin of the Museum of Natural History, a clipping service, Dunhill tobacco (his prescription was #A10432), a hood from Abercrombie's to thwart the elements, rum cakes, maple sugar, chocolates, grapefruit peel.

Lillian was writing *The Searching Wind* and had to seek his advice, which she always depended upon, by mail:

> Aleutians
> 10 Mar 44

Dearest Lily,

You're practically breaking my heart with your letters about the play. I think we're going to have to make a rule that you're not to tackle any work when I'm not around to spur, quiet, goad, pacify and tease you, according to what's needed at the moment. It is obvious that you're not capable of handling yourself.

I am sorry, though, baby, and hope that now—since the die seems finally cast—you'll at least go fatalistic on the whole thing. And I will write you in great detail—if I can trick myself into thinking in terms of the theater from way up here—as soon as I've read the script. And I hope it comes soon. Meanwhile, what the hell—you did your best and you'll have to let it go at that no matter what you'd like to do. . . . Pessimism is the opium of the middle-class intellectual and you are to stop it.[17]

The staff of the *Adakian* made up a special Hammett birthday number (Vol. I, No. 50) and printed one copy, just for him:

HAMMETT HITS HALF CENTURY
Half-Century Claims Foul

Somewhere in the Aleutians, May 27 (AP)—T/5 Dashiell Hammett is 50 today.

Courtesy of Lillian Hellman

Hammett with members of the *Adakian* staff.

The author of "Blood Money" and former war correspondent for Godey's Lady's Book observed the occasion with a quiet scream and a light repast with his Aleutian haunt. . . .

The issue contained news reports:

Mountbatten Resigns. Kandy, Ceylong, May 27 (AP)—Admiral Lord Louis Mountbatten resigned today as a protest against the unsportsmanlike criticism of Dashiell Hammett, Aleutian editor.

When asked for comment, Hammett laughed heartily.

And movie reviews, here written by Hal Sykes:

Today, THE THIN MAN; a good thing the theater is aired daily, spindly's a word for this one. The main stink is the script by Dashiell Hammett and the liquid-dated characters effulging from his non-compassed mentis. Whoever heard of sleuths substituting scotch for the Holmes' needle, and how could Wm. Powell and Myrna Loy do anything but look guilty in this mattent hamstringing: This Thin Man has a bad case of rickets.

Today: THE MALTESE FALCON; Something not-kosher about this bird. Ample proof that Hackheel Spam-mitt will get nowhere as a writer, and fast. Humphrey Gocart perambulates stoically thru the writer's wheeze-whim-sickly dialogue but the ivory crapper aura of the plot funks up the fowl foully. D. H. should get his own bird.

Coming: THIN MAN RETURNS, ANOTHER THIN MAN, THINNER MAN, THINNEST MAN—four feature exhibit of Hasheesh Dammit features proving that merdre will out, sometimes as dysentery.

Today: THE GLASS KEY; Don't be guided by Gide for Hammett's obviously using a ghost-writer, Colodny or Sol Chain, and it's an improvement.

Tomorrow: RED HARVEST; Daschshund Harcroquett's preference for red runs pink. We'll take Random, anyway.

Someone invented "From DH's Prospectus—"

I am against people who push other people around and it's quieter with a knife. I am against Freud and Deceit and Abbott and Costello and the Articles of War and $50,000 offers. I am for people who are kind and courageous and honest and willing to bet on the second front. I do not believe that all mankind's problems are being solved but what do you expect in 50 years? I am in dead earnest about this. Dead. I am an American and I prefer democracy to any other form of government including Hammett-ism. Shut up.

Major Henry W. Hall, the intelligence officer, got Hammett and another soldier, Robert Colodny, together to write a little booklet *The Battle of the Aleutians*, with pictures by Sergeant Harry Fletcher, captions by Colodny, text by Hammett, for which they were commended:

29 July 1944

SUBJECT: Commendation.

TO: Commanding General, U.S. Troops, APO 980, U.S. Army.

1. I have noted with pleasure the high standard of workmanship in the publication "The Battle of the Aleutians" which was written and compiled by the following members of Post Head-

quarters and Headquarters Company, U.S. Troops, APO 980, U.S. Army:

>Major Henry W. Hall, o-247318
>T/4 Harry C. Fletcher, 39014124
>T/5 Robert G. Colodny, 39168898
>T/5 Samuel D. Hammett, 3118358

2. This publication is an excellent historical record of the United States Armed Forces in the North Pacific. It has been selected by the War Department for distribution to United States Army Forces in all theaters and is a source of pride to all who have served and are serving so faithfully in barren, uninhabited and isolated locations of this Department.

3. The efficient manner in which this booklet is compiled reflects credit upon these men and this Command.

>/s/ Delos C. Emmons
>/t/ DELOS C. Emmons
>Lieutenant General, U.S. Army
>Commanding

HEADQUARTERS U.S. TROOPS, APO 980, c/o PM, Seattle Wash., 11 August 1944.

TO: Tec Five Samuel D. Hammett, 3118358, Post Headquarters Company, D.E.M.L., this station.

1. It is with great pleasure that I pass on to you the above commendation from Lieutenant General Emmons, Commanding General, Alaskan Department.

2. Publishing of the booklet "Battle of The Aleutians" was accomplished only by considerable effort in gathering and compiling the necessary data. This booklet has been highly commended by all who have had the privilege of reading it and you may be justly proud of your work on this concise and accurate record of the Aleutian Campaign.

3. A copy of this correspondence will be attached to your records.

>/s/ Harry F. Thompson
>Brigadier General, U.S. Army
>Commanding

In August 1944, with the *Adakian* running smoothly, Hammett was transferred to Fort Richardson, on the Alaskan mainland about six miles from Anchorage, a change that at first seemed welcome.

His new assignment was with an orientation unit that would send him, with three other enlisted men, up and down the Aleutian chain giving speeches to the troops, who, isolated in a hostile climate and isolated from the war, had a serious morale problem. Hammett and his companions enlightened and enlivened. One of the others was Lew Valentine, who had been "Dr. I.Q." on a popular radio quiz program.

Hammett wrote to Lillian:

I'm now near a town, a very small one, but to me, after a year and more out on the tip of the world, it is a completely satisfactory metropolis. Saloons, stores, restaurants, taxis, cement sidewalks—boy, oh, boy!
smallness is really surprising, but, still smaller even is a grade of
   I find that civilians come in three sizes. The largest are men. Then there is what is called the opposite sex and they are smaller. That is about the only thing one forgets about women, and their civilian known as the child. I'd forgotten them completely and was quite shocked at having forgotten them.
   Things one knew one missed—newspapers, saloons, restaurants, running water and so on—are no longer novelties after a few minutes. On the other hand, things you haven't thought about, like cement sidewalks, continue to be amazing. For the first time in more than a year you can actually walk without having to look down at your footing. It's a whole new way of walking—with your face in the air. Another still astonishing thing is being in buildings that don't need artificial illumination in the day time.[18]

A story you may like: the last time I was in town I was standing in a bar when a soldier came in with a native girl. Both were tight, but she could hardly walk. He half-carried her over to a booth and they had three quick drinks. When they got up to go she couldn't make it at all and toppled over backwards, sprawling out face upward on the floor. He turned around and with an air of utter surprise asked, "What the hell's the matter with you?"
   Another, which I don't think I've told you. A man I know down on the island was riding in a jeep with a friend who really deeply hates being in the Army and everything connected with it. It began to rain and the man I know noticed that the Army hater hadn't pulled his feet in where they wouldn't get wet—it was pouring by now. Then the Army hater saw my friend was looking curiously at him and he smiled delightedly at my friend and, looking at his feet again, said in a tone of complete satisfaction, "Look at it raining on their shoes!"[19]

The boys back on Adak heard about Sam in the city: "a procession of bars and liquor stores . . . Smashed, crocked, jugged, loud, boisterous, talking nonsense, then eloquence, then just four-letter words. The gamut, including weeping."[20]

"I'm a little worn out" he wrote a friend, "from celebrating the holidays. . . . The holidays were nice, if a bit hectic, but I'm just as well pleased to see them past. I was never too nuts about official feast days. I like ruts."[21]

January 1, 1945. Hammett was bored and hung over in Fort Richardson, near Anchorage, in Alaska. He wished something would happen, and hoped that a rumor he had heard was true that he might be sent back to Adak again to the routine of running his newspaper. He welcomed the prospect of work. He had been leading a completely nonmilitary life for three months—three months of giving orientation lectures to enlisted men and of hard drinking. He had nothing against such a life for people who weren't in the army, but for an army man like him, it offended his notions of orderliness and made him feel insecure. "You know what the rules are, but you can never be sure how far you can go, when you don't have to obey them very strictly, without jamming up."

He foresaw uneasily that if he stayed on this course he would jam up, and he decided to go on the wagon. It always surprised him to find that he could have a good time staying sober, and it was nice to wake up hungry every morning and feel good all day. He resolved to stay nonalcoholic for a long time. But he didn't.

He was too bored. He did a lot of reading, wrote letters, wrote Lillian even though she wouldn't get his letters in Russia or wherever she was by now, on a lengthy trip that would actually bring her to Alaska. It was lonesome not to write, and it was his habit to write letters. He liked ruts but not this one, "fooling around this damned Headquarters with a lot of jokers who don't know what in the name of God they're doing, only they vaguely hope it'll somehow please the General."[22] He hated Headquarters, but in fact Headquarters had put in a request that he be permanently stationed there. It figured.

He complained to Lillian:

When they ask me, "But what did you do in the second World War, Granddaddy?" I shall hem and haw and reply, "Well, now you take the last Saturday in April 1945 for instance. I got up in time for breakfast and then after making my bed and sweeping round it and tidying up with special care because Saturday is inspection day I went down to the latrine where it was my turn to be latrine orderly—or one of a couple of orderlies—and we washed bowls and scrubbed floors and such still with special care because it was inspection day, and so by the time I got to the office there wasn't time to do much but cut 1000 words out of an article somebody else had written before it was time for me to take off for my company again for chow, which is about a ten or twelve-minute walk. Well, then, bub, after I came back from eating there were a lot of British Information pamphlets on what the limeys had done in Burma and we figured it was only worth while to distribute 100 of them, so I spent all afternoon burning the rest of them because there were a hell of a lot of them and that thick coated paper burns slowly in bulk." That's what I'll answer . . . and let history sit in judgment if it's got nothing else to do.[23]

By the end of January 1945 he was confined to the base for coming in late on too many passes, and this made him feel quite pleasantly small-boyishly wicked. He had been spending a lot of time in Anchorage, in the fleshpots, he said.

Then, miraculously, he was sent back to Adak, and it was like old times, staying up all night to get the paper out, then hanging around the mess hall in the dawn waiting for it to open before going back to the hut to bed and his desk, with not a pin-up over it but Zuloaga's "The Actress Consuelo" and Rembrandt's "Young Girl at an Open Half-Door," and doughnuts and the barrage of letters and lots of time for reading. He heard Lillian on the radio "talking just like life and sounding fine and stirring and better than music to my old ears." The boys in the local radio station, thinking he might have missed it, recorded her talk for him in case he wanted to hear it over and over.[24]

In March he noted a "small dark distant political cloud" on his military horizon, which might fade or loom large but was very interesting indeed: he and some others had been denounced in the right-wing Chicago *Tribune* as Communist propagandists in the army, implying that Hammett was scouting Alaska for the Russians. Anti-Communists demanded investigations. Hammett followed developments rather anxiously in the newspapers, but meantime he wasn't in the guardhouse and nobody took away his dog tags.[25]

He had a lot of time for reading, and much of it was unabashedly left. Of Glenway Wescott's *Apartment in Athens* he said it was "an adequate enough description of how his grandmother in Minnesota felt when she had to take in boarders"; of Richard Wright's *Notes of a Native Son* that Wright was "a blackface Cliff Odets who never had any roller skates either"; and of Howard Fast's *Freedom Road* that it was "pretty much like his other works with the exception of *The Last Frontier*—pretty much on the right side, but oversimplified to death." He also read *The Red Cock Crows* and Selsam's *Socialists and Ethics*.[26] He had a subscription to the *New Masses* and Cockburn's *The Week* (airmailed from London). In a letter to Lillian:

> Aleutians
> 25 Feb 45
>
> . . . I also read somebody's STORY OF A SECRET STATE, a foolish and empty attempt to make believe the Polish Government in Exile had something to do with a legitimate underground movement in Poland. An amazing book in that nobody even faintly resembling a worker has anything to do—except perhaps by accident—with the resistance movement. I tell you, sister, the gentry can be trusted to save our world. Now, for a change of pace and something to enjoy, I'm reading DONOVAN'S BRAIN, a pulp horror tale.

His happiness at being back on Adak, where, he had to admit, the paper now needed him like a hole in the head, was interrupted abruptly in April by a transfer back to Fort Richardson and Headquarters, which had wanted to keep him all along. Immediately he was restive and unhappy again. "There is a good deal to be said for and against life. . . . it is comfortable living in a barracks with a built-in latrine, but looking out for haircuts and shoeshines and neat bed-making and wearing neckties and sweeping and mopping floors and washing windows and showing up for classes are nuisances after a couple of years of doing nothing of the sort." His work was interesting enough—a weekly roundtable for enlisted men on the local radio station, editing a magazine for Information-Education personnel, and writing another pamphlet about Alaska. These seemed pleasant and respectable occupations, "but keeping-office-hours-obeying-tiny-regulations sits uneasily on my free Aleutian soul. When I don't show up for a day or two—or even for a fraction of a day—as sometimes happens," he wrote to Bill Glackin back on Adak, "folks are very shocked and I am talked to firmly and I'm sure—unless I reform—to find myself one of these days standing in a corner with a tapering paper cap on."[27]

Trivial office work seemed mighty silly for a man of his age to be doing, but he guessed the same thing could be said about some of the things he did by choice on his off-duty hours. He found himself embroiled in Anchorage high life, such as it was, and in drinking again. Joe Louis came through, and Hammett liked him.

Thoughts of the outside world began again to impinge. Rumors and counter-rumors of surrenders and nonsurrenders made the return to the peaceful world imminent, and with it the prospect of getting out of the army. "I'd kind of like to see the European end wound up," he wrote Lillian, "so I'll know whether it really will tempt me to get out of the Army, something I haven't thought about hitherto but which I've been thinking about the last couple of days . . . probably only because I'm bored pissless just now with what I'm doing . . . or, perhaps, with the way I'm having to do it.

"The life of a fighting man, my darling, is not all blood and skirmishes."[28]

In July a U.S. congressional subcommittee (with testimony by H. Ralph Barton) learned for sure that certain commissioned officers in the U.S. army had Communist connections and that Sergeant Samuel D. Hammett, editor of a camp newspaper—what a spot for propaganda—was a well-known Commie. How had this happened?

Christian Science Monitor, Monday July 23, 1945:

LEFTIST EDITING ARMY PAPER
By Howard Rushmore

Sgt. Dashiell Hammett, now editor of an official Army paper, The Adakian, in Alaska, four years ago sponsored a Communist peace meeting which defied the American government to send soldiers abroad.

This was learned today from a documented report of a Congressional subcommittee in Washington which rebuked the War Department for permitting 16 well-known Communists and fellow-travelers to serve as officers and non-coms in the Army overseas.

All of the 16 Reds, the report charged, have a long list of affiliations with Communist "front" groups, many of which in past years have called for destruction of the American way of life.

From Alaska, Hammett could view political events with a certain dispassionate objectivity. Roosevelt's death, it seemed to him, occasioned the panicked mourning of his friends, to judge by their letters, "as if their sorrow were based on the fact that without him in the driver's seat they might be driven by fear into having to *do* something themselves."[29] His own opinion about Truman was cautiously optimistic: "My elderly statesman advice to you on the new President and international, as well as domestic, affairs, is to wait and see before you start shivering. He's not likely to become a great man, but, unless there is a lot I don't know about him (that's a hell of an unless: there are millions of things I don't know about him) he could turn out to be an able one."[30]

The world also let it be known that it expected a new novel from him. Lillian wrote him hopefully. Publishers queried. Hammett parried—and drank. He claimed that his novel had been blighted by his transfer to Fort Richardson: "You don't have to worry too much about the titles: it's not very likely that I'll have time to do anything on the novel in the immediate future. I'm not too disappointed, since I had from the beginning thought of it in terms of *if* I stayed on the island." This made a good excuse for a while. "There isn't any news of the novel for reasons already conveyed to you. If I don't get some part of my way on how I think this job ought to be done and decide to sulk in my tent I may turn to the novel again. Otherwise it's likely to rest in the egg for a while. (I've no immediate intention of sulking; it ain't that hopeless.)"[31]

Yank printed a story about this expected new novel. He wrote to Jo: "They didn't misquote me about the new novel, but it is a lie just the same."[32]

His old confusions began surely to surface as he thought of life as a civilian again, as a writer.

I slept till noon, then breakfasted on a shot of bourbon—how do you pronounce that?—and roast chicken—pronounced chicken—and came over to the office. . . . Last night I did Anchorage mildly, this evening I shall probably spend on the Post, unless, of course, some 1-volt temptation should ambush me. . . .

Yesterday, for an hour or two, I had a wrestling-match with the question of whether I should get out of the Army when they start whittling it down after the European War is over. It wound up by my deciding that even with 2,000,000 fewer men in it the Army will still represent the heart and guts of American manhood or something and I belong with it. I'm not sure to what extent my decision was influenced by personal desires, but, anyhow, there it is. And one thing I am sure of is that if I convinced myself I ought to get out and did so I could look forward to blackish periods of dissatisfaction with myself now and then.[33]

This accurate prediction did not foresee, however, how black and dissatisfied the next period would be, perhaps the worst of his life.

Meantime he wrote to his friend and favorite colleague back on Adak, Bill Glackin, that

things have at last worked out OK for me here, at least for the time being. A couple of weeks ago we had a sort of blowup and I said the hell with it, I'm too old for this kind of foolishness and I'm going home. So they said close the door and sit down and have a cigarette and what's really the matter. So I told them and they said, well all right, let's try it your way and see how it works out and I said let me think it over this afternoon and went back and asked my unit personnel officer if the age thing was always good or did I have to make up my mind right away and he said no as far as he knew it could just lie there waiting for my signature and so I came back to the office and said I'd give it a try and to find out if they'd meant what they said about my not having to keep office hours and stuff I took off for Anchorage that night—Monday—phoned in Wednesday to say I'd be in the next day, but actually didn't get back to the Post till Friday, and nobody even frowned at me, so I guess maybe they did mean what they'd said. But to make sure I vanished into town for a couple of days the following week, and again nobody frowned or asked where I'd been or anything, so I guess again they're on the level, so I've stayed on the Post for a week now like a good boy without a drink or anything getting some work out to keep my end of the bargain. (This, of course, isn't to be bruited around too much, though, come to think of it, a lot of folks know about it up here.) Now I'm in course of finding out if they meant the rest of what they said: that we could try to get out an I-E program that would be of some use to the enlisted man and not merely impress the high command. At best I don't expect things to work out too completely god-damned well—this is still the Alaskan Department—but it's beginning to look as if it's going to be fun and worth trying.[34]

The young officers attached to the Information and Education unit at Fort Richardson had been jittery when they heard that Hammett was to join them, this famous man about whom the terrifying tales had reached them, of an eccentric and iconoclastic soldier who did as he pleased, and did not return salutes unless he felt like it, and skipped drill and was said to have a gypsy radio station out on the tundra broadcasting disrespect for officers.[35] The young officer in charge could envision the crumbling discipline, vanished rapport of his unit, himself losing control, disasters. They said Hammett might not even get up from his bunk when an officer came to talk to him if he didn't feel like it.[36] Hammet was reported to have said to a chaplain who complained about their taking the name of God in vain that God was lucky to have got his name in the *Adakian* newspaper at all.

So when Hammett turned up, in complete uniform, with a correct salute, the officers of his new unit were relieved; the Aleutians were a rumor factory, and the exaggerations were often as vast as the terrain; this Hammett was perfectly nice and settled into his work, writing for the biweekly paper, the *Army of the North*. Of course his articles were better than anyone else's; that contributed to little rumblings of jealousy, but otherwise Hammett was a great success, and turned in his articles meticulously on time. No one ever changed them, naturally.

Sometimes they would see not Hammett himself but just the manuscript, which appeared, as if it had been done in the night by magic. Sometimes they saw Hammett at a baseball game, and Hammett would sometimes compliment the players. One night some members of the unit came upon Hammett in a bar and there saw Hammett, by himself and so plastered he couldn't talk or stand, hands shaking, speech unintelligible. Suddenly they understood Hammett's odd work habits, and why he never seemed to come around in the daytime to the office where he was supposed to be working.

So later when it was time to get higher ratings for the good job they'd all been doing, and one person could become Technical Sergeant 3, another soldier was chosen for that promotion, a good guy who kept to the straight and narrow and had a wife and family and could use the extra money and didn't give any trouble, though he didn't, it was true, do the writing Hammett did or have the seniority. The officers were surprised when Hammett pulled himself together and came in perfectly sober and pointed out that because he was senior and did the work, he should have the promotion, a matter of principle, and of course it was true.

"Now I've got to go see about having a Tec 3 sign sewed on my arm," Hammett wrote to Bill Glackin. "Sometimes I feel there *is* a real future for me in the Army . . . if only I had another 51 years ahead of me."[37]

But then it got harder and harder to deal with Hammett. His stuff got to be late, and the rumors were stronger. The drunks that Hammett went on became longer and longer. Once when he was being sent to Edmonton on a special mission, drunk, he missed the airplane and got the unit in a lot of trouble. They had to sober him up and rush him out on another plane, which, however, didn't get there on time. They could see that it was going to be like this with Hammett from now on. The young lieutenant in charge knew he had to talk to Hammett, scold or discipline him, but how could he do that to a famous man twice his age?

Nervously he called Sergeant Hammett in and took him aside. "Do you really think you are doing right for this unit and the country? Would you say this is the way to behave?" Hammett considered the young man's words in a perfectly nice way and then replied that he was not, in fact, doing much of any use for his country or the army or himself and it was time to get out of the service. So he went within the day to the right parties and got his separation papers and left the service without further ado in a very short time, and people said that as he got off the ship at Seattle he tossed his duffel bag into the bay.[38]

16

1945-1948

In the spring of 1944 Hammett had written Lillian:

> As always, however, I like most in your letters the parts—when any—which speak favorably of me, for that too is somehow an integral part of my conception of freedom of speech. (By god, I'm going to get some good out of the otherwise slightly fantastic notion of the importance of freedom of speech if it's the last thing I do!) But what you had to say this time pleased me very much, and you are a cutie-pie, and, if I had any sense, I would stay away forever so that you could build up a kind of dream picture of me without ever coming up against old bubble-prickler reality, but I haven't got sense enough, so do not throw away the clothes and things I left around the house.[1]

Christmas, 1945. Last year at Christmas he had been a military man, a soldier far away; now he was home at Hardscrabble Farm, and the greatest danger he was in was from the leaky roof, his most severe duty was to empty vessels of rainwater into the wee hours of a rainy night. The war was over. He got out of the army in August a Technical Sergeant 3, with a letter of commendation and the right to wear medals.[2] In August the atomic bomb was dropped on two Japanese cities, and the new world began for the worse.

Like other men home from the army, Hammett found the world had changed in small ways too, but some of those were for the good. There were fiberglass fishing rods, for instance. In Baltimore at a political dinner, more than a third who attended were Negroes,[3] and that could never have happened in the days he lived there—

progress owing, doubtless, to the wartime integration. He bought a little house in West Los Angeles for Jose and the girls. It had a pretty kitchen with yellow tile and a backyard. Jose was pleased.

But the old emptiness remained. He was trying to write a book about a man named Helm, an artist, who had just got out of the Army and had been on a drunk since his discharge and had been locked out of his hotel. Helm, unlike Hammett, had a son, a captain in the Eighth Air Force. Hammett wasn't exactly sure what this book was about. And he was going to write a story about a couple of men just discharged from the Eighth Air Force, "one of whom wants the other to marry his sister so they can hang around on the farm together and shoot ducks and stuff, and the other one likes the sister well enough, only she reminds him of a girl he knows down South so he thinks he'll go down there and see *her*. I don't know what that proves. . . ."[4]

And he had a couple of more books in his head, and he might actually do at least one of them—"All right, all right, I know that sounds alcoholic," he writes to Jo—but he hadn't had a drink since October first.

But he went back to it soon enough. The times encouraged drinking. It seemed to many people that hypocrisy, villainy and self-serving dishonor were the national afflictions; a war that had been fought against fascism seemed instead to have made the world safe for fascism in the form of persecutions by the American government of people living in America.

Moreover, events moving swiftly in Hollywood, within the American Communist Party and on the East Coast would have confused any committed man as to where his loyalties lay. Hammett had to decide whether he should be most loyal to the causes of civil rights and labor—what had originally attracted him to the Communist Party—or to the charitable causes that had involved him in fund-raising for orphans, refugees, summer camp for children of the lynched, or to the Communist Party or Marxism itself or America. In Hollywood the Party—in this case the Conference of Studio Unions—remained more interested in Russia than in the American worker and failed to support the association of more than ten thousand studio workers, whose legitimate grievances erupted in a bloody strike in October 1945, when pickets were attacked by armed Burbank police and sheriff's men.[5] More generally, a letter from the influential French Communist Jacques Duclos, denouncing the American Communist Party leadership of

Earl Browder, for whose cause Hammett had worked before the war, created a split in the American party between Browder's American-style mainstream political coalition and the hard-line Communists who followed the international party line and turned on Browder now. "It comes down to this—either Lenin was right and Browder was wrong, or Browder was right and Lenin was wrong. I prefer to believe that Lenin was right," the screenwriter Dalton Trumbo said,[6] and that was what those who stayed in the Party had to feel. Hammett, never much interested in parties or meetings anyway, drifted among causes, gave his name here and there, hoped for little.

About this time, Congressman John Rankin and the House Un-American Activities Committee decided to investigate Hollywood to track down the "footprints of Karl Marx." "We are out to expose those elements that are insidiously trying to spread subversive propaganda, poison the minds of your children, distort the history of our country, and discredit Christianity." Rankin believed that there were "loathsome, filthy, insinuating un-American undercurrents that are running through various pictures," and would later tell the House that Scotland Yard had written him to call attention to "the fact" that during the war "there were coded German messages going through moving pictures that were shown all over England, and some of them were made in Hollywood." The House would try to prove that Communists had infiltrated the movie industry and the Screen Writers Guild.[7]

In February 1946 Hammett must have read an article by Albert Maltz in the *New Masses*, suggesting that works of art should not be judged on the political allegiance of the writer, and that the aim of art is not to serve politics or provide propaganda; perhaps it was a view held by Hammett, who had so excitedly propounded art for art's sake in his youth. But the infuriated Party, especially the New York faction, demanded and got a recantation from Maltz. Where Hammett stood was unclear. No one, meeting him for the first time, would think he stood for anything much.

He missed the Aleutians. There was something he had always loved about islands—the sense of isolation or protection, the independence, a self-contained world. He was always happiest on islands and sought even imaginary ones, like Couffignal, the island stronghold in his story "The Gutting of Couffignal." Now, there was an island in Maine he wanted very badly for his own: four miles long, three miles wide, it had houses, roads, pastures, docks, boats, shooting, fishing, everything. It would cost $160,000—he'd had that much money in his life and then some, but now he didn't. There ought to be a way, he thought, to make the money for it. But this was just a longing, just a wish, that like most other wishes didn't come true.

Instead he was moving into a new apartment at 15 East Sixty-sixth Street and dividing his time between the city and Hard-scrabble Farm, where Lillian was leading the life of a famous play-wright. The Zilboorgs—Lillian's psychiatrist, Gregory, and his wife—might come on a Sunday, or Dorothy Parker, or Arthur and Maggie Kober or the Jerome Weidmans or strangers. Lillian would return from town each week with he didn't know what "gro-tesques," and he ignored them or mingled as he pleased. That sum-mer of 1946, Lillian's play *Another Part of the Forest* went into production. The cast included beautiful Patricia Neal, whom Ham-mett couldn't keep his eyes off. The cast got used to seeing him at the theater day after day, usually dead drunk. He was funny and could make helpful remarks, but it often seemed to anger Lillian, who knew he just hung around to see Pat. Pat liked him too.

Drunk or sober, he did his political tasks. The cold-war hysteria was worsening; witch-hunting was in the air. In June the Attorney General, Tom Clark, pronounced that the whole country was the target of a "sinister and deep-seated plot" devised by Communists and radicals. J. Parnell Thomas and the House Un-American Activities Committee were beginning to rampage; they looked at, among other things, the Joint Anti-Fascist Refugee Committee, whose board Hammett had served on. His name went on many lists about now, but he went on quite openly with causes he believed in. He thought that you change things to make them better not just because you don't like them.

Pleasantville, 10 October 1946

Dear Princess-Pie [Jo]

This afternoon I returned from three days of citying—mostly spent squirming on hard chairs at meetings and such or trying to wheedle money for one no-doubt worthy purpose or another out of this or that group of prospects, many of whom possibly only showed up for the food and/or drinks—and very nice it was to get back. Of course it's barely possible that I don't knock myself out working in New York to the extent I think I do, but you're three thousand miles away and can't check up . . . I would be less than human if I didn't put it on a little thick. I came back looking to a long or British weekend here—from today, Thursday, until Tuesday, when I have to go in for my class at the Jefferson School—but it seems there is a modern invention called the telephone and in a moment of absent-mindedness somebody had one installed here and, having inadvertently answered it this afternoon, I was weak enough to promise I'd go in to a political dinner in Brooklyn Saturday night and do fifteen minutes of jabbering over the radio in an attempt to help a fellow named Mead get himself elected to a job named governor. The campaign is very hot stuff indeed here this year, with registrations running some fifty per cent higher than usual. Ordinarily a heavy vote helps the Democrats and I don't see any reason why this year should be different . . . I'm saying that hopefully. Come to think of it, I haven't registered yet: I must do that when I go in Saturday. In this state I'm a member of the American Labor Party, which has been and still sometimes is the custodian of what's known as the balance of power at the polls. Mead is our candidate as well as the Democrats'. He is far from being as good as he might be and the Republican candidate—that louse Dewey—is no pushover, so we go ahead working and sweating and talking and talking and talking, and hope for the best. Next week, far as I know, I've got a relatively silent week. Outside of my weekly spiel to the students, I'll only get a chance to beat my gums Thursday night at the Hotel Pennsylvania, where Paul Robeson, Helen Gahagan, a newspaper editor from Mississippi named Greene and I will stir up some enthusiasm—and funds—for the "Unseat Bilbo" drive, which has a fair chance of getting somewhere even if the Senate doesn't really expel him. And the following week will also—unless something new pops up, as it always does—be one of comparative silence: outside my school I'm only scheduled for a political speech on the 23d in Rochester. Gabby Hammett, that's me.[8]

A month after this, Richard Nixon was elected in California to the U.S. House of Representatives.

Hammett would always sober up by Thursday night, the night he taught his class in mystery writing at the Jefferson School for Social Science. This was a school devoted to teaching "in the spirit of democracy, peace and socialism. It teaches Marxism as the philosophy and social science of the working class. . . ."[9] Hammett was deeply committed to the school; he taught mystery writing there for a decade and served on the board. He had a shabby classroom upstairs in the back, where people would crowd in. Here he would read students' manuscripts and make comments, usually mild. Once he tried a lecture class but decided the other system worked better.

David Goldway, who was then connected with the Jefferson School, recalls:

> In his relations with me and with Dr. Howard Selsam and others . . . Dash was always cordial—and embarrassingly respectful. Viewing us, I suppose, as the personification of Marxist theory and scholarship, he put on a show of great deference. When he finished his class on Thursday nights, he generally headed straight for his favorite bar on University Place, frequently taking one of us along. In conversation he always pretended that he knew nothing of theory of philosophy, but none of us was fooled. A laconic comment now and then revealed that he had read widely and his fliply expressed opinions were usually soundly based. He liked to listen, and it was always salutary to try to expound some philosophical principle or political strategy to Dash. Both his manner and his occasional mumbled interruptions forced you to steer clear of abstract generalizations and empty phrase-mongering. It was clear that he had no use for anything that smacked of phoniness.[10]

Morris Hershman remembers:

> Most of the questions he fielded in class were fan questions, but when asked if he himself was working on any fiction he said he was writing a play to be called "The Good Meal," from a proverb: a good meal is worth hanging for. When a student who was knowledgeable in play-construction matters asked if the difficulties weren't staggering, Hammett shook his head and insisted that writing plays wasn't hard work at all. I doubt if he believed it, but he could muster a very straight face indeed. . . . He had a talent for telling impossible stories and swearing that they were true. He told them skillfully. One that I remember concerned a radio actor with a Jewish accent who was the only one available to play the role of a priest, causing an executive to remark, "—and that priest with the Jewish accent—Hammett is a genius!"[11]

He didn't claim to be much of a teacher—his style was vague, permissive. But he believed in his task. People always wanted to get into the class, sometimes a couple of hundred; but he could take only fifteen, and they'd read one another's manuscripts and discuss them, and Hammett would add a word or two laconically.

Sometimes a guest would come—Howard Fast, or John Howard Lawson; once Frederic Dannay, one of the two mystery writers who wrote under the pseudonym Ellery Queen, came. Dannay was an admirer of Hammett's stories and had contributed to their survival by reprinting them in *Ellery Queen's Mystery Magazine*, which had absorbed *Black Mask* in 1941. Once, when the Jefferson School took up a subscription for an elevator and the class was too poor or indifferent to contribute, Hammett made up its quota from his own pocket. He brought a voluptuous young woman with him from time to time—"my secretary," he said. This was Marjorie May. Marge was proprietary and fended off other ladies, who wanted things from him, such as the one who wrote to him:

Dear Dashil,

I have applied to the bank for a loan against my business for 2,000, I need a good co-maker I will have to pay $97.00 a month back, for which I am capable.

Everything I have is in pawn and most of it is over due and is going on auction in few days, I am mailing you the tickets so you may see that I am sincere about everything I am telling you all of my coats and jewelry.

Please sign these papers as a co maker, I will guarentee you, I will pay the $97.00 a month back.

I pawned these when I needed money for taxes last year.

Dashil please help me I am working very hard and I am over board.

If you help me this time I will never come for help again

Enclosed you will see tickets for everything I own.

If you can borrow the money I will pay back $100.00 a month.[12]

15 East 66 Street
New York City
Dec. 18, 1946

Dear Miss ——:

While he wishes he might be able to help, in connection with the mortgage on your store, Mr. Hammett has asked me to advise you that he is unable to do so. He has held up on a reply in order to give the matter thought and regrets that it is not possible to say "yes".

> Sincerely,
> Marjorie May for Dashiell Hammett[13]

Nevertheless Hammett sent this woman a thousand dollars.

He had never seemed so alone, yet he was surrounded by others. He wrote letters signed Love, Love and kisses, Kisses and hugs, Many kisses, Lots of love. But it was real love that he could never speak of, except when drinking; a drink enabled him sometimes, to call a man a liar or a fool, or to speak of love. Once, about now, drinking, he wrote a letter to Jo in which he said:

> I don't suppose it's been a secret that I've loved you since I first saw you half-an-hour fresh from the womb and looking very much like my father whom I don't love; but now you've grown into the kind of woman I'd always hoped you'd grow up into— only better, of course. Once, while I was in California, I said fumblingly that I was proud of you, which sounded a little like a parent taking some sort of credit. I didn't mean that, honey: I meant I was proud of being your father, which, if you understand me, is a bit different. . . . The other things I said—that you're not only lovely to look at, but also lovely—I stand by; and when your face lights up with laughter you are to me the loveliest thing I've ever seen; but if on that account, you go round lighting your face all the time like a Cheshire Cat all the time I can see how people are going to think you're a gibbering idiot. . . . I love you, darling, deeply and completely. . . .[14]

In October 1947 HUAC hearings began in Hollywood. Congressman Nixon was on the committee. Everyone came. It might have been a wedding or a bullfight. The congressmen wanted to find out why all these well-paid people in Hollywood would want to be Communists. This baffled them. Louis B. Mayer said, "In my opinion, Mr. Congressman, which I have expressed many times, I think they are cracked." Ronald Reagan and Robert Montgomery assured the committee there were no Commies in the Screen Actors Guild; Gary Cooper, Robert Taylor and others had plenty to say too. Nineteen possible Communists were fingered to testify, of whom ten would become the Hollywood Ten.[15] Then the jailings began. Everyone was inclined to blame the Communists for all the things that were going wrong in the country, and the Republicans saw a fine chance to come to power at last. The Oscar that year for the best movie had been given to *The Best Years of Our Lives*, in which a crippled veteran comes back to wonderful America.

PROGRESSIVE PROTEST
Dashiell Hammett
President of the New York Civil Rights Congress

The proposal outlawing the Communist Party is a direct assault on American democracy, on American tradition of civil rights and liberties and of electoral freedom.

It must be assumed that the Secretary of Labor acted as spokesman for the Truman administration, of which he is a member, in making his statement before the House Labor Committee.

President Truman and the Republican leadership to whom the proposal was directed need not be reminded that outlawing of the Communist Party was the first step taken by the Hitler administration to establish itself in power.

We urge that every American now make his voice heard in defense of his country against the attack which is being leveled against it on the Hitler pattern from Washington itself. The chorus of American voices demanding that President Truman repudiate this proposal can stop the attack in its tracks.[16]

From Burrelle's Press Clipping Service: "Dear Mr. Hammett, due to the increases in our operating expenses, we have found it necessary to revise our charge for clippings. As of April 1, 1948 our rate will be eights cents per clipping with a minimum charge of eight dollars per month...."

April 8, from Miss May: "Mr. Hammett's monthly bill seems to be at the $15.00 rate—and yet, this could not possibly be based on a minimum rate, I don't believe for these last few months particularly, it has been only five or six or ten clippings he receives...."

"Dear Miss May: Mr. Hammett's former rate was $15.00 for one hundred fifty (150) clippings with a time limit of three months. ... For your information we wish to advise that Mr. Hammett received five hundred thirty-six (536) clippings during the period of April 1, 1947 to March 31, 1948."

Many of the numerous clippings concerned various ongoing

radio shows based on Hammett's characters. People had the impression he was writing or supervising these programs. A recent *Thin Man* ("The Case of the Frightened Fullback") was a story "that would have insulted the intelligence of a moron," a critic complained. "It is hard to believe that Dashiell Hammett, originator of the 'Thin Man' series, was responsible for this particular show. If he was, it is time he retire from the mystery script writing business. If not, he should give writer's credit to the man responsible or else lift his name from the series." But, says another critic, Sam Spade is still the best show in the whodunit class: "One reason may be that Hammett supervises the scripting." John Crosby believed that Dashiell Hammett "still writes the Spade Series." Believing this, the *Daily Compass* took him to task for an anti-Semitic segment where Spade says to a Jewish character, "Your kind don't take chances." Hammett confessed that he hadn't listened to Sam Spade lately, "but I will certainly listen more often in the future." The new *Fat Man* series was a success,[17] because the fat detective "of engaging personality was created especially for ABC by Dashiell Hammett, outstanding present day writer of detective fiction."

Little Jo was going to get married. It startled him. It pleased him too that she had gone to college and had found a nice young man, Loyd Marshall. He was proud of her. He went to Los Angeles for the wedding in July and stayed with Jose and the girls at the little house he had bought them. It ought to have been a happy time, with the family together again, but it was not. Hammett, who had never been cruel to Jose, not, anyway, in little ways, was cruel now. He made caustic remarks and unreasonable demands, to which she always acceded. "See how I've got your mother trained," he'd say. He went unshaven for days; his daughters had never seen him like this. And he wept, when he was drunk, and regretted that he had no sons and made dreadful scenes, so that Jo was happy that she was getting married and out of there. But he was lovely at the wedding, so handsome and famous and charming to everyone.

Then Jo and Loyd went off to Hawaii, where Loyd, an engineer, would be working. Hammett stayed with Jose and Mary awhile longer, drinking. He wrote to Jo in her new home: "We all miss you a great deal and speak of you often—whenever we happen to think of it. Some of us remember you quite clearly—a plump redhaired girl with two ears, as I recall. . . . Feeling restless

Hammett and Jo at her
wedding to Loyd Marshall,
Los Angeles, 1948.

today, I thought up a plot for a novel which I hope one day to get
around to doing. Meanwhile it's swell having a new novel not to
do: I was getting pretty bored with just not working on that half
a dozen or so old ones. . . ."

Back in New York he moved to an apartment at 28 West Tenth
Street. His ménage consisted of Marge and the housekeeper, Rose
Evans, and the poodle Salud. Rose Evans told him she thought he
should pay more attention to his family, and Hammett, stung by
this truth, perhaps influenced by a desperate letter Jose sent him
now, arranged for Mary to come East for some needed dental work
and some treatment for her emotional problems too. Jose grate-
fully put Mary on the plane.

His feelings for Mary were again strange and violent. Feelings of
love and combat all came back now. She was both tough and
fragile; he wanted to help her and at times to kill her. He had
written about tough girls like Mary; it was as if she had grown into
a character in one of his books, perhaps Gabrielle Dain. Mary
moved in with him on Tenth Street.

He and Mary fought. So did he and Marge, and one day Marge threw a glass of whiskey in his face and Mary got scared and called her doctor to see if whiskey could hurt his eyes. The doctor laughed and said it would probably open them.

Salud, the poodle he loved, died. Marge bought him another dog, a bloodhound named Babette, a nice enough dog, but things somehow didn't seem the same without Salud.

He tried to write. He would send Mary out for pencils, buy a new typewriter, have a drink, change the color of the paper, try ink, another typewriter, no drink until afterward, various stratagems. The blank hours passed. He spent a lot of time in those newspaper bars on East Forty-fourth.[18]

His friends remembering:

[Franklin Folsom said:] I did see him drinking on the last night before he went into the army. I met him by appointment at a bar on Seventh Ave. in the Village. He made out and gave me a check for $1000 at that time—a check to be used for a Win the War Congress of Writers which the League was initiating but which we hoped would be under broader auspices. With Dash in the booth in the bar was a woman I did not know. They seemed to be on intimate terms, and he told her about a technique he had used for getting rid of women who wanted to go to bed with him—women in whom he was not interested. Dash would say that he and the unwanted woman might have different venereal diseases so they had better not go to bed together. I doubt that Dash had any venereal disease.[19]

[A woman who knew him in Alaska said:] When I was in New York I called him up, this would be in '48 or so, and we went on the town—dinner, and clubs, and then more clubs and more clubs and he got hard to handle—loud, and sarcastic and abusive to waiters and weaving and wobbling, and when I couldn't take it I said call me a cab, and he said he wouldn't, so I called a cab, and when the cab came and he saw I was going to get in it and go, he said "Please don't leave me alone."[20]

[Ed Rosenberg said:] I remember once I was putting him on the train for San Francisco and Hammett had a drink, waiting for the train, and then another and another, and God he was sloshed and an hour to wait before the train, and I said Dash, why don't you wait, you can get something on the train, and he said, "Oh, I will."[21]

[Hannah Weinstein remembered:] He'd get drunk in airports and send telegrams. Or, I remember once in a restaurant in Chicago, he ordered everything on the menu. This restaurant—is it the Pump Room where their specialties are flambéed? Some waiter came along, and Hammett had something against him. Waiter said "What do you want?" and Hammett said, "How do we know till we've tried what you have?" and he ordered one of everything, and there were these trains of waiters bringing up little side tables to put the dishes on, and other waiters coming along with things flaming on swords, and Hammett waving them on, and us trying to call them off, and I could have died of shame, and everyone in the restaurant staring.[22]

[Mary said:] I remember the time he made me eat four dozen snails. Luckily I liked them.[23]

[Jo said:] He was so drunk in this restaurant once—and I was sitting between him and some producer's wife, kind of a tart he kept propositioning, and it was so embarrassing I went to the ladies' room and never came back. I thought he wouldn't speak to me after that, but he did, he apologized. "I guess I was bad last night," he said.[24]

[Bud Freeman:] We played concerts and he'd come along. He was a good friend and, in fact, after the war, when I was playing with Condon down in the Village, he came down with Lillian Hellman to say hello. He had been drinking very heavily. . . .[25]

[Dorothy Nebel wrote:] A bunch of the boys were in a bar one evening and they were discussing the indifference of New Yorkers to other people on the street. Someone said he could probably walk down the street naked and no one would turn to look—fortunately they didn't try to prove that! Dash got the idea that, though it was a beautiful clear evening, he could walk down the street under an open umbrella and no one would notice. The bartender had one of those large black ones, which he loaned them and Fred and Dash started off under it (that alone must have been a funny sight, for Fred was a head shorter than Dash). At any rate they claimed that they walked—I can't recall the number of blocks—up Lexington to 42nd Street, over to Fifth and back to the bar, and not a single person turned to stare.[26]

[Ed Rosenberg said:] He'd just slide off his chair onto the floor and go to sleep. He slept through a lot of parties in his drinking days. I've seen him fall in the gutter, too, and lie there.

Drunk, in the gutter, and it was disgusting. He was a disgusting drunk.[27]

Lillian later wrote that "the years after the war, from 1945 to 1948, were not good years; the drinking grew wilder and there was a lost, thoughtless quality I had never seen before. I knew then that I had to go my own way. I do not mean that we were separated, I mean only that we saw less of each other, were less close to each other."[28]

A telegram came for Hammett, and he threw it on his desk un-opened and did not look at it as the days passed. Mary could not help seeing it and thinking about it; there was something ominous and frightening about Hammett's unconcern, as if he knew what it would say. She would never touch things on his desk, but she finally decided that he should open the telegram, and when he would not, she opened it herself. It was from Aunt Reba: Papa's father was dead. It told about the funeral and about his end. Mary wondered, was Papa going to the funeral? "No. I'm paying for it, let somebody else do the crying." Hammett made this remark be-cause he was drinking. Mary understood. Hammett did not go to the funeral, though, or speak of it later. He said he had not loved his father.

One day Lillian drove Mary and Hammett to Pleasantville. It was hard to say which of them was drunker, Hammett or Mary. Their screaming quarrels shattered Lillian's concentration, split her ears, and when it seemed to her she couldn't bear it any longer, suddenly Hammett got out of the car and vanished. Lillian took Mary to Pleasantville and locked her in the little bedroom. She took her her meals three times a day and wondered if she might jump out the window. She didn't. She ate the meals with docility and promised not to drink anymore. Lillian kept her in there until Sunday night and then drove her back to town, thinking to hell with this crazy pair.

Mary didn't like Marge, her father's secretary, and Marge didn't like Mary. Rose, the housekeeper, liked Mary but not Marge. "We can get along without Marge here," Mary said, so Marge went. Now Rose had the charge account and did all the shopping for Hammett.

Mary loved someone. He was handsome, and he loved her back; he was so handsome he could be an actor or a model. But Papa and the doctor said cruel things about him. They said he wasn't stable or well. They said she wasn't stable or well enough yet to marry him. She thought she would always love him, next to Papa, or maybe she might love him more.[29]

Reba came to visit Hammett and Mary. She was as thin as Hammett, and her hair as white. She asked Mary to come on a trip with her, but Mary didn't want to leave the doctor or Papa. She and Hammett took Reba to the New Yorker Hotel, and to plays and tried to show her a good time.

Johnnie Walker Red. He liked to have cases of it in the closet, a comforting presence. He could drink more than one bottle in a night. Mary could get through quite a bit too.

Rose thought that if Hammett wanted to sit all day reading and not go out, that was his business, he was a famous man. When he finished a book, he would throw it in the fireplace. "Why you do that?" Rose would ask. "I'll take them home if you don't want them." Well, he'd finished with them, why else? A book burning slowly in the grate, charring slowly, only gradually breaking into flame. He would sit by the fire sipping his Scotch in the alluring light of the burning book. Women came around, tried to get money out of him; Rose tried her best to keep them away, but they came around at night too when Rose had gone home. She didn't know what went on when she wasn't there. Gold diggers. She knew what they were.[30]

Lillian told Hammett she didn't want to see him anymore. It may be that she was able to envision a peaceful life, success, perhaps love without him. He would now become so grossly drunk as to be unendurable. People worried about Mary, living down there with him. They were afraid he might harm her in his drunken rages, or worse, or perhaps had already. The situation was ugly. The girl was hard to handle too and defensive of her father. Someone saw dark bruises around her eyes; she would not say where they came from.

Sober, he couldn't remember things that had happened the night before, passages with Mary, the import of her looks of hate, fear, defiance, love. Sober, he panicked when he thought of the dimly remembered drunken time. He hated and loved his daughter; it was a kind of curse. Like other writers, he knew the odd way that life catches up with things that you write, after you have written them.

A man Mary recognized came for her one night—a friend of Lillian's—who looked the situation over. "Get some things in a bag," he said; and he made her go to a hotel and, the next day, took her to Lillian, who grimly kept her. The doctor, too, said she shouldn't go back to her father. But she knew he didn't mean the things he said and did; he just couldn't drink, and the things he did when he drank didn't count. Mary understood Papa because she was like him, and the others weren't. But like him, she was alone. She went back to him for a time, and then got an apartment of her own. They all thought it best.[31]

Everyone now let him alone. Lillian refused to see him. Mary had moved out; the secretary was gone. Rose came every day to look after things. Ed Rosenberg, the producer of his Sam Spade radio plays, would stop in from time to time and find him in bed and the place a mess. There wasn't much anyone could do. Hammett stayed in bed, drinking, keeping himself alive on beer.

Rose began to get frightened when he could hardly make it to the bathroom and he wouldn't stop drinking and didn't move. Each day when she arrived she expected to find him dead. "Don't call Lillian," he said, but she did.

Lillian's secretary answered and said she'd give Miss Hellman the message; the message was "Please come down here and see to Mr. Hammett because I think he's going to die," and Lillian said, "No, I'm not going to go." But the secretary was so worried that she was about to go and Lillian realized that wasn't fair, so she went.

It took both Lillian and Rose to load him into his clothes and drag him to the taxi and into Lillian's house, and there Lillian called the doctor. She was frightened, for it was obvious that Rose was right, he might die. He had begun to shake and scream.

He couldn't go to the hospital with DT's—there'd be a scandal, and also you had to get over them before you could be admitted, and the doctor was worried about that. He told Lillian how to give him paraldehyde so he would calm down.

At the hospital the doctor looked him over and told him he'd be dead in a month or two if he didn't stop drinking. He came out of the room and said with a sad wink at Lillian, "He's never going to drink again," which he took to mean the usual alcoholic resolution that would last until Tuesday. But Lillian knew it meant that Hammett would never have a drink again:

> Five or six years later, I told Hammett that the doctor had said he wouldn't stay on the wagon.
> Dash looked puzzled. "But I gave my word that day."
> I said, "Have you always kept your word?"
> "Most of the time," he said, "maybe because I've so seldom given it."[32]

Hammett forswore drinking because there was no choice before him, but it was a decision he had rehearsed a hundred times.

17

1949-June 1951

Hammett was in the hospital over Christmas of 1948 and New Year's, and convalesced in January at Hardscrabble Farm. It had been a mild winter—the lawn remained green, but the pond was frozen and the temperature brisk. Mornings he woke late, spent a long time over breakfast and the papers, dressed in the afternoon to roam outside; he carried a slingshot as he wandered in the bare woods. Lillian stayed mostly in town at work; with Norman Mailer she had been adapting *The Naked and the Dead* for the screen. Hammett rode into town with her sometimes to see Mary, but otherwise he relished the solitude. Each day he felt better, but the better he felt, the more he felt he should be working. "It would be good to say that as his life changed the productivity increased, but it didn't," Lillian wrote later. "Perhaps the vigor and the force had dissipated. But good as it is, productivity is not the only proof of a serious life, and now, more than ever, he sat down to read. He read everything and anything."[1] He read his horoscope.

What to Expect Today Jan. 25, 1949

THE SUN IN AQUARIUS. Romances would be affected by careless words and would need time for recovery. Best interests for today seem to be mechanical or scientific doings—and this includes housekeeping, which is truly a science these days—also the planning of research or any detailed writing or study. Be sure that your performance equals your standards today, as there are slips showing here.

Well—Lillian was coming back from town for dinner; maybe her petticoats would be dragging. "Affecting" a "romance" seemed like nice work, but he couldn't think up a "careless" word: such words all seemed so sort of premeditated. . . . Planning—what else had he been doing exclusively for years and years? He guessed he'd saw some wood. He still tired easily and speedily, and got out of breath—but at least that kept you from getting blisters on your hands.

On Thursdays, however ill, he faithfully turned up as usual at the Jefferson School. Then he would have dinner with Mary and come back as soon as possible to Pleasantville. He was mildly irritated by his conviction that Mary was having an affair with her dentist. "Lillian was in Washington over the weekend, being feted by the Yugoslav and Russian embassies, I think, and possibly by other subversive elements as well," he joked to Jo in February.[2]

His own health improved, and his family anxieties were for the moment lessened. Mary settled into a New York routine. With Jo happily married, he wished for a grandchild. Jose traveled to Hawaii to visit Jo. "The Hawaiian men have wonderful healthy bodies and are nice," she wrote innocently to Hammett. He wrote to Jo: "Just as well she's heading back towards the States, unless you want a native step-father. . . . She'd better get back to looking at those fairies doing handstands on the Santa Monica beach."[3]

In February Death of a Salesman, in which Hammett had invested, opened to great acclaim, which was nice, though "he didn't think much" of Arthur Miller's writing. He himself was hoping to do a stage version of The Maltese Falcon, and liked the idea of Peter Lorre for Gutman if possible. "We'll ignore the written-in fatness," he said. A play he had promised to write for Kermit Bloomgarden, "The Good Meal," was by now several seasons late, and people remarked its absence. He had actually written some of it; he knew he wouldn't write any more.

I'm still mightily occupied putting up birdhouses and feeding boxes. It seems to me there was a comparative shortage of the feathered dopes last year and I'm trying to woo 'em back . . . especially bluebirds and purple martins, which I haven't seen for several years. This afternoon I saw a song sparrow outside the study windows—there are plenty of chickadees and nuthatches (nuthatches are my favorites this year though I used to be a pretty staunch chickadee man); robins and juncos (who ought to be getting hell back of north if winter's really over) and redwing blackbirds are easy to find; and I've seen a couple of wood-peckers, though I am not sure one of 'em wasn't a flicker.[4]

The spring 1949 enrollment in his Jefferson School class was down. Either he wasn't as much of a draw as he used to be or the climate of red-baiting was worsening, he didn't know which. "Fear of arrest or reprisal keeps the space between floors and beds fairly well filled with otherwise intrepid characters." He and Lillian invited people who might be compromising—Yugoslavians and Russians and Henry Wallace—to Hardscrabble. A pamphlet published by the congressional committee on Un-American Activi-ties on a recent peace conference (which Hammett didn't attend, though he was a sponsor) listed Lillian among a group of sponsors affiliated with from 31 to 40 red-front organizations.[5] It amused Hammett when she took to her bed—sulking, he teased, because he was listed in the "smaller and more elite 41 to 50 group, includ-ing something—where I seem to be alone—called The Crown Heights Committee for A Democratic Spain. . . . From now on whenever I get involved in one of those Committee arguments I'm going to mow down the opposition by pointing out that, 'Now, up in Crown Heights (I wish I could remember where it is or was) we always did it thisaway.' "[6]

He made light of his political involvement, but he continued to put his name to things, or donate money, or appear on a platform. He was a member of the American Labor Party, and in June 1949 he was the chairman of the Conference for Civil and Human Rights and a member of its resolutions committee. The political climate worried him, but it did not worry him enough. However pessimistic his temperament, he respected America too much to see to what depths it would yet sink.

An FBI agent, assigned to watch him, noted that at a Communist dinner given for the campaign to recall or impeach racist Senator Theodore Bilbo, Hammett contributed $1,000. Another recorded that at a mass meeting in Madison Square Garden on June 28, 1950, for the purpose of stopping the war in Korea and granting amnesty to political prisoners, Hammett contributed another $1,000.

His old properties were still supporting him. Earlier, in the Hollywood days, he had become acquainted with E. J. Rosenberg, a successful producer who sold his *Sam Spade* series to radio and helped develop another series, *The Fat Man*, inspired by Gutman of *The Maltese Falcon*, which featured a fat detective called Brad

Runyan. The *Fat Man* series began in January 1946 and ran till 1950.[7] A Fat Man movie deal hung fire; Mutual Broadcasting wanted to put *Thin Man* radio programs on five times a week. A Continental Op television series was talked of, and Hammett had presented a couple of new ideas for radio and television shows to agents and producers. "A new idea with me, you must understand," he said, "is usually based on something I did back in the 20s. My sole duty in regard to these programs, is to look in the mail for a check once a week. I don't even listen to them. If I did, I'd complain about how they were being handled, and then I'd fall into the trap of being asked to come down and help. I don't want to have anything to do with the radio. It's a dizzy world—makes the movies seem highly intellectual."[8]

He and Lillian had settled into the chaste affection of the long married, happy enough in the close but separate way they lived. In the summer of 1949, they went to Martha's Vineyard, where they had rented a house on Gay Head. It was to him a perfect summer, and in the fall he had a new prospect for work in Hollywood, which had received word that Hammett was now sober and reasonable. Over the summer he did some play-doctoring for producer Kermit Bloomgarden,[9] and made plans to go to the Coast early in 1950 to work with his old friend William Wyler on a new movie for Paramount, *Detective Story*. He planned to stay at the Beverly Hills or the Beverly Wilshire, as in the old days, for about a week of discussion, then come back East again in time for his class at the Jefferson School on the nineteenth of January. He would do the writing, he figured, in New York. By the end of 1949, then, life seemed brighter, where exactly a year before he had been near death.

DASHIELL HAMMETT HAS HARD WORDS
FOR TOUGH STUFF HE USED TO WRITE

"This hard-boiled stuff—it is a menace."

Dashiell Hammett made that remark—or confession—yesterday at the Beverly Wilshire Hotel.

Hammett is a first-class writing man from Manhattan. He has written five mysteries and innumerable short stories of various sorts. He is now working on a sixth novel to be titled "December 1."

In a period when most writers reside in remodeled barns in

Connecticut and Vermont, Hammett lives on Lower Manhattan and plays the table d'hotes. He seldom gets farther west than Philadelphia.

He came out to see his daughter, Mrs. Josephine Marshall of Westchester, who is the wife of a Douglas Aircraft mechanical engineer.

"Are you up to something in Hollywood?" he was asked.

"Positively not," he replied, and that was that.

The reason Hammett denounces the hard-boiled stuff he used to write with such relish and profit is that it has become old hat.

"It went all right in the Terrible 20s," he explained. "The bootlegger days. The racketeering days. There are racketeers now, to be sure, but they are nice, refined people. They belong to country clubs."

Hammett paused and looked as if he were going to say something unexpected. He did.

Tribute to Belgian

"Do you know," he went on, "the best mystery writer today is a Belgian who writes in French? His name is Georges Simenon. His latest book, which has been translated into English, is titled 'The Snow Was Black.'"

"What makes him the best?"

"Well, he is more intelligent. There is something of the Edgar Allan Poe about him."

After that tribute to a rival, Hammett toddled off to meet his daughter to go on a trip to the beach. Papas are about the same, whatever they do for a living.[10]

Beautiful Pat Neal was in Los Angeles. He took her to dinner every night, to restaurants whose expense and elegance amazed her. He took her to dinner rather more often than he recounted to Lillian, to whom he wrote: "Pat's an awfully pretty girl if you don't look at her hands and feet and can ignore that incredible carriage. She's very much the earnest future star at the moment and thus not too entirely fascinating if you don't think her career the most important thing in the world."[11] Their meals were rather silent. Pat would think desperately of things to say to break the silence, but it was hard because Hammett was so intelligent and she felt she was not intellectual enough for him, but she looked up to him and she had no boyfriend at the moment, so it was nice to go out to dinner, and at the end he would kiss her nicely, rather wistfully, but that was all. Of course, she thought, he was so *old*.[12]

Each afternoon he would go to the hospital to see Maggie

Kober, who was dying of a chronic neurological disease but was brave and cheerful and looked forward each day to his visit. And he'd write letters to Lillian and to Mary, who was still in New York, and he read. He liked Joyce Cary's novel *The Horse's Mouth*. In between all this he really did begin work on his cops-and-robbers script, and then realized he couldn't do it and gave back the money, the $10,000 they'd given him in advance. What powers he had left he did not want to expend in Hollywood.

Hammett was back in New York in the late spring and was overjoyed at the arrival of Jo's baby, Ann, on June 2, 1950. He rushed to California to see her when she was a week old. Conversations with Mary's doctor were encouraging, and Mary had lost weight and gone on the wagon.[13] His school teaching was over until fall, and he hoped to get somewhere on his novel, which he thought of as "The Hunting Boy, or December 1." He bought a new IBM electric typewriter, hired a new secretary, Muriel Alexander, and organized his apartment on West Tenth for working in earnest, although world events were distracting.

> Korea's the big news just now, which makes conversation pretty tough, since nobody seems to know what happened or is happening. I'm old enough to be pretty placid about the whole thing: it's not difficult for me to be placid about unpleasant things happening to Dr. Rhee's government: he's a stinker even among Koreans and generally speaking I've never been able to consider them God's masterpieces. The truth is, I suppose, I'm not too appalled by the thought of a possible World War III. We've had two of those World War things and both were silly and wicked, but not much more silly and wicked than most large-scale things we tackle in our present childish state. The way we live, I dare say war can be considered as normal as peace.
>
> There's nothing like that kind of deep thinking to rest up your back and legs: now I feel able to face that walk to the pond. . . .[14]

> July 12, 1950 Rumors that we're about to pop the Koreans with the atom bomb are floating around. It's unreasonable enough to seem reasonable: we think of some mighty peculiar things to do and I don't see why this should not be one of them. . . . I'm anxious to get back to work on a novel called DECEMBER FIRST I started some months ago, but somehow my anxiousness doesn't seem to keep me from spending most of my time doing other things like trying to work out a new formulation of the

always-with-us problems of Marxist culture and messing around with the fight that goes on between theoretic physicists over the relativity and quantum contradictions. I suspect the quantum boys are more nearly right in a strictly scientific way, while his truths are more mixed with philosophy and maybe even esthetics. (I know you give a damn about all this!)[15]

In the autumn Mary had a worrying episode; he writes to Jo:

There's nothing to say about Mary yet, so perhaps it would be just as well if you didn't say anything at all to your mother. Mary had some sort of convulsions—seemingly non-alcoholic in origin—and spent a week in the hospital being checked up on. The medical men don't altogether agree on what happened or on what's the best thing to do about what happened, and the chances are she'll have to take some more tests. (I don't think she knows about this.) None of this seems too immediately serious. The chief thing to decide at the moment will be whether she's most in need of physical or psychical treatment, or both; and I don't want to make any unnecessarily silly decisions. So I'm listening to the experts, hoping I don't do what practically everybody always does in such cases—take the opinion of whichever expert comes closest to my own. I hope to know more about this—I can hardly know less—later in the week and will let you know.[16]

Christmas, 1950. Rather apologetically, Hammett sends Jo and Loyd a blank check for a television set. Not an altogether respectable item, but it fascinates him. ("The descent from radio to television is certainly not as great as from bridge to canasta!") He thinks they should get one with a large screen, and probably an RCA Victor, which has a better repair service, the most important item in television owning, and he hopes it won't cost more than $1,000. He's also sending a huge doll for Ann from F. A. O. Schwartz. He has a fixed belief "that every little girl should at some time have a doll larger than she is. And naturally this is a lot easier before she's grown too much."[17]

The previous summer Lillian had begun work on a new and so far untitled play, which was to interest and involve him. She'd nearly finished the first act by mid-July, and the first few pages seemed "pretty good." By November, the final version of Act I was "kind of wonderful," and she was on Act II. She wanted him

Jo and Mary, c. 1930.

to direct it, but he told Jo, "I don't feel too sure that I should start a new career till I'm in my sixties, and I'm three years away from that."

A new career. The older he got, it seemed to him, the fewer things happened to him that didn't seem to have happened and happened and happened before. Still, slight variations on familiar themes were, he thought, his meat, and he distrusted anything new. So maybe he wouldn't direct a play. He would write.

At Christmas a new edition of his novels came out in England and was reviewed in the London *Times Literary Supplement*. He wrote to Jo that the review was

awfully stuffy and pompous, of course, but I guess it's still the most influential publication in the world, so . . . it makes me out quite a fellow in a writing way . . . and this is a time in history when I can stand being made out quite a fellow. If I can get hold of an extra copy I'll send it to you because I do not wish you to go through life not thinking I'm quite a fellow, and there is Ann, too, who must be taught to think the same thing without any foolish juvenile notions of her own.

The Times said "Mr. Hammett has not published a novel for more than 16 years, and it is to be hoped that he will soon complete the major work on which he is rumored to be engaged," so I reckon I'd better quit this and get engaged.[18]

At his best, the *Times* had gone on to say, "he is an artist intent on presenting his intensely personal vision, in terms of action rather than psychology, of the violent, cruel and treacherous world we live in to-day." (A world where he can imagine America dropping the bomb on Korea. It seems to him that a world at peace was not too much better than a world at war.) *The Glass Key* was his most important novel, it said, and Hammett agreed with that, though it sometimes seemed to him that his favorite was always the one he'd reread most recently. "The nihilistic intransigence of Mr. Hammett's heroes is, however, unbacked by any philosophy, and perhaps the more terrible for that. . . ."

It must have seemed to him that the *Times* had somewhat misunderstood his work. His heroes were not nihilistic but principled in a world where, it was true, principle had disappeared but could be restored again. His was a Manichaean and not a nihilistic view. The loyal Op followed through on his tasks in a West as poisoned as the old Eastern world by playing the bad elements against other bad elements; he straightened out the life of the enchanted Gabrielle in the same way because all you have to do is wait for evil to destroy itself, or help it along a little. You do what you have to do. Sam Spade's flippant remark about finding the killer of his partner because not to do so was bad for business was just that, a flippant remark. Just like any nice old-fashioned moralist, Spade was against killing, he was against scoundrels and women who used their sexual wiles for deceitful gain; and at the end of Hammett's stories the world was not put back in order but shown up for the disorderly place it was, as in a sermon or a prayer.

In January Lillian was still at work on the final revisions of her play, which Hammett wanted to call "Some of Us," but which was called *The Autumn Garden* by the time it opened for trials in Philadelphia in February. Fredric March and Florence Eldridge were pretty good in it, if hammy, he wrote to Maggie Kober.[19] Hammett had been interested in this play from the beginning—and his criticism had led Lillian to discard an early draft. He had also patched up some of the dialogue, including, Lillian remembers, a long speech in the last act in which the character, Griggs, regrets the missed opportunities of his life:

> So at any given moment you're only the sum of your life up to then. There are no big moments you can reach unless you've a pile of smaller moments to stand on. That big hour of decision, the turning point in your life, the someday you've counted on when you'd suddenly wipe out your past mistakes, do the work you'd never done, think the way you'd never thought, have what you'd never had—it just doesn't come suddenly. You've trained yourself for it while you waited—or you've let it all run past you and frittered yourself away. I've frittered myself away. . . .[20]

Hammet had a royalty share in the play. He went to Philadelphia for the opening and again a few days later to be with Lillian during this nervous time. It reminded him of his dislike of travel.

He was invited by the Comité National des Ecrivains to Paris, and then, he wrote to Maggie, to Renaud de Jouvenel's château in the Corrèze district for a week, and then to Paris again to discuss the salient topic "Intellectual Comfort versus Conscience." All expenses paid. But he decided not to go, annoying Lillian, who had a firm belief that one should go almost anywhere for almost any purpose if it was free, and she had been trying to get him to France for years. He was tempted—he wanted in particular to meet Pablo Neruda. On the other hand, he doubted if he could get a passport. Something in him did not want to go to France; he had never wanted to go abroad.[21]

He was now, he claimed to his friends, "very much the nice-old-man-puttering-around-in-suburbia. I planted some gloxinias and cut some sprays of forsythia for indoor forcing and put out fresh suet cakes and seed for the birds and was just too sweet for words all the way around. Maybe I can find a ladybird on the study windowsill and kick it around to show I'm young and vigorous."[22] He watched more and more TV.

In April of 1951 Hammett has been visiting in California. Now he is at the Los Angeles airport, carrying a small baby. The baby's anxious parents wave as Hammett with the bundled-up baby ascends the steps of the airplane and vanishes inside. The baby begins to scream. She screams her head off. The other passengers glare at Hammett, and perhaps also wonder what this old guy, white-haired and skinny, is doing with an infant, and also why he is letting her scream like that.

Hammett is unperturbed. He jiggles and rocks her, his grand-daughter Ann, whom he is carrying off to New York. When the plane begins to taxi, her screams subside into sobs. When they are twenty feet airborne she falls asleep, immediately, and Hammett feels a certain triumph. He probably imagines that people are envious of the man with the beautiful baby. He has fallen in love.

He puts her in the berth and reads, and Ann sleeps until they land in Chicago, at five in the morning, but she doesn't cry. She likes the berth, her grandpa and the traveling. At seven he changes her diapers and feeds her a bottle, which the stewardess, full of solicitous amusement, has warmed for the elderly gentleman with the baby. Ann goes back to sleep, and at eight-thirty they are in New York. She sleeps in the taxi to Lillian's, but then wakes up very satisfactorily and makes a kind of regal entrance. She is a huge success.[23]

Lillian adored her, which amused Hammett. Sometimes she bored even him with her infatuation. She went around asking everyone if Ann wasn't beautiful, and those who didn't say that Ann was the most beautiful child ever were forthwith on her son-of-a-bitch list. Hammett himself was inordinately proud, and he buttonholed strangers in elevators to tell them she was his grand-daughter. They were a couple with a baby.

They took Ann up to Pleasantville, and there Hammett played with her all day, or waited for her to wake up from her naps so they could go for walks down to the pond, through the woods, in the sunny spring weather. Once the baby picked up a bee, between thumb and forefinger, and it scared her when it tried to get away, and Hammett leaped to assist, but the bee had already escaped without stinging her. This pleased him. "A true descendant, I told myself, who can handle bugs and such without harm coming to either!" He put out some new wren houses and shelters for the robins and wood thrushes. Each spring he felt a certain touch of anxiousness, before the summer birds arrived, that perhaps they had decided to go somewhere else for once. He wondered what he did with his time without a baby to waste it on.

Jo arrived—he had mixed feelings about seeing her, since it

Hammett with grandchild, c. 1950.

meant she would take Ann away again. He snapped at her too sharply once, and she remembered how she'd had this same feeling in the past when he would turn his disapproval on her that she could not bear it.

He had gone to California ostensibly for legal reasons. Warner Brothers had made three films of *The Maltese Falcon*, two with that title (in 1931 and 1941), and one called *Satan Met a Lady* in 1936. Warner believed that having bought the motion picture rights to the book, they owned both the story and the character Sam Spade, and that Hammett's using Sam Spade in a radio series was an infringement of their ownership of Spade. Hammett contended that Spade was his property—he had been used in stories before and after *The Maltese Falcon*, and that there was, moreover, a literary tradition in detective fiction that not only allowed reuse of the detective character but even required it. The outcome of this case had important implications for other writers. In 1949 a New York court had upheld Warner Brothers, but the matter was moved to California, where eventually the trial and appellate courts upheld Hammett. Now, in 1951, he had to appear in court in California—but it made a nice excuse to go.

In mid-May Jo and Ann returned to California a few days ahead of him; Mary, too, better than she had been in some time, went back to California. It was an occasion to pay more visits to the baby, to Jose and Mary at Purdue Avenue, and to a fellow he remembered from the Aleutians, and to Maggie Kober. He gave his court testimony and returned to New York.

Enjoying the lovely June weather of Pleasantville again, Hammett thought he would never go into the city unless he had to—though the world, he complained, paid very little attention to the desires of elderly men. His gloxinias flourished, and there was no domestic drama more serious than the spaying of a favorite poodle, Flora, and a wonderful new puppy, Gregory, who was learning to come fishing with him in the boat.

Of course there was, as always, the void of work. "Dull matters," he would say, interfered with his writing, or he'd stayed up too late. Sometimes an excuse like that would strike him as so useful that he would use it in letters to several people: "Having the dopiness of youth without youth's vigor isn't always the most satisfactory thing," or, always the careful stylist, reducing and polishing: "the dopiness of youth without youth's vigor isn't too satisfactory." Whatever it was, he found it hard to write, after all these years. In his mind there was the artist's excitement at the prospect of the work; on paper there would be only the tense little phrases that did not please him. Maybe tomorrow.

July–December 1951
THE TRIAL

There are no big moments you can reach, says Griggs in the play *The Autumn Garden*, unless you have a pile of smaller moments you can stand on. Now, in 1951, indeed since the late forties, if you did not wish to stand on the pile of your accumulated deeds and wished instead that you had not done them, or tried to convince others you had not done them, you had to busy yourself with the task of changing your face. And a number of people were busy trying to do just that. In the thirties many had been Communists, the way they might have been Bull Moose or voted Peace and Freedom at other times, depending on what the parties were in their towns and how they saw the problem of replacing capitalism at a time it wasn't working well for millions of people. In the forties, if you regretted your behavior or were afraid of trouble, you had to disclaim history, investigate it, excoriate it and rewrite it. You got out of the Party and pretended you hadn't been in it or admitted you had and repented of your error, or managed some odd combination of these; unless you denounced your former friends, tracked down Communists and jailed them, you found yourself out of work. Formerly reasonable judges now appeared or pretended to believe that the Communist Party was "a clear and present danger." Communists were hunted for and found in Hollywood, in the government, in the army, in the State Department. And when found they took the Fifth, formerly the recourse of gangsters and crooks, so respectable people now thought of Commies as gangsters and crooks.

In the autumn of 1948 eleven Communist leaders, including Robert G. Thompson, Gilbert Green, Gus Hall and Henry Winston, had been indicted under the Smith Act and were brought to trial in January 1949. The Smith Act, passed in 1940,[1] demanded the registering and fingerprinting of aliens and, among other penalties, provided for deportation of those convicted of un-American or subversive activities. Depending on the definition of subversion, the Act was thus a ready tool for the political persecution of Communist Party members, many of whom were Europeans who were not American citizens. The Supreme Court had not yet reviewed the constitutionality of the Smith Act, so when the defendants were convicted, after a trial of nearly seven months, and each was sentenced to five years in prison and fined $10,000, they were released on bail (refused initially by Judge Harold Medina but granted by an Appeals Court).

Hammett, in 1950, wrote an introduction, perhaps his last published piece of writing, to George Marion's account, *The Communist Trial: An American Crossroads:*

> The methods often seemed the methods of Alice in Wonderland, but there was no charming dreamlike irresponsibility in the Federal Court at Foley Square. Here upsidedownness served a grim purpose and whimsy carried concealed weapons. No matter how often the State said this was an ordinary criminal trial, it was never that. From the indictment of the Communist leaders on July 20, 1948—just as the presidential election campaigns were getting well under way—until the verdict of Guilty on October 14, 1949, politics was the whole show. The indictment was political, the trial was political, the verdict was political. Only the defense was not allowed to be political.
>
> George Marion has told the story here in good solid exciting prose. He is not neutral and doesn't pretend he is. I don't know anybody who was neutral, though I know quite a few who pretended they were. The daily newspapers were a godsend to these folks: with few exceptions the press handled the trial with such inept dishonesty that they soon bored everybody stiff and it was easy for their readers to think it was the trial itself—and not the reporting—that was dull. So we had a lot of people going around saying, "I don't care how it comes out just so they get it over with."
>
> Pro or con, you ought to care what happened; at the very least you ought to find out what happened so you'll know whether to care.[2]

The Supreme Court heard the case and upheld the conviction in June of 1951. Four of the convicted defendants then jumped bail at the beginning of July, 1951, around Independence Day.

Bail of $20,000 each had been supplied by the Civil Rights Congress, a broad-based organization dedicated to the civil rights—mainly voting rights—mostly of Communist Party members. Judge Sylvester Ryan declared the bail forfeit when the four did not show up for sentencing, and summoned the bail-fund trustees of the Civil Rights Congress to explain. The first of these trustees was Frederick Vanderbilt Field; the others were Alpheus Hunton, Abner Green and Hammett.

Contributions to the bail fund had been made by hundreds of people who were alarmed by the Smith Act and were sorry for the many harmless and inpecunious people whose freedom it threatened and who would not be able to afford bail as the Act became more and more broadly used for political persecutions and threatened people with jail or deportation for their (usually left-wing) political beliefs. It seemed to Hammett and the other trustees that the government would initiate prosecutions against bail-fund contributors themselves, most of whom were also harmless and impecunious. The government for its part believed that some of the contributors were probably hiding the four Communist officials, but thought it most likely that the trustees themselves might be harboring the fugitives. So Hammett watched with concern when Fred Field was arrested for contempt of court after his appearance at a court session on July 6, and was not surprised when the FBI showed up at Pleasantville to have a look around.

The three FBI men admitted they had no search warrant. Hammett told them to look around anyway. Lillian, coldly polite, drove them around in her car, insisting they look everywhere, that they talk with the farmer, Gus Benson, and his wife and go up in the attic. No Communists, of course; but it was horrible to realize they had been denounced by neighbors, perhaps someone quite close by.

> It is interesting to note [wrote columnist Tom Blair] how the FBI has been whitewashed of any guilt in letting the Reds slip through their fingers. In an effort to save the FBI embarrassment Attorney General McGrath said the FBI isn't required to keep tabs on men who are out on bond. If any other government agency had committed such a giant faux pas it would be pilloried and declared subversive.
>
> These are queer times; the FBI is supposed to protect us from subversives, and if we criticize them for being negligent in pursuing subversives we are accused of being subversives.[3]

Frederick Field had been subpoenaed and had testified before Judge Ryan, who, sympathetic to the FBI's efforts to find the reds, was willing to turn the court into an interrogation session about the whereabouts of the missing Communists. When Field refused to cooperate, he was arrested and jailed on Friday, July 6. The court expressed the view that Hammett was evading service because the subpoena servers couldn't find him, though the FBI knew he was at Pleasantville; in any case he preferred to go back into town, to Tenth Street, and to await the subpoena there. Driving Hammett into town, Willy Wyler had spotted a wood turtle by the side of the road. It was supposed to be bad luck, but they picked her up and took her along.

The night before he was to appear in court on Monday, July 9, 1951, Lillian asked him why he didn't simply tell the court that he didn't know the names of the contributors, because, as she wrote later, "the truth was that Hammett had never been in the office of the Congress, and did not know the name of a single contributor."

"No, I can't say that" [she remembers him saying].

"Why?"

"I don't know why. I guess it has something to do with keeping my word, but I don't want to talk about that. Nothing much will happen, although I think we'll go to jail for a while, but you're not to worry because—" and then suddenly I couldn't understand him because the voice had dropped and the words were coming in a most untypical nervous rush. I said I couldn't hear him, and he raised his voice and dropped his head. "I hate this damn kind of talk, but maybe I better tell you that if it were more than jail, if it were my life, I would give it for what I think democracy is, and I don't let cops or judges tell me what I think democracy is." Then he went home to bed, and the next day he went to jail.[4]

The proceedings were not without comic overtones. One of Hammett's lawyers, Victor Rabinowitz, moved to quash the subpoena on the grounds that it was inadvertently made out to one of the defendants—*United States* v. *Hall*.

"The witness is present in court. The Court will now proceed to examine him irrespective of the validity of any subpoena served upon him," insisted Judge Ryan.

The prosecutor then began to question Hammett, but the eager judge kept interrupting to correct him:

[IRVING] SAYPOL [the prosecutor]: Mr. Hammett, are you one of the five trustees of the bail fund of the Congress of Civil Rights?

HAMMETT: I decline to answer that question on the ground that the answer might tend to incriminate me. I am exercising my rights under the Fifth Amendment of the Constitution.

JUDGE: Mr. Saypol, I think the name of the fund was not correctly given by you in your question. I therefore suggest that you ask the question again.

SAYPOL: All right. Mr. Hammett, I show you this . . .

JUDGE: No, ask the question again so that we may get an answer to it.

SAYPOL: Are you one of the five trustees . . .

JUDGE: No. One of the trustees. Are you one of the trustees of the . . .

SAYPOL: Bail fund of the Civil Rights Congress of New York?

HAMMETT: I decline to answer. Do I have to repeat my reasons for declining to answer?

JUDGE: Yes.

The lawyers now produced the minutes and account books of the Civil Rights Congress and directed Hammett to inspect them, which he did, and asked him to look particularly at a group of initials—"four to be exact"—in the left-hand margin. Did he see them?

I do.

Do you recognize those?

I decline to answer that—now I would like before I decline[,] to ask, do I recognize them as initials? I would say yes.

But he declined to acknowledge whether he recognized the handwriting and so on, or whether "D.H." referred to himself, or anything else.

JUDGE: Let me ask you one question, Mr. Hammett—is that the name?

HAMMETT: It is.

JUDGE: Have you in any way conspired, aided or abetted or arranged or assisted in the arrangements for the non-appearance of Robert G. Thompson, Gilbert Green, Gus Hall and Henry Winston, or any of them in this cause since the issuance of process against them?

But Hammett declined to give the answer that it would have been easy to give: Of course not. He believed in the law and would not have hidden fugitives.

JUDGE: Mr. Hammett, a bond was given in this court, four bonds were given in this court by the bail fund of the Civil Rights Congress of New York, to secure the appearance or to assure the appearance of these four individuals whose names I have just given you. The testimony before this court is that you functioned as one of the trustees of that fund, that you have functioned as one of the officers and trustees of that fund for some time past. When these men were released on bail, they were released in the custody of the bondsmen, and since the bondsmen are members of an unincorporated association, in effect it means that they were released in the custody of those who operated and managed the affairs of this bail fund, and that they were released in the custody of the trustees, and the testimony before the Court indicates that you were one of the trustees, and by your refusal to answer you are not only violating the trust imposed in you, that you voluntarily assumed when you acted as a trustee for this fund, but you are thwarting the processes of this court. I feel that your claim of immunity has neither legal basis nor factual foundation. It is the intention of the Court, if you persist in your refusal to answer these questions which have been put to you, particularly those questions concerning the present whereabouts of these four men who were released under bail given by the bail fund of the Civil Rights Congress of New York, to deal with you just as drastically as the law permits. I trust that you will not make that necessary.

Hammett took the Fifth throughout the proceedings, as others had been doing, on the advice of the lawyers, though it was his own opinion that he had a First Amendment issue: that of free speech, or right to silence. The Hollywood Ten, among others, had believed the same thing, to no avail. But the Fifth did not offer protection either, if, as here, a witness had been summoned not on an issue where he was himself the accused but only as a witness. The law holds that a citizen is obliged to act as a witness in a hearing or court when called upon to do so, and even if a citizen feels that his testimony would lead to indictments and harassment of himself in later situations quite apart from the present one, he must cooperate with the court proceedings or be in contempt.

Here was the heart of the matter:

Mr. Hammett, the Court is desirous here of obtaining for its examination records of the bail fund of the Civil Rights Congress of New York of which you are one of the trustees and the chairman of the fund, and those records which indicate the deposit of money and the sources of these deposits, and I ask you whether you are willing to produce those?

HAMMETT: Without conceding that I have the ability to or can produce such documents I must decline to produce them.

JUDGE: Step down, Mr. Hammett, before the bar of the Court. Mr. Hammett, I find you guilty of contempt of court for your failure and refusal to comply with the directions of the Court and to make answer to questions asked of you, and to directions of the Court made to you to produce books, documents and records [of] the bail fund of the Civil Rights Congress of New York.

The minutes of this proceeding in which you committed contempt and in which your contumacious conduct has occurred have not as yet been transcribed. The hearing has not yet been concluded. I commit you now to the custody of the marshall, to be incarcerated by him until 8 o'clock this evening, at which time you will be arraigned before me, and I will impose sentence. . . .[5]

There is considerable satisfaction in being right and behaving well at a time when almost everyone else, on all sides, is behaving contemptibly. Hammett saw the right of the issue in two ways: that cops and judges couldn't make him talk about anything he didn't want to talk about; and that he should protect the names (which he didn't know anyway) of the little people who had given money in good faith.[6] The courts, on the other hand, maintained that if you put up bail for someone who skips bail, you have an obligation to help the court recover the fugitive, that "the claim of privilege against self-incrimination has no application to the contemnor's refusal to produce books held by him in a representative capacity," and that refusal was therefore contempt of court.

Moreover, since the bail-fund officers would not help the law recover the fugitives, the bail fund wasn't a responsible bonding agent and the people already bailed out by it were no longer bailed out and must find bond elsewhere, and that went for the trustees for the fund itself; and you couldn't get bail from just anywhere, you had to say where it came from and the court had to like where it came from. Fred Field was refused bail offered by Lloyd's of London—it sounded perhaps too foreign for the judge—but his wife could bail him out. A Communist and founder of the Civil Rights Congress, Grace Hutchins, could bail out Elizabeth Gurley

Flynn because she had inherited the money for it from her father, but Hammett's secretary, Muriel Alexander, didn't look like the kind of girl who would have $10,000—the first figure set—even though she said it was hers, and she couldn't bail out Hammett.

Toward noon of the day after Hammett's arrest, it was rumored that Judge Ryan was sympathetic to the plea of Assistant U.S. Attorney Roy M. Cohn—soon to become famous as Senator Mc-Carthy's counsel—that in view of the refusal by the trustees of the bail fund to say "whether they even knew the four convicted men for whom they had vouched, for whose appearance when required, they had guaranteed," any assurance that the bail bond fund might give for future defendants was "not worth the paper it is written on." The fund was, in fact, disqualified from posting bail for a new batch of fifteen people who had been indicted and described in the press as "second-string reds."

The legal argument was complicated on both sides, but never before had bail been refused in a case like this, so it was also rumored that Judge Ryan could not refuse bail for Hammett, Field and Hunton, but that he would set it very high.

As Lillian now recalls, she spent the afternoon trying to raise $100,000, although she has no memory of where that figure came from. She herself did not have $100,000, but she set about immediately trying to find it.

At the Chase Bank she learned that it would take more than half an afternoon to get a mortgage on the house on Eighty-second Street, so she went home and gathered up all her jewelry, including the pieces she had inherited from her mother, took it all to a pawn-shop on Fifty-ninth Street and came out with $17,000. It was not enough.

She then called a few people, who either were not at home or didn't have the large sums of money available to them in their bank accounts. Then she called Gerald Murphy, who owned the fashionable Mark Cross store on Fifth Avenue, and together they went down to remove all the money the store had taken in that day, plus an extra check from Gerald for $10,000 to be cashed anywhere she could find to cash it. She now had over $27,000, plus the possible $10,000 check—still a long way from $100,000.

She telephoned her old friend William Wyler, the director, who had been fond of Hammett, and he said, of course, she could have anything she needed and he would wire as much as he had in the bank that day. He called her back to say that it would be $14,000.

By Saturday dinnertime Lillian was in a bad state and had a

hangover. She had been pacing up and down the Eighty-second Street house, trying to think of people who had wanted to buy it and who would have quick cash. She tried the only very rich man she knew, an oil millionaire, only to find that he was in Europe.

Then the phone rang. It was her friend Leo Huberman,[7] calling from Martha's Vineyard. He had just heard the news of Hammett's arrest on the radio. He suggested that Lillian fly up to the Vineyard immediately and stay with him and his wife and their friends Sarah Greenebaum and Sybil May.

Leo had been a schoolteacher, then gone to work for the Maritime Union and had written a book on the working class that Lillian also admired. Sybil May, who was working on Leo's magazine, the *Monthly Review*, and had been a schoolteacher, was spending the summer with them. Perhaps the most impressive of the group, according to Lillian, was Sarah Greenebaum, who taught at the Parkinson School in Chicago.

The May-Greenebaum-Huberman friendship was a very old one. Lillian says she does not think any of them knew what it was to say, "I bought yesterday's dinner. You buy tomorrow's," but that all money was pooled and that that was how they lived.

She cried as she told them the story of Hammett's arrest and her attempts to raise money for bail.

It was a custom in that house to sit around the pleasant, old, ugly dining room table, as there were really no other good chairs to sit in. Somewhere around six, after perhaps an hour's tears, Huberman rapped sharply on the table, as Lillian recalls, and said that he wanted to see Sarah alone. He asked the others to clear out of the room. They had been gone only about ten minutes, when he called them back, taking Lillian by the hand to lead her in first. He said, "You will have the money tomorrow morning. We have called the bank. They will give enough mortgage on this house and on my little house to make up the hundred thousand dollars."

Lillian knew what the houses meant to them. It was all they really had in the world and she cried some more, until Leo finally rapped on the table again. In a very sharp voice he said, "Stop it. We are not doing it for you, or for Hammett. We are doing it for what we believe in. That is our duty, not to you or to Hammett, but our duty to ourselves. Hammett is right. You must not be seen in the courtroom, or you yourself will be arrested. I will get the money on Monday morning, fly down with you and take the bail money to court."

The next morning, protesting—not this time for Hammett but

for the sacrifice her friends had made—she cried all the way to the airport. Finally, Huberman said, "Lilly, you're a bore."

They parted at the airport in New York. Leo was to call the minute bail was put up and accepted. But when he did call, it was to say that Judge Ryan had decided to accept no bail whatsoever.

On the night of the second day, Hammett's lawyer sent Lillian a note:

> Do not come into this courtroom. If you do, I will say I do not know you. Get out of 82nd Street and Pleasantville. Take one of the trips to Europe that you love so much. You do not have to prove to me that you love me, at this late date.
>
> DH

And so the money was returned, Lillian booked passage to Europe, and after a year or two bailed out her jewelry.

After he was jailed, Hammett was kept busy with hearings to which he and Fred and Alpheus Hunton were taken, hither and

Hammett and Hunton going to jail, July 1951.

thither in Black Marias, always handcuffed. They used to hope to meet old friends on the way, so as to shake hands handcuffed. In elevators when people saw the handcuffs, they would always get off at the next floor, which would make Hammett and Hunton and Field laugh, and their guards too.[8]

Legal matters proceeded rapidly, confusingly, at first solely on the matter of bail. Judge Ryan had canceled it for the fifteen other defendants on July 11; they were jailed the next day but were ordered released by Judge Learned Hand, who held that a substantial question existed as to whether this was a Fifth Amendment situation. The defense counsel proceeded with Hand's order for the fifteen to the Federal House of Detention, but the jail refused to let them go. Field was taken to face the House Un-American Activities Committee on the twelfth, and also on this day the Treasury Department, working harmoniously with the Justice Department, filed notice of an income tax lien for $100,629.03 against Hammett.[9] The Treasury Department said proudly that "it was the first such action taken against any one involved in an investigation of subversive activity."

Field had been bailed out briefly with his own money, though not Hammett because of Muriel's appearance, but on Tuesday the seventeenth, Field was back in jail too. Meanwhile the state superintendent of banking tried his hand at subpoenaing the records of the Civil Rights Congress bail fund. On the same day the legislative branch, working in tandem with other departments of the federal government, did its part; Representative Francis Walter (R., Pa.) introduced a bill in Congress to bar any organization on the Attorney General's list from acting as bondsman in any federal case.

That same day, too, Judge Swan of the appellate court decided that "the giving of security is not the full measure of the bail's obligation; it is hornbook law that the accused is delivered into the custody of the bail and the bail is bound to deliver him so far as he can.

"It does not discharge the bail from that duty merely to abandon the security. The bail must assist in arresting the convict so far as possible; security is not a substitute.

"This being true, the bail can have no constitutional privilege to conceal from the court all that he knows of the whereabouts of the convict, and that necessarily includes an inquiry into his relations with him at the time when the security was posted." Hammett, of course, had refused to say whether he'd seen the four since they jumped bail, and refused to identify his own signature. "The claim of privilege against self-incrimination has no application here," held the judge.

The next day, July 18, Hammett, Field and Hunton were taken before a federal grand jury and made to testify there.

On July 19, Victor Rabinowitz moved to ask the Supreme Court to set bail and hear the issue, and on the twentieth, a Friday, Justice Stanley Reed, at home in Kentucky, agreed to hear the case but reserved decision on the question of bail. On Monday Reed denied bail, and on Thursday the twenty-sixth agreed that Hunton, Hammett and Field were indeed "contemptuous." And another judge, of the state supreme court of New York, ruled that the Civil Rights Congress had to give its records to the State Banking Department. Hammett had by now been in jail since the ninth of July—eighteen days.

The next day, July 27, the FBI seized twelve more reds, including a woman in her nightie, who was dragged off without being allowed to arrange for a baby-sitter for her small children.

Jose minded that Dash was going to prison. She hoped people wouldn't hold it against the girls, or imagine that she or they were Communists. And she worried about his health. The Kellys acted as if they had always expected something like this. She wrote him faithfully. The other nurses where she worked were nice about it; they knew it didn't have anything to do with her.

In *Hollywood Life*, July 13, 1951:

> Dashiell Hammett, noted author and creator of the "Thin Man" stories and "Sam Spade," deserves an American Tragedy title. Hammett is one of the most dangerous (if not THE) influential communists in America. Communism has been his first love for many years, and he has aided the Moscow methods with thousands of dollars, and most of his spare time. Hammett is said to be responsible for selling the red banner to dozens of men and women including actor Howard Duff, alias Sam Spade. Duff is also a member of one or more red fronts, and a definite red sympathizer.
>
> Truthfully, Dashiell Hammett should be indicted for participating in subversive activities and aiding in matters which seek and conspire to overthrow the United States Government. Earlier

this week, he was jailed for refusing to reveal the secret communist bankroll used to free commies and red fellow travelers whenever jailed. Proving over again that Hammett is without any question one of the red masterminds of the nation, with main headquarters in Hollywood and a sub-office in New York.

The actual record of the numerous red fronts of which Hammett is a member, executive or organizer, runs far past 35 organizations. I doubt if there is any notorious communist front organization that doesn't bear the phony Dashiell Hammett name.

When you're a commie and a member of more than 35 red organizations, you're in the high, top brackets of the caviar-vodka set.

CRUMMIE DASHIELL HAMMETT has been a member and has helped organize more than 35 organizations and, for the sake of the record, here are a few important ones: Citizens Committee for Harry Bridges, Hollywood Writers' Congress, Civil Rights Congress, Abraham Lincoln Brigade, Motion Picture Artists' Committee, American Committee for the Protection of the Foreign Born, Jefferson School of Social Science, and he once signed a letter, sent to President Roosevelt, protesting the alleged persecution of communist leaders. The above amounts to approximately 10% of Dashiell Hammett's efforts to help further the cause of communism.[10]

The New York *Mirror* commented on the fate of the Pink Plutocrats: "Too many American lives have been lost in Korea and undoubtedly will be lost elsewhere, fighting for us, to give one single, solitary damn for any stuffed-shirt who got mixed up with the smart, brilliant young Communists, and who now want out." Many people were jubilant to think how much safer America was now, with the smart and brilliant behind bars.

Mr. J. Edgar Hoover,
F.B.I.
Washington, D.C.

Dear Mr. Hoover,

I have in two instances advised your N.Y., or local (White Plains) of persons I believed to have acted suspiciously and who might be in some sense or other subversives.

In both instances the replies by your men were not definite nor was I advised that they would communicate with me if anything occurred. This is not a complaint. Your men were courteous,

& could claim that they had advised me that neither of my suspects were on their lists. In other words if I should otherwise later see or hear of something suspicious,—I would have no way of knowing whether or not such (my) suspects had been so carefully screened that the something suspicious was merely a coincidence.

We have, in my belief, subversives who are not Communists,—but even more dangerous? I am more apt to meet such latter, i.e. the Alger Hiss' friends,—than the type ordinarily read about in the newspapers. To put it another way if I knew the names of subversives & suspects I might be in a position to furnish your office with information. I am told that a Miss Lillian Hellman & a Dashiell Hammett, both of whom I understand live near here are suspected of having subversive tendencies ? I doubt that I will meet the former, & the latter I understand is living at Uncle Sam's expense. Of course, if desirable I might create the opportunity. I have done so before, in other matters.

I appreciate that your agents cannot disclose their records to everyone.
However,—I am told that in certain places there are watch-dog committees of citizens,—who keep your office informed ?
If there is one such here, I have not heard of it ? And if I knew who was on such,—I could give you my re-actions for what such were worth.

Perhaps,—to arrive at anything worthwhile,—it may be better to postpone an answer, in full, until you are to be in New York City,—if in the near-future?

May I hear from you at your early convenience ?

cordially yours,
[Deleted]

ps. I assume that you can inform yourself as to me ? If not I can supply the data.
At one time there use to be a number of [deleted],—some of whom caused me some bother.
For the present, I may say that my forbears were known since the beginnings of Our Country & in New York City or thereabouts since more 100 years. At my age, going-on-to 70, I doubt that anyone could vouch as to my birth & such.

Someone wrote to Walter Winchell, who had asked in his column, "Why would a pro-Commy enlist in our Army at his age?" The reply: "You ask 'why a pro-Commy (Hammett) enlist in our Army—' That's easy. Because our Army was fighting for Russia.

In other words: Only the Commies knew what the last war was all about—a war to make the world safe for Communism. (Don't mention it.) (Just call me professor.)"[11]

And one of the nice lads Hammett had known on Adak wrote, on VETERANS OF ADAK stationery:

This may not be worth a damn . . . but, this organization has never solicited or accepted the membership of Dashiell Hammett.

His financial help would have aided us in our drive for increased membership but we are Americans first, last, and always. . . .

Well it was common knowledge up in Adak, that even at $80 per bottle, there was more liquor under his bed than anywhere on the Rock. He was the Editor of the Island paper and the fact that a few drinks can open lips of any GI to another there must be a lot he must have learned.

If we can be of any help in the fight to rid this country of the COMMISCUM let me know.[12]

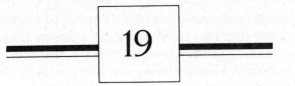

19

December 1951-1952
FALSE HOPES

It was December, colder now. Hammett, in prison, was told that the Supreme Court had refused to hear his plea for bail. He didn't much care; he was due to get out in a few days. "If there's any god this should be the last letter I send you from this address," he wrote to Jo. But as the preparations and symbols of deliverance gathered outside the walls his apprehensiveness increased. What had been happening while he was in here? "Being in jail is really being out of the world, since even your friends begin to think they're helping you by not telling you anything that might 'worry' you, and even when they do try to tell you something they are either so cryptic, or so take for granted your knowledge of things you don't know, that you can't make heads or tails of what they're say-ing. . . ." And how was he actually to get out of here? "As nearly as I understood my lawyer—by no means as easy a task as it may seem to those who don't know him—the last time he was down, L. is not coming to meet me and my airplane transportation from Charleston, W. Va. (which is only a couple of hours from here by bus) is either to be mailed me here ahead of time or be waiting for me at the airport in Charleston. Will you check on this with L. for me?" He needed clothes. Rose Evans sent him two suits, two shirts, two pairs of shoes from his closet so he'd have a choice. And: "My lawyer came down to see me last week, with no great amount of news, but with a topcoat to go home in, which is no doubt better. . . . The real trouble, perhaps: I still haven't—and won't have until I've had a chance to look the situation over in NYC—any idea of what I'm going to do when I get out or when I'm coming to California."[1]

Now he was delivered, or expelled, from the prison alone. When the hour came to report to the warden's office to take the ticket and the overcoat and the fifty dollars for a new start, Hammett wasn't quite ready. He made them wait a little, maybe just wanting to leave the place on his own terms. "When I'm finished talking here," he said. Alone, he caught the Greyhound bus to Charleston, and there ran into a guy he'd known inside who was now outside and down on his luck. So Hammett gave him the fifty. Perhaps he wasn't ready in his mind for money and tickets. Getting off the plane in New York, he seemed to falter, to stagger on the steps, was obliged to hold on to the rail. Then he was swept by waves of nausea and went off to be sick in the airport men's room; so much for wonderful homecomings. Lillian, who had come to meet him in a fancy car with a driver, had to send the driver in to check on him. A bad hamburger, something he ate, Hammett said. She'd made a supper of quail and oysters.

A newspaper reported a gala party organized by his friends. "The only one who wasn't there was Hammett himself. Maybe they forgot to serve him a subpoena," it said. He was sick, maybe just sick to be out, with no particular plans, broke, and nothing changed. He went back to his apartment on Tenth Street, alone except for Willy the turtle and Rose Evans to do for him. He bought three hundred worms to put out in the backyard for Willy.

Even the one little auspicious sign, after New Year's, the settlement in his favor of the Los Angeles suit that had dragged on, made no real difference to his situation at the moment. A judge in Los Angeles finally decided that Hammett did indeed own Sam Spade, the point that had been at issue since the Sam Spade radio series was begun by Regis Radio and CBS. But as Sam Spade had gone off the air again anyhow, it made little practical difference, and even if winning the suit had meant money coming in, the Feds and New York State income tax people had slapped liens on him anyhow. He would never have any money from now on.

The Civil Rights Congress had a nice reception you could go to for a dollar to pay tribute to the "three heroic Civil Rights Bail Fund Trustees who accepted imprisonment rather than become informers," as the *Daily Worker* described the occasion, and Hammett submitted to the role of hero at the Hotel Brevoort at Fifth Avenue and Eighth Street. The *Daily Worker* said that five hundred people came. There was oratory: "These men were not summer soldiers or sunshine patriots," said Mrs. Angie Dickerson, assistant secretary of the Civil Rights Congress, "but on the month of our Declaration of Independence, Hammett, Hunton, Green and Field—these great Americans—stood firm, knowing the grey walls of prison faced them," and Hammett, pressed for a word, observed that "they send you to prison to change your mind, but going to prison doesn't change anybody's mind about anything." Afterwards there was a reading by Beulah Richardson, "Negro poet and actress," the music of Bach and Chopin, played on the piano by Lucy Brown, and a group of songs by Al Moss.

A couple of months later the Jefferson School of Social Science got up a banquet too, for Hammett, Field, Hunton and Alexander Trachtenberg, "front line fighters for the preservation of the Civil Liberties of the American people," in the Carnival Room of the Capitol Hotel. Frail impassioned immigrants and indomitable society ladies with large busts and flowered dresses and principles were photographed attending. This gala cost $7.50 and had Paul Robeson and poetry by Whitman.

Hammett as prisoner, 1951.

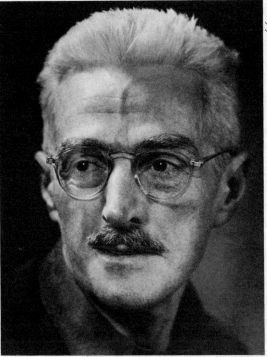

About the same time, in March, living alone in his old apartment on West Tenth Street, Hammett became acutely ill for several weeks with fever and nausea and couldn't finish his teaching term. "Things seemed to be piling up on me and I guess I was frailer than I thought,"[2] he apologized to the director, Howard Selsam, on April 10, when he first felt well enough to write, and on the same day he wrote to Jo about another sorrow, the sale of the farm, which Lillian, blacklisted and heavily in debt after paying Hammett's legal expenses, had decided was necessary: "Lillian's been moving P'ville this week, will probably wind up the job this weekend. I haven't thought about it much except to know it's going to leave quite a hole in life. I think she suspects me of having taken to bed to avoid the unpleasantness of helping her move." Indeed it would leave quite a hole in life. But it was, after all, Lillian's farm, not his; she was more concerned than he about money. He tried not to think about it. "She's coming down for dinner tomorrow night: I haven't seen her since last Sunday, haven't seen anybody: I'm not a man who likes his friends when he's sickish." It occurred to him that he hadn't written to Jo for a long time, maybe since he got out of prison. This surprised him. "I miss hearing from you and miss photographs of the youngsters and hope this sounds pathetic enough to touch you into doing something about it such as forgiving me for seeming to be such a non-caring non-corresponding father for so long."[3]

He finally got out of bed on a Friday, and on Monday morning he was obliged to appear before a federal grand jury to talk about the bail fund again. "By no means a difficult session and—though I was told to hold myself ready for a possible recall—I have no special reason for supposing anything will happen in the immediate future."[4]

In this he was wrong.

In the general climate of hysteria, persecution and prosecution, Hammett and the other bail-fund trustees would have refused to reveal the names of the bail-fund contributors, even if they had known them, because they did know that many of the contributors were aliens and vulnerable to deportation. But during their time in the West Street jail they had in fact been made to turn over the bail-fund records to the State Banking Department, which seemed to be at least a relatively honorable and responsible body with no political interests; it was entrusted with sorting out the financial aspects of the problems caused by the expensive defection of Green, Winston, Hall and Thompson.

Joseph McCarthy's was only the most conspicuous of the careers made from Communist-hunting; there were enough Communists around to support a number of careers. Now the records of the bail fund, in the possession of the State Banking Department, became especially interesting to the attorney general of New York, Nathaniel L. Goldstein, who called the fund "detrimental to the welfare of the public," felt it should be "erased as a public nuisance," and got the New York supreme court to freeze the rest of the money, about $717,000. He then named Hammett and the other trustees in a civil action, and he was considering criminal prosecution. He said they had violated the state banking law in soliciting and receiving deposits without license or authority, violated the Martin Act by failing to file certain necessary documents with the attorney general and secretary of state of New York and by indulging in "fraudulent practice," and had been unfaithful to their trust by not only refusing to cooperate with authorities in helping to recapture the four fugitives but failing to keep proper records of deposits.

So the possibility of jail arose again. Moreover, when Goldstein by legal maneuvers got the bail-fund records from the State Banking Department, he promptly turned them over to the FBI. "I came to the conclusion," said this Communist-fighting New York State attorney general, "that in the interest of national security, these records and names should immediately be made available to the FBI. . . . The FBI is equipped and in a position of being best able to determine whether the lists disclose any subversive elements."[5] This was exactly what Hammett and others had feared.

"In a way, I suppose the Bail Fund of the Civil Rights Congress was more fortunate in dealing with the Republican Attorney General of the State of New York than it would have been dealing with the Democratic U.S. Attorney of the New York Federal District" was I. F. Stone's view. "Judging from the past conduct of the U.S. Attorney's Office [the office that had sent Hammett up], I think it is safe to assume that it would have released the names of the 6,442 bail fund depositors to be publicly smeared across the pages of the Hearst and Scripps-Howard press."[6]

The next month Lillian was called in her turn to testify before the House Un-American Activities Committee, and she did what she thought Hammett should have done in the first place—offered to testify about herself but refused to testify about others. When this formulation was not acceptable to the committee, she took the Fifth but was not prosecuted.

Since jail, Hammett had got used to finding his character denounced in newspapers; now he found his work being questioned too. When he went to prison, people in buses had torn down ads for the film *The Maltese Falcon*. In February 1952 Robert Ruark, in a piece in the New York *World Telegram* mildly enough entitled "But Is It Art?" remarked he was "beginning to wish that Mr. Hammett and Mr. Chandler had never popularized the brutal beating and the cold killing and the kiss-'em-first-and-kill-'em-later method of dealing with dames, shameless hussies though they may be. The eager imitators [he meant mainly the almost parodic Mickey Spillane] have coarsened the tough school into a fatuous farce." In May a more serious article, by *Black Mask* writer Ben Ray Redman in the *Saturday Review*, extolled the fiction of gentleman-detectives and ratiocination and clues, complaining that "something happened to the detective story. What happened was a man named Hammett. The impact was terrific. We live today among conditions and convulsions that may be traced directly to the shock."[7]

And of his character, Hammett now read, in Hy Gardner's column in the New York *Herald Tribune*: "Talk is that Dashiell Hammett, whodunit writer jailed for contempt will renounce his Red companions by issuing a torrid denunciation of communism."[8] "You can't believe everything you read in the newspapers," Hammett commented to Jo.

In October he saw in another newspaper: "Reading over the list of the supporters for the movement to save the convicted Rosenbergs, we note the significant absence of names of prominent radio, teevee and show people who in other years were the first to lend their weight to all dubious and subversive causes. But some of the old reliables make their expected appearance on the roster. Howard Da Silva, for instance, Dashiell Hammett, Howard Fast, Ring Lardner, Jr., John Howard Lawson—and of course, that fine loyal citizen, Paul Robeson!"[9] He took this, of course, as a compliment to his character. People had run squeaking in every direction away from the listing left during this heyday of the House Un-American Activities Committee. Hammett continued meticulously to sign petitions, lend his name to causes, put up a couple of dollars when he could. He joined a movement to end the Korean War that would have required him, if it got off the ground, to go on a peace-lecturing circuit abroad; he signed a petition on behalf of jailed Communists that noted, truly enough, that "increasing multitudes of people . . . consider . . . that the government of the United States

fears the American people, and is no longer strong enough to tolerate freedom of speech and political association." He headed a
defense committee for V. J. Jerome, Communist Party theorist indicted under the Smith Act for activities no more dangerous than
a "Culture Fights Back rally of the arts," and whose "overt act"
against the government was an article entitled "Grasp the Weapon
of Culture." Hammett often didn't actually go to the rallies and
meetings of causes he worked for, but he went to a rally to protest
the death sentence of the Rosenbergs and he did a lot of other
things too, because prison doesn't change your mind about anything, a point he wanted to make. If he believed anything, he believed a man should stick by his views. But he didn't believe in
anything too much.

Lillian Hellman has written that she "was frightened that his
official connection with the [Jefferson] School would send him
back to jail and was saying so as [she and Hammett] walked down
52nd Street:"

> When we were a few steps from Sixth Avenue, he stopped and
> said, "Lilly, when we reach the corner you are going to have to
> make up your mind that I must go my way. You've been more
> than, more than, well, more than something-or-other good to me,
> but now I'm trouble and a nuisance to you. I won't ever blame
> you if you say goodbye to me now. But if you don't, then we
> must never have this conversation again." When we got to the
> corner, I began to cry and he looked as if he might. I was not
> able to speak, so he touched my shoulder and turned downtown.
> I stood on the corner until I couldn't see him anymore and then
> I began to run. When I caught up with him, he said, "I haven't
> thought about a drink in years. But I'd like one. Anyway, let's go
> buy one for you."[10]

Hammett could not talk about things that truly mattered to him.
He avoided sounding heroic. He could make an occasional revela-
tion, or he could admit to Fred Field that when he tried to write,
nothing much came of it, for he was nothing if not honest—in fact,
his honesty was considered a fault or a species of rudeness. But
mostly his innermost thoughts were sealed within him, trapped by
a habit of silence—the silent messenger boy reserves judgment on
the fat bosses; the sleuth must use his silence and stealth; the people
at a meeting or a party speak so inanely there is no point in re-

plying. There was so much speech in the world—he did nothing but listen to speeches these days. So few actions. It was men of deeds whom he respected, and men of words, of course, the writers who took words seriously. But words themselves could go wrong—the two-faced words of Dorothy Parker, for example, who would show someone sweetly to the door and no sooner would the door close than she would ridicule the guest. He disliked hypocrisy, disliked complaining.

Lillian always complained.

> I like her, so her complaints often seem cute to me, but the truth is as I grow older I have less and less understanding—of which I never had much, though I suppose I thought I did because the young hate to think they're mudheads—of either the reason behind complaints or the reason for them. They seem to me just talk, or quotations from the scripture. You improve an automobile or a civilization or a way of making soup because you think it will be better that way, not because you didn't like it the way it was; if you're disgusted with it it's a lot easier to walk or become a hermit or commit suicide or change your diet or something.[11]

He had contemplated, was to contemplate, was to try all these measures. Disgust is an immobilizing emotion.

He receives a post card from the Stork Club: "Just to remind you of our private room for parties."

The good ladies in Kentucky were worried when they found in their DAR magazine a list of Communists, including Hammett. Someone wrote on DAR stationery to check with J. Edgar Hoover: "I am going to visit all the Kentucky DAR districts and make a talk on Americanism—is this list accurate? Will it be alright to mention their names to be boycotted? I have heard that the Priest at Lynch Ky. knew the names of several Communists in Harlan Co. if 'the pressure were put on him' I don't know if you wish such information or not." Mr. Hoover, to his credit, declined her offer of boycott; nor did he encourage her to pressure the priest to inform on his parishioners.

Mary's recurrent nervous illness reasserted itself. In California the desperate Jose put her in the hospital. But there were nice things in Hammett's life at the same time: Pat Neal was in town—to appear in a revival of Lillian's *Children's Hour*. Best of all in the late spring he began to write a little at last. In April 1952 he wrote to Lillian, who was vacationing in Jamaica, that feeling good after a dinner party he "even took out the book and wrote about six lines on it before I went to bed," and the next night again after dinner out he left a blank space in his letter to her: "I was hoping I'd do enough on the book to brag about in this space. I did some, but not enough to brag about. So . . ." This halting pace notwithstanding, by August he was caught up in work—had good days, bad days, felt himself committed to a project. The "book," perhaps heretofore mythical, suddenly seemed in some measure to exist. To Lillian:

> It's looking a good deal like rain this afternoon although rain wouldn't make a great deal of difference since there are no local baseball games scheduled for today, which leaves me very little to do except maybe work at my writing, which is in good favor with me nowadays. I am looking on the book as something that might turn out to be very worth while having done, though I'd be one of the first to admit that my optimism may be based more on what I intend and hope to inject into it than what I've managed to get into it thus far, but that, I dare say, is more or less true of any writer's any book at any given time, and I hope that is true because I naturally . . . or it seems natural to me . . . wouldn't want to be—or to consider myself that, though after looking at this—as drunken-looking a page as ever was typed by a probably sober man I think I shall have to stop and brood over the whole tactical situation.[12]

Any writer's good days are followed by any writer's bad days, chagrin, depression:

> Let's see now what's news today that wasn't news some other day if any, outside of the fact that I've done very little work, which, while not setting the day off from all others as much as might be supposed still is generally speaking unsatisfactory. . . . I still haven't got up to your neighborhood, haven't been out of the house since along about this time last week, but I'll make it one of these days for sure. I stay in because I think I've got a lot of work to do . . . and I have, time's a-wasting . . . and then I don't get it done anyway. Explain that to me, Miss Hellman, though not just by saying it's too much like me to need explain-

ing; make up some fancier stuff even if it isn't perhaps as truthful. After all, what is truth? (I don't put quotation marks around
things like that—me and Adlai take what we want where we find
it, counting on our hearers being too uneducated to see that our
stuff lacks freshness.)

It's not too late to still do some of that work I'm bragging
about not having done, but the chances are I'll find some more or
less Proustian reason for not doing it. For instance, my watch
just stopped—and its stopping upset me. Do you think I can do
my best work when I'm upset? (Do you think I can ever do my
best work?)

I enclose some things, perhaps so the postage on this letter
won't be altogether wasted.[13]

And the next day:

I haven't been able to tear myself away from this work I keep
thinking about but not doing long enough to get outdoors to the
80's or the barber shop or anywhere. . . .

Now my conscience tells me that I ought to clear this typewriter for possible work on the novel that I'm supposed to be
writing.

I love you with the utmost extravagance even if I do set the
"Expand" key so that not too many words will take up a great
deal of room when I write, but it does not always seem to me
that such words as run through my head are at their best when
embalmed in black on white, and what are your problems as a
writer, Miss Hellman?[14]

On July 1 he signed his will, leaving half of everything he owned
to Jo and a quarter each to Mary and Lillian.[15]

24 August 52

Dear Lilishka,

. . . being back here in New York seems to have been more
of a waste of time than anything else as near as I can figure out,
but that's the way things go or something sometimes I suppose,
and if Proust doesn't get through with Albertine pretty soon now
—I'm almost up to "The Flight of Albertine" chapter and very
hopeful—I'm afraid he's going to lose a customer. Writers, not
only Proust, nearly all writers, make too much of things as a rule:
it's as if they took for granted that their readers lived in vacuums,

which may be true some of the time, but is at least an impolite assumption and very often leads to boredom. At the moment I take a dim view of writing and writers in general, but may feel better about it after I've scrubbed the little hand-shaker's teeth, shaved and bathed and had my little dinner—steak tonight, I guess, and maybe I'll go crazy and whip up a mess of potatoes, onions and lima beans to go with it. There's nobody around to dog-eye me if I don't eat much of 'em after I've cooked 'em— if I do—so why not? Isn't this Liberty Hall or something? On the other hand I barely may—after I've done those things that end with bathing—dress and got out for dinner, in which unlikely case I could mail this and you'd probably get it Tuesday whereas if I don't mail it till I go out tomorrow then you won't get it till . . . of course, the chances are I won't go out tonight, telling myself I should stay home and get some work done and—who knows?—maybe even telling myself that with some truth in it. I'm having a mess of trouble with my book, but it's the kind of trouble I suppose I ought to be having—what I hope and think I mean by that is that I'm having a hard time making it as nearly as good as I want it in the way I want it—so I guess there's nothing to do except go along sulking and cursing and writing and tearing up and writing and not tearing up and thinking I ought to be working harder on it and finding sulky reasons for not working on it at all and thinking it's going to be better than it's going to be and worse than it's going to be and different from what it's going to be and one minute sure that tomorrow or the next day I'll be better and the next minute just as sure that I'd've been better off writing it a few years ago when I had more stuff . . . all nice cute silly stuff that, I dare say, helps pass the time while the novel will get done—little better or worse than it ought to be—somehow somewhen. And with that bit of solemn bellyaching I leave you, my child, for what I hope is just a little while.

He had decided to leave New York, "because being back here in New York seems to have been more of a waste of time than anything else as near as I can figure out," and go and live instead in Katonah, not too far from the farm at Pleasantville he had loved so much. Some people he knew and liked, Sam and Helen Rosen, had offered a four-room guest cottage, with ten acres, near the entrance to their weekend place. The rent would be tiny—$75. Lillian told him to take it from her safe each month. In October he moved up there, taking his things—beds, chairs, tables, rugs, lamps and so on—"and here I am all more or less installed in what looks like it's going to turn out to be one of the nicest homes I've had."

And maybe this move would work. "Tomorrow I hope to get back to work on the book. My aim in life is now to be out of the trenches for Christmas, though the truth is I'll be more than satisfied if I've the first draft done by then. Its title—permanent I think—is TULIP, which is the principal character's last name, or, anyhow, what he says his name is."[16]

Jose started to work again, at St. John's Hospital. People did not know she had been the wife of a famous writer.

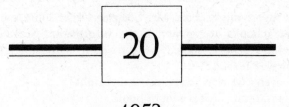

20

1953

THEATER

March 26, 1953. Joseph McCarthy's Senate subcommittee was looking into charges that pro-Communist books had found their way into a hundred and fifty overseas libraries run by the State Department. Three hundred copies of Hammett's books were on the shelves in seventy-three of the libraries. Hammett was questioned about this by Chairman Joseph McCarthy,[1] Senator John McClellan and the subcommittee's counsel, Roy Cohn:[2]

MR. COHN: Could we have your full name, please, sir?

MR. HAMMETT: Samuel Dashiell Hammett.

MR. COHN: Samuel Dashiell Hammett. Is that right?

MR. HAMMETT: That is right.

MR. COHN: And what is your occupation?

MR. HAMMETT: Writer.

MR. COHN: You are a writer. Is that correct?

MR. HAMMETT: That is right.

MR. COHN: And you are the author of a number of rather well-known detective stories. Is that correct?

MR. HAMMETT: That is right.

MR. COHN: In addition to that, you have written, I think, in your earlier period, on some social issues. Is that correct?

MR. HAMMETT: Well, I have written short stories that may have—you know, it is impossible to write anything without taking some sort of stand on social issues.

MR. COHN: You say it is impossible to write anything without taking some sort of stand on a social issue. Now, are you the author of a short story known as Nightshade?

MR. HAMMETT: I am.

MR. COHN: I might state, Mr. Chairman, that some 300 of Mr. Hammett's books are in use in the Information Service today located in, I believe, some 73 information centers; I am sorry, 300 copies, 18 books.

You haven't written 300 books; is that right?

MR. HAMMETT: That is a lot of books.

MR. COHN: There are 18 books in use, including some collections of short stories and other things, and there are some 300 copies of those located in some 73 information centers.

Now Mr. Hammett, when did you write your first published book?

MR. HAMMETT: The first book was Red Harvest. It was published in 1929. I think I wrote it in 1927, either 1927 or 1928.

MR. COHN: At the time you wrote that book, were you a member of the Communist Party?

MR. HAMMETT: I decline to answer, on the grounds that an answer might tend to incriminate me, relying on my rights under the fifth amendment to the Constitution of the United States.

MR. COHN: When did you write your last published book?

MR. HAMMETT: Well, I can't really answer that. Because some collections of short stories have been published. I imagine it was some time in the thirties, or perhaps the forties.

MR. COHN: In the thirties or forties. At the time you wrote your last published book were you a member of the Communist Party?

MR. HAMMETT: I decline to answer on the grounds that an answer might tend to incriminate me.

MR. COHN: If I were to ask you, with reference to these books, whether you were a member of the Communist Party at the time you wrote the books, what would your answer be?

MR. HAMMETT: Same answer. I would decline to answer on the grounds that an answer might tend to incriminate me.

CHAIRMAN MC CARTHY: Mr. Hammett, let me ask you this. Forgetting about yourself for the time being, it is a safe assumption that any member of the Communist Party, under Communist discipline, would propagandize the Communist cause, normally, regardless of whether he was writing fiction books or books on politics?

MR. HAMMETT: I can't answer that, because I honestly don't know.

CHAIRMAN MC CARTHY: Well, now, you have told us that you will not tell us whether you are a member of the Communist Party today or not, on the ground that if you told us the answer might incriminate you. That is normally taken by this committee and the country as a whole to mean that you are a member of the party, because if you were not you would simply say, "no," and it would not incriminate you. You see, the only reason that you have the right to refuse to answer is if you feel a truthful answer would incriminate you. An answer that you were not a Communist, if you were not a Communist, could not incriminate you. Therefore, you should know considerable about the Communist movement, I assume.

MR. HAMMETT: Was that a question, sir?

CHAIRMAN MC CARTHY: That is just a comment upon your statement.

Mr. Counsel, do you have anything further?

MR. COHN: Oh, yes.

Now, Mr. Hammett, from these various books you have written, have you received royalty payments?

MR. HAMMETT: I have.

MR. COHN: And I would assume that if the State Department purchased 300 books, or whatever it was, you would receive some royalties.

MR. HAMMETT: I should imagine so.

MR. COHN: Could you tell us, without violating some secret of the trade, just what your royalties are, by percentage?

MR. HAMMETT: Well, it is not a case of violating a secret of the trade. I would have to look up contracts. And they vary, as a matter of fact. On the books published by Alfred Knopf, $2 or $2.50 books, or whatever they were, I think it starts at 15 percent. On the short-story collections, most of which were reprints, the royalties are lower than that.

CHAIRMAN MC CARTHY: Did any of the money which you received from the State Department find its way into the coffers of the Communist Party?

MR. HAMMETT: I decline to answer, on the grounds that an answer might tend to incriminate me.

CHAIRMAN MC CARTHY: Let me put the question another way. Did you contribute any royalties received as a result of the purchase of these books by the State Department to the Communist Party?

MR. HAMMETT: I decline to answer, on the grounds that an answer might tend to incriminate me.

CHAIRMAN MC CARTHY: You have the right to decline.

MR. COHN: Now, is it a fair statement to make that you have received substantial sums of money from the royalties on all of the books you have written?

MR. HAMMETT: Yes, that is a fair statement.

MR. COHN: And you decline to tell us whether any of these moneys went to the Communist Party?

MR. HAMMETT: That is right.

MR. COHN: Now, Mr. Hammett, is it a fact that you have frequently allowed the use of your name as sponsor and member of governing bodies of Communist-front organizations?

MR. HAMMETT: I decline to answer, on the ground that an answer might tend to incriminate me.

MR. COHN: Mr. Hammett, is it a fact that you recently served a term in prison for contempt of court?

MR. HAMMETT: Yes.

MR. COHN: And from what did that arise?

MR. HAMMETT: From declining to answer whether or not I was a trustee of the bail bond fund of the Civil Rights Congress.

CHAIRMAN MC CARTHY: May I ask the photographers not to use any flash pictures while the witness is testifying?

MR. COHN: Now, you said it was for refusal to answer. The fact is: You were a trustee of the bail fund of the Civil Rights Congress. Is that right?

MR. HAMMETT: That was the question that I went to jail for not answering; yes.

MR. COHN: Well, let me ask you: Were you a trustee of the bail bond fund of the Civil Rights Congress?

MR. HAMMETT: I decline to answer on the grounds that an answer might tend to incriminate me.

MR. COHN: And is it a fact that the Government's allegation was that you were one of the sureties on the bond of four fugitive Communist leaders, that when they disappeared and ran away you were called in to see if you could aid the court in discovering where they were, and that a number of questions were put to you concerning their whereabouts, your activities as a surety, as a trustee of the group that had put up the money for the bail bond, and that you refused to answer?

MR. HAMMETT: I don't remember. I don't know whether I was asked anything about their whereabouts.

MR. COHN: Well, I will now ask you: Do you know the whereabouts of any of the fugitive Communist leaders.

MR. HAMMETT: No; Gus Hall, I read, is in jail.

MR. COHN: You know Gus Hall has been captured. How about the other three?

MR. HAMMETT: I don't know.

MR. COHN: You say you don't know?

MR. HAMMETT: I don't know.

CHAIRMAN MC CARTHY: You say you do not know where they are at this moment. Did you know where they were at any time while the Government was searching for them?

MR. HAMMETT: No.

CHAIRMAN MC CARTHY: You did not. Do I understand that you arranged the bail bond for the fugitives?

MR. HAMMETT: I decline to answer, on the grounds that an answer might tend to incriminate me.

MR. COHN: Did you contribute any of the money that went toward the bail, which made it possible for these Communist leaders to go free on bail, and later to abscond?

MR. HAMMETT: I decline to answer, on the grounds that an answer might tend to incriminate me.

CHAIRMAN MC CARTHY: Have you ever engaged in espionage against the United States?

MR. HAMMETT: No.

CHAIRMAN MC CARTHY: Have you ever engaged in sabotage?

MR. HAMMETT: No, sir.

CHAIRMAN MC CARTHY: Do you believe that the Communist system is better than the system in use in this country?

MR. HAMMETT: I can't answer that question, because I really don't know what it means: is the Communist system better than the system used in this country?

CHAIRMAN MC CARTHY: Do you believe that communism as practiced in Russia today is superior to our form of government?

MR. HAMMETT: Well, regardless of what I thought of communism in Russia today, it is doubtful if, you know, any one sort of thing—one is better for one country, and one is better for the other country. I don't think Russian communism is better for the United States, any more than I would think that some kind of imperialism were better for the United States.

CHAIRMAN MC CARTHY: You seem to distinguish between Russian communism and American communism. While I cannot see any distinction, I will assume there is for the purpose of the questioning. Would you think that American communism would be a good system to adopt in this country?

MR. HAMMETT: I will have to decline to answer that, on the grounds that an answer might tend to incriminate me. Because, I mean, that can't be answered "yes" or "no."

CHAIRMAN MC CARTHY: You could not answer that "yes" or "no," whether you think communism is superior to our form of government?

MR. HAMMETT: You see, I don't understand. Theoretical communism is no form of government. You know, there is no government. And I actually don't know, and I couldn't without—even in the end, I doubt if I could give a definite answer.

CHAIRMAN MC CARTHY: Would you favor the adoption of communism in this country?

MR. HAMMETT: You mean now?

CHAIRMAN MC CARTHY: Yes.

MR. HAMMETT: No.

CHAIRMAN MC CARTHY: You would not?

MR. HAMMETT: For one thing, it would seem to me impractical, if most people didn't want it.

CHAIRMAN MC CARTHY: Did you favor the Communist system when you were writing these books?

MR. HAMMETT: I decline to answer, on the grounds that an answer might tend to incriminate me.

CHAIRMAN MC CARTHY: Senator McClellan, did you have a question?

SENATOR MC CLELLAN: You are declining to answer many questions, taking refuge in the privileges of the fifth amendment of the Constitution, because you are afraid you might incriminate yourself if you answer the questions. Are you sincere and honest in making that statement under oath?

MR. HAMMETT: Very sincere, sir. I really am quite afraid that answers will incriminate me, or tend to incriminate me.

SENATOR MC CLELLAN: Since you say you are afraid: Do you not feel that your refusal to answer is a voluntary act of self-incrimination before the bar of public opinion? Are you not voluntarily, now, by taking refuge in the fifth amendment to the Constitution, committing an act of voluntary self-incrimination before the bar of public opinion, and do you not know that?

MR. HAMMETT: I do not think that is so, sir, and if it is so, unfortunately, or fortunately for me in those circumstances, the bar of public opinion did not send me to jail for 6 months.

SENATOR MC CLELLAN: Violation of law sent you to jail; being caught; is that what you mean? Public opinion, as against being caught? Is that what you are trying to tell us?

MR. HAMMETT: No, sir.

SENATOR MC CLELLAN: I did not want to misunderstand you. I thought maybe public opinion or at least judicial opinion had something to do with your going to jail. That was not a voluntary act, was it?

MR. HAMMETT: Going to jail?

SENATOR MC CLELLAN: Yes.

MR. HAMMETT: No, sir.

SENATOR MC CLELLAN: Well, public opinion must have had something to do with it, or judicial opinion at least.

I do not want to misjudge anyone. I do not think the public wants to. We want to give you every opportunity to be fair to the committee, to be fair to yourself, to be true to your country, if you care anything for this country. And I would like to ask you this question: Would this committee and the public in general be in error if they judged from your answers, or rather your lack of answers, to important questions, and from your demeanor on the witness stand here, that you are now a Communist, that you have been a Communist, and that you still follow and subscribe to the Communist philosophy? Would we be in error if we judged you that way from your actions?

MR. HAMMETT: I decline to answer, because the answer might tend to incriminate me.

CHAIRMAN MC CARTHY: Then we are free to judge according to our observations and conclusions based on your refusal to answer and your demeanor on the stand.

MR. HAMMETT: Is that a question, sir?

SENATOR MC CLELLAN: Well, if you want to answer it, it is a question. Do you want to take refuge under the Constitution again?

MR. HAMMETT: Yes, sir.

CHAIRMAN MC CARTHY: All right. That is all. . . .

CHAIRMAN MC CARTHY: For your information, in case you do not know it, Mr. [Louis] Budenz, the former editor of the Communist Daily Worker, gave you as one of those used by the Communist Party to further the Communist cause, and gave your name as a Communist under Communist Party discipline, recognized by him as such. If you care to comment on that, you may.

MR. HAMMETT: No, sir. I have no comment to make.

CHAIRMAN MC CARTHY: I have no further questions.

MR. COHN: I would like to ask: Is Mr. Budenz being truthful when he told us that you were a Communist?

MR. HAMMETT: I decline to answer, on the grounds that an answer might tend to incriminate me.

MR. COHN: When he told us that you were under Communist discipline?

MR. HAMMETT: I decline to answer, on the same grounds.

CHAIRMAN MC CARTHY: May I ask one further question: Mr. Hammett, if you were spending, as we are, over a hundred million dollars a year on an information program allegedly for the purpose of fighting communism, and if you were in charge of that program to fight communism, would you purchase the works of some 75 Communist authors and distribute their works throughout the world, placing our official stamp of approval upon those works?

Or would you rather not answer that question?

MR. HAMMETT: Well, I think—of course, I don't know—if I

were fighting communism. I don't think I would do it by giving people any books at all.

CHAIRMAN MC CARTHY: From an author, that sounds unusual. Thank you very much. You are excused.[3]

Hammett testifying before the House Un-American Activities Committee, 1952.

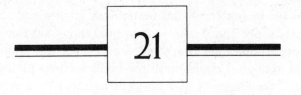

21

1953–1958
KATONAH

Hammett settled into a summer routine in his Katonah cottage. He had the woods to himself to wander in, enjoying the birds and small animals, devising feeding schemes. The cottage was little but cozy. He had three typewriters. He would go into town for provisions, or sometimes he'd go up to the Rosens' for dinner and sometimes he would not, depending on the company: "Barrows Dunham, author of *Man Against Myth* and *Giant in Chains* and in course of losing his lease on a professor's job at Temple, and Jack McManus, editor of *The Guardian*, are there for dinner and there will be much intellectual conversation about progressive political matters and I can get a bellyache just thinking about it." He had never been able to convince the Rosens that social change took lots of time. He took the long view and meantime would skip the discussions. "Outside of the necessary talk that goes with most of the things you work at, while you're working at them, I'm not sure talk oughtn't to be limited to women and sports . . . and I hope that's a sign of age because that way I can count on the notion staying with me and not being just a passing fancy. (I always get testy like this when I'm working, and I've been working a little—I never seem to work very hard, and do you want to make something of that?—on the book.)"[1]

With the move to Katonah and the congressional hearings, "Tulip" had lain untouched for some months now, but he had only a couple of months' work, he figured, to finish it up. Not working on it was "a sort of stage fright—"putting the finishing touches on a book can be kind of frightening, because that's that then—partly that I feel—most of the time—that it can be a very good job and

I don't want to botch it—and partly that from a financial stand-point there's not much use in my publishing anything till my income tax troubles get straightened out. That last reason is only half valid, though. I could finish the book without publishing it."[2]

"Tulip," the fragment of a novel, is narrated by a white-haired skinny guy named Pop who lives in the country on somebody's place, and life has contrived it so he hasn't got much choice left but to write. "I'm just out of jail," Pop says. "The last of my radio shows went off the air while I was doing my time, and the state and federal people slapped heavy income tax liens on me. Holly-wood's out during this red scare. So he [Tulip, a friend] figures I'll have to do another book—which doesn't take much figuring."

Pop's history is almost exactly Hammett's: "I've been in a couple of wars—or at least in the Army while they were going on—and in federal prisons and I had t.b. for seven years and have been married as often as I chose and have had children and grand-children and except for one fairly nice but pointless brief short story about a lunger going to Tijuana for an afternoon and eve-ning holiday from his hospital near San Diego I've never written a word about any of these things. Why? All I can say is they're not for me. Maybe not yet, maybe not ever. I used to try now and then—and I suppose I tried hard, the way I tried a lot of things—but they never came out meaning very much to me."[3]

Hammett wrote to Jo:

If you catch the Winchell broadcasts I suppose you heard him a couple of weeks ago tell about me worrying my friends with my thoughts of suicide. Well, quite a few people phoned me about it, but they didn't seem to be as bothered about my suicid-ing as about my not having told them. "You've always pretended to be a friend of mine: well, then, why didn't you. . . ." Just about this time last year Dorothy Kilgallen, another Hearstling, had the same item almost word for word in her column. Maybe Louis Sobol will have it next year. I'll try to be around to see.[4]

In the late spring of 1953 his income-tax troubles, which were never to straighten out, took him to New York for a few days as usual, during which he and the income-tax folk agreed pretty well as usual on how much blood you can get from a turnip. Lillian gave him money; it was, she said, a loan; he'd be back on his feet someday.

In town he saw Pat Neal, who he thought looked more beautiful than ever. She was getting married—he found this more irksome than he had a right to feel—in July, he told Jo,

to the guy Winchell mentioned, Roald Dahl, a tall ex-British flier who works for the New Yorker and has a book of short stories coming out this fall. I think he's a very silly dull fellow but Lillian—through whom Pat met him—and—I guess naturally— Pat both tell me I'm wrong and have only seen him at his worst. The ring isn't bad looking, though, and I told her I was glad she was getting that out of it because it didn't look as if she was getting much else. I guess the size Winchell gave is about right: it's a rather large marquise diamond—that's a sort of pointed oval shape, in case you've forgotten my Samuels training—of fairly good color: few big diamonds are really of pure color. She doesn't know whether to name her baby—regardless of which sex it picks out and it had better hurry or she'll go out and adopt one because this waiting around nine months might be well enough for some folks but it's a long time if you really want to play at motherhood—Neal Dashiell or Dashiell Neal.[5]

There were premonitions of worsening problems with his health. He'd had rheumatism or arthritis in his shoulder since '40 or '41, but the funny thing was it had never bothered him enough to make him notice it unless he was doing something he didn't especially like to do. In the army he'd had to go to the infirmary and have it baked before he went on the rifle range for target shooting, which he didn't particularly like, but it never bothered him when he went out with his shotgun in the woods. Now carrying firewood bothered his shoulder, and so did putting on coats. And at night when he couldn't go to sleep, his shoulder hurt. Not the other way around—it wasn't that the shoulder hurting kept him awake. It hadn't bothered him when he was in jail.[6]

In July he had a touch of pleurisy. That put him into a state of "halfwitted nostalgia"—he used to have it two or three times a year from the late twenties to fairly late in the thirties: "Maybe my youth's coming back, and I'm not sure I want to go through all that mishmash again."

He did feel, for the moment, invigorated. Lillian was in Europe for the summer to work on a film script for Alex Korda. In her absence Hammett was overseeing arrangements for the autumn road production of *The Children's Hour* and, among other things,

heard actresses read parts. He ran into old friends in restaurants—
Dorothy Parker, Rodgers and Hammerstein and, of course, Pat,
who had come back from her honeymoon and looked and acted
as if she were enjoying marriage. Pat still made him laugh, as he
wrote to Jo:

> She said that in London she was talking to a painter named Wood
> who was telling her something or other about Jacob Epstein, the
> sculptor, and mentioned that Epstein was currently interested in
> a mad way in Smuts and Pat said it was probably stupid of her not
> to know, but what was a smut? My guess would be that Pat
> deep in her mind thought maybe Epstein was going in for porno-
> graphic statuary.[7]

> I'm not sure how Pat's going to take it when she finds out that
> Priscilla Gillette has a remarkably fine stage voice. Pat likes her
> own voice a good deal, which I had counted on to keep her from
> paying any attention to Priscilla's, but that dope of a drama critic
> in the Wilmington paper had to go and comment on how nice
> Miss Gillette's voice was, so . . . I am very glad you are not an
> actor: they are capable of sillinesses unknown to the rest of the
> world and if I ever find out that I am wrong and that the rest of
> the world is capable of the same sort of silliness I am going to
> give up all political activity designed to benefit mankind and
> take up knitting.[8]

What might he not take up next? After the opening in Wil-
mington he had sat up and talked till after five in the morning and
he wasn't sleepy, so he wrote a letter and caught the seven o'clock
train north, got home in time to look at the World Series on TV,
was still up to look at the fights that night, went to bed with the
usual book and read till the usual time, and it was all the way it
was years ago, and he felt young.

June 22, 1953. Confidential directives from the State Department required books by subversive people to be withdrawn from
U.S. libraries overseas: books by Hammett, Hellman, Langston
Hughes, Theodore H. White and a number of others. The library
in Tokyo enthusiastically burned the books, but those in other
countries cautiously put them away for later. In America book
burning caught on. In San Antonio the "Minute Women" Committee demanded the burning of Albert Einstein's *Meaning of Rela-*

tivity and an edition of *Moby Dick* that had been illustrated by Rockwell Kent. Thomas Mann, living in California, who had seen his books burned in Nazi Germany, now saw them burned again in America. McCarthy was enthusiastic about such attacks on traitorous or obscene authors like Hammett: "Just because something is written on a piece of paper doesn't make it sacred."

President Eisenhower, being told about Hammett's books being barred from the overseas libraries, sensibly remarked that he wouldn't have removed them and that somebody must have been frightened. This provoked criticism of him. David Lawrence in the New York *Herald Tribune*:

> President Eisenhower is either the victim of mistakes by members of the White House staff who fail to inform him on controversial subjects before he enters his press conferences, or else he actually doesn't mind spending the taxpayers' money to give recognition on the shelves of overseas libraries of the American government to authors of books on subjects related to communism written by Communists or Communist sympathizers.
>
> It is difficult to accept the second assumption. It is easier to believe the first. . . .
>
> After the Press conference one correspondent asked a member of the White House staff if the President knew, when he was discussing Hammett's books, that the author had refused to answer questions before a Congressional committee. The reply from the member of the White House staff was that it could be assumed that the President knew that fact. . . .
>
> As for the voters of the United States, they would make short shrift of any candidate for Congress who said during his campaign that he approved of spending their money for detective stories written either by Communists or non-Communists.[9]

Unlike Lawrence, Hammett credited Eisenhower with courage and sense:

> It's early of course to see whether Eisenhour's—among other things I have given up spelling this year: let the letters fall where they may, the word or the name's the same as far as I'm concerned—mentioning my book has helped sales, but his position seems to me very vulnerable from his standpoint and I imagine he'll be slapped down, politely perhaps but slapped down just the same. The gent at times seems to talk a little like Adlai Steven-

son and it's not hard to know that that kind of thing helps anybody's political career.[10]

The FBI agent watching Hammett reported that "USA with
Dashiell Hammett as chairman, was formed by a group of individuals to assure that the young sons and daughters of Smith Act
prisoners and defendants, WALTER-MCCARRAN law victims
and children whose parents have been murdered by mob violence
or legal lynchings would be afforded 1953 summer activities."

Hammett spent the summer of 1954 with Lillian on Martha's
Vineyard. Warm days, a boat, a fishing pole, happy solitude and
less happy sociability, for the place was peopled as usual with
both friends and fools, whom Lillian collected in numbers, it
seemed to him.

There was a little tower in the house, and he went up in it
sometimes and stayed there for days at a time. Once he had gone
up to avoid the pontificating of an English writer who was pro-
nouncing ignorantly on fish, saying that the herring was related to
the mackerel. The man was clearly no fisherman and no ichthyolo-
gist, and his grand voice fluted queerly. Hammett forbore, then
could no longer restrain himself from pointing out that mackerel
and herring were not the same sort of fish. A quarrel began. He
hadn't meant to start it. He went to the encyclopedia to check
the matter, then started on upstairs. Were you wrong? laughed
the fellow. Hammett shrugged. He hadn't been wrong, but he
was unwilling to be down there with this ass, or any other self-
important ass. He spent more and more nights in the tower. He
did not feel lonely there; he read and slept a lot.

By the end of 1954 he was letting himself have a little drink,
just one each day, for relaxing. The year's end was a gloomy time
for him always, and now at this point each year he would think
of how he had stopped drinking and this would somehow fill him
with the impulse to drink a lot, and he would have to go into the
woods, far from things, until the feeling passed. As each year's end
approached he dreaded the return of the desire for alcohol, the
pangs of self-denial.[11] The anniversary reaction—it's common,
the doctor said.

In February of 1955 he had to testify again, this time before the
New York State Joint Legislative Committee, which was investi-

gating the Civil Rights Congress and other charitable organizations. Were there Communists in the Civil Rights Congress? Hammett said he didn't think so, but didn't care if there were: "Communism to me is not a dirty word. When you are working for the advance of mankind it never occurs to you whether a guy is a communist."

He had assumed, he said, that after he had gone to jail, such tribunals as this would let an old guy alone to get some rest. In the same month an appeal by Warner Brothers and Knopf on the Sam Spade matter was filed with the Supreme Court, and in March the Supreme Court upheld the appellate court and, by refusing to hear the case, decided in favor of Hammett. A great victory for private authors as well as private eyes, it was said. It didn't help Hammett's destitute circumstances, but it gave him some satisfaction.

In the summer of 1955 he went with Lillian to Martha's Vineyard again. On the last day of August he felt a terrible pain in his chest. It lasted all day, so that he felt he had to lie down, but he didn't call the doctor. He hoped the pain would leave him, and after a day it did, though he still didn't feel well and lay in bed a few more days. Afterward he was not the same; something had gone wrong.

After a month, when he still wasn't right, he went to the doctor and admitted that he hadn't been right, had been getting wronger for maybe ten years: short of breath, tired. Suddenly he was filled with a passionate desire that the doctor fix it. The doctor saw that Hammett had had a heart attack on the last day of August, so long ago that now he might as well continue resting up at home. So he couldn't go to Lillian's rehearsals—her adaptation of Anouilh's *The Lark*—and he couldn't go to his classes at the Jefferson School, "and the truth is that I don't want to much anyhow, feeling kind of weak and thus far very willing to spend most of my time in bed. Weakness is about all I do feel, however, and nobody seems to have any doubts that I will be as good as new once this take-it-easy period is over and I can go back to smoking and taking it easy again in my own way."[12]

What bothered him, he told the doctor, was that he always felt so tired. To move required a tremendous act of will. Why was he so tired? The doctor didn't know. Hammett was thin but seemed strong; the tiredness was odd. The doctor didn't think the cause was depression; he thought the symptoms were those of adrenal insufficiency. Otherwise there was no explanation.

To Jo on October 13, 1955: "Last month I had some sort of

heart attack—an *unserious* coronary embolism—and spent part of last week and part of this in dear old Lenox Hill Hospital and came back here yesterday on the promise to my doctors that I'd play invalid for at least three weeks, which is what I'm doing. . . .

Now I've got to go lie down. Give my best to Loyd and kiss the youngsters for me."

Katonah, 14 Oct 55

Dearest Jo,

That letter yesterday was just so you'd know I wasn't too badly off in case you heard that I'd had a heart attack because that can be made to sound sort of ominous—it has nice bullying possibilities that I must explore for possible future use—and there wasn't much news in it—the letter—so here I am trying to bring you up to date about what's been going on in my world since long long ago when I last wrote you . . . only nothing much of anything seems to have happened . . . but we can't all live full lives, I guess . . .

Pat had a baby last spring, a kind of cute little girl that I saw when she was maybe a week old, christened Olivia Twenty Dahl for God knows what reason. Pat, whose new show, "A Roomful of Roses," opens here next week, phoned me while I was in the hospital and promised to send me the youngster's picture—she says she looks like Ann, but then that's probably the only baby Pat ever saw—but it hasn't come yet. (It seemed to me that when Pat spoke of the baby it was a little remotely, as if she were speaking of last month's baby, but I'm probably doing her an injustice.)

Judy Rosen, now Judy Rubin, also had a baby in London last week, a boy named David as a great many boys seem to be named. A lot of other people I know seem to be breeding too, but I don't guess there's much use of telling you about those you don't know like Felicia Montealegre, who's an actress married to Leonard Bernstein, who's a composer-conductor married to her, so I'll just stick to my statement that a lot of people I know seem to be breeding.

I was up before some kind of state joint-legislative committee in the spring to keep up my franchise and the income tax people both federal and state bother me just enough to keep my blood more or less circulating and that heart attack—I'm beginning to roll that phrase around in my mouth quite unctuously—made me skip this term at the school and I haven't done much work on the book for more or less obvious reasons, none of which has to do with publishers, because, regardless of what's often said, they're folks who have nothing against making an honest dollar and are always willing to print anything that'll sell, and have been taking life easy.

Lily is up to her ears in rehearsals of "The Lark" which opens in Boston in a couple of weeks and comes into the big city some time next month, and in conferences with Tyrone Guthrie, who is going to direct the opera that she and Lennie Bernstein made out of "Candide," probably next year. I miss all this fun, if that's what you want to call it, by being on the sick list, though I've hopes of getting up to Boston in time to see "The Lark" before they bring it to town.

Frances Goodrich and Albert Hackett got smash-hit notices for the opening of their "Diary of Ann Frank" and everybody is very happy about it—those that aren't jealous—and that's every last bit of news I can remember unless you want me to make up some for you.

My best to Loyd and kiss the children for me—isn't it about time you sent me a snapshot of them?—and take care of yourself for me. . . .

Love—Pop

He was well enough to go to Martha's Vineyard in February of 1956 to see the house Lillian was buying there. New England was nice in winter. To one in precarious health, life is suddenly sweet and precious.

Nothing untoward happens to me however: I just go along in my usual on-this-hand-not-too-good-on-that-hand-not-too-bad shape, looking forward to some sort of gradual decline till I die in my eighties, though I'll spread it out as long as I can because having been born in the last century I'd naturally like to see this one through and die in the next, but since I was six years old when this one came in I'd be pretty old and people around me would probably get pretty impatient and you couldn't blame them too much . . . though I guess I would.[13]

In April of 1956 he wrote to Jo that his heart had recovered, and now all he had to worry about was that his lungs or something wouldn't manufacture enough oxygen for his big muscles. But he was weak and couldn't lead that fantastically active life to which he tried to make himself remember he was accustomed. He guessed the doctors weren't taking it too seriously—they more or less wrote it off as advancing age, incurable—but he had no intention of playing *that* game. He went again to Martha's Vineyard, and it was so pleasant there that he stayed until June. Then he went to New York, to the hospital again, and tried to get the doctors to fix whatever it was that made him so weak and short of breath, not the way he wanted himself to be:

> the general weakness that bothers me into thinking that I'd like to climb mountains or something—which isn't too bad, but the trouble is I get to thinking that I used to climb mountains or do many equivalent things (and you don't have to tell me I never did; I know it) and that's a kind of softening of the brain that probably does a lot of harm in the long run. The world's too full now of old fuffs who go around believing—or at least saying in the absence of witnesses—that they were once hell-a-mile. My guess, of course, remains the same, that old age is catching up with me a little prematurely and I'd better find out about it so I can nurse myself along and try to do at least a little better than my father, whom I'd like to beat at the longevity racket and who was about 83 when he popped off.[14]

The doctors couldn't find anything to fix. "It's hard to talk to doctors sometimes. For instance, I complained of weakness—w e a k n e s s—and they ask me about pain, of which I don't have any, and about tiredness, of which I'm not complaining. So we start all over, with pretty much the same results." So he gave up on doctors. If they want to go on thinking he's a man of sixty-two complaining because he doesn't feel like thirty-two, let them.

His doctor, still thinking he might have an adrenal insufficiency, put him on a saltier diet, and it made him feel a little better. And he was made happy by the news, in July, that Jo was to have a third baby.[15]

Jo kept writing her father, but he wouldn't answer. It was like sending letters off into the void. Then a letter would come out of the blue, as if no time had passed. Her life was full anyway, with babies and housekeeping. It was too bad about Papa, but he was quite old now, perhaps this always happened with the old. Mama and Mary behaved as if he still oversaw their every decision. Not Jo. She had her life.

He had been sued a lot, sometimes it seemed to him through faults of his own and sometimes not. When you are rich and famous you are vulnerable to suits. People want your money and also want to diminish and embarrass you.

Now, though he had a telephone, he didn't always answer it. He might be sitting outside, or maybe he just didn't feel like talking to anyone. He'd answer if he knew it was going to be Lillian or a daughter, but often it would be Helen or Sam Rosen from the big house, proposing his customary Saturday-night or Sunday-morning visit. More and more often they'd have somebody else up there he didn't feel like seeing, and if he wasn't going up, then why answer the phone? It was the same with the mail, but this day he did answer, and it was a reporter asking what he was going to do about the suit for $350. This was the first he'd heard of it. It was only then that he learned of the judgment against him in a county court in New York State—$350, for Burrelle's Clipping Service—and then when he didn't show up in court, a contempt fine of $250 and costs. The judge said he could pay it off at $10 a week.

It was the view of Burrelle's Clipping Service that it had served Mr. Hammett very well over the years, ten years or more now, even if Mr. Hammett was a Communist and a convict and disposed to complain of his bills. Mr. Hammett had complained, for instance, in 1948, when they raised his bill to $8 a month, not a very large sum in the opinion of Burrelle's, even if he did get only six or eight clippings a month. Plenty of months in earlier days he'd got tons of clippings, and you never knew when he might again. But now Mr. Hammett had not paid his bill for years, and he'd ignored very reasonable pleas, and so, finally, it seemed to Burrelle's, they had no choice but to sue.

The reporter came over to see Hammett and wrote it up, and Hammett sent the clipping, from the Mt. Kisco *Patent Trader*, to Jo:

> The man who earned a million dollars as creator of Sam Spade and the Thin Man is penniless and ill today, living quietly at the home of a friend in a secluded section of this town. . . .[16]

Jo was aghast, and talked very seriously with Loyd about her father. It wasn't the best time, with a baby on the way and many difficulties, but they knew what they had to do and wrote suggesting a visit.

7 Aug 56

Dear Princess,

You're a dear sweet girl and I'd love to see you and the youngsters but the plan your letter suggests doesn't, I'm afraid, seem
practicable just now, for various reasons, none of which have
much to do with with [sic] the things "covered" by that dopey
newspaper story I sent you, and which I foolishly took for
granted you'd take with a grain of salt. I guess I forgot the power
of the press. Anyhow, I'm not yet the pathetic figure the story
makes me seem with its "ill and penniless" angle. So I'm ill! Well,
I have had a couple of years of more or less progressive breath-
lessness and weakness—and a heart attack or something that certainly wasn't very bad and seemed to have nothing to do with
the other things—and it was a nuisance, but not as much of a
nuisance as it would have been if I'd had to do things when I
didn't feel like doing them—like working for a living—and I had
been sick before—for longer periods—and no doubt will be again
—and could wait it out even if I got a little impatient now and
then, and I did, and I seem to be on the mend now and have felt
stronger for the past month or so and how strong do you expect
to get anyhow? So I'm broke! Well, I am, but I still move around
New York City when I go there by taxicab and usually have a
steak and some caviar and whatever I happen to think of in the
ice-box and don't have to worry about the price of anything
unless it's fifty dollars or something—phooey on that kind of
being broke!

Lillian's still on Martha's Vineyard, working on "Candide"
with her colaborator [sic] and the director, and will prbably
[sic] be down to New York later this month when they start
rehearsals or wind up the casting or something. She sounded all
right when I talked to her on the phone last week.

Now I've got to go down to Katonah to get my hair cut. Give
my love to everybody, and I'm sorry about this summer, but
maybe I'll see you before too long anyhow. Much love, honey . . .

Pop

He still had the three typewriters there, gathering dust. A young
Englishman, James Cooper, came to talk to him. "Still in pyjamas
at noon," he told his readers. "In keeping with his own description
now of being a 'two-fisted loafer,' Mr. Hammett shows no signs
of the old spark that ignited his fame. Why did he keep those
typewriters around?"

"I keep them chiefly to remind myself I was once a writer."
Answers to other questions:

All my royalties are blocked. I am living on money borrowed
from friends.

I found I could sell the stories easily when it became known I
had been a Pinkerton man. People thought my stuff was authentic.

[I did not write in jail because] I was never bored enough.
I found the crooks had not changed since I was a Pinkerton man.
Going to prison was like going home.

The best detectives are the ones who do not get into trouble.

I am concentrating on my health. I am learning to be a hypo-
chondriac. I stopped writing because I found I was repeating
myself. It is the beginning of the end when you discover you
have style. But the thing that ruined me was the writing of the
last third of "The Glass Key" in one sitting of 30 hours. Ever
since then I have told myself: "I could do it again if I had to."

Yet, Cooper surmised, "As he gazes listlessly over the lonely
countryside from his isolated cottage there must be times when
he reviews a life as bizarre as any of his whodunits."[17]

In January of 1957, on a cold and sunny day, with an inch or two
of snow, he felt well enough to go into the village to do his shopping and mail a letter. The place was quiet—the Rosens weren't
coming this weekend. He liked the Rosens but he liked it quiet
better.

Yesterday his shoulder had hurt him—rheumatism, he guessed—
so he spent the day lying in bed looking at television. It wasn't
very good, but better than on some Sundays, or maybe he was
feeling more tolerant. He began by watching a girl sing "The
St. Louis Blues" on a church show, and then the Reverend Albert
Kersaw explaining that God was implicit in the song, making
Hammett think of the Song of Solomon, the same kind of situation. Then the high spots from *Troilus and Cressida* as done
by both Chaucer and Shakespeare, all this in half an hour—then
somebody called Pud and somebody called Ginger going through
the Indonesian embassy in Washington—and Hammett was amazed
as usual by the slick bad manners of television folk and the way

In Katonah, N.Y., c. 1953.

people put up with it; then he listened to a woman named Elizabeth Boyd talk about *Madame Bovary*—in a series called *Report from Rutgers*—in a way that was neither interesting nor uninteresting. Then something called *Odyssey*, which seemed to be Channel Two's answer to *The Wide Wide World* on Channel Four, a program he had always thought too dull to need an answer. *Odyssey* dealt in a boring way with the Comstock Lode and Virginia City, which you wouldn't have thought could have been that boring, and then Christopher Plummer did a Walter Kerr version of *Oedipus Rex*, on *Omnibus*, which was not bad except maybe for a kind of repulsive overdoing of makeup after Oedipus had blinded himself, with Carol Goodner playing Jocasta, and she was just a kind of puppet; so was a guy named Goodier who played Creon.[18]

So the long days passed. A neighbor, Jeremy Gury, remembers looking in on him one day.

There was a light on and I headed towards it on foot—even the jeep couldn't have got through the snow, dragassing the basket [of provisions] and a few logs, no mean feat. I knocked and waited, and waited. I had horrible visions. . . . I knocked again —this time the door was opened about four inches. No hearty greetings, neighbor. "Miss Hellman asked us to see if we'd look in to find out if you needed anything. I'm pretty good at making a fire." . . . If he had been drinking there was no sign of it. But the pile of cigarette butts was mountainous. He sat down in an old leather chair alongside the bleak fireplace and simply stared across the room. He seemed almost catatonic. I once had succeeded in keeping my mind blank for a fraction of a second and felt triumphant. Dash looked as if he was permanently in that state. No effort could elicit a word from him. I stacked the three logs next to the fireplace having decided that it would be unwise and surely unsafe to build a fire.[19]

Lillian wrote to Jo that she had consulted the doctor, who believed there was no danger in his living in the country alone. "The best thing to do is let him do what he wants to do. He is no longer very strong and his life is now the life of a semi-invalid. To put it bluntly, I don't believe the condition of his health will now ever change, although I do believe he has a long life ahead of him. . . . (You know your father well enough to know that the wise thing is to omit any mention of this report I have given you on his health.)"[20]

He could still, if he liked, read of his decline in the papers, even without Burrelle's Clipping Service. One Saturday he picked up the *Daily News* and read that he had bought a house in Mexico and planned to live there permanently. He hadn't been to Mexico since those trips to Tijuana when he was hospitalized after the first war. Another day in the paper he read that he was refusing to pay a long-standing bill to a swank New York restaurant because the management had put up the velvet rope to him.

March 1, 1957, New York *Times*:

A default judgment for $104,795 was entered in Federal Court yesterday against Dashiell Hammett, 62-year-old author of Katonah, N.Y. Mr. Hammett failed to appear or answer the Government's suit for the taxes filed last Dec. 10. The suit sought $103,486 in back taxes that the author was said to have owed for 1950, 1951, 1953, and 1954. The order to pay $104,795 included the taxes, interest, and costs.

A court deputy investigated him:

> Judgment #61,466   Samuel Dashiell Hammett
> Civ. 115-278   "Arcady" Estate, Orchard Hill Rd.
> June 5, 1957   Katonah, N.Y.
> This is a statement of my findings on above named person.

I spoke to Doctor Rosen on whose property Mr. Hammett is living in a small house. Dr. Rosen told me that Mr. Hammett is down and out both in finances and health. The Doctor told me he is living there because he and Hammett are good friends and he would not turn him out knowing he is in such shape.

I spoke to Mr. Hammett at the little house on "Arcady" Estate Orchard Hill Road Katonah N.Y. I made a demaned [sic] on him (as per instruction and according to the writ) for the sum stated of writ. He said he did not have the money. I asked him if he had any real property or posessons [sic] that could be turned into cash to pay the sum demanded of him. He told me all he had was a few pictures, a few sticke [sic] of furnture, [sic] which would add up to about two hundred dollars. I inquiried [sic] about his health (to substantiate the Doctors [sic] statement about him) Mr. Hammett told me he had had a heart attack and is now having trouble with his chest. In my opinion after my investagation [sic] I was speaking to a broken man.

The FBI continued to investigate him:

> FEDERAL BUREAU OF INVESTIGATION
> Title of Case SAMUEL DASHIELL HAMMETT

Subject contributed $1.00 to the American Committee for the Protection of Foreign Born on an unknown date. Subject signed a resolution condemning armed aggression against Guatemala sponsored by the National Council of the Arts, Sciences and Professions (NCASP) on an unknown date. Subject one of the sponsors of a newly formed organization known as "Watchdog Committee for Legislation in the National Interest."

Details: April 5, 1957

Hammett lives in the gate cottage located on the estate of Dr. SAMUEL ROSEN located at Orchard Hill Road, Katonah, New York. He has lived there for about 4 1/2 years rent free. He is single, having been divorced in 1936, and has no bank accounts or safe deposit vaults or boxes whatsoever. He has no boarders or subtenants living with him and lives alone.

. . . HAMMETT is not presently employed as the result of a

heart attack which he suffered about 1 1/2 years ago resulting in a shortness of breath and complications with his lungs and diaphragm.

He is not presently receiving royalties from any books or literary productions, and has not done so for several years because of tax liens imposed by federal and state income tax agencies. He stated that his income for the last year had been somewhere around $30, from an investment in the play "Death of a Salesman." He stated that he has been living on loans from friends since December, 1951, when he got out of jail.

He stated that he has no stocks, bonds or other securities, and receives no pensions of any kind. According to HAMMETT, he holds no mortgages, has no insurance policies of any type, and is not presently engaged in any business venture either actively or passively. He explained that he had a book which he had started some years ago, but that he had done nothing for the past couple of years. This book is entitled "Tulip," and is the only book on which he is presently working.

. . . According to the report of the Examination, the government made an application to direct HAMMETT to fully disclose the identity of all persons to whom he is obligated, including those making loans to him for his present subsistence. This application was denied by United States District Judge NOONAN. . . .

This "captioned debtor" has had charge accounts with the following stores:

> Tripler and Company;
> A. Sulka and Company
> Bloomingdale's
> Abercrombie and Fitch
> Finchley, Incorporated
> Holliday Book Shop
> Hotel Pierre
> Brentano's Book Stores
> McCutcheons

These stores report that his accounts are inactive, but one [deleted] reveals that Hammett made a purchase in the amount of $159.65 on July 3, 1957, paying by personal Money Order check dated February 1957, and another store disclosed that Hammett's account was utilized once in June of 1953, for $10.30, and that he didn't pay until December.[21]

January 14, 1958

Dear Lillibelle,

I meant to write you last week but life ain't always good even to tall goys and I had a kind of a go of it and am just getting my head above water again. No pain, or anything like that, but a kind of maximum discomfort. I was right in thinking I was picking up a cold . . . that's the first cold I've had in a couple of years and it wasn't bad as colds go, but it sure made a bum out of me while it lasted. . . .

There's a popular song called You're my Destiny that has a second line I kind of like . . . "You are what you are to me," because it's got that kind of ambiguity that I like.[22]

The mention of maximum discomfort, given Hammett's inclination to understatement, animated Lillian's fears.

Katonah, the last day
of January in 1958

Dear Lilishka,

Well, here it is Friday again and I needs must go into Katonah on another shopping expedition—that's the way I talk sometimes when there's nobody listening, highfalluting but not making much sense and no truthful sense at all. "Needs must" forsooth! What's the matter with the phone? It snowed a little this morning but now it's bright and sunny, and I can get a haircut and everything. . . . What's "everything"? What's wrong with just wanting to go down to Katonah?

It seems like a long time since I've heard from you, though it was only last Sunday. Maybe there'll be a letter from you today before I go shopping, or maybe not. I guess not.

Love anyhow . . .
SDH

In March he got bad again and went to the hospital, and when he got out he wasn't much better. "The ugly little country cottage grew uglier with books piled on every chair and no place to sit, the desk a foot high with unanswered mail. The signs of sickness were all around: now the phonograph was unplayed, the typewriter untouched, the beloved, foolish gadgets unopened in their packages. When I went for my weekly visits," Lillian recalls, "we didn't talk much and when he came for his weekly visits to me he was worn out from the short journey."[23] The Rosens' daughter, glancing at the window as she approached the cottage, believed she saw Hammett standing there in his pajamas with a gun in his hand. But then when she knocked and he opened the door, there was no gun. Sam Rosen, full of concern, called Lillian about it and confirmed Lillian's fears. Whether or not he'd had a gun, he ought not to be there alone anymore.

He knew this too. ". . . he suddenly looked embarrassed—he

N.Y. Daily News

Hammett, probably after 1955.

always looked embarrassed when he had something emotional to say—and he said, 'I can't live alone anymore. I've been falling. I'm going to a Veterans Hospital. It will be O.K., we'll see each other all the time, and I don't want any tears from you.' "[24]

Lillian asked Gregory Zilboorg how she could get Hammett to come to her, how to overcome his pride and independence. Zilboorg said she should tell him that she needed him in New York, so Lillian told him this, and she talked to Sam and Helen Rosen and they cooked up a story that they needed the cottage for their daughter. Hammett, though he didn't like to say so, felt relieved, a little, and made plans to go to Martha's Vineyard for the summer. To Jo:

17 May 1958

Dear Toots,

After five years and a half I finally tore myself, or got torn, I'm not sure which, from Katonah and came back to the big city where my address will be this until next month when I'll try Martha's Vineyard for awhile.

22

1958–1961

DEATH

Lillian moved him to New York.

He did not like being beholden, and applied to activate his pension so he would have at least a little income. The reply:

> Veterans Administration
> June 5, 1959

> Your disability prevents you from following substantially gainful employment. . . . The statutory award of $67.00 monthly for your respiratory condition has been authorized from April 3, 1959. Non-service connection pension benefit for $78.75 monthly is payable from May 27, 1959, date you attained age 65, to pay you the greater benefit since you cannot receive both pension and compensation.

Lillian gave him her room, which had a little dressing room adjacent to it, and she moved her bed to the room that had been the study, and the new study was the living room. Invalids require arrangements. Hammett tried not to require anything but kept to himself, mostly reading. The manuscript of "Tulip" lay on his desk.

"*You* try to get him to go out," Lillian would say to her secretary, Selma. "Mr. Hammett, you ought to get out, go out to dinner," Selma would say, and it had worked a few times—Hammett would dress, slowly, for all his movements were now very slow, and when dressed in his beautiful clothes, he would still look handsome. She would watch him go off in a taxi to a nearby Longchamps.

Veterans Administration
January 27, 1960

Dear Mr. Hammett:

The award letter to you dated June 5, 1959 was based upon your examination of May 6, 1959, which shows your respiratory condition to be arrested, inactive.

The appeal filed by you has been cancelled in our records since it is not in affect [sic] an appeal, but rather a request that your service connection for your respiratory condition be reopened. In order to reopen your claim, you should submit current medical evidence to show whether your respiratory condition is active since the previous examination, as above stated, shows that it was in an arrested state.

Upon receipt of this medical evidence, your claim will be reivewed, and you will be advised as to any determination made.

Lillian's play *Toys in the Attic* was opening in February 1960. He wanted to go and bought a new dinner suit to wear to it. He didn't feel well at the play but he got through it. After this he didn't go out anymore.

One evening he didn't want his nightly martini. Lillian remarked she never thought that could happen, in the bright tones one uses in speaking to dying people so they will not know you know. "I never thought I'd turn one down," he said, his expression, as ever, inscrutable. She had never understood him.

It was a difficult time, "indeed some of it was very bad," Lillian wrote, "but it was an unspoken pleasure that having come together so many years before, ruined so much, and repaired a little, we had endured. Sometimes I would resent the understated or seldom stated side of us and, guessing death wasn't too far away, I would try for something to have afterwards. One day I said, 'We've done fine, haven't we?'

"He said, 'Fine's too big a word for me. Why don't we just say we've done better than most people?' "[1]

Once when Lillian was away she telephoned Hammett, and he ran to the telephone in his eagerness to talk to her. Selma, the secretary, seeing this, wondered why he could not show his affection when she was around. She didn't seem to know how he felt about her. Or maybe she did, maybe they both did. An odd pair, it seemed to Selma, and so sad with him sick now, and it was bound to end the way it would end.

In May 1960 Lillian went to London to supervise the English production of *Toys in the Attic*, scheduled to open in November.

In the summer, Loyd, encouraged by Lillian, flew Jo and the children back to see Hammett. It would be, they knew, the last time.

You could see death on his face. "He doesn't know it," Lillian had said. Jo was shy around him, sad and appalled and hoped he wouldn't mention dying. He didn't. He looked forward toward life. "I have something I want to write," he told her. "I want to write but my fingers won't—won't type the words." Jo didn't know what to say. "We all have our crosses to bear," she heard herself say, a phrase that Mama used to say, or the priest—she hardly knew where it came from. He looked at her for a long moment and then laughed. "I guess you're right at that," he said. It had been a perfectly Hammett-like thing to say.

In September the doctor called Lillian to tell her what he did not tell Hammett, that they had found on his X-rays a cancer on his lung that had not been there even a few months before and could not be operated on, and there was nothing to be done. "I decided not to tell him about the cancer," Lillian wrote.

In the fall, Lillian woke early one morning and wrote a little note on her typewriter and gave it to him.

Nov. 25, 1960
7:10 am

On this thirtieth anniversary of the beginning of everything, I wish to state:

The love that started on that day was greater than all love anywhere, anytime, and all poetry cannot include it.

I did not then know what treasure I had, could not, and thus occasionally violated the grandeur of this bond.

For which I regret.

But I give deep thanks for the glorious day, and thus the name "Thanks-giving."

What but an unknown force could have given me, a sinner, this woman?

Praise God.

Signed.

It made him laugh.

He signed it and added a postscript: "If this seems incomplete it is probably because I couldn't think of anything else at the time. DH." His hand was large and strange, the letters wobbly.

In California, Jose and Jo and Mary discussed Papa's impending death. They wondered if they should attend. Lillian wrote them. Sometimes she would write that in their letters to him they were not to let him know that they knew there was anything wrong. Then again she would write or call, reproachfully, desperately, saying that other people had sent him flowers. Why didn't they? Didn't they care for him? What must he think? She was distraught, they said among themselves. Should they go to him?

Jo had three babies and another on the way. Mary? But Lillian did not think her presence would soothe him. Jose wondered if she was the one who should go—after all, she was the wife. But where would she get the money to go? And she had to work each day at her nurse's job in the hospital in Santa Monica. And would seeing her give him any pleasure? It had been nearly ten years now since she had seen him. She wondered if her presence had ever given him pleasure. But she was a nurse, on the other hand, and could be of help with the nursing. "But what could you *do*, Mother?" the girls said, talking against it. "There are nurses in New York."

From the window he could look down on the elegant street. His father had died alone in a boardinghouse in Virginia, or maybe —he hoped—Reba and Dick had been somewhere nearby. He himself would die in the East Eighties. He hadn't seen Reba and Dick for a while. Probably he owed them a letter. He should write some letters. He had trouble reading these days, his mind wandered, his eyes were bad. He should have gone to the old man's funeral. He hadn't seen Mary in a while. Mary had a husband now. This Selma, Lillian's secretary, was a nice girl and gave him a kiss when she came to work in the morning. She had her troubles with her son, and he could talk to her about Mary.[2]

He spent more and more time in bed, but got up to cross the room or sit near his desk, a book upside down on his lap. The manuscript of "Tulip" lay on the bed, unfinished. Lillian later wrote:

He did not wish to die and I like to think he didn't know he was dying. But I keep from myself even now the possible meaning of a night, very late, a short time before his death. I came into his room and for the only time in the years I knew him, there were tears in his eyes and the book was lying unread. I sat down beside him and waited a long time before I could say, "Do you want to talk about it?" He said, almost with anger, "No. My only chance is not to talk about it." And he never did. His patience, his courage, his dignity in those suffering months were very great. It was as if all that makes a man's life had come together to prove itself: suffering was a private matter and there was to be no invasion of it. He would seldom even ask for anything he needed, and so the most we did—my secretary and my cook who were devoted to him, as most women always had been—was to carry up the meals he barely touched, the books he now could hardly read, the afternoon coffee, and the martini that I insisted upon before the dinner that wasn't eaten.[3]

"An upside-down book should have told me the end had come," Lillian wrote," but I didn't want to think that way, and so I flew to Cambridge," where she was to teach a seminar at Harvard,

found a nursing-home for Dash, and flew back that night to tell him about it. He said, "But how are we going to get to Boston?" I said we'd take an ambulance and I guess for the first time in his life he said, "That will cost too much." I said, "If it does, then we'll take a covered wagon." He smiled and said, "Maybe that's the way we should have gone places anyway."[4]

Some nights a nurse sat with him, sometimes Lillian nodded at the foot of his bed, afraid to leave the room. Early in December she went out one night, but they called her home. The doctor said Hammett had to go to the hospital. As they were putting him on a stretcher in the elevator, he opened his eyes and asked her in surprise if she was coming, as if he hadn't expected that she would be. It seemed unkind that he could think she would not go with him. He was preoccupied, though, with death, and not with tact or gratitude.

This time he did not die. There was a little moment—here a space of two weeks—in which to consider whether the price of the flamboyant life had been too high. There was a flatness, an attitude of waiting, an atmosphere of silence and good manners. Lillian rubbed his sore shoulder, which seemed to have rheumatism in it.

At the end of the year 1960, on New Year's Eve, he went into the hospital again.

Pat Neal's new baby, while being pushed in his pram by his nurse, had been struck by a taxi and lay in the Lenox Hill Hospital and perhaps would die, and would never be the same even if he survived. Pat went each day to sit by her baby, and sometimes, having heard that her old friend Dash Hammett was in the same hospital, went up to see him. He could not say much. He was weakening and dying, but he was glad to see her and would smile. Now he knew that he was dying, or so it seemed to her. It did not seem to her that he cared.

The telephone rang for Lillian before dawn on January 8. She went out in the darkness to go to the hospital. It was the crisis. "Run quickly to the bed," said the nurse, "shout in his ear, as loud as you can." Lillian ran, shouting. Pulled back from death for a second, he looked at her, startled. On his face she saw a look of terror; for a second, profound terror. Then he was in a coma the doctor said he would not return from. Lillian waited in case it was not true, but it was true, and she didn't know what else to do, so she went home to think. He died two days later.

Hammett would not have wanted a funeral, and yet it seemed to her he should have one. He would not have wanted fine words, and yet some words must be said. He was dressed in the dinner clothes he bought for *Toys in the Attic*; this was the second time they were worn. Lillian was surprised at the number of people who came, people standing outside the door of the tiny chapel of the funeral home.[5] She wrote a eulogy and read it in a firm voice: "Dash wrote about violence but he had contempt for it and thus he had contempt for heroics. . . . He believed in man's right to dignity and never in all the years did he play anybody's game but his own—he never lied, he never faked, he never stooped," said Lillian at his funeral.[6]

Hammet was a veteran of two wars and could thus be buried as he wished in Arlington National Cemetery.

January 17, 1961

TO: Mr. A. H. Belmont, Federal Bureau of Investigation
FROM: [deleted]

It is thought Mr. DeLoach might wish to call the attention of one or more of his press contacts to the incongruous situation which exists wherein one who has been a member of an organization which believes in the overthrow of our government by force and violence receives a hero's burial among those who gave their lives to support this government.

"Hammett is dead now and his ideological sins may be buried with him. We had no original intention to speak ill of the dead but only to remark that Hammett's genius changed the form of the detective story and—without meaning dishonor to the classics by saying it—for the better," said the Los Angeles *Times*.[7]

"Dashiell Hammett, who died the other day," the columnist John Crosby wrote, "was that rare thing—a shaker of the earth, an authentic. 'The Maltese Falcon' was one of the best books of its kind ever written. It struck the publishing world and reading world—which is something entirely distinct from the literary world—like a thunderclap. Nothing has been the same since.

"Realism. Vigor. Vitality. Callousness. Immorality. Amorality. Muscular. Hard-boiled. They were all words applied to Hammett at various times. But authentic fits him better."[8]

SELECT BIBLIOGRAPHY

Adams, Donald K., "The First Thin Man," in *Mystery and Detective Annual*, n.d.

Bazelon, David T. "Dashiell Hammett's 'Private Eye.' No Loyalty Beyond the Job." *Commentary*, May 1949.

Bazin, André. "Mort d'Humphrey Bogart." *Cahiers du Cinéma*, February 1957.

Behlmer, Rudy, ed. *Memo from David O. Selznick*. New York: Viking, 1972.

Belfrage, Cedric. *The American Inquisition 1945–1960*. Indianapolis: Bobbs-Merrill, 1973.

Bentley, Eric. *Thirty Years of Treason*. Excerpts from Hearings Before the House Committee on Un-American Activities, 1938–1968. New York: Viking, 1971.

Blair, Walter. "Dashiell Hammett: Themes and Techniques." In Clarence Gohdes, ed., *Essays on American Literature in Honor of Jay B. Hubbell*. Durham, N.C.: Duke University Press, 1967.

Boyd, Rick. "The Thin Man of St. Mary's," *Lexington Park Enterprise*, December 5, 1979.

Carr, Robert K. *The House Committee on Un-American Activities*. Ithaca, N.Y.: Cornell University Press, 1952.

Cawelti, John G. *Adventure, Mystery and Romance: Formula Stories as Art and Popular Culture*. Chicago: University of Chicago Press, 1976.

Chandler, Raymond. *Selected Letters*. Edited by Frank MacShane. New York: Columbia University Press, 1981.

Edenbaum, Robert I. "The Poetics of the Private Eye: The Novels of Dashiell Hammett." In David Madden, ed., *Tough Guy Writers of the Thirties*. Carbondale: Southern Illinois University Press, 1968.

Ephron, Nora. "Lillian Hellman Walking, Talking, Cooking, Writing, Walking." *New York Times Book Review*, September 23, 1973.

Evans, L. O. "Speech before the Chamber of Commerce, Missoula, Montana," August 29, 1917. (Pamphlet.) Missoula, Mont.

Gardiner, Dorothy, and Walker, Kathrine S., eds., *Raymond Chandler Speaking*. Boston: Houghton Mifflin, 1962.

Gregory, Sinda J. "The Mystery of Mystery: The Novels of Dashiell Hammett." Unpublished dissertation, University of Illinois Press, Champaign: 1979.

Hammett, Dashiell. *The Big Knockover*. Edited with an introduction by Lillian Hellman. New York: Random House, Vintage Books, 1972. Includes "The Gutting of Couffignal," "Fly Paper," "The Scorched Face," "This King Business," "The Gatewood Caper," "Dead Yellow Women," "Corkscrew," "Tulip," "The Big Knockover," and "$106,000 Blood Money."

———. *The Continental Op*. Edited with an introduction by Steven Marcus. New York: Random House, Vintage Books, 1974. Includes "The Tenth Clew," "The Golden Horseshoe," "The House in Turk Street," "The Girl with the Silver Eyes," The Whosis Kid," "The Main Death," and "The Farewell Murder."

———, ed. *Creeps by Night*. New York: John Day, 1931.

———. *The Dain Curse*. New York and London: Knopf, 1929. Reprint. New York: Random House, Vintage Books, 1972.

———. *Dead Yellow Women*. Edited by Ellery Queen. New York: Spivak, 1946. Includes "Dead Yellow Women," "The Golden Horseshoe," "House Dick," "Who Killed Bob Teal?," "The Green Elephant," and "The Hairy One."

———. *The Glass Key*. New York and London: Knopf, 1931. Reprint. New York: Random House, Vintage Books, 1972

———. *The Maltese Falcon*. New York and London: Knopf, 1930. Reprint. New York: Random House, Vintage Books, 1972.

———. *Red Harvest*. New York and London: Knopf, 1929. Reprint. New York: Random House, Vintage Books, 1972.

———. *The Thin Man*. New York: Knopf, 1934. Reprint. New York: Random House, Vintage Books, 1972.

———. *Woman in the Dark*. Edited by Ellery Queen. New York: Spivak, 1951. Includes "Arson Plus," "Slippery Fingers," "The Black Hat That Wasn't There," "Woman in the Dark," "Afraid of a Gun," "Holiday," and "The Man Who Stood in the Way."

Hellman, Lillian. *Three*. Boston: Little, Brown, 1979. Includes *An Unfinished Woman, Pentimento*, and *Scoundrel Time*.

Howe, Irving, and Coser, Lewis. *The American Communist Party*. New York: Praeger, 1962.

Johnson, Nunnally. *The Letters of Nunnally Johnson*. Selected and edited by Doris Johnson and Ellen Leventhal. New York: Knopf, 1981.

Kalb, Bernard. "Remembering the Dashiell Hammett of 'Julia.'" *New York Times Book Review*, September 25, 1977, pp. 15–16.

Layman, Richard. *Dashiell Hammett: A Descriptive Bibliography*. Pittsburgh, Pa.: University of Pittsburgh Press, 1979.

———. *Shadow Man: The Life of Dashiell Hammett*. New York: Harcourt Brace Jovanovich, 1981.

Leverence, John. "The Continental Op." *Journal of Popular Culture*, Winter 1958.

Levinger, Larry. Interview with Albert Samuels, Jr. *City of San Francisco Magazine*, November 1975.

Macdonald, Ross. *On Crime Writing*. Santa Barbara, Calif.: Capra Press, 1973.

Madden, David, ed. *Tough Guy Writers of the Thirties*. Carbondale: Southern Illinois University Press, 1968.

Marcus, Steven. "Dashiell Hammett and the Continental Op." *Partisan Review*, vol. 2, no. 3, 1974.

Martin, Jay. *Nathanael West: The Art of His Life*. New York: Farrar, Straus & Giroux, 1970.

Miller, Perry. "Europe's Faith in American Fiction." *Atlantic Monthly*, December 1951.

Naremore, James. "John Huston and The Maltese Falcon." *Literature/Film Quarterly*, vol. 50, 1973.

Navasky, Victor S. *Naming Names*. New York: Viking, 1980.

Nolan, William F. *Dashiell Hammett: A Casebook*. Santa Barbara, Calif.: McNally & Loftin, 1969.

Paterson, J. "Cosmic View of the Private Eye," *Saturday Review of Literature*, August 22, 1953.

Perelman, S. J. *The Last Laugh*. New York: Simon & Schuster, 1981.

Porter, Joseph. "The End of the Trail: The American West of Dashiell Hammett and Raymond Chandler." *Western Historical Quarterly*, October 1975.

Potter, Jean. *The Flying North*. New York: Macmillan, 1947.

Pryce-Jones, Alan. "The English Have a Different Accent." *New York Times Book Review*, December 23, 1951.

Redman, B. R. "Decline and Fall of the Whodunit." *Saturday Review of Literature*, May 31, 1952.

Reilly, John M. "The Politics of Tough Guy Mysteries." *University of Dayton Review*, vol. 10, 1973.

Roughead, William. *Bad Companions*. Edinburgh: W. Green, 1930.

Ruehlmann, William. *Saint with a Gun: The Unlawful American Private Eye.* New York: New York University Press, 1974.

Sanderson, E. "Ex-Detective Hammett." *Bookman*, January 1932.

Schwartz, Nancy Lynn. (Completed by Sheila Schwartz.) *The Hollywood Writers' Wars.* New York: Knopf, 1982.

Spitzer, Erwin. "Remembrance: With Corporal Hammett on Adak." *Nation*, January 5, 1974.

Stein, Gertrude, *Everybody's Autobiography.* New York: Random House, 1937.

Stewart, Kenneth. *News Is What We Make It.* Westport, Conn.: 1943.

Symons, Julian. *The Mortal Consequences: A History from the Detective Story to the Crime Novel.* New York: Harper & Row, 1972.

———. "The Tough Guy at the Typewriter." *Times Literary Supplement*, June 5, 1981.

Tuska, Jon. *The Detective in Hollywood.* New York: Doubleday, 1978.

Wolfe, Peter. *Beams Falling: The Art of Dashiell Hammett.* Bowling Green, Ohio: Bowling Green University, Popular Press, 1979.

Woollcott, Alexander. *Letters.* New York: Viking, 1944.

NOTES

Unless otherwise specified, the letters cited are in the possession of the recipients. The following abbreviations are used throughout:

AK	Alfred Knopf
BK	Blanche Knopf
DH	Dashiell Hammett
HB	Harry Block
HRC	Humanities Research Center, University of Texas
JDH	Josephine Dolan Hammett
JHM	Josephine Hammett Marshall
LH	Lillian Hellman
MJHM	Mary Jane Hammett Miller

Quotations from Lillian Hellman's *An Unfinished Woman*, *Pentimento* and *Scoundrel Time* are taken from *Three* (Boston: Little, Brown, 1979), which includes these works with some additional observations by Miss Hellman.

Introduction

[1] John Crosby, "Death of an Authentic," New York *Herald Tribune*, January 18, 1961.
[2] John M. Reilly, "The Politics of Tough Guy Mysteries," *University of Dayton Review*, vol. 10, 1973.
[3] André Bazin, "Mort d'Humphrey Bogart," *Cahiers du Cinéma*, Février 1957, p. 81: "*quand il entre dans le film c'est déjà l'aube blème du lendemain, dérisoirement victorieux du macabre combat avec l'ange, le visage marqué par ce qu'il a vu et la démarche lourde de tout ce qu'il sait. Ayant dix fois triomphé de sa mort, il survivra bien sans doute pour nous une fois de plus.*"

Chapter 1

[1] DH to JHM, September 27, 1951.
[2] This account of Hammett's prison stay depends mainly on an interview by the author with Frederick Vanderbilt Field, Hammett's companion there, as well as on his letters to Mrs. Marshall.
[3] DH to JHM, November 8, 1951.
[4] Letter to the author from John Waters, then a correctional officer at Ashland, July 15, 1979.
[5] Muriel Alexander to JHM, August 1, 1951.
[6] DH to JHM, October 27, 1951.
[7] Ibid., November 8, 1951.
[8] Alan Rankin, in the Montgomery, Ala., *Journal*, October 2, 1951, re-

ferring to mention of Willard Motley in the fifth House Un-American Activities report: "Some other favorite writers of mine are listed in this jarring document. Mystery writer Dashiell Hammett, it says, is affiliated with from 41 to 50 Communist Front Organizations. . . . Is my new-found hero and genius Willard Motley . . . the same as the WM found worthy of mention in this 'Un-American Activities' volume? I don't know. And for the purpose of enjoying and appraising his book, I don't care."

[9] DH to JHM, October 18, 1951.

[10] Ibid., October 12, 1951.

[11] Ibid., November 12, 1951, and November 8, 1951.

[12] Ibid., October 12, 1951.

Chapter 2

[1] Hammett's mother, Annie Bond Dashiell, daughter of John V. Dashiell and Anne R. Evans, was born June 3, 1864, in Baltimore, Md., and died there August 3, 1922. She was married May 18, 1892, to Richard T. Hammett, son of Samuel Biscoe Hammett and Ann Rebecca Hammett, his first cousin. Richard T. was born February 19, 1863, and died March 13, 1948. Aronia Rebecca, Hammett's sister, was born February 8, 1893, and Richard Thomas, Jr., on September 7, 1896. See *The Dashiell Family Records* (Baltimore, Md., 1932), compiled by Benjamin Dashiell, for additional information on the Dashiells. Other family information comes from the St. Marys County Historical Society; Rick Boyd's "The Thin Man of St. Marys," p. C-1; and the State of Maryland Department of General Services, Hall of Records.

[2] U.S. Census, 1900.

[3] Boyd, "The Thin Man of St. Mary's," p. C-1.

[4] Baltimore City directories, 1900–1921. Hammett is listed there as living with his parents through 1921. It is probable that the family home remained his official address while he traveled West.

[5] Richard Layman, *Shadow Man*, pp. 8–9.

[6] Layman, among other biographers, has reported Richard T. Hammett as a hard-drinking womanizer, but his daughter (Hammett's sister, Reba), interviewed in the Baltimore *Sun*, May 8, 1966, by James Bready, says, "Dashiell was a wild one. . . . Father didn't like it—he never touched a drop." Considering Hammett's pattern of rebelling against authority, the teetotaling father makes a certain sense of Hammett's alcoholism.

[7] *Black Mask*, March 1, 1924.

[8] "Our Readers' Private Corner," *Black Mask*, June 1925, p. 128.

[9] L. O. Evans, chief counsel of the Anaconda Copper Mining Company, "Speech before the Chamber of Commerce, Missoula, Montana, August 29, 1917" (pamphlet, New York Public Library, p. 8).

[10] "Through the years he was to repeat that bribe offer so many times," Lillian Hellman wrote, "that I came to believe, knowing him now, that it was a kind of key to his life. He had given a man the right to think he would murder, and the fact that Frank Little was lynched with three other men in what was known as the Everett Massacre must have been, for

Hammett, an abiding horror. I think I can date Hammett's belief that he was living in a corrupt society from Little's murder" (*Scoundrel Time* [*Three*, p. 614]).

Chapter 3

[1] Evans, "Speech before Missoula Chamber of Commerce," p. 1.

[2] Treasury Department, Bureau of War Risk Insurance Award of Compensation, June 10, 1920. Military records do not reveal the accident with the ambulance. Hammett enlisted July 12, 1918, and was discharged May 28, 1919, the day after his twenty-fifth birthday.

[3] Josephine Marshall corrects Richard Layman's account: Josephine Dolan's father did not desert the family after her birth (February 27, 1896) —there were in fact two younger brothers. Josephine Dolan's mother died when she was four, her father when she was nine. The material here comes from the author's interview with Josephine Dolan Hammett and from her daughters' recollections of conversations with her.

[4] Cushman Hospital, Tacoma, Wash.

[5] "Tulip" (*The Big Knockover*, pp. 337-39).

[6] "Seven Pages," unpublished MS (HRC).

[7] "Women Are a Lot of Fun Too," unpublished story (HRC). Hammett's daughter Josephine Marshall doubts that this description could refer to her mother, at least not in every detail—in particular, Mrs. Hammett did not use strong language.

[8] Ibid.

[9] "Tulip" (*The Big Knockover*, p. 344).

Chapter 4

[1] The Crawford Apartments, no. 35, at 620 Eddy Street. According to Mrs. Hammett, they also lived later in another apartment at the same address.

[2] Interview with Mrs. Hammett.

[3] This account, from the San Francisco *Chronicle* (November 30, 1921, p. 13), is preserved among a number of Hammett papers given to me by a previous researcher, Professor Steven Marcus, of which I have not been able to establish the provenance. Hammett saved newspaper clippings, though he did not, apparently, preserve letters. So it is possible that it was he who preserved this; but it is equally possible that this clipping was dug out by the previous researcher. Hammett also said that he himself put an ad in the newspaper including the hopeful words "I can write." This ad has not been found.

[4] "Seven Pages," unpublished MS, n.d. (HRC).

[5] The story of the *Sonoma* gold was one that Hammett would tell in various versions in later years (see Lillian Hellman's Introduction to *The Big Knockover*, pp. xiii–xiv).

[6] Hammett's close reading of James is illustrated in the following, from his Introduction to a collection of mystery stories, *Creeps By Night* (New York: John Day, 1931): "This business of making the reader feel that what

cannot happen can and should not is a tremendously difficult one for the author. Addressing himself, as we have assumed he must, to the orderly minded reader, he cannot count on any native credulity or superstition to be taken advantage of.

"Atmosphere may be used to set the stage, but is seldom a great help thereafter and in fact more often an encumbrance than not.

"Brutality, often an excellent accompaniment and a means to an end, is never properly more than that in this field, and some of the finest effects have been secured with the daintiest touches. The most authentic single touch in 'The Turn of the Screw'—too well known as well as a bit too long for inclusion here—is not when the child sees the ghost across the lake, but when she turns her back to it, pretending interest in some rubbish at her feet, to keep her governess from knowing she has seen it."

James Benet remembers hearing Hammett discuss James and surprise others with his minute and close acquaintance with James's work. According to William F. Nolan (*Dashiell Hammett*, p. 60), on another occasion Hammett told James Thurber that the plot of *The Maltese Falcon* owed a great deal to *The Wings of the Dove*.

[7] Ellery Queen, Preface to *Woman in the Dark*, p. 9.

[8] Hammett was presumably there for Pinkerton; he stayed at 1117 Third Avenue.

[9] "Holiday," in *Woman in the Dark*. First published in *The New Pearsons*, July 1923, pp. 30–32.

[10] A photostat of this advertisement is among the Hammett papers. Nolan, in *Dashiell Hammett*, gives the traditional view that Hammett put an ad in the paper, listing his work experience and adding, "And I can write." The actual dates of Hammett's employment at Samuels are in doubt. It seems that it may have been, at first, part-time.

[11] San Francisco *Chronicle*, November 1922.

[12] San Francisco *Chronicle*, July 26, 1925; signed "Albert Samuels."

[13] Oakland *Post*, September 20, 1924; signed "Albert Samuels."

[14] Oakland *Post*, September 6, 1924; unsigned.

[15] Oakland *Post-Enquirer*, April 26, 1925; signed "Albert Samuels."

[16] Among the Hammett papers are photostats of two poems published in *Argosy All-Story Weekly*, July or August 1922. If this very Hammettesque poem is indeed his, this would be earlier than "The Parthian Shot," usually believed to be his first publication.

By Practised Skill

Surely he who loves but once
    Is a clumsy clown;
Trembles like a silly dunce
    At a woman's frown.

Kisses when she'd rather not,
    Doesn't when she would
Always cold when she is hot,
    Crosses every mood.

Either tries to go too far,
   Gets her in a huff;
Or his weak entreaties are
   Scarcely bold enough.

Loving is a subtle art,
   Intricate its lore;
And he wins a woman's heart
   Who has won before.

The same periodical published another, shorter poem in July or August 1923.

A CLINCHER

By one decisive argument,
   Giles gained his lovely Kate's consent
      To fix the bridal day.
"Why in such haste, dear Giles, to wed?
I shall not change my mind," she said.
      "But then," said he, "I may!"

[17] In 1946 Raymond Chandler wrote Erle Stanley Gardner about Shaw: "I don't think I ever knew that Phil Cody had been editor of the BM or that Hammett and you and others had been in the book for years. I didn't know the magazine until 1932 or 1933, although I later picked up a few older copies. In view of the fact that I was raised on Latin and Greek and once wrote essays and book reviews for a *very* highbrow English weekly, the story of how I became a multiple murderer may have a certain piquancy, but there's not time to go into it now. Nor did I know that Cody was the real discoverer of Hammett and his first strong encouragement. I think these things need airing. I have always received from Shaw the definite impression (borne out by his projected introduction to his projected anthology) that he invented the hardboiled dick story with a ready assist from Hammett. Certainly nothing of Shaw's own fiction that I have seen has any such germs in it. It's about the deadest writing I ever saw, on a supposedly professional level. I don't know what Hammett was writing before he and Shaw had the brainwave, but it is now obvious to me and would have been earlier if I had really done any serious thinking on the subject, that it did not happen all at once. There must have been experiments and discussions and a need to get an okay from the boss. Shaw's gifts as an editor seem to me now to be exactly what you rate them. He was a warm editor and always seemed to have time to write at length and to argue with you. To some of us I think he was indeed a genuine inspiration in that, just as you say, we wrote better for him than we could have written for anybody else" (Chandler, *Selected Letters*, 67–68).

[18] Josephine Marshall remembers Hammett saying that he blamed himself for the eclipse in Daly's fortunes, and that Daly blamed him; Hammett's greater talent must have been obvious to all.

[19] *The Smart Set*, January 1923, p. 56.

[20] Hammett, "The Gutting of Couffignal" (*The Big Knockover*, p. 34).

[21] *Smart Set*, March 1923, pp. 88–90. No other Hammett anecdote has been repeated and distorted more frequently than item 28, about the Ferris wheel. Details vary hopelessly, the discrepancies often attributed to Hammett himself. He found or lost the Ferris wheel, was promoted or fired for his success or failure.

Chapter 5

[1] Author's interview with Josephine Dolan Hammett.

[2] *Sunset Magazine*, October 1925.

[3] *Western Advertising*, December 1925, pp. 82–83.

[4] *Writer's Digest*, June 1924, p. 7.

[5] *Forum*, August 1925, p. 317.

[6] "Our Own Short Story Course," *Black Mask*, August 1924, pp. 127–28.

[7] "The Advertisement Is Literature," *Western Advertising*, October 1926, pp. 35–36.

[8] The reviews in *Western Advertising* have not previously been attributed to Hammett. My assumption that he wrote them is based on the style as well as the fact that they came out under his initials in a magazine with which he was associated at this particular time, a time when he was also writing reviews for other periodicals.

[9] *Western Advertising*, December 1925, p. 80.

[10] Ibid., June 1928, p. 83.

[11] Ibid., July 1926, p. 74.

[12] Elfinstone MS (HRC). These manuscripts pertaining to "The Secret Emperor" throw some light on Hammett's habits of composition. He has provided himself with character descriptions (quoted), a short and a second more elaborate outline. Then he writes a scene mostly in dialogue, without action or description, evidently planning to combine the dialogue with the action in a fuller draft. Hammett may have preserved these working materials with the intention of returning to the novel at some point.

[13] DH to JHM, April 30, 1947.

[14] Josephine Hammett Marshall says that a trip to Montana was never described to her, in later years, as a precautionary measure against the danger of infection.

[15] In a letter to Willis Wing, Gardner's agent, January 17, 1946, quoted in Philip Durham's Preface to *The Boys in the Black Mask*, which accompanied an exhibition at the UCLA Library, January 6–February 10, 1961. Other *Black Mask* writers included W. T. Ballard, Charles G. Booth, William E. Brandon, Paul Cain, Raymond Chandler, George Harmon Coxe, Carroll John Daly, Norbert Davis, Lester Dent, Gardner, Frank Gruber, Horace McCoy, Frederick Nebel, Shaw himself, Thomas Walsh, Raoul Whitfield and Cornell Woolrich.

Gardner was right that Shaw was Hammettizing the *Black Mask* as best he could. He tried to cure the others of what he considered verbosity by giving them a story by Chandler or Hammett and suggesting they cut it a little; he was sure they would realize that these stories had not a word to spare. Shaw said: "It was only when Hammett began to set character before situation, and led some others along that path, did he in any way attain recognition. This change, as can readily be seen by an examination of all his republished stories, shall I say, chanced to happen shortly after I came to the magazine, in 1926."

Alfred Knopf apparently wielded Hammett's example to good effect too. "Knopf seems to think that if somebody comes along who can write as well as Hammett, he should have Hammett's success," Raymond Chandler complained. "My feeling is that somebody might come along who wrote a great deal better than Hammett and still not have anything like Hammett's success" (Chandler, *Selected Letters*, pp. 5–6).

16 Author's interview with Mary Jane Hammett Miller.

Chapter 6

1 *Stratford Magazine*, March 1927, p. 30.

2 *Bookman*, September 1927, p. 75. One of Hammett's few stories from the female point of view, "Weekend" (HRC, University of Texas, probably 1928), portrays a young woman on an illicit weekend with a man who may share some of the characteristics of Hammett himself: "Harry had bought some magazines and the Sunday papers. He lay across the bed smoking and reading to her. She wondered with how many women he had spent days and nights like this. The matter-of-factness that made it bearable for her testified, she thought, to familiarity with the situation. But that, of course, was all right. He had never disguised his attitude toward this part of life. Perhaps that was why he had always had his way with her. She would have liked to have had him more ardent now, but that was not to be expected. He had never seriously said he loved her—not like that. He was not like that" (p. 6).

3 *Saturday Review of Literature*, June 11, 1927, p. 901.

4 Ibid., October 20, 1928, p. 282.

5 Ibid.

6 Ibid., December 1, 1928, p. 440.

7 Ibid., April 27, 1929, p. 961.

8 Ibid., January 12, 1929, p. 591.

9 Ibid., January 15, 1927, p. 510.

10 Ibid., February 5, 1927, p. 570.

11 This account is drawn from the recollections of Albert Samuels, Jr., who was interviewed by Larry Levinger for *City of San Francisco Magazine*, November 4, 1975, p. 24, and from Hammett's letters to Jose, apparently describing the same occasion.

12 DH to JH, n.d.

13 Ibid., late June? 1927.

14 Ibid., June 1, 1927.

15 Ellery Queen writes in his Introduction to *Dead Yellow Women*, pp. 3–4:

Dashiell Hammett occasionally succumbed to this editor-baiting temptation, and he worked out a clever psychological method of "having the last word." Here is the way he managed it; he would deliberately inject into his dialogue two different words (or phrases); one word seemed to be an obvious violation of good taste; the other word had a completely innocent air. The editor would promptly delete the word which seemed indelicate or offensive. Having thus satisfied all his inner bowdlerian instincts, the editor would then pass by the innocent-looking word without even bothering to question or check it.

The trap was now sprung, but good. You see, the word that seemed "off-color" was really a perfectly innocent term; and the word that seemed perfectly innocent was really a censorable one. The editor fell hook-line-and-eraser for the "red herring" word, the smokescreen; once he was convinced in his own mind that he had blue-penciled the "bad" word, the *really* "bad" word escaped almost unnoticed.

Two such expressions were "the gooseberry lay" and "gunsel." The first meant stealing wash off a clothesline; the second, a boy kept for immoral purposes. But it was the first, of course, that the editor crossed out; so gunsel came into the language as a synonym for gunman.

[16] *Stratford Magazine*, June 1927, p. 30.

[17] DH to JH, n.d.

[18] Ibid.

[19] Shaw to DH, July 22, 1927, preserved among Josephine Dolan Hammett's papers.

[20] DH to JDH, n.d.

[21] HB to DH, July 10, 1928 (HRC).

[22] Quoted in Nolan, *Dashiell Hammett*, p. 50.

[23] Hammett, *The Dain Curse*.

[24] Knopf files, June 1929.

[25] DH to HB, July 14, 1929 (HRC).

[26] *Lovers Should Marry* was published in 1933 by Macauley, in New York. Other works by Martin were *The Constant Simp, Lord Byron of Broadway, The Mosaic Earring* and *The Other Side of the Fence*.

Chapter 7

[1] Introduction to *The Maltese Falcon* (1930 edition), pp. vii–viii.

[2] DH to Herbert Asbury, February 6, 1930 (HRC).

[3] *The Glass Key* (Vintage edition), pp. 9–10.

[4] In March 1931 he wrote Lillian Hellman (letter at HRC): "Beginning of a thousand-stanza narrative verse:"

In San Francisco, Elfinstone
　　Fell in with a red-haired slut
Whose eyes were bright as the devil's own
　　With green-eyed greed, whose jaw was cut
Wolfishly. Her body was lean and tough as a whip.
With little of breast and little of hip,
And her voice was thin and hard as her lip,
　　And her lip was as hard as bone.

[5] *Saturday Review of Literature*, June 7, 1930, p. 54; July 3, 1930, p. 55. The first nineteen items were printed in the first issue, and the rest in the second.

Chapter 8

[1] Lillian Hellman, *Unfinished Woman* (*Three*, p. 72).

[2] Behlmer, ed., *Memo from David O. Selznick*, pp. 26–27.

[3] DH to AK, December 20, 1930.

[4] Hellman, *Unfinished Woman* (*Three*, p. 280).

[5] Mrs. Frederick Nebel remembers Martin and Hammett in about 1935: "A mutual friend called Fred to tell him that Dash couldn't pay his hotel bill (at the Waldorf) and was going to be asked to leave. Everyone chipped in, the bill was paid and we asked him to stay with us in Connecticult but he refused to leave New York at that time, so Nell took him in. . . . She was a very good friend to him, cared for him when he was sick and let him stay in her place when he was sick or broke."

[6] San Francisco *Examiner*, June 29, 1932.

[7] AK to DH, May 7, 1931.

[8] DH to AK, June 6, 1931.

[9] AK to DH, June 16, 1931.

[10] DH to AK, April 27, 1931. Hammett says he has been in San Francisco "a few weeks."

[11] Telegram, DH to AK, April 29, 1931.

[12] MS of *The Thin Man* (Occidental College Library), p. 22.

[13] DH to LH, May 3, 1931.

[14] Ibid., April 30, 1931.

[15] Ibid., "a Tuesday," n.d. (HRC). Hammett was already ill at this time, possibly with this attack of gonorrhea. "My headache is gone, my respiration seems normal, and if I had a thermometer I'd give you a report on my temperature. I think I've been to the toilet twice since you left: I'll try to keep more complete records hereafter. . . . I've been to the toilet again." These references to toileting refer to the treatment, with silver nitrate, then current.

[16] DH to LH, April 30, 1931 (HRC).

[17] Dorothy Parker, *The Portable Dorothy Parker* (New York: Penguin, 1980), pp. 538–40.

[18] DH to AK, September 1, 1931.

[19] DH to LH, "a Tuesday," 1931.

[20] This episode is reported by Lillian Hellman, who is uncertain of the date. 1931 is likely because of details that seem to fit the two hotels: he had lived in both at this time.

Chapter 9

[1] Hammett had a movie agent, Daniel Leonardson. Ben Wasson had been Faulkner's agent.

[2] DH to LH, February 23, 1932, on Hotel Elysée stationery.

[3] Undated; in Knopf files.

[4] Los Angeles *Times*, June 30, 1932, p. 18.

[5] Hellman, *Unfinished Woman* (*Three*, p. 290), gives the name of the suite as the Diplomat; Jay Martin, in *Nathanael West*, calls it the Royal Suite.

[6] S. J. Perelman, *The Last Laugh*, p. 161.

[7] *American Magazine*, July 1932.

[8] Ibid., October 1933.

[9] *Collier's*, April 8, 1933.

[10] *Mystery League Magazine*, October 1, 1933.

[11] *Esquire*, Autumn 1933, p. 34.

[12] *Liberty*, April 8, 1933. *Woman in the Dark* was filmed by RKO in 1934.

[13] Roughead, *Bad Companions*, pp. 111–46.

[14] Hellman, *Unfinished Woman* (*Three*, p. 292).

[15] Hellman credits Hammett with several alterations in her script; Hammett worked on it but did not receive film credit.

[16] *The Thin Man* by 1950 had sold 750,000 in paperback, 120,000 reprints and 300,000 of a comic-book adaptation (data concerning the lawsuit from Warner files).

[17] This line does not appear in the 1972 Vintage edition.

[18] Layman, p. 14.

[19] The text in fact gives Nora's age as twenty-six. The letter's author, "Dorothy Mackaill," may have been the actress of that name.

[20] Hellman, *Unfinished Woman* (*Three*, p. 290).

[21] *The Thin Man* (Vintage edition), pp. 7–9.

[22] Frances Goodrich and Albert Hackett were a prominent husband-and-wife writing team primarily associated with Broadway. They were to write three of the Thin Man scripts, and became good friends of Hammett's. One of their most notable successes was the stage version of *The Diary of Anne Frank*.

[23] Hammett's association with *X-9* lasted from January 29, 1934, to April 1935. Alex Raymond carried it on longer, for a time, without Hammett.

[24] Philbrick would become famous later as the author of *I Led Three Lives*, about his life as FBI agent, Communist Party member and ordinary citizen.

[25] This reference is evidently in error. This film (*Private Detective 62*) was made from a story by Raoul Whitfield. It is not impossible that Hammett worked on it; but he did not receive film credit.

[26] Screenplay by Doris Malloy and Harry Clork. The film was released in 1935 and starred Edmund Lowe as the detective, Gene Richmond, whose name in the film is Thompson.

[27] DH to LH, October 31, 1934.

[28] Ibid., November 5, 1934.

Chapter 10

[1] Recollections of Mildred Lewis Le Vaux, Hammett's secretary at this time (1935) and earlier. This period followed the completion of *The Thin Man*; the original 34 pages of the sequel had been expanded to 115 pages by September 17, 1935.

[2] AK to DH, March 26, 1935 (Knopf files).

[3] Ibid., June 11, 1935 (Knopf files).

[4] DH to AK, September 24, 1935 (Knopf files).

5 Martin, *Nathanael West*, p. 268. See also *The Letters of Alexander Woollcott* (New York: Viking, 1944), p. 152, for mention of Hammett's party.

6 Taped interview with Frances Goodrich.

7 Letter from Dorothy Nebel to author.

8 Steven Marcus' taped interview with Albert Hackett.

9 Author's conversation with Mildred Le Vaux.

10 Steven Marcus' taped interview with Albert Hackett.

11 Hellman, *Unfinished Woman(Three*, p. 74).

12 Steven Marcus' taped interview with Albert Hackett.

13 Author's conversation with Hannah Weinstein.

14 Nunnally Johnson, *Letters*, pp. 187–88 (letter to Julian Symons).
Johnson writes further:

Hammett told me that he stopped writing (at the top of his career and success) because he saw no more reason to write when he not only had all the money he needed but was assured of all that he would ever need for the remainder of his life. This turned out to be a mistake, but it was a sound enough belief at the time, for the curious reason that I think I can explain. Money was pouring in. . . .

Apparently there was nothing in writing that interested him but the money. He had none of the usual incentives that keep writers at their typewriters for as long as they have the strength to hit the keys. He had no impulse to tell any more stories, no ambition to accomplish more as a writer, no interest in keeping his name alive, as it is often described, or any other vanity about himself or his work. This is not to say that he was not gratified by the respect with which his stories were received, nor should it be taken to mean that he did not apply to his work all the conscientiousness of a self-respecting craftsman. But once he had made his pile, that was all there was to it. Out went the typewriter and he never wrote another book or story. If there is a precedent for a decision like this in a writer I have never heard of it, and as a writer myself, with all the urges and secret vanities of a writer, it took me a long time to be convinced of the truth of it. But time provided the proof. And I can tell you how awed I was and always have been by such astonishing resolution.

To say that the decision turned out to be a mistake calls for a second explanation, and my testimony on this point I must confess is speculation, but speculation based on a good deal of knowledge. From the day I met Hammett, in the late twenties, his behavior could be accounted for only by an assumption that he had no expectation of being alive much beyond Thursday. He had had a severe case of tuberculosis and he told me that he now had but one lung. Once this assumption was accepted, Hammett's way of life made a form of sense. Even allowing for exuberance and the headiness of the certain approach of success, not to mention the daffiness of the twenties, no one could have spent himself and his money with such recklessness who expected to be alive much longer. For once in my life I knew a man who was clearly convinced that there would never be a tomorrow.

The money rolled in and out just as fast. And it would continue to do so for many years to come, long after he expected to be here to collect it. But life persisted in him. Lusty friends sickened and died, and Hammett, for whom we all drew a deep sigh every other day, survived and carried on. As frail as he was, as appallingly as he mistreated himself for many years, he came to be accepted by the Army and served during World War II in the harsh outpost of Alaska. I would give much to have shared his amused reflections then, with his financial springs running dry and him still here (though now very well behaved) when so many of those who had sighed for him were long since with their fathers.

I suppose that by the time he came to realize that he would in all likelihood be here not only next Thursday but for many Thursdays to come it was too late to sit down at the typewriter again with much confidence. When the end approached, it was thirty years later than he expected it, and Death owed him a genuine apology when eventually it made its tardy appearance.

[15] *The Glass Key*, p. 23.

[16] E. J. Rosenberg, quoted in Hellman, *Unfinished Woman* (Three, p. 298).

[17] Hellman, *Unfinished Woman* (Three, p. 75).

[18] Ibid., p. 289.

[19] Gertrude Stein, *Everybody's Autobiography* (New York: Random House, 1937).

[20] Schwartz, *The Hollywood Writers' Wars*, p. 33. The song is by Henry Myers.

[21] Ibid., p. 30.

[22] Chandler, *Selected Letters*, pp. 23, 165.

[23] BK to DH, January 31, 1936 (HRC).

[24] DH to JHM, March 14, 1936.

[25] Ibid., February 21, 1936.

[26] DH to LH, June 6, 1936.

[27] Ibid., June 11, 1936.

[28] Records of Lenox Hill Hospital, in New York City.

[29] Hellman, *Unfinished Woman* (Three, chapter 16).

[30] *Daily Princetonian*, November 11, 1936, pp. 1, 4.

[31] DH to LH, sometime in December 1936 (HRC).

[32] Ibid., December 28, 1936.

[33] Ibid., December 29, 1936.

[34] Ibid., December 30, 1936.

Chapter 11

[1] Letter concerning a contract with MGM, February 11, 1937, p. 1. This contract allowed Hammett to keep radio serialization rights, and a *Thin Man* radio serial was produced in 1941.

[2] DH to LH, March 13, 1937 (HRC).

[3] Interview with Frances Goodrich.

[4] DH to LH, January 15, 1938. Dudley Nichols was an important screenwriter (*Stagecoach*, *Bringing Up Baby*). He was the president of the Screenwriters Guild 1937–38.

[5] The manuscript of *Another Thin Man*, in MGM files, was finished May 13, 1938. It is written in the form of a short novel, beginning with Nora chattering on the telephone, and ending, as so many of Hammett's

stories do, with the beautiful but deadly woman guilty, being taken off to justice. Guilty Lois, here, however, is more philosophical than her forerunners: "Oh, well, all you can do is try to play the breaks as far as you get them."

6 Schwartz, *The Hollywood Writers' Wars*, p. 90. Lillian Hellman has denied either that the Berkeley meeting took place or that they were at it. Hellman has written that she herself did not know whether Hammett joined the Party. Josephine Marshall and Frederick Field believe from things Hammett said that he did, probably in 1937.

7 Both the Schulberg and Lardner quotes are from Schwartz, p. 92.

8 DH to LH, January 15, 1938.

9 *Film Daily*, New York, March 18, 1938.

10 DH to LH, September 9, 1937 (HRC).

11 Ibid., November 27, 1937.

12 Los Angeles *Evening News*, December 1, 1937.

13 Ibid.

14 DH to LH, December 26, 1937 (HRC).

15 *The Lariat*, November 1925, p. 507.

16 *Argosy All-Story Weekly*, July or August 1923, p. 562.

Chapter 12

1 Accounts vary as to the name of this suite, but all suggest some image of Oriental royalty.

2 Interview with Frances Goodrich.

3 Schwartz, *The Hollywood Writers' Wars*, p. 124.

4 Hollywood *Citizen News*, March 24, 1938.

5 DH to LH, January 15, 1938.

6 DH to JHM, February 22, 1938.

7 Although there is little literature on the connection of sexual impotence and writer's block, a psychiatrist whom Hammett consulted says that he and other psychiatrists have long noticed that the two symptoms very often appear together.

8 DH to LH, May 12, 1938. *The Foundry* was to have been made from Albert Halper's novel, with Hunt Stromberg directing.

9 "The Advertisement IS Literature," *Western Advertising*, October 1926, pp. 35-36; January 1928, p. 61. What was his style by habit now had once been a subject he had studied and written up: "Meiosis—to give understatement of this sort its technical name—has nothing to do with modesty of moderation in speech as such, with conservative statement, with strict adherence to the truth. It is a rhetorical trick, the employment of understatement, not to deceive, but to increase the impression made on reader or hearer. In using it the object is, not to be believed, but to be disbelieved to one's advantage. One says to his reader: 'I am deliberately telling you less than the truth. Here is something you can't believe literally. You've got to believe more than this.' This is in contrast to the method of hyperbole, which says, to itself at least: 'I'll pile it on good and thick, and some of it's bound to stick.' "

[10] DH to LH, May 14, 1938.

[11] Diagnosis of metabolic disorder was common at this period. Judging from later medical records, the likelihood here is that this was an emotional problem.

[12] Perhaps in revenge, when Stewart was once in an auto accident, Hammett remarked, "You gave all your friends an anxious fifteen minutes, Donald."

[13] Maslin's column was widely syndicated. This article was taken from the Staten Island, N.Y., *Advance*, May 7, 1938.

Chapter 13

[1] DH to Bennett Cerf, January 14, 1939; Cerf to DH, January 16, 1939 (Columbia University, special manuscript collection). Knopf and Hammett had parted company over money and the fact that Knopf, having published Lillian's first two plays, declined to publish the third. Bennett Cerf then offered a $5,000 advance for a book on which Knopf had an option, at which point Knopf said good riddance—he wanted no more to do with Hammett, he said, he's a terrible man (Bennett Cerf, *At Random* [New York: Random House, 1977], p. 206).

[2] DH to JHM, December 27, 1945.

[3] The speculation about the underlying causes of Hammett's failure to write after 1934—indeed after 1930—is based on Hammett's discussions with a psychiatrist, who prefers not to be mentioned by name, who treated Mary Hammett, and whom Hammett also consulted for his own benefit.

[4] A list of people who owed him money was compiled by his secretary in 1952, in connection with his tax troubles. By her calculation the figure exceeded $35,000.

[5] DH to LH, December 29, 1936.

[6] See Sidney Skolsky in the Detroit, Mich., *Swing*, June 1939:

> Harlem's Plantation Club, hottest of the uptown sepian spots, has the most extravagant show since the days of the old Cotton Club, the premises of which it occupies. The new opus, designed for the World's Fair trade (everyone is now World's Fair minded—you just can't keep them away from the place), is called SEE HARLEM FIRST. Dashiell Hammett, "the thin man," is a regular visitor that way, as are Arline Judge and hubby, Dan Topping, and many others. Don't miss the music which is wild and barbaric.

[7] FBI files.

[8] DH to Cerf, June 1, 1939; Cerf to DH, June 7, 1939 (Columbia University, special manuscript collection). Hammett's review of *Finnegans Wake*, which would be of great interest, has not been found.

[9] A clipping preserved among Hammett's papers, by its style apparently from *Time* or *Newsweek*.

[10] *New Republic*, June 21, 1939, p. 192.

[11] *New Masses*, June 20, 1939.

[12] League of American Writers papers (Bancroft Library, University of California, Berkeley).

[13] *Nation*, August 26, 1939, p. 228.

[14] He apparently accepted the Hitler-Stalin pact in accordance with the Party position. People who discussed politics with Hammett remember that, as Hannah Weinstein put it, he had a notably long view of political events, remaining sanguine when many of the people he and Hellman knew were precipitated into varying crises of spirit. According to Sam and Helen Rosen, benefactors of Hammett's in his later years, the long and the short view of world events formed the topic of many discussions with Hammett as late as 1957.

[15] Hellman *Pentimento* (*Three*, pp. 569–70). Hammett did not publish any short stories at this time. Reference could be to "The Thin Man and the Flack," a photo story in *Click*, December 1941, pp. 30–32.

[16] Manuscripts Department, Lilly Library, Indiana University, Bloomington. Another excerpt from the text:

> We the undersigned believe that civil liberties are the distinguishing mark of American democracy. We believe furthermore that the Bill of Rights must apply to the rights of all Americans—or that it will prove a cheat for all. We do not accept the dangerous proposition, now being broadcast from certain quarters, that civil rights can be withheld from this dissident minority or that, at the pleasure of those who may have the power to do so.
>
> Therefore we feel compelled to speak out sharply and boldly at this moment. When forces exist, as we believe they do exist, whose objective effect, if not their secret purpose, is the destruction of civil liberties, blindness to facts becomes dangerous, pious protestation of liberalism becomes mockery, and failure to speak out courageously becomes criminal. The objective effect furthermore is to create war hysteria and to incite witch hunts at a time when unity for peace in the face of international events is a condition of our further progress as a nation of free men.
>
> We recognize the following blunt facts:
>
> 1. That the Dies Committee is talking openly of the suppression of dissident groups, and that in this it has secured the support of influential newspapers throughout the country.
>
> 2. That open incitement to vigilante activity against labor, against minority radical groups, against national and religious groups, is increasing shamefully in this country.
>
> 3. That various discriminatory and repressive measures against the alien have been passed by the House of Representatives and have become law in many states.

Whether or not Hammett wrote the text is not clear; but he actively solicited support for it among influential literary people, such as Theodore Dreiser, and Upton Sinclair, who replied,

> My dear Hammett,
>
> Many thanks for your friendly letter. You may quote me as saying that I am in complete sympathy with all the general principles stated in your letter; but I have to add the statement that I am not familiar with all the facts concerning the details which are mentioned in your letter.
>
> I feel that I have to make the above statement in common honesty, because, to give one illustration, I have not read the speech which Browder delivered in Boston, and only glanced at what the newspapers said about it.

I must tell you that I am buried in work on a long novel with scenes laid in Europe during the past twenty-five years; it requires a great deal of research, and I have to keep my mind on it, and it is impossible for me to do all the other things that I am asked to do, and that I should have to do in order to sign your manifesto as it stands.

[17] From the collection of David Werman.

[18] *New Masses*, November 26, 1940.

[19] Kenneth Stewart, *News Is What We Make It*, pp. 242–43.

[20] An earlier version, directed by Roy del Ruth, had appeared in 1931, starring Ricardo Cortez as Sam Spade and Bebe Daniels as "Ruth Wonderly" in the film. In 1936 *Satan Met a Lady*, starring Bette Davis, reworked the story again.

[21] At least once he found this 1941 version, when he did see it, "boring," and later, in a better frame of mind, admired it. For a good discussion of the adaptation, see James Naremore, "John Huston and *The Maltese Falcon*," *Literature/Film Quarterly*, vol. 50, 1973, pp. 239–49. The first version of *The Glass Key* was released in 1935.

[22] Pine was a songwriter. See Schwartz, p. 189.

[23] Recollection by Franklin Folsom, the secretary of LAW, in a letter, December 27, 1978. The LAW papers are in the Bancroft Library, University of California at Berkeley.

[24] LAW papers, Bancroft Library, University of California at Berkeley.

[25] Hellman, *Pentimento* (*Three*, p. 488).

[26] Ibid., p. 492.

[27] New York *Herald Tribune*, July 14, 1942.

[28] DH to JHM (n.d.), 1944.

[29] Hellman, *Unfinished Woman* (*Three*, p. 292).

[30] Perhaps explicit or pornographic acts. This account of Hammett's situation derives mostly from his psychiatrist; that he liked prostitutes, and especially black or Oriental ones, was well known among his acquaintances. This predilection is common, and was, as Freud called it, the "primary degradation" of erotic life among men in Freud's period. It is not surprising that there should have been brothels specializing in helping men with sexual problems then as there are now.

[31] Author's interview with Hellman.

[32] Ibid.

Chapter 14

[1] Hammett went first to the Reception Center, Camp Upton, L.I.; then to a signal corps training regiment at Fort Monmouth (with its subposts Camp Edison and Camp Charles Wood), N.J., until June 29, 1943; then to Company A, Twelfth Battalion at Camp Shenango, in Transfer, Pa.; then to Fort Lawton, in Fort Lewis, Wash.; then to Alaska, to Forts Randall and Richardson.

[2] Letter from Edward Langley, December 10, 1978.

[3] Private conversation; see also Leonard Lyons, "In the Lyons Den," syndicated column July 15, 1951.

[4] DH to LH, October 1, 1942.

[5] Ibid., October 4, 1942. There is also some testimony that Hammett was also at this time sent to miltary governors school in Charlottesville.

[6] The first names of Gottlieb, Stewart, Senecal and Fingatti are not mentioned. Among others who knew Hammett at this period were Bernie Stavis, Paul Monasch, Alexander MacDougal, Richard Webb, Edward Langley.

[7] Robert Boltwood quoted a passage from the Bible. Hammett bet Lillian $50 she couldn't identify it, and she couldn't. Hammett insisted Boltwood take the money. Hammett's *The Complete Dashiell Hammett* had come out just then, so he gave Private Boltwood one: "For Robert Boltwood, who fought shoulder to shoulder with me through the bitter training standards campaigns, with thanks for having made my days less empty." Lillian sent a copy of her plays: "It is more profitable for you to read the Bible, but this comes with my warm regards."

[8] DH to LH, December 28, 1942.

[9] Ibid., January 4, 1943.

[10] Ibid., n.d.

[11] Ibid., n.d.

[12] Ibid., May 9, 1943.

[13] FBI files, 1944.

[14] DH to LH, n.d.

[15] Ibid., August 14, 1943.

[16] Ibid., n.d.

[17] Ibid., October 2, 1943.

[18] Ibid., October 3, 1943.

[19] Ibid., October 25, 1943.

[20] Ibid., October 27, 1943.

[21] Ibid., November 6, 1943.

[22] Ibid., December 31, 1943.

[23] Ibid., n.d.

[24] FBI files, 1944.

Chapter 15

[1] DH to LH, March 1, 1944.

[2] Ibid., March 6, 1944.

[3] DH to MJHM, May 13, 1944.

[4] DH to LH, January 2(?), 1944.

[5] Ibid., May 25, 1944.

[6] Ibid., August 2, 1944.

[7] Ibid., March 12, 1944. André Gide, in *Imaginary Interviews*, translated from the French by Malcolm Cowley (New York: Knopf, 1944):

And speaking at random, there is one recent author, Dashiell Hammett, who is doubtless not in the same class as the four great figures we began by discussing. Again it was Malraux who drew my attention to him; but for the last two years I have been vainly trying to find a copy of *The Glass Key*, which Malraux specially recommended; it couldn't be procured either in the original or in translation, whether on the Riviera or in North Africa. Hammett, it is true, squanders his great talent on detective stories; they are unusually good ones, no doubt, like *The Thin Man* and *The Maltese Falcon*, but a little cheap—and one could say the same of Simenon. For all of that, I regard his *Red Harvest* as a remarkable achievement, the last word in atrocity, cynicism, and horror. Dashiell Hammett's dialogues, in which every character is trying to deceive all the others and in which the truth slowly becomes visible through the haze of deception, can be compared only with the best in Hemingway. If I speak of Hammett, it is because I seldom hear his name mentioned [pp. 145–46].

The French found in the hard-boiled American writing the same loneliness and anxiety they admired in Gide or Malraux and they admired the stylistic qualities of Faulkner, Hammett, Hemingway, Erskine Caldwell and Steinbeck. The American critic Perry Miller, in "Europe's Faith in American Fiction," *Atlantic Monthly*, December 1951, pp. 50–56, noted the admiration felt by Gide and other European intellectuals for "violent" American fiction, that is, our romantic fiction rather than the realistic fiction of, say, Willa Cather or Edith Wharton; and a European tendency to believe that it both reported reliably on American life and therefore offered, in Gide's imaginary interviewer's phrase "a foretaste of Hell," an intimation of destiny which includes, at least, vitality.

Alan Pryce-Jones, in "The English Have a Different Accent," *New York Times Book Review*, December 23, 1951, p. 1, commenting on American fiction from the English point of view, is less approving. "We have no first-hand knowledge of the Southern life which makes a Joe Christmas possible. . . ." The English find themselves, therefore, more comfortable with genre literature—"Dashiell Hammett in one field and James Thurber in another."

[8] William Glackin, Bernard Kalb, E. E. Spitzer, among others.

[9] Bud Freeman, interviewed by Jay Robert Nash, *Chicago Tribune Magazine*, February 28, 1982, pp. 19–20.

[10] DH to LH, n.d.

[11] Letter from Jean Potter to Stephen Talbot, March 8, 1982:

Hammett's kindness to "struggling writers" is a legend: I'm a case in point. I met him in Fairbanks, Alaska, in 1944, when he was a Staff Sergeant who had enlisted in the Army and was editing an Army newspaper. I was a highly nervous fledgling writer. (Nine years as a *Fortune* researcher in the Luce empire of that day where only men were paid to write had done little for my writing confidence. Finally resigned from *Fortune*, I had spent more than a year in Alaska preparing a book on the early pioneering of aviation there, under contract to Macmillan.) I had just completed a first draft of the manuscript and was shaky about it. Shaky enough to ask Hammett if he might possibly be willing to read and criticize it. He agreed, read it at one sitting while I paced the streets. He told me it was a "fine" book; "breathtaking." (Note: He was cold sober; this was not during one of his tragic bouts with alcoholism. I think he meant that the record of the pioneer pilots was "breathtaking" and that he appreciated my concern to tell it without exaggeration.) But the manuscript could do with some editing, he said, and offered to "go over it" with me. So he did; page by page, line by line, word by word.

I shall never forget those daily working sessions, especially Hammett's sharp eye and often biting wit in his relentless drive for the least words possible and the right word. His total honesty and regard for fact. His scorn for overuse of adjectives, for murky thinking. He seldom did the changing himself but propelled me into doing it by questions. Lillian Hellman has written that Hammett was "tender" toward all writers because he remembered his own early struggles. "Tender," yes, but rather rough. Samples: "Here we have our white, spruce-patched mountains again. Haven't you flown enough over Alaska to give the reader a break?" . . . "I'd say this page is pretty much a piece of cheese—what did you mean by it?" . . . "What's this word, do we really need it?" I was surprised by Hammett's obvious pleasure, even exhilaration, as he worked with my words, my book. He was so dedicated a craftsman I wondered why he himself had not written a book for more than ten years.

Hammett surprised me in several ways. Perhaps I had expected this dean of the "hardboiled" school of detective fiction to be cynical. I soon noted that he was genuinely moved, no less, by the biographies of Alaska's pioneer pilots, those men who had risked their lives in a land without airports—for a buck, of course, but in emergency without payment. Also surprising: this white-haired celebrity who was lionized in cities like New York and Hollywood *liked* life on the frontier that Alaska still was (relatively speaking) in that day. I recall that he looked askance at a sentence in my preface that referred to the "democratic, energetic, curious, ingenious, fearless spirit of the frontier." He raised his eyebrows, of course, at so many adjectives; then said he thought I could go ahead and leave the sentence as was. I felt it was because he thought every word counted. Hammett even liked the wind-and-fog-swept Aleutian Islands, which most servicemen detested. On return to his base there he wrote describing the stark, stormy place with affection adding: "Coming back here is like coming home." I had the impression in the short time that I knew Hammett that this masterful writer was as a man sensitive, idealistic, lonesome and contradictory.

Hammett's generosity to me continued in New York, where we both returned after the War, after I had delivered the ms of my book—entitled *The Flying North*—to Macmillan. Hammett by this time had started to write a novel, tentatively entitled "Tulip." Late in 1946 I was about to sail for Europe to marry Anatole Chelnov. Hoping to write another book abroad, I sought another advance from Macmillan; as I had no specific subject in mind Macmillan refused. Hearing this, Hammett scoffed, referring to Macmillan with some of his typical unprintable epithets; I could find a much better publisher, he told me, when the time came. He sat down and scribbled a generous check. "Take it," he insisted. "I know you'll pay it back because you'll always write and if you write you'll sell." (Since my return from Alaska I had sold a number of magazine articles.)

His generous attitude continued during the years after my marriage and the birth of two children when for a while I did *not* write. He wrote me in early 1950: "Thanks for the checks" (I had already returned some of the loan) "but I wish you wouldn't get yourself so lathered up about that lousy debt. So you haven't written anything for three years. So what? So a lot of people skip a lot of years. There's always plenty of time: nobody dies young any more." His novel, he also wrote in that letter, had a new title: "December First." There is a terrible poignancy to his attempt, above, to reassure a younger writer, for the years ahead for him were to be dark.

¹² DH to LH, May 27, 1944.

¹³ DH to JHM May 24, 1944.

¹⁴ While Hammett served his country in this remote place, the world poured money into his bank account as usual, and would later insist on having some of it back: the Internal Revenue Service would claim he owed $25,609.30 in unpaid income taxes for the year 1943; $30,280.57 for 1944; and $37,217.14 for 1945.

¹⁵ DH to LH, February 22, 1944.

¹⁶ LH to DH, July 6, 1944.

¹⁷ His detailed comments are as follows:

15 Mar 44

Last night the play came, so I pushed the War up a couple of hours so I could read it before breakfast. Now, having breakfasted, I report as follows:

You must understand first that I am not a man who knows very much about polite comedy and what makes it tick. You have, in this one, a defter touch than in any of your other plays, and it may well be that that is what makes light comedy tick and will make this one click. I don't know. It doesn't seem to me that you make your points, but it may be the nature of light comedy that its points aren't so much made as revealed in passing.

My feeling is that you should have told your story in chronological order, running the triangle straight through with history from the dawn of Mussolini up to today. The best of the play is in the historical scenes and, in the present form, they seem to me to be in effect subordinated to the triangle—and to make the closing of the play anti-climactical. Now, one section of the play is seen in the light of the other; it is said, and is of course inherent in the whole thing, that each had a bearing on the other—but for me that part is not sufficiently shown.

Another thing: catching these characters now here, now there, doesn't—it may be different seeing them on the stage—give me a chance to know, to *feel* them and what they do to one another. Cas, as a matter of fact, seems to me a not altogether necessary character in the play. What I'm trying to say is that there are too many things—too much rounding out of personality and even event—I have to supply for myself, and I'm not sure that audiences can be trusted to do that accurately.

The essential frivolity that fucked things up—and I take it that's the real point—isn't *shown*. No answer is provided to the question, "But what else could these people have done?" and there isn't—except of course by inference—any statement that the kind of people who couldn't do anything else should never have been there.

(You understand, of course, that I read the script for the first time only a few hours ago, knew very little beforehand of what you were trying to do, and am coming to the whole thing not only cold but with practically no time to have let it sink in or to have thought it over. This kind of snap judgment is not likely to be of the best. I'm just putting down what I feel on practically the spur of the moment, and I hope you don't give it any more value than that. There's no excuse for either of us considering this anything like considered judgment.)

Characters of the sort you've chosen here are—you've learned before now—sons of bitches to handle on the stage unless, of course, you load them down with idiosyncrasies or something, because they are essentially characterless characters. I don't know how you're having the two gals directed, but they don't come through to me from the typed sheet with any bite to them.

None of this is doing you much good, of course, and I'll try to do better after I've had a little while to think, but I dare say we'd be better off if I just kept my big mouth shut. After all, if you're opening on the 26th and this, at the fastest, can't get to you before the 22d—how can it do anything but perhaps disturb you?

I will try, though, to get something maybe useful to you as soon as I can.

And it is in ways the most interesting play you've done, and it's got swell stuff in it, and, as I said before, it's defter than any of the others, and you are a cutie.

Much love.

SDH

(who does not always know as much about everything as he acts like he does and who hopes the play gets its points over in a manner that'll make this letter sound like the work of a smart-aleck)

[18] DH to LH, August 23, 1944.

[19] Ibid., September 5, 1944.

[20] E. E. Spitzer, *Nation*, January 6, 1974, p. 9.

[21] DH to Nancy Bragdon, January 1, 1945. Nancy Bragdon was Lillian Hellman's secretary, and was helpful to Hammett as well. He wrote Bragdon a number of letters at this period while Hellman was traveling in Russia.

[22] DH to Nancy Bragden, January 10, 1945.

[23] DH to LH, April 28, 1945.

[24] Ibid., March 10, 1945.

[25] Ibid., March 13, 1945.

[26] Ibid., March 29, 1945.

[27] DH to William Glackin, April 29, 1945.

[28] DH to LH, April 28, 1945.

[29] Ibid., April 23, 1945.

[30] Ibid.

[31] Ibid., May 3, 1945.

[32] DH to JHM, December 27, 1945.

[33] DH to LH, May 6 ,1945.

[34] DH to William Glackin, June 2, 1945. He seldom mentioned his Alaskan companions in letters home, but he wrote in a letter to Lillian on February 22, 1944: "I let one of your admirers read your letter and it quite overwhelmed him. Do you wish to marry a young man of perhaps 24, certainly not handsome, but very interested in films and the stage? Your name would be Mrs. Glackin, which in itself would be no mean inducement."

[35] Communication with Harold Edinberg.

[36] In an article in *Yank* (n.d.), Al Weisman wrote:

The major approached Hammett and said, "I've been doing a little bit of mystery writing myself, and I wonder if you would come over to my quarters this evening and share a steak with me. I'd like to show you my stuff." Hammett replied, "Certainly, if you've got enough for all of us," pointing to the four EM accompanying him. "Well, I don't know," stuttered the major. "Oh, well, some other time, sir," said Hammett, as he saluted and walked off.

[37] Hammett was promoted June 27, 1945.

[38] In other reports he left his GI toilet articles on the dock at Anchorage.

Chapter 16

[1] DH to LH, May 10, 1944.

[2] The Asiatic-Pacific Service Medal, four overseas bars and a Good Conduct Medal.

[3] DH to JHM, July 29, 1947.

[4] DH to LH, February 27, 1945. The letter also says: "I like the Alaskan mainland and am as likely as not to come back to it some day. There's a Major up here who thinks I should ranch on one of the islands after the war—he promises to get me all the backing I'd need from Maury Maverick —but, as much as I like the islands, I don't think that would make too much sense. Of course Kodiak, possibly my favorite spot in all Alaska, is an island, but that's different." The substance of this excerpt appears in "Tulip" (*The Big Knockover*, pp. 309–10).

[5] Schwartz, *The Hollywood Writers' Wars*, pp. 227–30.

[6] Ibid., p. 225.

[7] Robert Carr, *The House Committee on Un-American Activities*, pp. 55–58.

[8] DH to JHM, October 10, 1946.

[9] The Jefferson School catalog, 1946, quoted in Layman, p. 206.

[10] Letter from David Goldway to the author.

[11] Letter from Morris Hershman to the author.

[12] Letter in the possession of Stephen Talbot.

[13] Marjorie May to Miss ——, December 18, 1946.

[14] DH to JHM, April 30, 1947.

[15] The Hollywood Ten were John Howard Lawson, Dalton Trumbo, Alvah Bessie, Ring Lardner, Jr., Samuel Ornitz, Albert Maltz, Adrian Scott, Edward Dmytryk, Herbert Biberman, and Lester Cole.

Lillian Hellman wrote an editorial in the Screenwriters Guild pamphlet against HUAC entitled "The Judas Goats":

> Why this particular industry, these particular people?
> Has it anything to do with Communism? Of course not.
> There has never been a single line or word of Communism in any American picture at any time. There has never or seldom been ideas of *any kind*. Naturally, men scared to make pictures about the American Negro, men who have only in the last year allowed the word Jew to be spoken in a picture, who took more than ten years to make an anti-Fascist picture, these are frightened men and you pick frightened men to frighten first. Judas goats, they'll lead the others, maybe, to the slaughter for you. The others will be the radio, the press, the publishers, the trade unions, the colleges, the scientists, the churches—all of us. All of us who believe

in this lovely land and its freedoms and rights, and who wish to keep it good and make it better.

They frighten mighty easy, and they talk mighty bad. For one week they made us, of course, the laughingstock of the educated and decent world. I suggest the rest of us don't frighten so easy. It's still not un-American to fight the enemies of one's country. Let's fight [Quoted in Stefan Kanfer, *A Journal of the Plague Years* (New York: Atheneum, 1973), pp. 82–83].

[16] *Daily Worker*, March 12, 1947, p. 3.

[17] Bee Offiner, in Akron, Ohio, *Beacon Journal*, October 29, 1946; *Tide*, October 1, 1945; John Crosby, New York *Herald Tribune*, December 3, 1946; Fred Rayfields, in *Daily Compass*, January 25, 1950.

[18] Interviews with Mary Jane Hammett Miller and Rose Evans; Hammett's description of his day to the psychiatrist.

[19] Letter from Franklin Folsom to the author.

[20] Quoted in Layman, *Dashiell Hammett*, p. 204.

[21] Author's interview with Ed Rosenberg, the producer of the Sam Spade radio show.

[22] Author's interview with Hannah Weinstein.

[23] Author's interview with Mary Jane Hammett Miller.

[24] Author's interview with Josephine Hammett Marshall.

[25] Bud Freeman, interviewed by Jay Robert Nash, *Chicago Tribune Magazine*, February 28, 1982, pp. 19–20.

[26] Letter from Dorothy Nebel to the author.

[27] Author's interview with Ed Rosenberg.

[28] Hellman, *Unfinished Woman* (*Three*, p. 296).

[29] Author's interview with Mary Jane Hammett Miller.

[30] Author's interview with Rose Evans.

[31] Author's interview with Mary Jane Hammett Miller.

[32] Hellman, *Unfinished Woman* (*Three*, p. 281).

Chapter 17

[1] Hellman, *Unfinished Woman* (*Three*, p. 285).

[2] DH to JHM, February 13, 1949.

[3] Ibid., April 18, 1949.

[4] Ibid., March 21, 1949.

[5] Ibid., April 25, 1949.

[6] Ibid.

[7] *The Thin Man* radio series ran July 2, 1941–42, 1946–48 on CBS, 1940–50 on ABC. *The Fat Man* ran 1946–50; *The Adventures of Sam Spade*, 1946–51.

[8] Martha's Vineyard, Mass., *Gazette*, September 6, 1949.

[9] Hammett's analysis of Sean O'Casey's *Purple Dust* illustrates the kind of critical analysis he supplied also to Hellman's plays:

28 West 10th Street, New York City 11, 2 Oct 49

Dear Kermit,

Here's what I think ought to be done to Purple Dust, boiled down as far as I can, because I don't imagine you feel like reading a book about it at the moment, but you can have as much act-by-act detail as you want whenever you want it, and as far as I know I'll be available for talking about it almost any time that suits you within the next few weeks either here or in Philadelphia.

Still seeing the play as a slapstick allegory with music, I've tried to resist my natural tendency toward tight plotting; I think a lot of the play's charm hangs on its seeming haphazard quality.

About the music: the three pieces in Act I are jammed together (pages 1-5, 1-11, and 1-17) in the first third of the act, and then there's no more music until O'Killigain's brief song to Souhaun far along in Act II (page 2-31). In Act III there's a work chant (far too short) on page 3-16 and the "Faraway o!" song on page 3-35. If O'Casey can't be persuaded to write—or permit—more songs, then the songs in Act I should be put further apart—which shouldn't be very difficult—because they—especially "Deep In the Bosky Countrie"—prepare the audience for a good deal of music. If, as I hope, O'Casey agrees to more songs, here's a rough schedule of possibilities, though there are other spots that would do just as good. (1) A work-song or ballad by workmen, off-stage at first and then brought on by the 1st and 3rd Workmen as they enter, top of page 1-32. Instead of peering around the corner hunting for Poges, as now, they would, of course, be surprised to find him there, but I don't think that need make any difference to the following scene. (2) Avril and Basil do a riding-song (parallelling the "Bosky Countrie" song) as they set out for the horses on page 1-38. (3) In the beginning of—or early in—Act II "Deep In The Bosky Countrie" might be done again, bitterly, perhaps by Cloyne and Barney. O'Killigain's song to Souhaun (page 31) should be lengthened. (4) Poges's and the 1st Workman's conversation about past glories could wind up (page 2-20) in a song. (5) In Act III, I think the scene between Poges and the Canon would be helped by bringing Avril, Souhaun and Basil on (page 3-6) singing a bawdy song. (This scene bothers me a little in its present form: Avril seems to step out of character—anything for a laugh—but I don't think that would be true if she and the others were tight—and the Canon has already included drinking among the things he disapproves of.) (6) The workmen's shanty on page 3-16 should be longer of course.

The rains, the rising of the river, the expected flood are mentioned too casually—and too infrequently—to make enough impression on the audience, so that the inundation at the end of the play now seems—or will seem to an audience—more fortuitous than inevitable. This doesn't need much fixing. The 1st Workman in the opening speech (page 1-2) could include marks of water among the things hidden by the black and white prints; and again in his first speech on page 2-18 he could put the water in with the wind; and so on wherever there's an opening. (I think the thing to get across is that the house is generally uninhabitable when the water rises during the rainy seasons—some years worse than others—and it's only a matter of time before a fullgrown flood will knock it over.) The rain should begin in Act II.

Of the Irish mistresses, Souhaun is the larger character—as she should be—but I think Avril's running-off with O'Killigrain at the end of Act I is passed over too lightly, and, in any event, I think there should be one, or possibly two, hair-down scenes between the pair. The first one could easily be spotted by keeping them on-stage instead of withdrawing (bottom of page 2-4) after Stoke and Poges have gone off. They should discuss Avril's adventure, with Avril possibly attaching no importance to it or seeming not to. The relationship between them remains the game, of course, mentor and pupil, mother and daughter. Souhaun, as I see her, would realise that they had about played their string out with the two Englishmen and—a point of pride with trollops—shouldn't want to wait for Stoke and Poges to come to the same conclusion. Since Avril won't admit that she cares too much about O'Killigain—a point of pride with young trollops—Souhaun makes a play for him (just as it's now written) but when that's no go she turns to the 2nd Workman as her next best bet. (To keep this from seeming too abrupt—as her turning to him is in the present version—she could very easily stay on stage instead of exiting (page 2-23)—Poges going off at that point—and play pretty much the same part Poges now plays with the 2nd Workman until Poges comes in at top of page 2-28 with, "My own great grandfather was Irish, etc.").

The second scene between Souhaun and Avril could come right at the end of Souhaun's scene with O'Killigain (page 2-31), Avril coming on right after the kiss, Poges's entrance with the roller being held off to interrupt the scene between the two women when we've had enough of that. Souhaun now knows that, warm as he is to her, O'Killigain has no more interest in her than he'd have in any goodlooking woman who was handy, and that the real thing—if there is any real thing involved—is between him and Avril. She urges Avril to run off with him, but Avril— perhaps because she does think her feeling for O'Killigain is real and has had no experience in that sort of relationship—can't make up her mind until—in Act III—the whole situation, including the flood, pushes her into it. Souhaun, I think, should wait till after Avril's gone to clear out with the 2nd Workman—a sort of guardian according to her lights till the end. (The 2nd Workman, if he needs any explaining, patiently waited until Souhaun had made her play for O'Killigain, knowing the younger man would make off with the younger girl in the end and Souhaun would fall in his lap.) None of this stuff, of course, should be on any higher emotional level than is necessary to carry it off.

Now I've got some production difficulties for you that you're going to love—live stock. In the beginning of Act II, where there are now off-stage animal and bird noises, I'd like to see chickens, ducks, pigs, perhaps a sheep, roam into the room where the two Englishmen are abed. Where the "Bull puts a stylized head with long curving horns over the barricade and lets out a loud bellow" (page 2-13) I'd like to see the head and shoulders of as pretty and gentle a cow as you can get hold of. And at the finale of Act III I'd like to have the 2nd Workman ride in on a very big white plowhorse—with water from the rising river sloshing around its legs—haul Souhaun up behind him and ride off.

The Act I and Act II curtains are weak, but I'm not sure that isn't as it should be. (I like the buildup of the "naked" stuff at the end of Act I— it's very Irish and is why other folk always think the Irish are liars—and wish there had been more of that sort of thing throughout the play. This is an anti-British play but the Irish will find it more insulting to them than to anybody else: all good Irish writers manage to do that.)

The "precious vase" sequence didn't hold me very well, and I think it could very well be either cut out completely or whittled down to a mere additional catastrophe. A good deal of cutting could be done throughout— many of the funny scenes are too long—but perhaps you can get a permit out of O'Casey to cut that stuff to fit.

The telephone troubles should be increased throughout to build to the Postmaster's entrance, but that's simply a matter of spotting them wherever there's a hole and I can easily do that when I get down to details.

I don't know just what you think is the best way to deal with O'Casey—I mean I don't know what shape you want to put your suggestions in or how much detail you want to go into—so if you'll let me know . . . as I said in the first paragraph of this letter . . .

[10] Los Angeles *Times*, January 7, 1950.
[11] DH to LH, January 31, 1950.
[12] Author's interview with Patricia Neal.
[13] DH to JHM, June 22, 1950.
[14] Ibid., June 27, 1950.
[15] Ibid., July 12, 1950.
[16] Ibid., November 19, 1950.
[17] Ibid., December 11, 1950.
[18] Ibid., December 4, 1950.
[19] DH to Maggie Kober, February 24, 1951.
[20] *The Autumn Garden*, in *Six Plays by Lillian Hellman* (New York: Vintage, 1979), p. 490.
[21] DH to Maggie Kober, April 16, 1951. When Josephine Marshall commented to him that he had never been abroad, he reminded her that he had been to Cuba. But it is true that he passed up numerous opportunities to go abroad.
[22] Ibid., February 24, 1951.
[23] Hammett's description of his journey, to Maggie Kober, April 23, 1951.

Chapter 18

[1] Smith Act (Alien Registration Act of 1940):

Sec. 2. (a) It shall be unlawful for any person—
   1. to knowingly or willfully advocate, abet, advise, or teach the duty, necessity, desirability, or propriety of overthrowing or destroying any government in the United States by force or violence. . . .
   2. with the intent to cause the overthrow or destruction of any government in the United States, to print, publish, edit, issue, circulate, sell, distribute, or publicly display any written or printed matter advocating, advising, or teaching the duty, necessity, desirability, or propriety of overthrowing or destroying any government in the United States by force or violence;
   3. to organize or help to organize any society, group, or assembly of persons who teach, advocate, or encourage the overthrow or destruction of any government in the United States by force or violence; or to be or become a member of, or affiliate with, any such society, group, or assembly of persons, knowing the purposes thereof.
Sec. 3. It shall be unlawful for any person to attempt to commit, or to conspire to commit, any of the acts prohibited by the provisions of this title.

[2] Hammett's Introduction to George Marion, *The Communist Trial* (New York: Fairplay, 1950), p. 2.
[3] Tom Blair, "Through the Haze," Boston *Chronicle*, July 14, 1951.

⁴ Hellman, *Unfinished Woman* (*Three*, pp. 282–83).

⁵ Extracts from the transcript of court testimony, July 9, 1951, pp. 172–241a.

⁶ Author's interview with Charles Haydon.

⁷ Leo Huberman and Paul Sweezy, his co-editor of the *Monthly Review*, were called about a year later before the Senate Internal Security Committee and were represented by Ephraim London, one of the few lawyers who would take the cases in those days.

According to Hellman, when asked by the Internal Security Committee if they were Communists, one spoke also for the other when he answered, "No, we are not Communists and we never have been. Now that you've asked that question, we must warn you that we have no intention of answering any others. We answered that question only to tell you that there are non-Communists who do not believe that you have the right to ask the questions. You may now do anything you like, sirs, but no further questions will be answered."

No harm came to them, in Lillian Hellman's memory.

⁸ Interview with Frederick V. Field.

⁹ At the time of his death in 1961, the figure was $163.286.46:

INCOME 1943	$25,609.30
Interest 12/22/50 to 6/30/61	17,480.76
INCOME 1944	30,280.57
Interest 12/22/50 to 6/30/61	19,207.52
INCOME 1945	37,217.14
Interest 12/22/50 to 6/30/61	23,495.55
INCOME 1947—Int.	207.23
INCOME 1948 Add'l	3,607.43
Interest 3/2/51 to 6/30/61	2,235.16
INCOME 1949 Add'l	352.70
Interest 3/6/53 to 6/30/61	1,001.67
INCOME 1950 Add'l	1,540.11
Interest 2/26/54 to 6/30/61	1,051.32
TOTAL	$163,286.46

PLUS INTEREST ACCRUED AT 6% PER ANNUM TO DATE OF PAYMENT

¹⁰ Quoted in Eric Bentley, *Thirty Years of Treason* (New York: Viking, 1971), pp. 303–4.

¹¹ Winchell's column, July 17, 1951.

¹² FBI records, July 6, 1951.

Chapter 19

¹ DH to JHM, November 27, 1951.

² DH to Howard Selsam, April 10, 1952, Butler Library Collection, Columbia University.

³ DH to JHM, April 10, 1952.

⁴ Ibid., April 16, 1952.

⁵ New York *World Telegram* editorial, May 6, 1952, p. 30.

⁶ *Daily Compass*, July 19, 1952.

[7] "Decline and Fall of the Whodunit," *Saturday Review*, May 31, 1952, pp. 8–9, 31–32.

[8] New York *Herald Tribune*, October 20, 1952.

[9] Louis Sobol, New York *Journal American*, October 20, 1952.

[10] *Unfinished Woman* (*Three*, p. 134).

[11] DH to JHM, November 23, 1953.

[12] DH to LH, August 18, 1952.

[13] Ibid., August 20, 1952.

[14] Ibid., August 21, 1952.

[15] Layman, *Dashiell Hammett*, pp. 237–39.

[16] DH to JHM, October 20, 1952. The details of Hammett's rent are obscured by controversy. The FBI apparently believed he lived rent-free.

Chapter 20

[1] The senator from Wisconsin, whose career as a Communist hunter was ended in disgrace by a motion of censure by the U.S. Senate.

[2] Cohn still practices law in New York.

[3] From the hearing before the permanent subcommittee on investigation of the committee on government operations, U.S. Senate 83rd Congress (U.S. Government Printing Office, 1953), pp. 83–88.

Chapter 21

[1] DH to JHM, July 18, 1953.

[2] Ibid., June 14, 1953.

[3] "Tulip" (*The Big Knockover*, p. 336).

[4] DH to JHM, June 5, 1953.

[5] Ibid., June 6, 1953.

[6] Ibid., June 14, 1953.

[7] Ibid., September 16, 1953.

[8] Ibid., October 3, 1953. Priscilla Gillette was co-starring with Patricia Neal in this production of *The Children's Hour*.

[9] New York *Herald Tribune*, July 7, 1953.

[10] DH to JHM, July 7, 1953.

[11] Hammett's medical records, Lenox Hill Hospital, in New York City, and his psychiatrist's account.

[12] DH to JHM, October 13, 1955.

[13] Ibid., February (n.d.) 1956.

[14] Ibid., April 6, 1956.

[15] Ibid., July 30, 1956.

[16] Mt. Kisco, N.Y., *Patent Trader*, July 29, 1956, p. 16.

[17] James Cooper in the London *Daily Express*, March 22, 1957.

[18] DH to LH, January 7, 1957.

[19] Letter to author from Jeremy Gury, July 18, 1979.

[20] LH to JHM, February 21, 1957.

[21] FBI report, April 1957.

[22] DH to LH, January 14, 1958.

[23] *Unfinished Woman* (*Three*, p. 297).

[24] Ibid.

Chapter 22

[1] Hellman, *Unfinished Woman* (*Three*, p. 298).
[2] Steven Marcus' interview with Selma.
[3] Hellman, *Unfinished Woman* (*Three*, p. 299).
[4] Hellman, *Pentimento* (*Three*, p. 510).
[5] The funeral was held at Frank E. Campbell, Madison at 81st St., New York. The invoice for the funeral:

Estate of Dashiell Hammett
c/o Miss Lillian Hellman
63 East 82nd Street
New York 28, New York.

January 12, 1961

FOR THE FUNERAL OF SAMUEL DASHIELL HAMMETT

Funeral including use of our facilities; our professional services; hearse to Pennsylvania Railroad Station; and casket as selected:

The sum of	$395.00
Outer case	65.00
Brought forward	460.00
Five transcripts of death certificate	$5.00
Transportation for deceased to Washington, D.C.	30.58
Long distance telephone tolls	4.62
Newspaper notices	26.03
New York City Sales Tax (Except $250. Veterans Burial Allowance)	6.30
TOTAL CASH DISBURSEMENTS ADVANCED	$72.50
Brought forward	460.00
	$532.50
Veterans Burial Allowance applied for	250.00
	$282.50

[6] The text of the eulogy:

A few weeks ago, on a night when he was having a tough time, I said, "You're a brave man." I had never said such a thing before and as he came out of that half doze the very sick have from minute to minute, he smiled and said, "Better keep words like that for the end." The end has come and he would not have wanted words today. This small funeral, this small tribute, I arranged for my sake. He was a man who respected words in books and suspected them in life: he believed that words sometimes took the place of thought and almost always took the place of action, and he deeply believed in both.

With very little school behind him, Dashiell Hammett had the greatest respect for knowledge of anybody I have ever known. He read enormously, sometimes five and six books a week, and anything that came to hand. There were the years when there were stacks of books on mathematics. And then on chess, teaching himself by memorizing the problems and mumbling them to himself; there was a year when he was interested in the retina of the eye, and another year when he bought a hearing aid and wandered in the woods trying to find out if it would make the sounds of birds and animals come clearer. Poetry, fiction, science, philosophy—any book that came to hand. He believed in the salvation of knowledge and intelligence, and he tried to live it out.

I have asked myself many times in these last thirty years why he seemed to me a great man. Perhaps because the combinations in the nature were so unexpected and so interesting. He didn't always think well of people and yet I've never known anybody else who gave away anything he had to anybody who needed it, or even wanted it, who accepted everybody with tolerance. He didn't, as you know, think well of the society we live in and yet when it punished him he made no complaint against it, and had no anger about the punishment. The night before he went to jail, he told me that no matter what anybody thought he had no political reason for the stand he took, that he had simply come to the conclusion that a man should keep his word.

He was sick the night he came out of jail and it took me years to find out that wandering around the Kentucky town from which he was to catch the plane back to New York, he had met a moonshiner who had been in jail with him and was walking the streets with his wife because he couldn't find work. Dash gave him all the money he had in his pocket and he arrived in New York sick because he had kept no money to eat with. Many people would do just that, but most of us would have talked about it.

Dash wrote about violence but he had contempt for it and thus he had contempt for heroics. And yet he enlisted in the Second World War at the age of forty-eight because he was a patriotic man, very involved in America. He went through three basic training courses with men young enough to be his grandsons, and told me later that his major contribution to the war had been to sit in the Aleutians and convince the young that the lack of ladies didn't necessarily have anything to do with baldness or toothache.

He was a gay man, funny, witty. Most of his life was wide open and adventurous, and most of it he enjoyed. He learned and acted on what he learned. He believed in man's right to dignity and never in all the years did he play anybody's game but his own. "Anything for a buck" was his sneer at those who did. In the thirty years I knew him I never heard him tell a lie of any kind and that sometimes made me angry when I wasn't envying the courage it takes. He saw through other people's lies but he dismissed them with a kind of tolerant contempt. He was a man of simple honor and bravery. Blessed are they, I hope, who leave good work behind. And who leave behind a life that is so worthy of respect. Whoever runs the blessing department, may they have sense enough to bless a good man this last day he is on earth.

[7] Los Angeles *Times*, January 12, 1961.
[8] John Crosby, New York *Herald Tribune*, January 18, 1961.

INDEX